砲神
エグザクソン

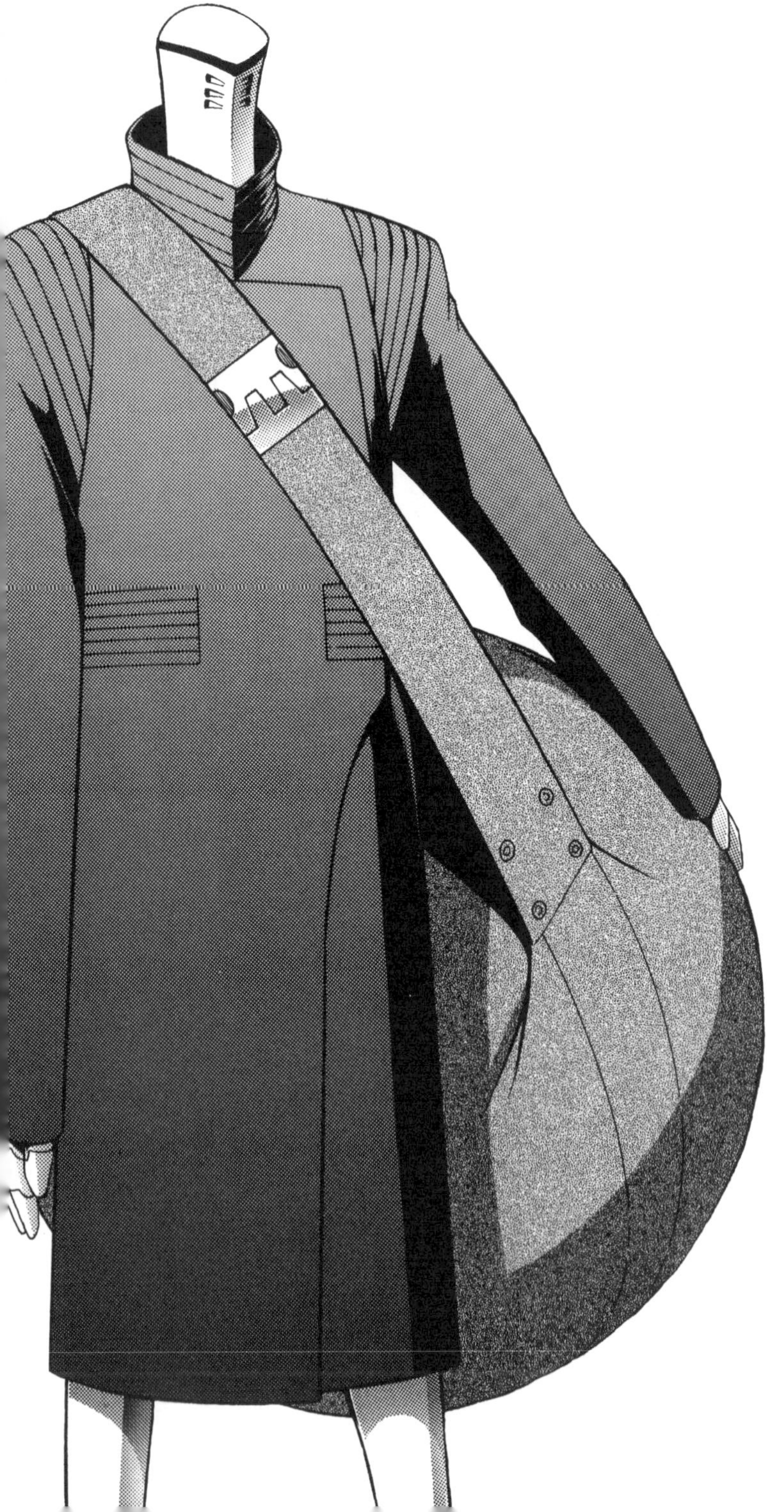

CANNON GOD EXAXXION

STORY AND ART BY
KENICHI SONODA

TRANSLATION BY
DANA LEWIS & ADAM WARREN

LETTERING AND TOUCH-UP
SUSIE LEE with TOM 2K

STAGE 2

™

DARK HORSE MANGA™

CANNON GOD EXAXXION: STAGE 2

FIRST EDITION: AUGUST 2003 | ISBN: 1-56971-966-7 | 1 2 3 4 5 6 7 8 9 10 | PRINTED IN CANADA

PUBLISHER
MIKE RICHARDSON

SERIES EDITOR
TIM ERVIN-GORE

SERIES EXECUTIVE EDITOR
TOREN SMITH
FOR STUDIO PROTEUS

COLLECTION EDITOR
CHRIS WARNER

COLLECTION DESIGNER
LIA RIBACCHI

ART DIRECTOR
MARK COX

ENGLISH-LANGUAGE VERSION PRODUCED BY STUDIO PROTEUS FOR DARK HORSE COMICS, INC.

THIS VOLUME COLLECTS ISSUES NINE THROUGH THIRTEEN OF THE DARK HORSE COMIC-BOOK SERIES *CANNON GOD EXAXXION.*

PUBLISHED BY DARK HORSE MANGA A DIVISION OF DARK HORSE COMICS, INC.,10956 SE MAIN STREET, MILWAUKIE, OR 97222

D A R K H O R S E . C O M

TO FIND A COMICS SHOP IN YOUR AREA, CALL THE COMIC SHOP LOCATOR SERVICE TOLL-FREE AT 1-888-266-4226

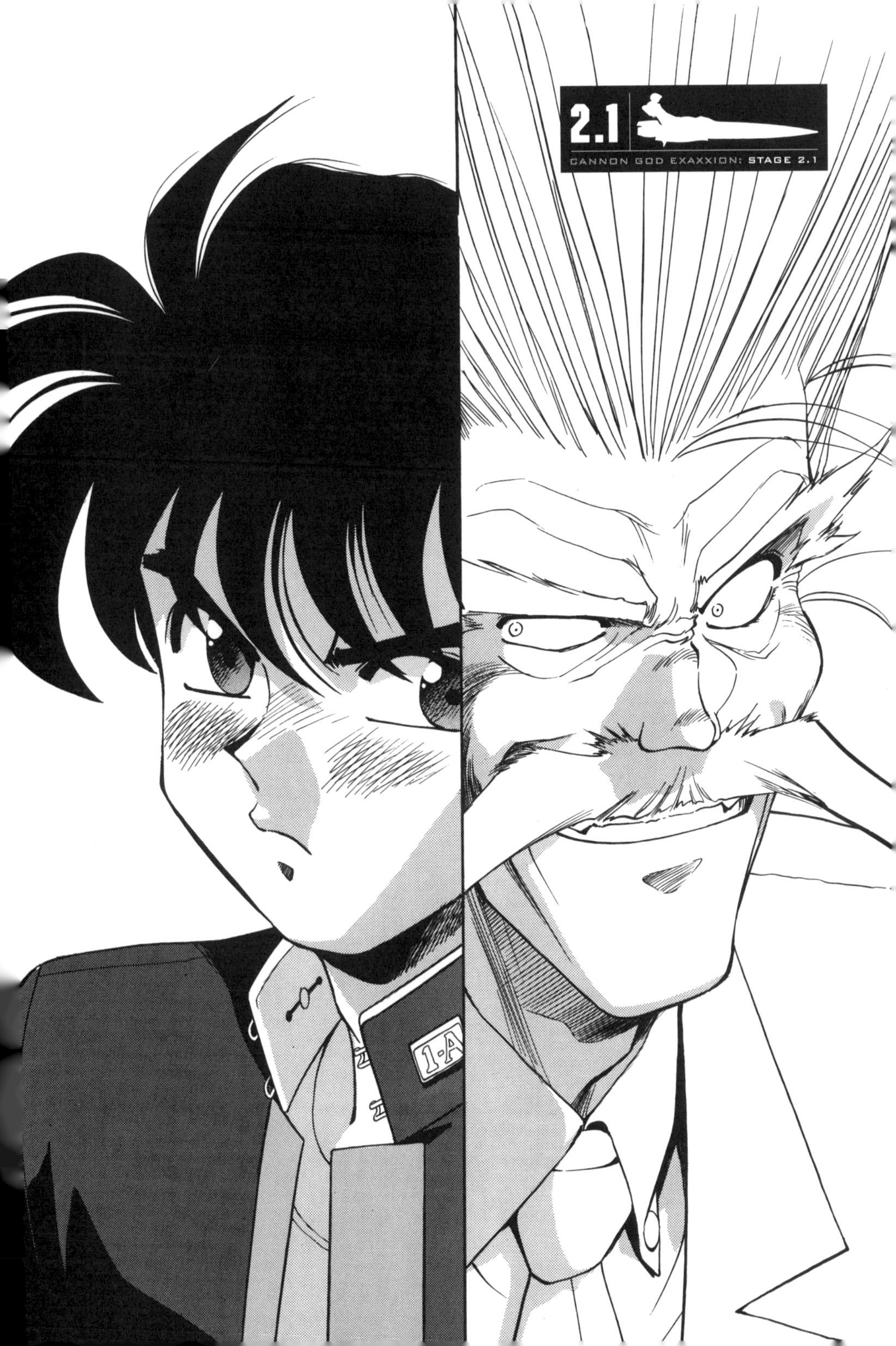
2.1
CANNON GOD EXAXXION: STAGE 2.1
1-A

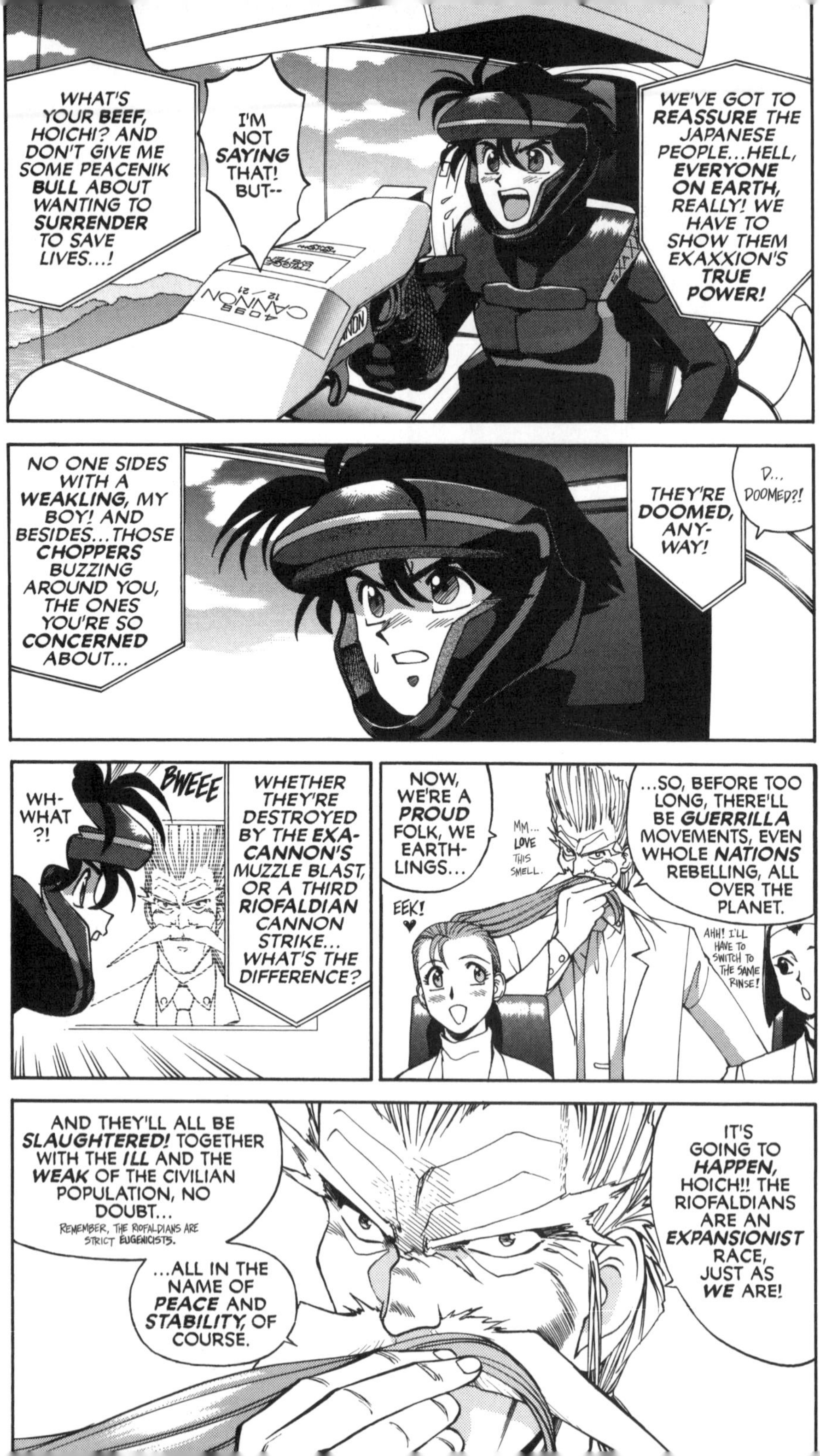
WHAT'S YOUR **BEEF**, HOICHI? AND DON'T GIVE ME SOME PEACENIK **BULL** ABOUT WANTING TO **SURRENDER** TO SAVE LIVES...!
I'M NOT **SAYING** THAT! BUT--
WE'VE GOT TO **REASSURE** THE JAPANESE PEOPLE...HELL, **EVERYONE ON EARTH,** REALLY! WE HAVE TO SHOW THEM EXAXXION'S **TRUE POWER!**
NO ONE SIDES WITH A **WEAKLING,** MY BOY! AND BESIDES...THOSE **CHOPPERS** BUZZING AROUND YOU, THE ONES YOU'RE SO **CONCERNED** ABOUT...
THEY'RE **DOOMED,** ANY-WAY!
D... DOOMED?!
WH-WHAT ?!
BWEEE
WHETHER THEY'RE DESTROYED BY THE **EXA-CANNON'S** MUZZLE BLAST, OR A THIRD **RIOFALDIAN** CANNON STRIKE... WHAT'S THE DIFFERENCE?
NOW, WE'RE A **PROUD** FOLK, WE EARTH-LINGS...
MM... LOVE THIS SMELL.
EEK! ♥
...SO, BEFORE TOO LONG, THERE'LL BE **GUERRILLA** MOVEMENTS, EVEN WHOLE **NATIONS** REBELLING, ALL OVER THE PLANET.
AHH! I'LL HAVE TO SWITCH TO THE SAME RINSE!
AND THEY'LL ALL BE ***SLAUGHTERED!*** TOGETHER WITH THE ***ILL*** AND THE ***WEAK*** OF THE CIVILIAN POPULATION, NO DOUBT...
REMEMBER, THE RIOFALDIANS ARE STRICT EUGENICISTS.
...ALL IN THE NAME OF ***PEACE*** AND ***STABILITY,*** OF COURSE.
IT'S GOING TO ***HAPPEN,*** HOICHI! THE RIOFALDIANS ARE AN ***EXPANSIONIST*** RACE, JUST AS ***WE*** ARE!

OKAY! GOT IT, GRANDPA...!

BUT...THIS *EXA-CANNON*... CAN IT *REALLY* PUNCH RIGHT THROUGH THE ARMOR OF THAT *ROBOT* BACK AT THE SPACE ELEVATOR TERMINAL...?

OF *COURSE*, LADDIE!

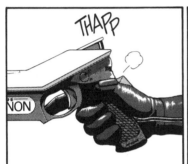

THAPP

ISAKA!

YES, MASTER HOICHI...?

BWEEE

TARGET THAT *ROBOT* AT THE ELEVATOR BASE, OKAY?

YES, SIR!

NOW, KEEP IN MIND THAT RAIL GUNS AREN'T *RIFLED*... INSTEAD OF SPIN STABILIZATION, WE USE *MORPHING ROUNDS*.

HUH? WHAT'RE *THOSE*?

THINK--OUR ROUND'S *TRAJECTORY* HAS TO FOLLOW THE CURVATURE OF THE EARTH, RIGHT? SO WE FEED THE PROJECTILE A STREAM OF COMMANDS-- USING HACKED COMSATS-- TO CONTINUOUSLY *RESHAPE* ITS AERODYNAMIC PROFILE IN FLIGHT...!

EARTH

NOW LOADING ONE 4096SR *ARMOR-PIERCING* ROUND!

MASTER HOICHI, ORIENT *EXAXXION* EAST-SOUTHEAST, PLEASE. I'LL HANDLE THE *FINE ADJUSTMENTS* FOR TARGETING.

YOU *GOT* IT!

SHNKK

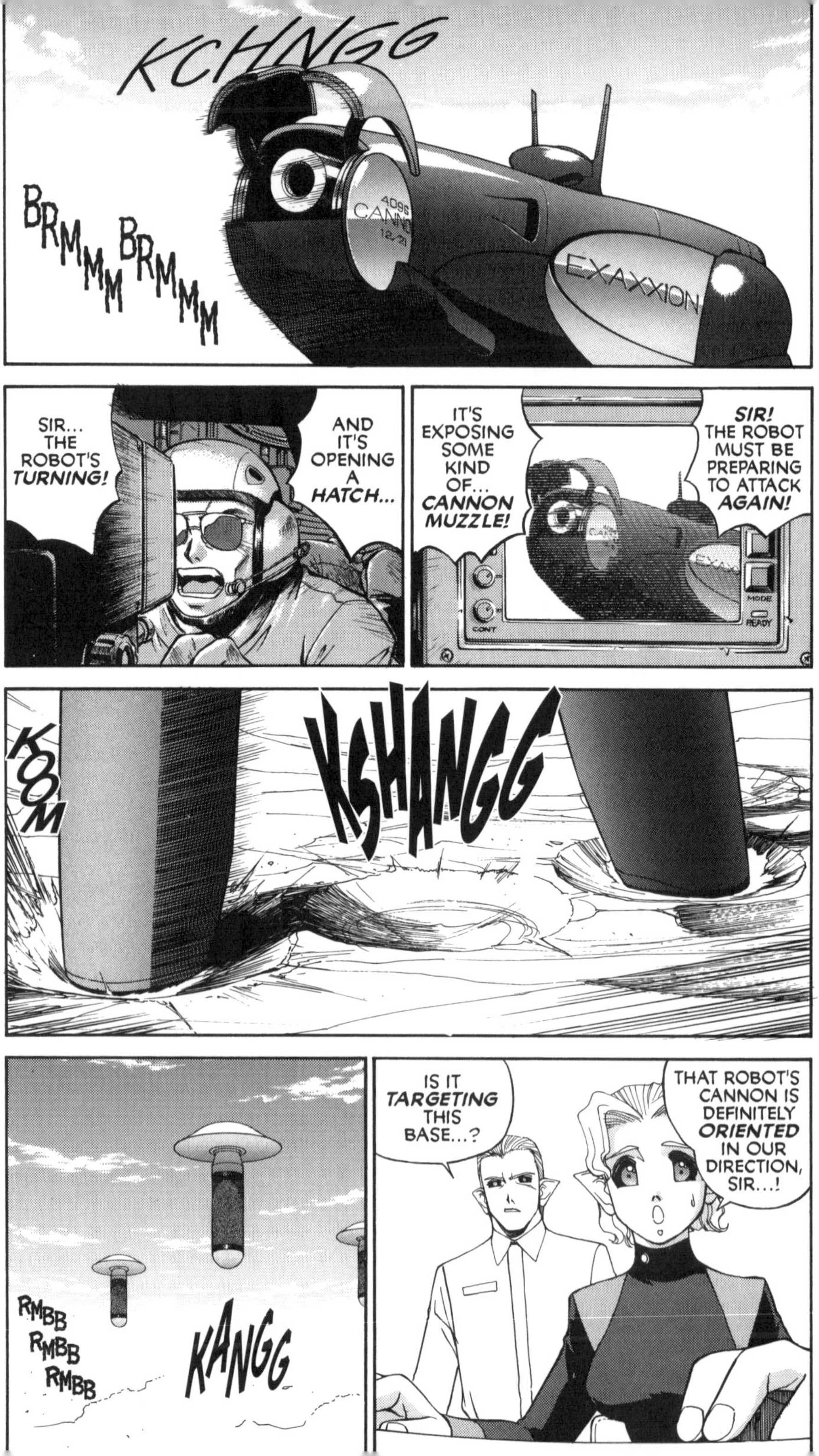
KCHNGG
BRMMM BRMMM
4096 CANN 12/21
EXAXXION
SIR... THE ROBOT'S *TURNING!*
AND IT'S OPENING A *HATCH...*
IT'S EXPOSING SOME KIND OF... *CANNON MUZZLE!*
SIR! THE ROBOT MUST BE PREPARING TO ATTACK *AGAIN!*
MODE
READY
CONT
KOOM
KSHANGG
RMBB RMBB RMBB
KANGG
IS IT *TARGETING* THIS BASE...?
THAT ROBOT'S CANNON IS DEFINITELY *ORIENTED* IN OUR DIRECTION, SIR...!

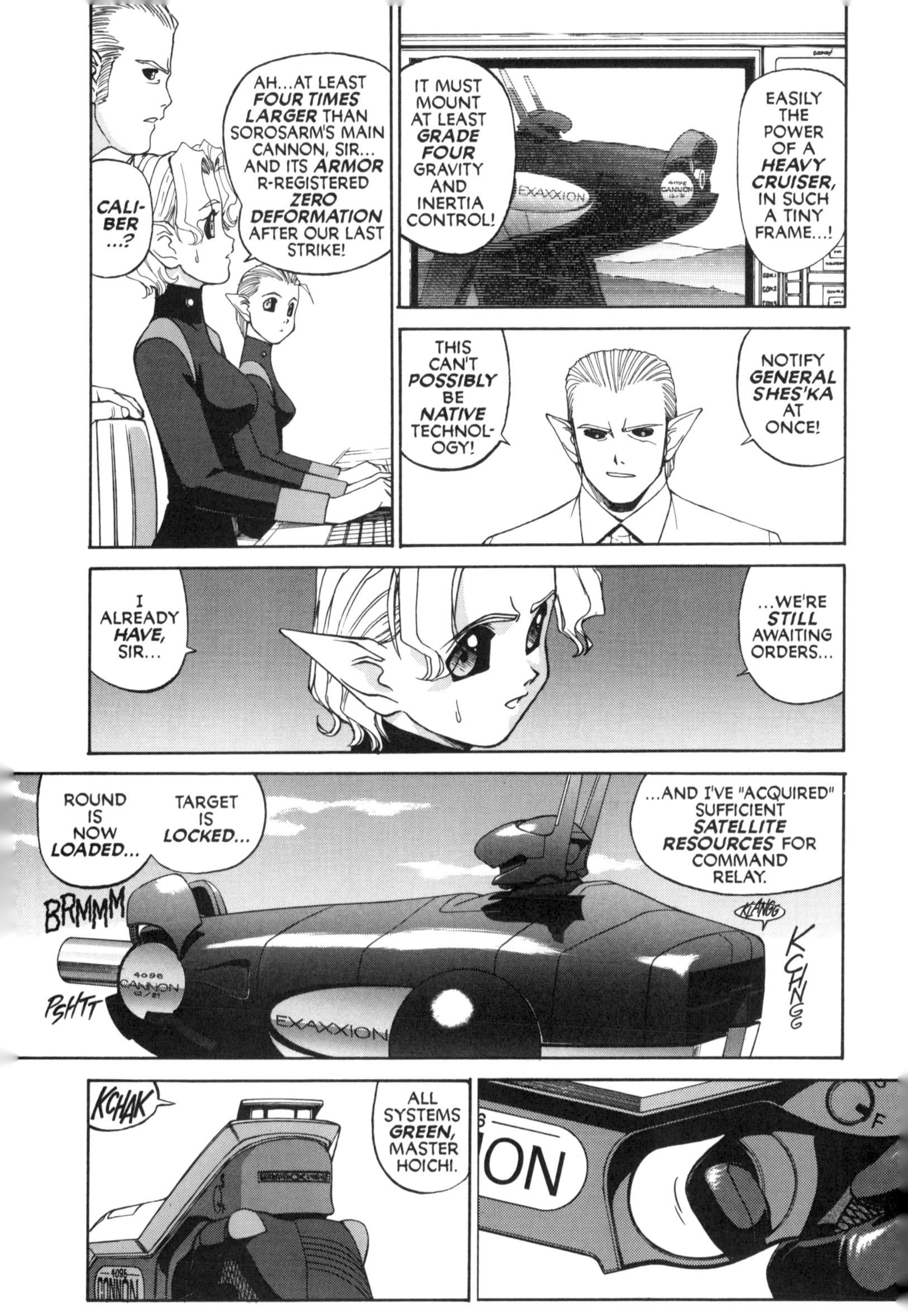
CALI-BER ...?
AH...AT LEAST FOUR TIMES LARGER THAN SOROSARM'S MAIN CANNON, SIR... AND ITS ARMOR R-REGISTERED ZERO DEFORMATION AFTER OUR LAST STRIKE!
IT MUST MOUNT AT LEAST GRADE FOUR GRAVITY AND INERTIA CONTROL!
EXAXXION
EASILY THE POWER OF A HEAVY CRUISER, IN SUCH A TINY FRAME...!
THIS CAN'T POSSIBLY BE NATIVE TECHNOL-OGY!
NOTIFY GENERAL SHES'KA AT ONCE!
I ALREADY HAVE, SIR...
...WE'RE STILL AWAITING ORDERS...
ROUND IS NOW LOADED...
TARGET IS LOCKED...
BRMMM
...AND I'VE "ACQUIRED" SUFFICIENT SATELLITE RESOURCES FOR COMMAND RELAY.
KLANGG
KCHNGG
4096 CANNON
PSHTT
EXAXXION
KCHAK
ALL SYSTEMS GREEN, MASTER HOICHI.
ON

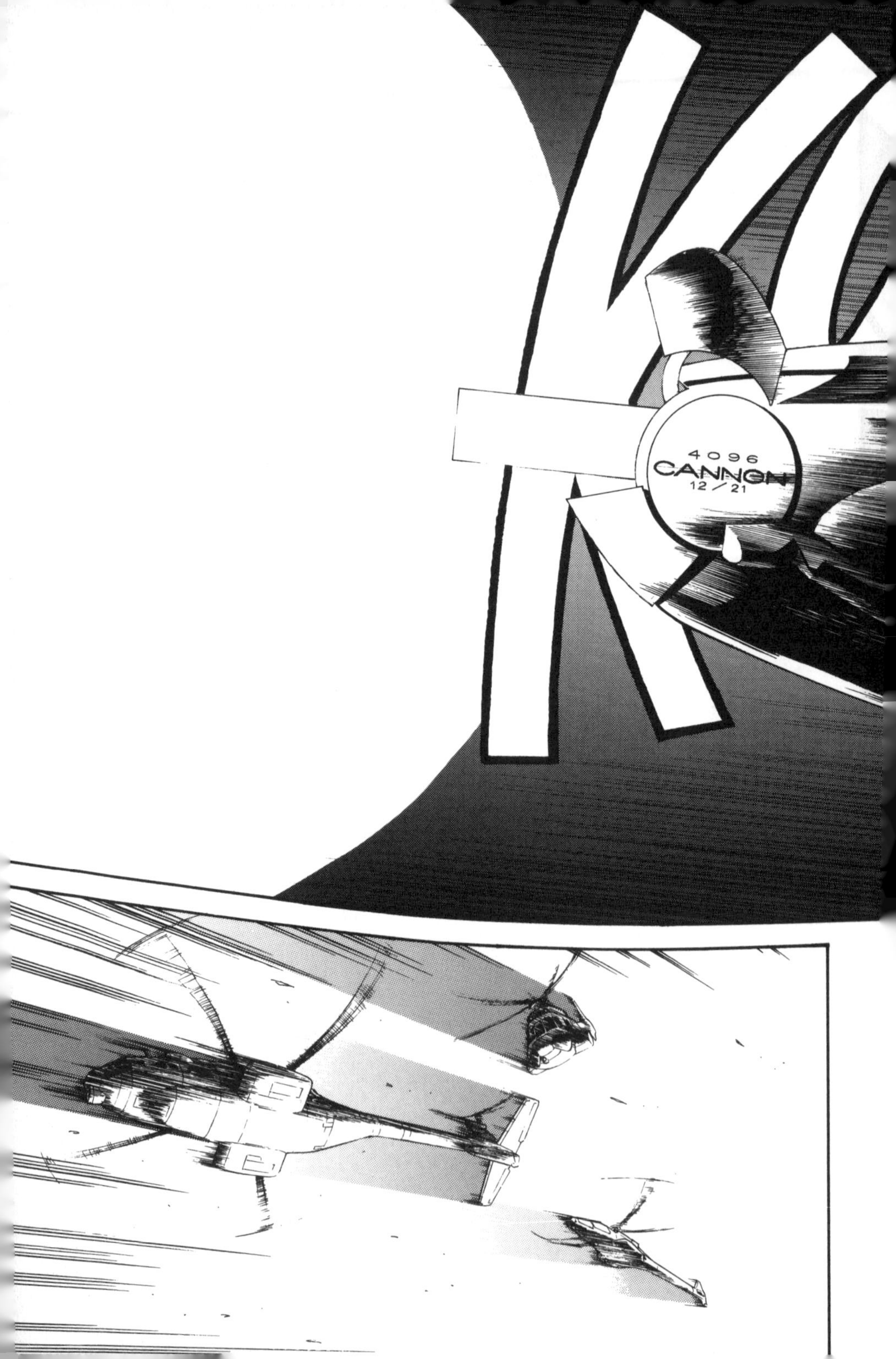
4096
CANNON
12/21

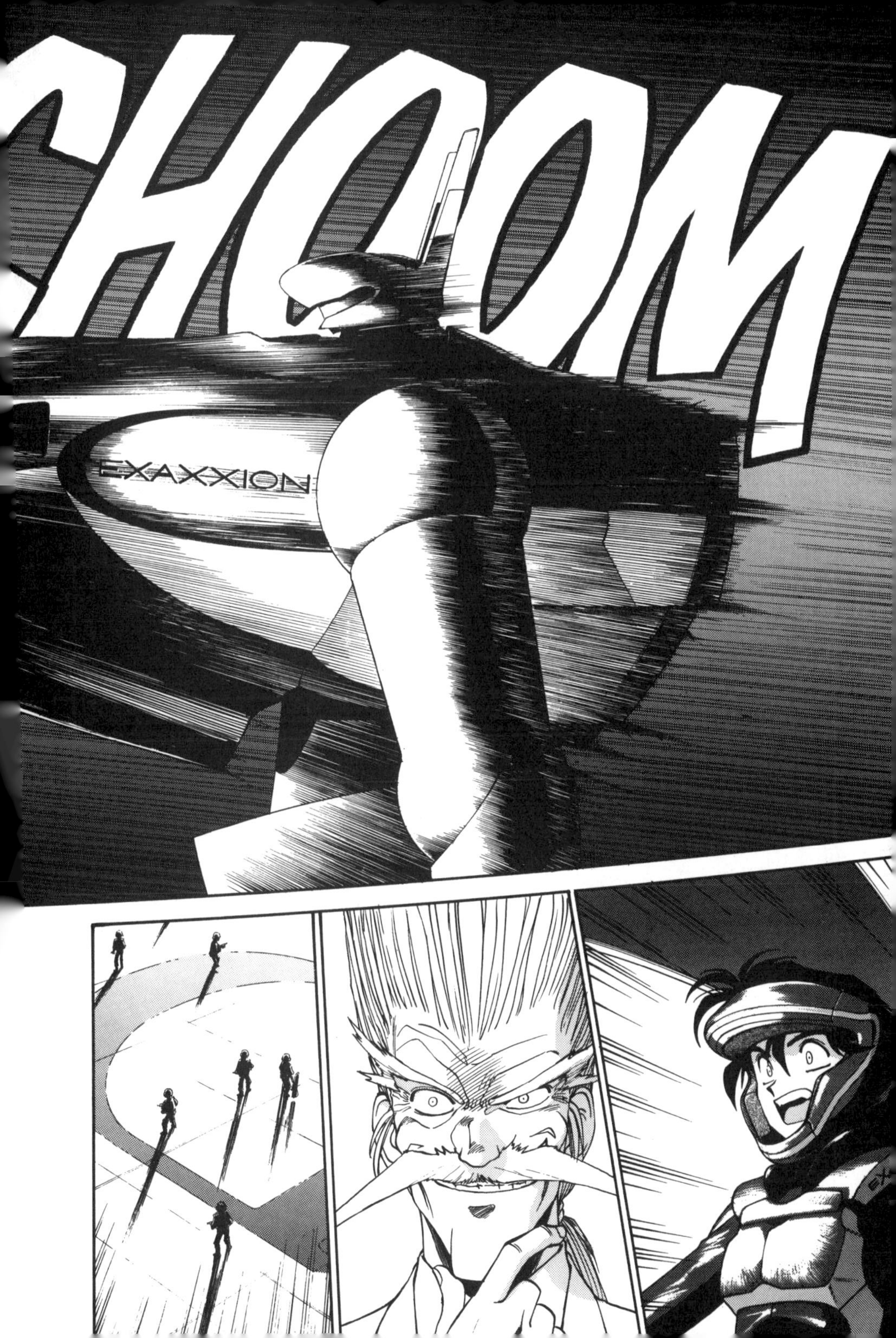
CHOOM
EXAXXION

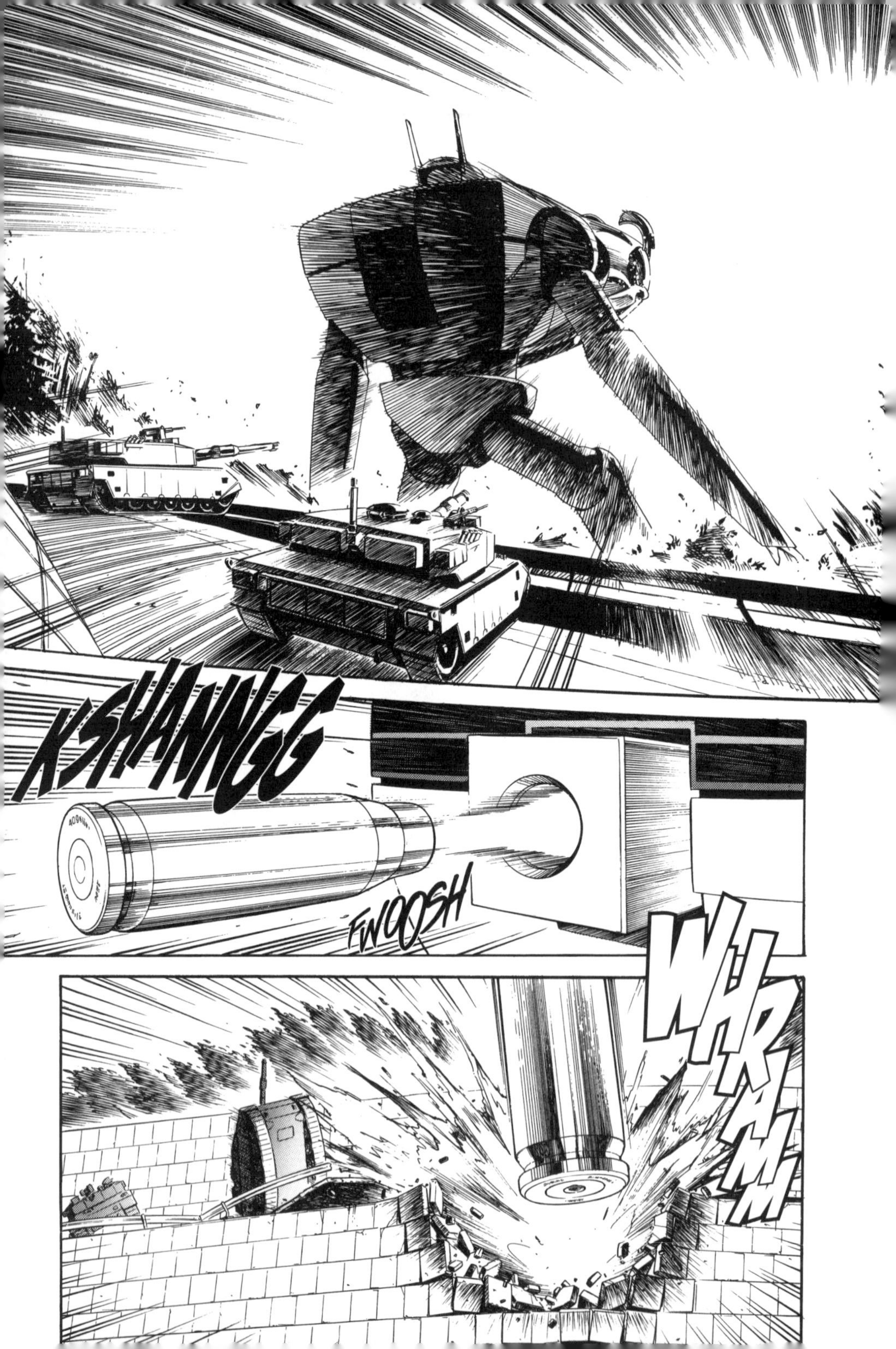
KSHANNGG
FWOOSH
WHRAMM

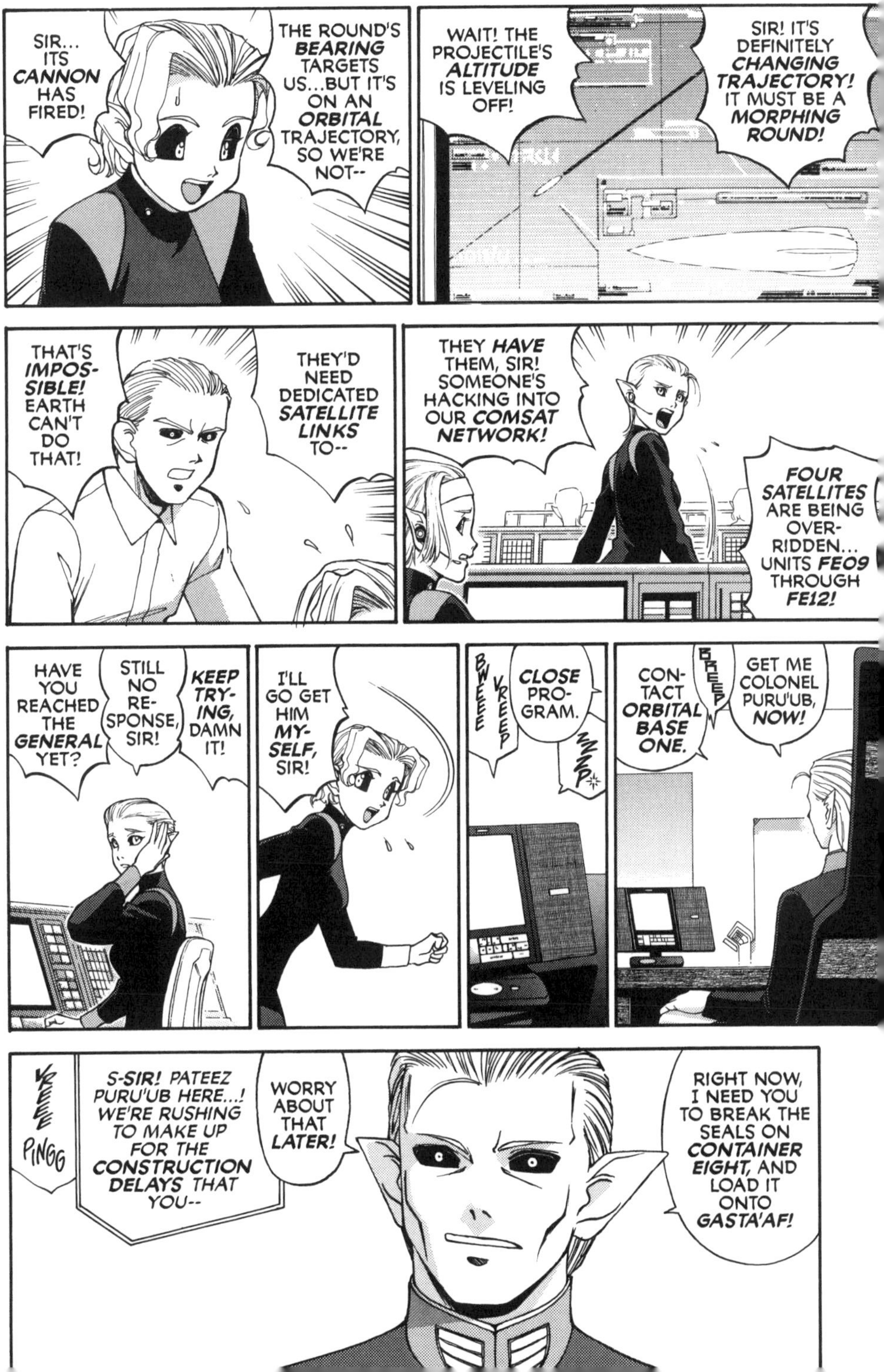
SIR... ITS CANNON HAS FIRED!
THE ROUND'S BEARING TARGETS US...BUT IT'S ON AN ORBITAL TRAJECTORY, SO WE'RE NOT--
WAIT! THE PROJECTILE'S ALTITUDE IS LEVELING OFF!
SIR! IT'S DEFINITELY CHANGING TRAJECTORY! IT MUST BE A MORPHING ROUND!
THAT'S IMPOS-SIBLE! EARTH CAN'T DO THAT!
THEY'D NEED DEDICATED SATELLITE LINKS TO--
THEY HAVE THEM, SIR! SOMEONE'S HACKING INTO OUR COMSAT NETWORK!
FOUR SATELLITES ARE BEING OVER-RIDDEN... UNITS FE09 THROUGH FE12!
HAVE YOU REACHED THE GENERAL YET?
STILL NO RE-SPONSE, SIR!
KEEP TRY-ING, DAMN IT!
I'LL GO GET HIM MY-SELF, SIR!
BWEEE
VREEP
CLOSE PRO-GRAM.
ZZZP
CON-TACT ORBITAL BASE ONE.
BREEP
GET ME COLONEL PURU'UB, NOW!
VREEE
PINGG
S-SIR! PATEEZ PURU'UB HERE...! WE'RE RUSHING TO MAKE UP FOR THE CONSTRUCTION DELAYS THAT YOU--
WORRY ABOUT THAT LATER!
RIGHT NOW, I NEED YOU TO BREAK THE SEALS ON CONTAINER EIGHT, AND LOAD IT ONTO GASTA'AF!

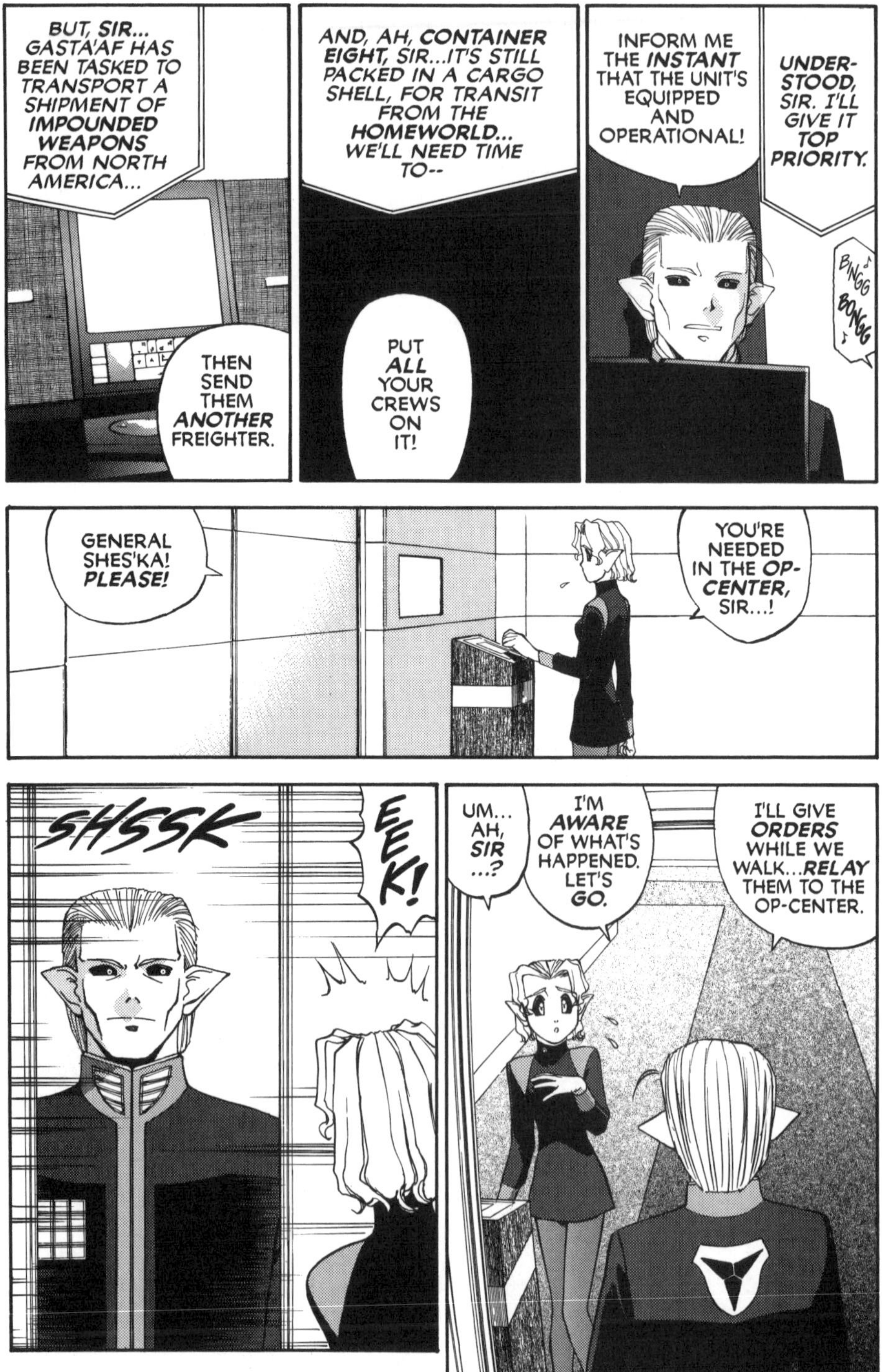
BUT, SIR... GASTA'AF HAS BEEN TASKED TO TRANSPORT A SHIPMENT OF IMPOUNDED WEAPONS FROM NORTH AMERICA...
THEN SEND THEM ANOTHER FREIGHTER.
AND, AH, CONTAINER EIGHT, SIR...IT'S STILL PACKED IN A CARGO SHELL, FOR TRANSIT FROM THE HOMEWORLD... WE'LL NEED TIME TO--
PUT ALL YOUR CREWS ON IT!
INFORM ME THE INSTANT THAT THE UNIT'S EQUIPPED AND OPERATIONAL!
UNDER-STOOD, SIR. I'LL GIVE IT TOP PRIORITY.
BINGG BONGG
GENERAL SHES'KA! PLEASE!
YOU'RE NEEDED IN THE OP-CENTER, SIR...!
SHSSK
EEEK!
UM... AH, SIR ...?
I'M AWARE OF WHAT'S HAPPENED. LET'S GO.
I'LL GIVE ORDERS WHILE WE WALK...RELAY THEM TO THE OP-CENTER.

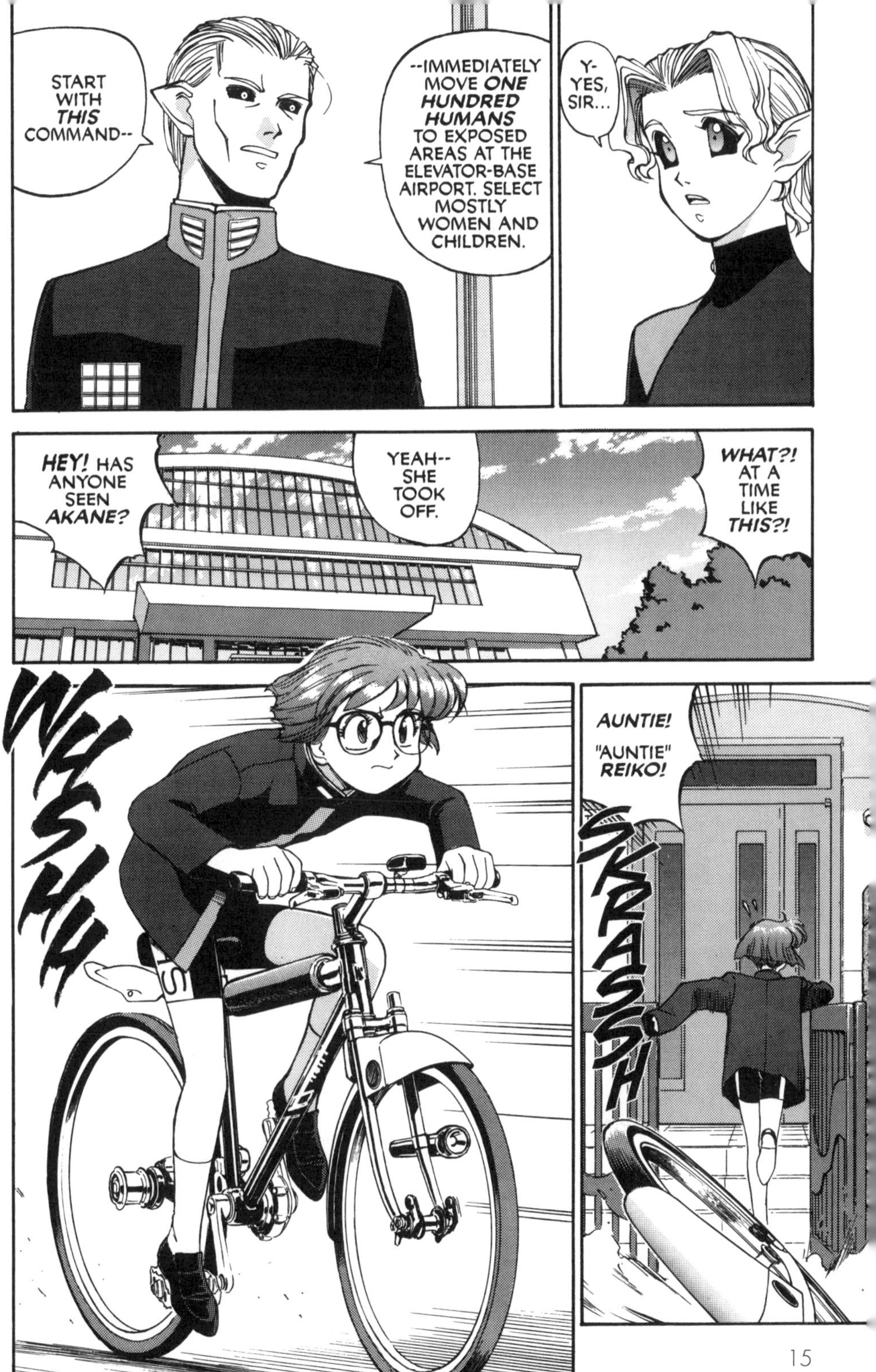
START WITH *THIS* COMMAND--
--IMMEDIATELY MOVE ***ONE HUNDRED HUMANS*** TO EXPOSED AREAS AT THE ELEVATOR-BASE AIRPORT. SELECT MOSTLY WOMEN AND CHILDREN.
Y-YES, SIR...
HEY! HAS ANYONE SEEN ***AKANE?***
YEAH-- SHE TOOK OFF.
WHAT?! AT A TIME LIKE ***THIS?!***
WHSHH
AUNTIE!
"AUNTIE" ***REIKO!***
SKRASSH

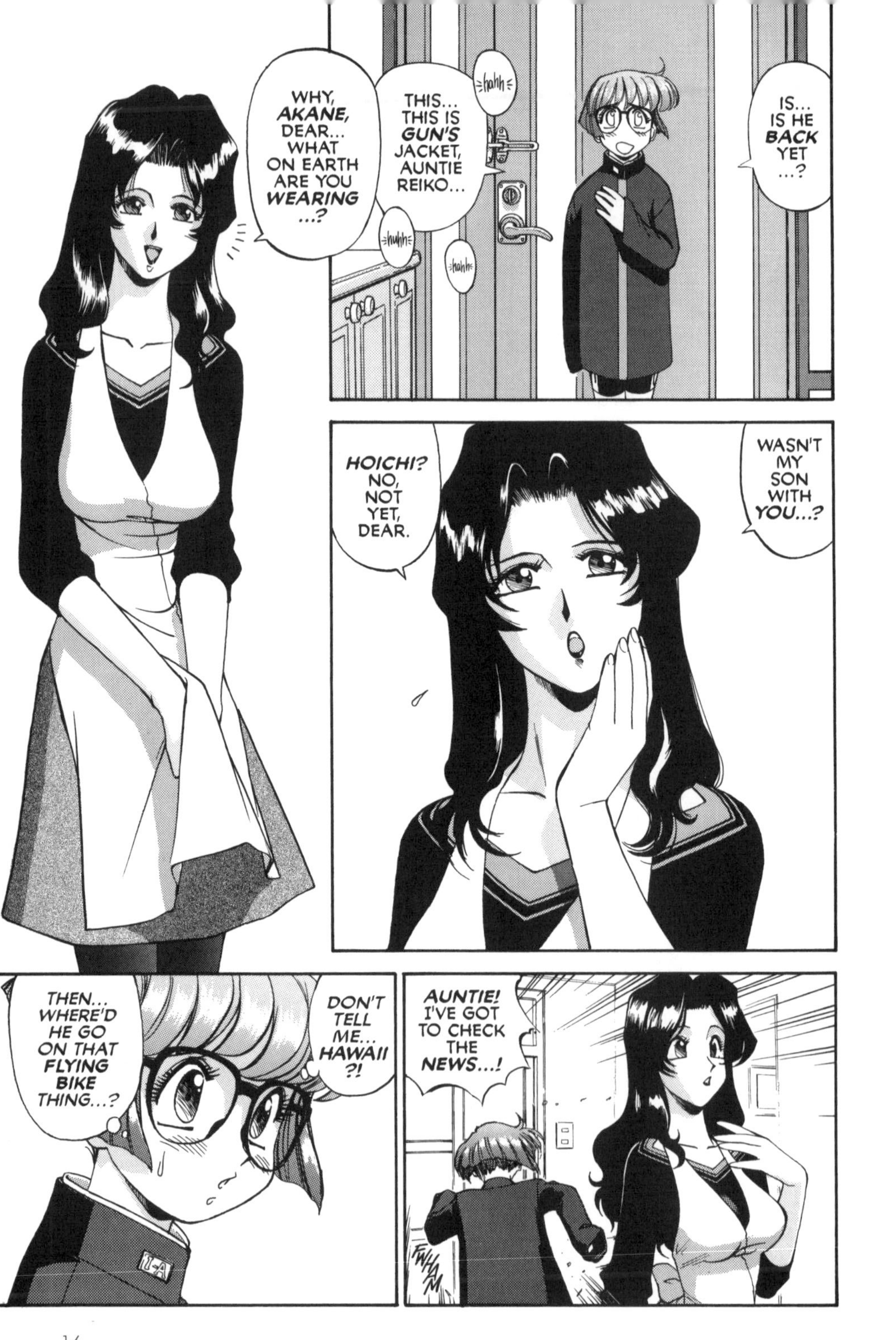
WHY, AKANE, DEAR... WHAT ON EARTH ARE YOU WEARING...?
hahh
THIS... THIS IS GUN'S JACKET, AUNTIE REIKO...
huhh
hahh
IS... IS HE BACK YET...?
HOICHI? NO, NOT YET, DEAR.
WASN'T MY SON WITH YOU...?
THEN... WHERE'D HE GO ON THAT FLYING BIKE THING...?
DON'T TELL ME... HAWAII?!
AUNTIE! I'VE GOT TO CHECK THE NEWS...!
FWHAM

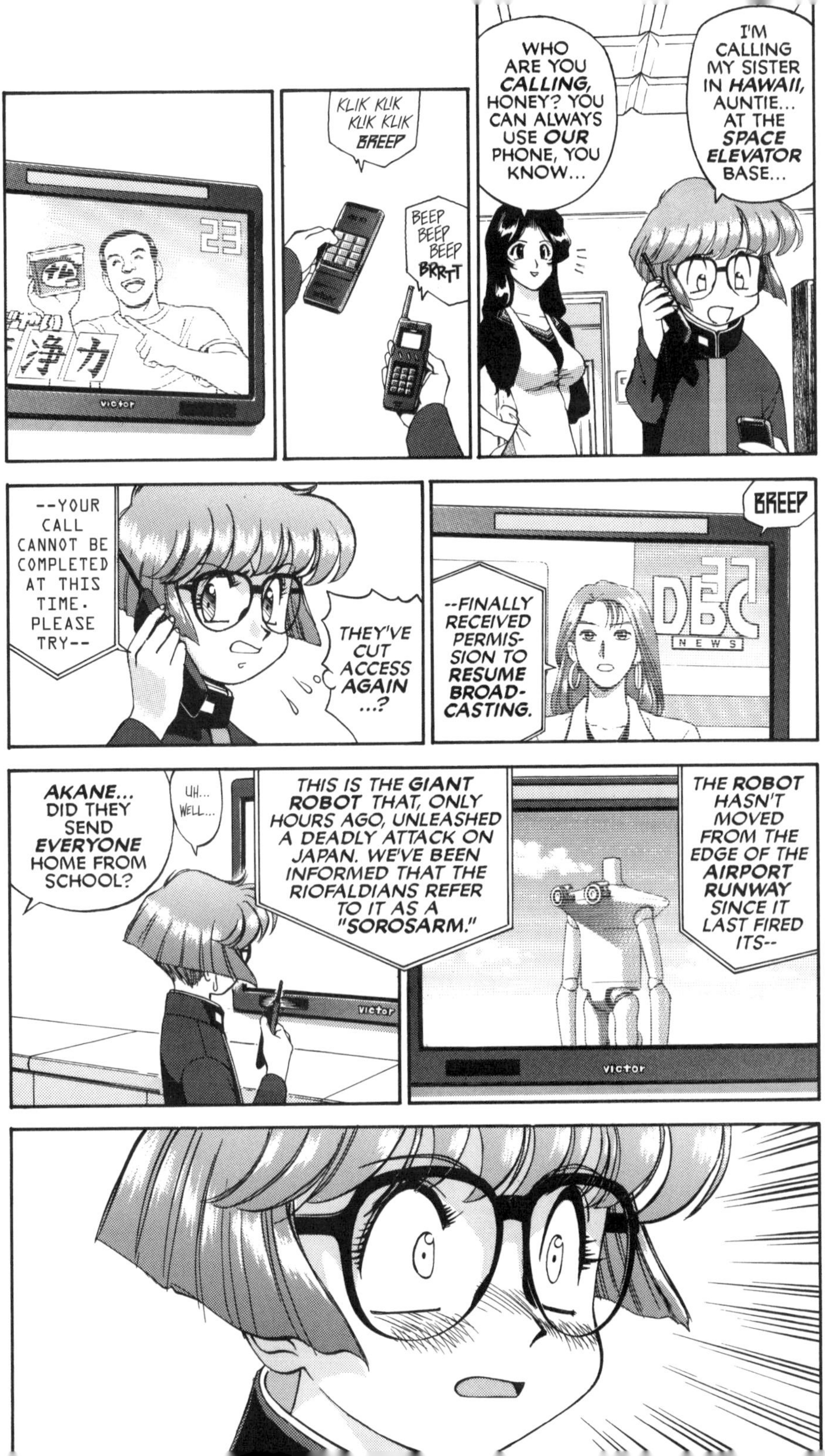
KLIK KLIK KLIK KLIK BREEP
BEEP BEEP BEEP BRRTT
WHO ARE YOU CALLING, HONEY? YOU CAN ALWAYS USE OUR PHONE, YOU KNOW...
I'M CALLING MY SISTER IN HAWAII, AUNTIE... AT THE SPACE ELEVATOR BASE...
--YOUR CALL CANNOT BE COMPLETED AT THIS TIME. PLEASE TRY--
THEY'VE CUT ACCESS AGAIN ...?
BREEP
--FINALLY RECEIVED PERMISSION TO RESUME BROADCASTING.
DBC NEWS
AKANE... DID THEY SEND EVERYONE HOME FROM SCHOOL?
UH... WELL...
THIS IS THE GIANT ROBOT THAT, ONLY HOURS AGO, UNLEASHED A DEADLY ATTACK ON JAPAN. WE'VE BEEN INFORMED THAT THE RIOFALDIANS REFER TO IT AS A "SOROSARM."
THE ROBOT HASN'T MOVED FROM THE EDGE OF THE AIRPORT RUNWAY SINCE IT LAST FIRED ITS--

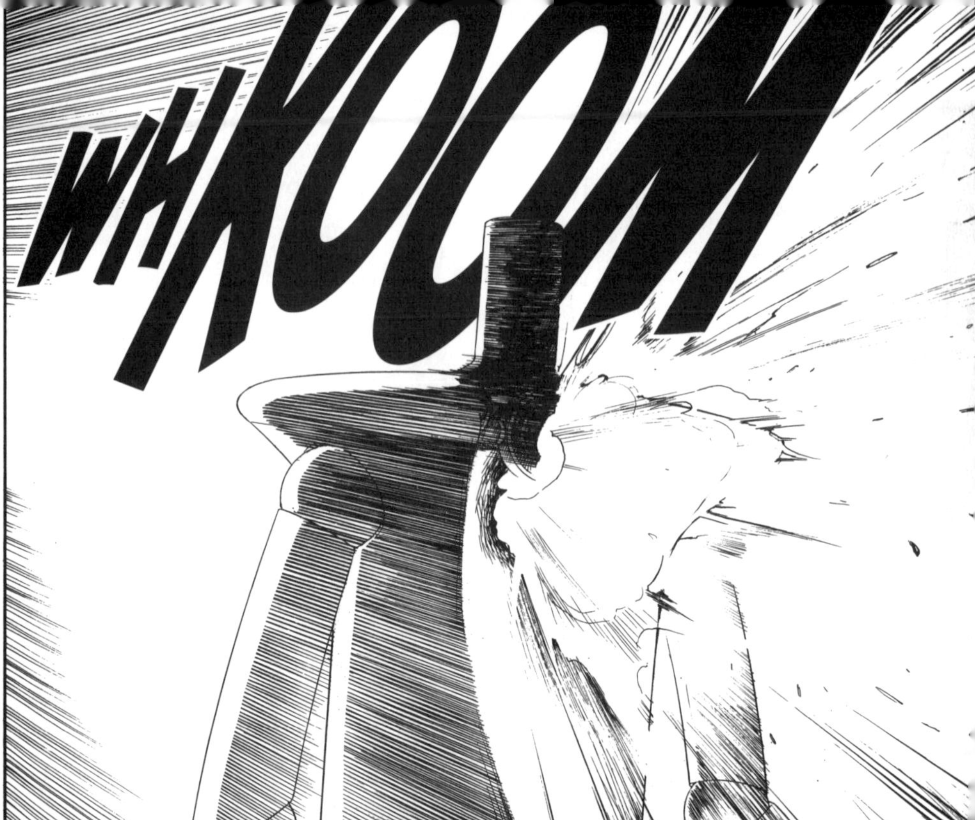

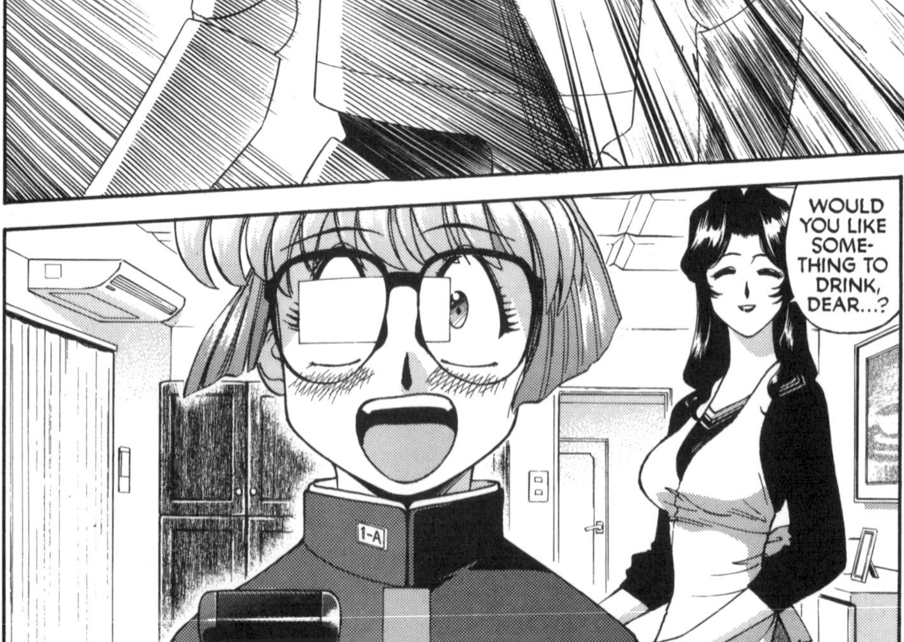
WOULD YOU LIKE SOME-THING TO DRINK, DEAR...?

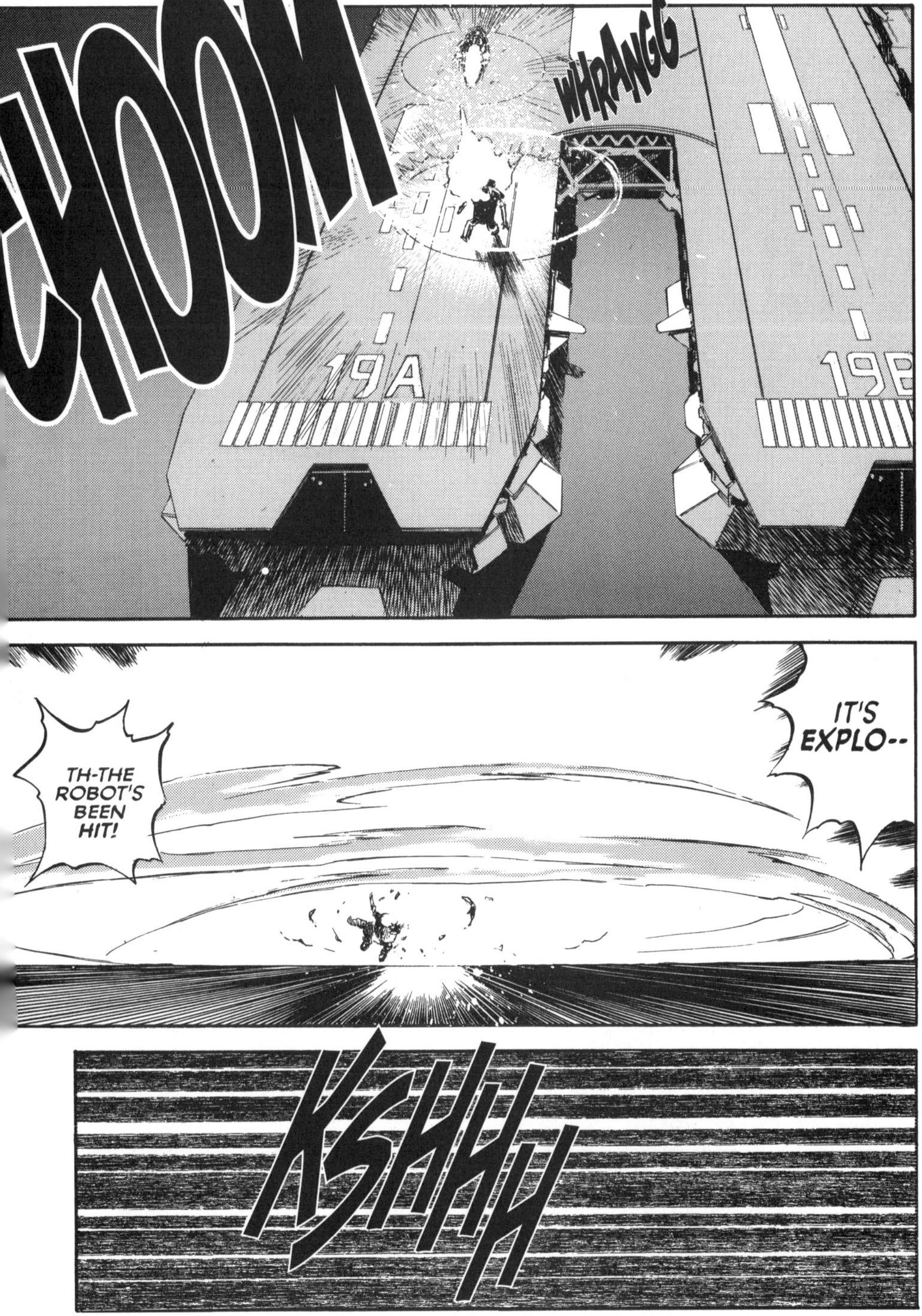
CHOOM
WHRANGG
19A
19B
TH-THE ROBOT'S BEEN HIT!
IT'S EXPLO--
KSHHH

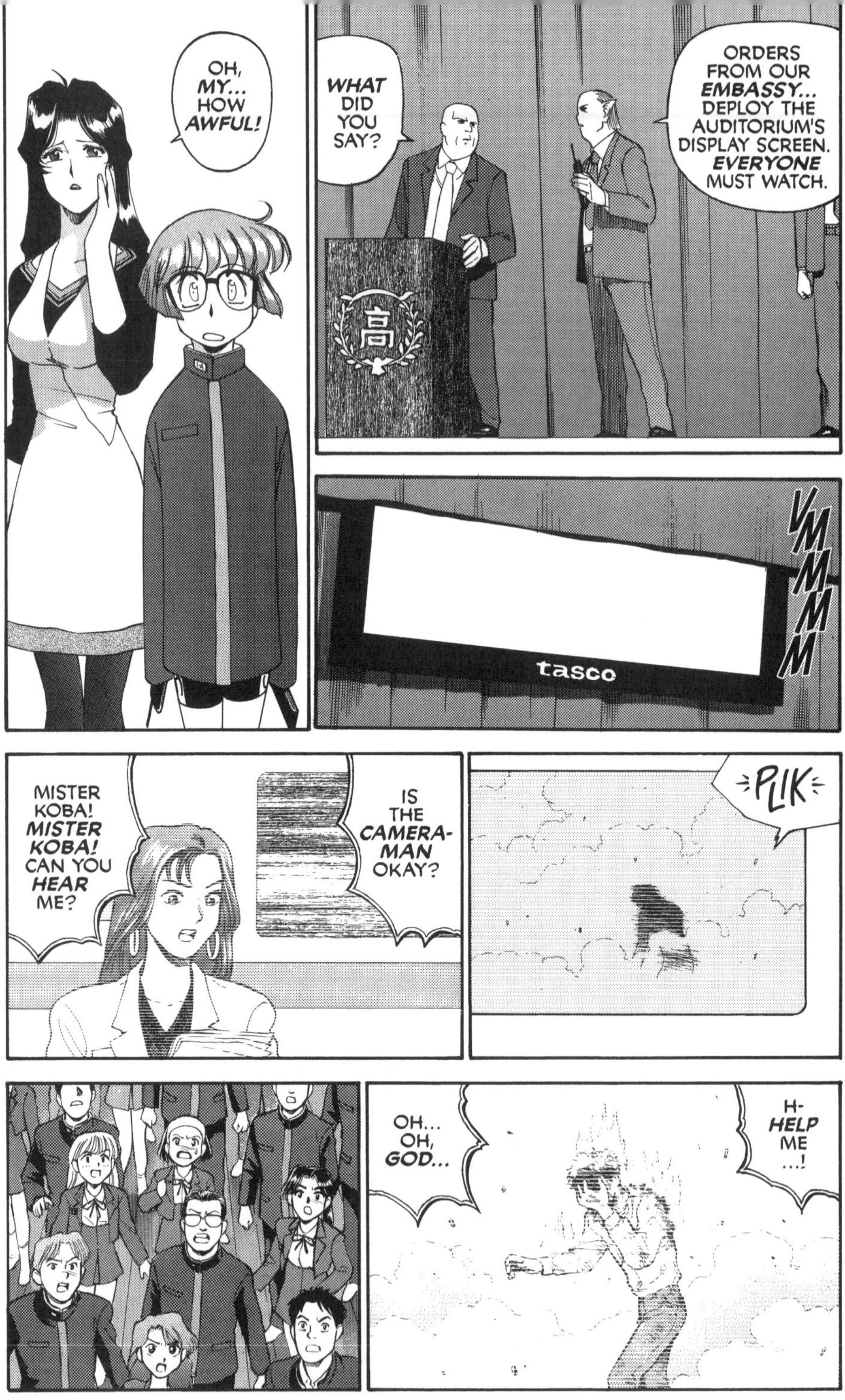
OH, MY... HOW AWFUL!
WHAT DID YOU SAY?
ORDERS FROM OUR EMBASSY... DEPLOY THE AUDITORIUM'S DISPLAY SCREEN. EVERYONE MUST WATCH.
VMMMMM
tasco
MISTER KOBA! MISTER KOBA! CAN YOU HEAR ME?
IS THE CAMERA-MAN OKAY?
PLIK
OH... OH, GOD...
H-HELP ME ...!

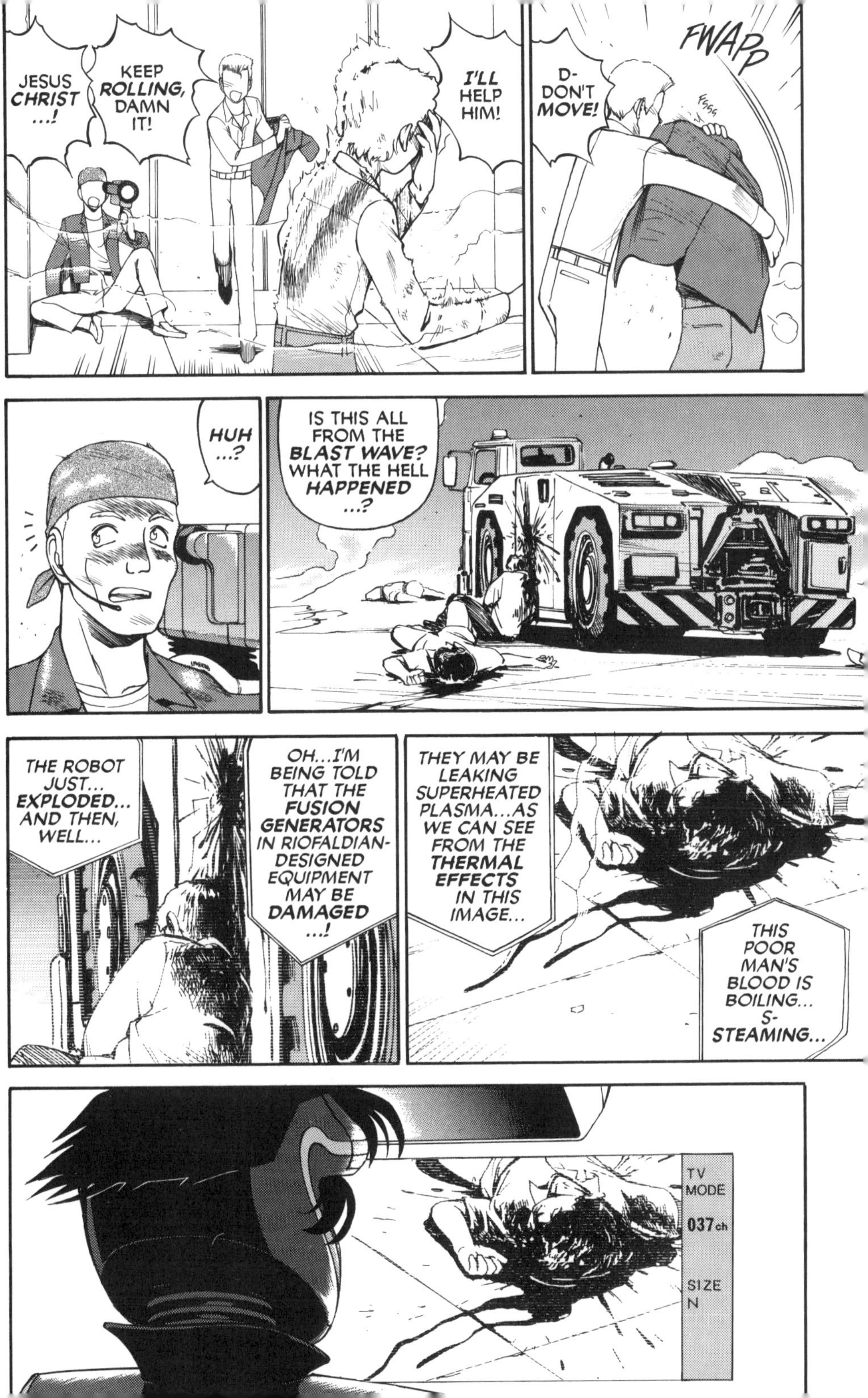
JESUS CHRIST ...!
KEEP ROLLING, DAMN IT!
I'LL HELP HIM!
D- DON'T MOVE!
FWAPP
HUH ...?
IS THIS ALL FROM THE BLAST WAVE? WHAT THE HELL HAPPENED ...?
THE ROBOT JUST... EXPLODED... AND THEN, WELL...
OH...I'M BEING TOLD THAT THE FUSION GENERATORS IN RIOFALDIAN-DESIGNED EQUIPMENT MAY BE DAMAGED ...!
THEY MAY BE LEAKING SUPERHEATED PLASMA...AS WE CAN SEE FROM THE THERMAL EFFECTS IN THIS IMAGE...
THIS POOR MAN'S BLOOD IS BOILING... S-STEAMING...
TV MODE
037ch
SIZE
N

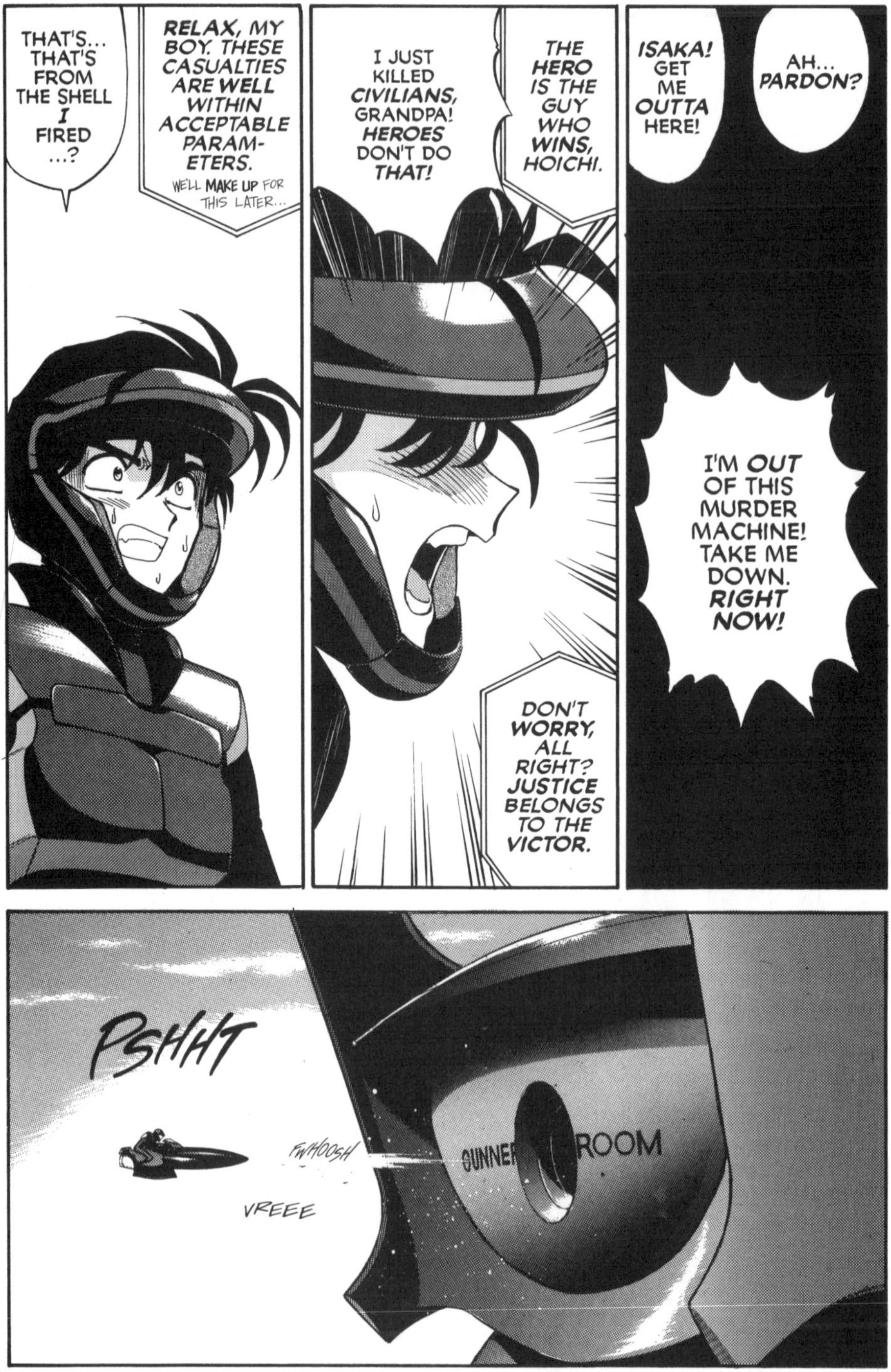
THAT'S... THAT'S FROM THE SHELL I FIRED ...?
RELAX, MY BOY. THESE CASUALTIES ARE WELL WITHIN ACCEPTABLE PARAM-ETERS.
WE'LL MAKE UP FOR THIS LATER...
I JUST KILLED CIVILIANS, GRANDPA! HEROES DON'T DO THAT!
THE HERO IS THE GUY WHO WINS, HOICHI.
DON'T WORRY, ALL RIGHT? JUSTICE BELONGS TO THE VICTOR.
ISAKA! GET ME OUTTA HERE!
AH... PARDON?
I'M OUT OF THIS MURDER MACHINE! TAKE ME DOWN. RIGHT NOW!
PSHHT
FWHOOSH
VREEE
GUNNER ROOM

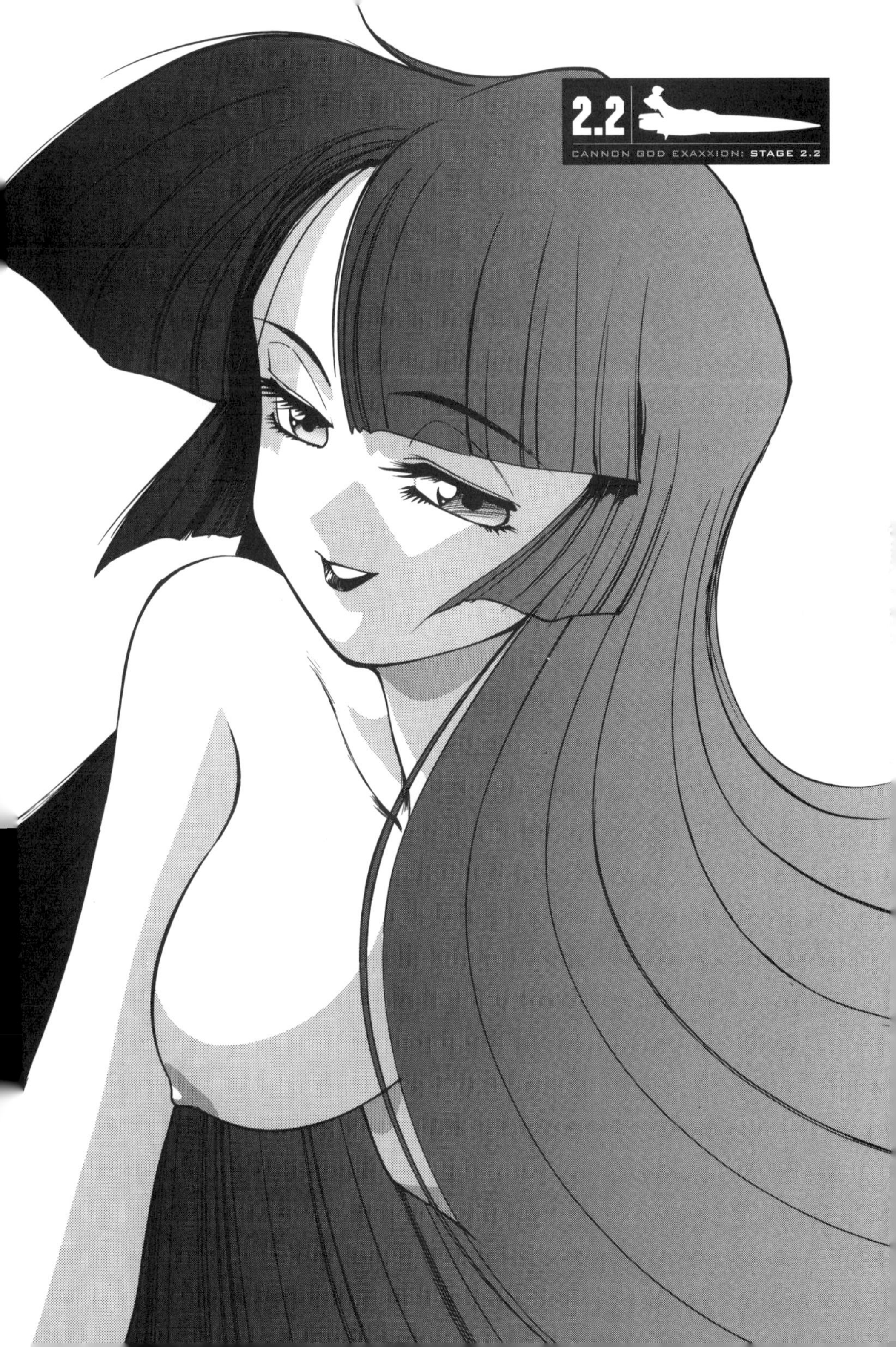
2.2
CANNON GOD EXAXXION: STAGE 2.2

KRKK
DAMN IT--!
USING THIS ROBOT...
...I'M JUST A FRIGGIN' MURDERER!
WHOOSH
I'M NO BETTER THAN THE DAMN ALIENS!
HEY, GRANDPA...
...WHAT THE HELL'S "HEROIC" ABOUT THAT, HUH?
FSHOOM

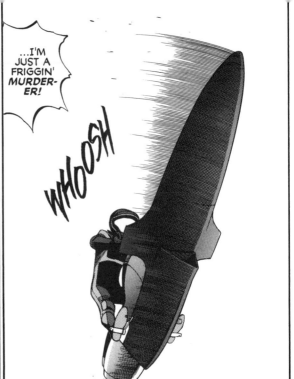

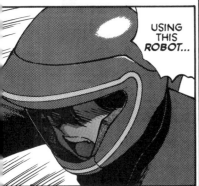

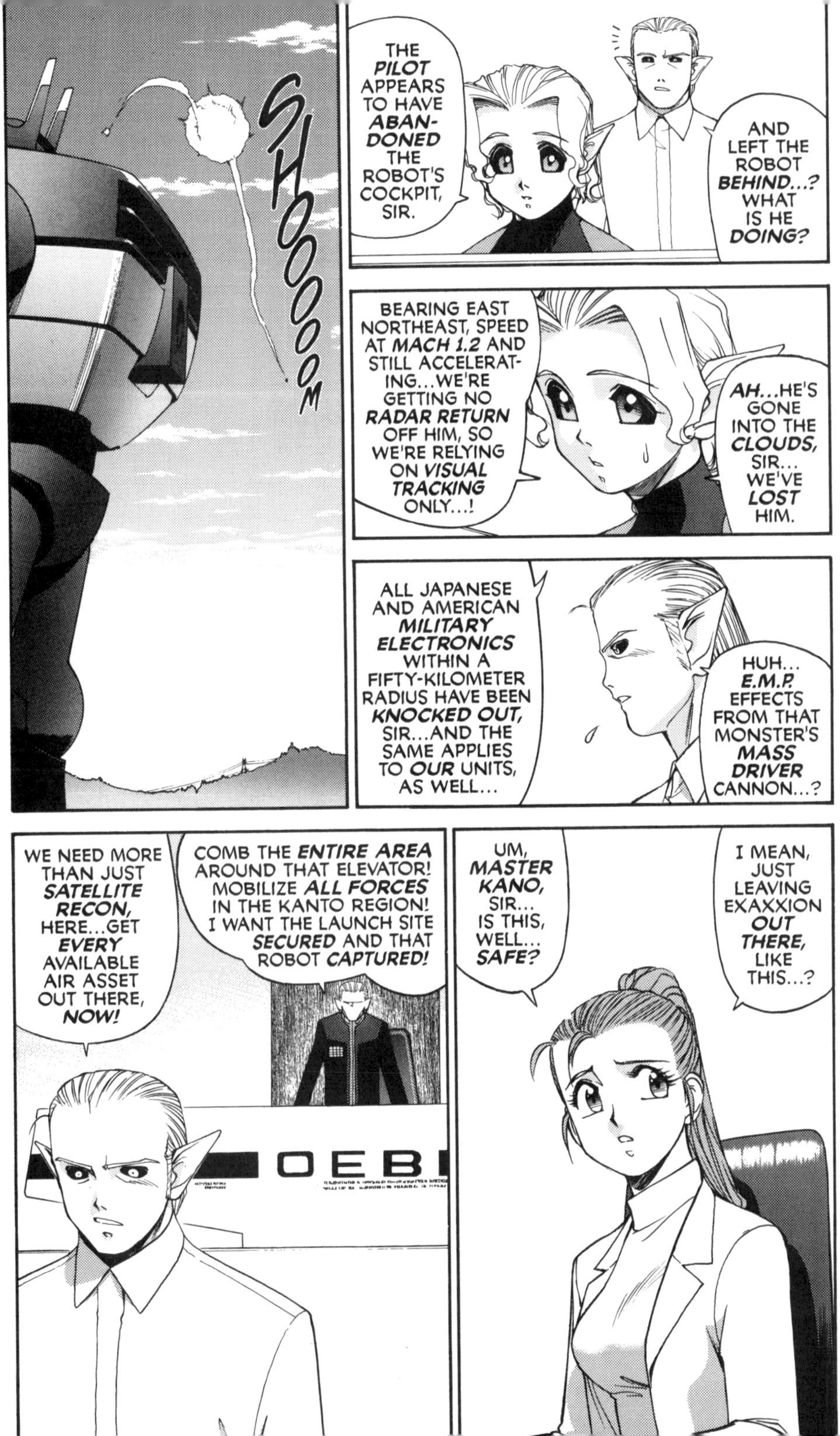
SHOOOOOOM
THE PILOT APPEARS TO HAVE ABAN-DONED THE ROBOT'S COCKPIT, SIR.
AND LEFT THE ROBOT BEHIND...? WHAT IS HE DOING?
BEARING EAST NORTHEAST, SPEED AT MACH 1.2 AND STILL ACCELERAT-ING...WE'RE GETTING NO RADAR RETURN OFF HIM, SO WE'RE RELYING ON VISUAL TRACKING ONLY...!
AH...HE'S GONE INTO THE CLOUDS, SIR... WE'VE LOST HIM.
ALL JAPANESE AND AMERICAN MILITARY ELECTRONICS WITHIN A FIFTY-KILOMETER RADIUS HAVE BEEN KNOCKED OUT, SIR...AND THE SAME APPLIES TO OUR UNITS, AS WELL...
HUH... E.M.P. EFFECTS FROM THAT MONSTER'S MASS DRIVER CANNON...?
WE NEED MORE THAN JUST SATELLITE RECON, HERE...GET EVERY AVAILABLE AIR ASSET OUT THERE, NOW!
COMB THE ENTIRE AREA AROUND THAT ELEVATOR! MOBILIZE ALL FORCES IN THE KANTO REGION! I WANT THE LAUNCH SITE SECURED AND THAT ROBOT CAPTURED!
OEB
UM, MASTER KANO, SIR... IS THIS, WELL... SAFE?
I MEAN, JUST LEAVING EXAXXION OUT THERE, LIKE THIS...?

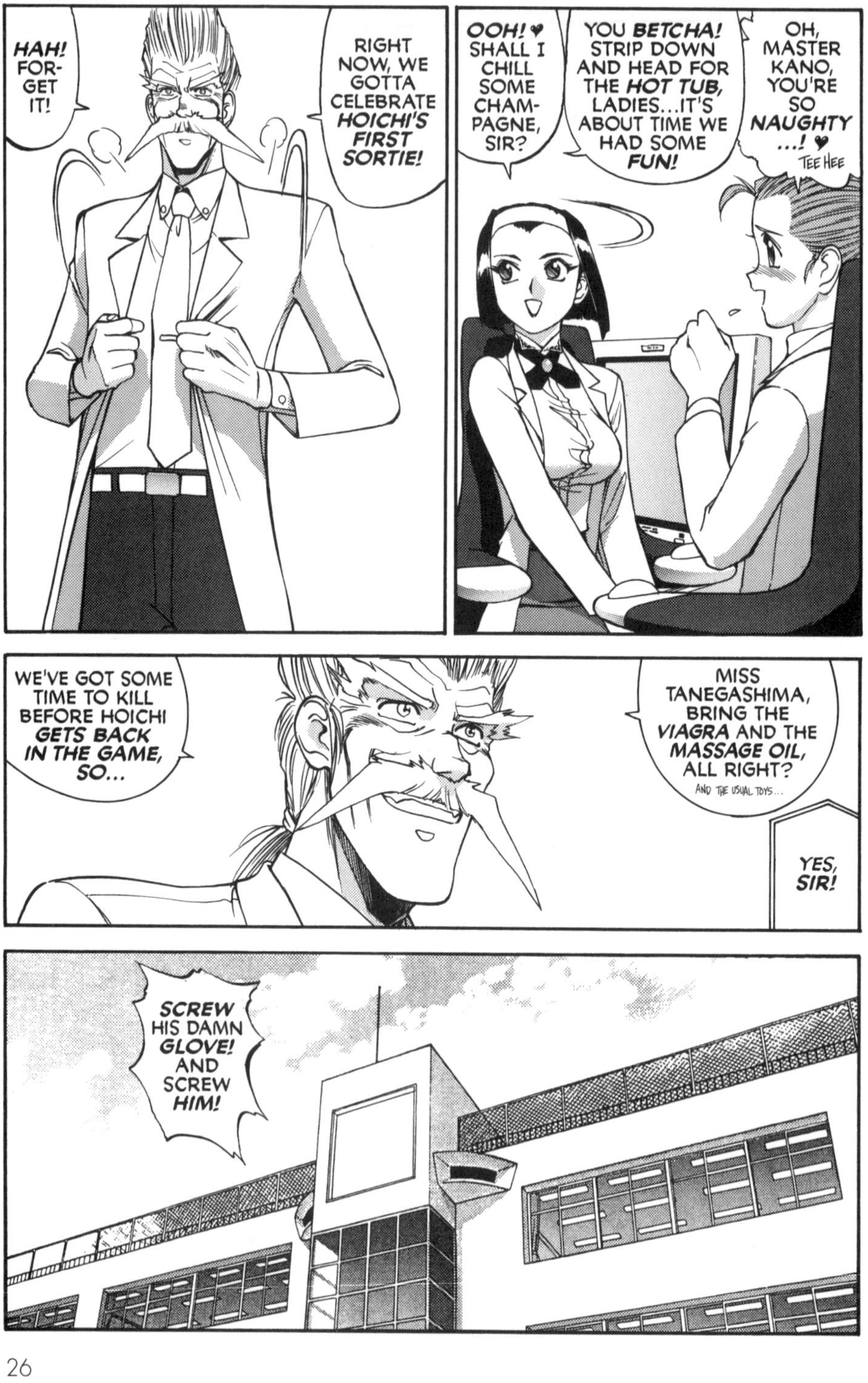
HAH! FORGET IT!
RIGHT NOW, WE GOTTA CELEBRATE HOICHI'S FIRST SORTIE!
OOH! ♥ SHALL I CHILL SOME CHAMPAGNE, SIR?
YOU BETCHA! STRIP DOWN AND HEAD FOR THE HOT TUB, LADIES...IT'S ABOUT TIME WE HAD SOME FUN!
OH, MASTER KANO, YOU'RE SO NAUGHTY ...! ♥
TEE HEE
WE'VE GOT SOME TIME TO KILL BEFORE HOICHI GETS BACK IN THE GAME, SO...
MISS TANEGASHIMA, BRING THE VIAGRA AND THE MASSAGE OIL, ALL RIGHT?
AND THE USUAL TOYS...
YES, SIR!
SCREW HIS DAMN GLOVE! AND SCREW HIM!

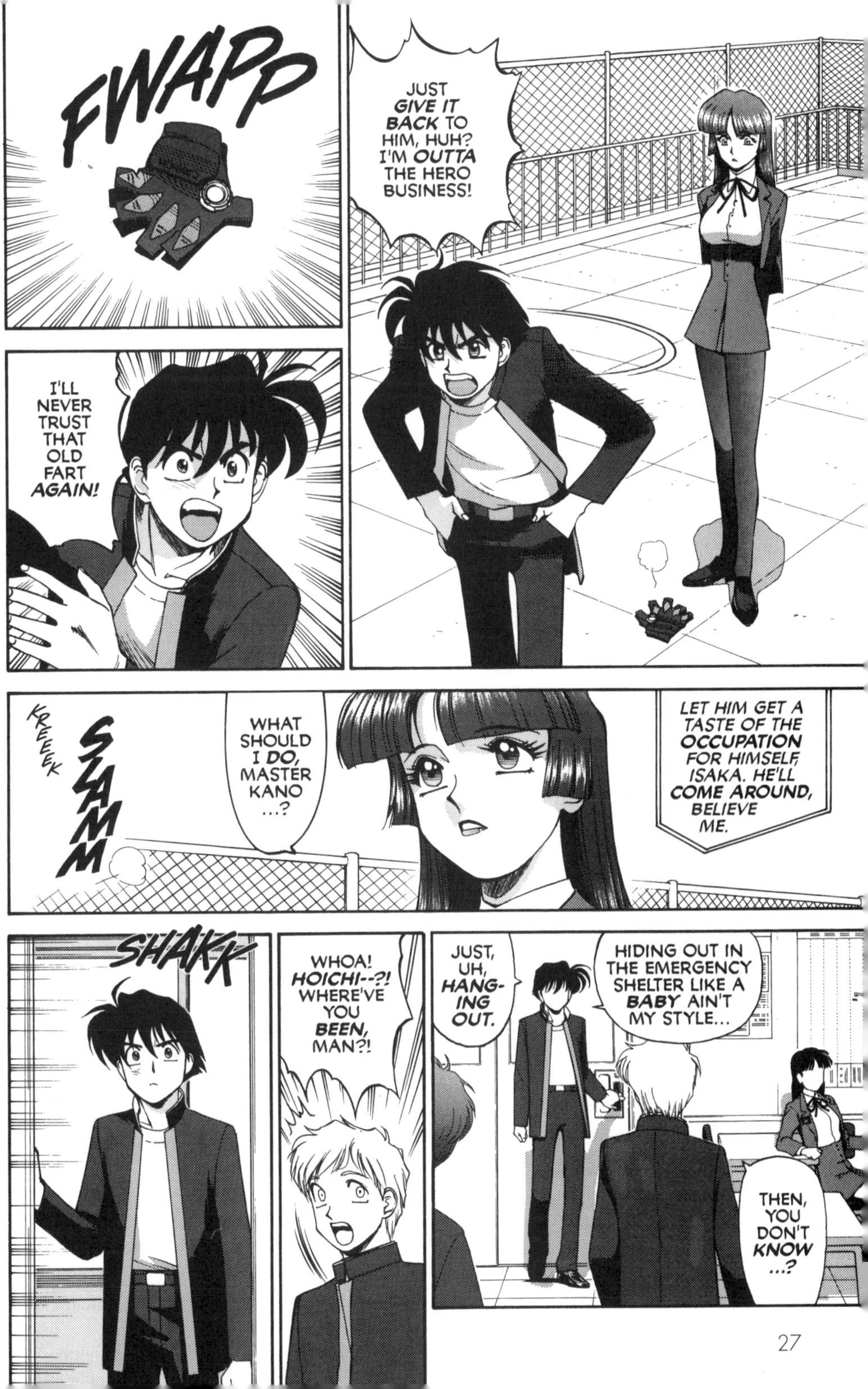
FWAPP
I'LL NEVER TRUST THAT OLD FART AGAIN!
JUST GIVE IT BACK TO HIM, HUH? I'M OUTTA THE HERO BUSINESS!
KREEEK
SLAMM
WHAT SHOULD I DO, MASTER KANO ...?
LET HIM GET A TASTE OF THE OCCUPATION FOR HIMSELF, ISAKA. HE'LL COME AROUND, BELIEVE ME.
SHAKK
WHOA! HOICHI--?! WHERE'VE YOU BEEN, MAN?!
JUST, UH, HANGING OUT.
HIDING OUT IN THE EMERGENCY SHELTER LIKE A BABY AIN'T MY STYLE...
THEN, YOU DON'T KNOW ...?

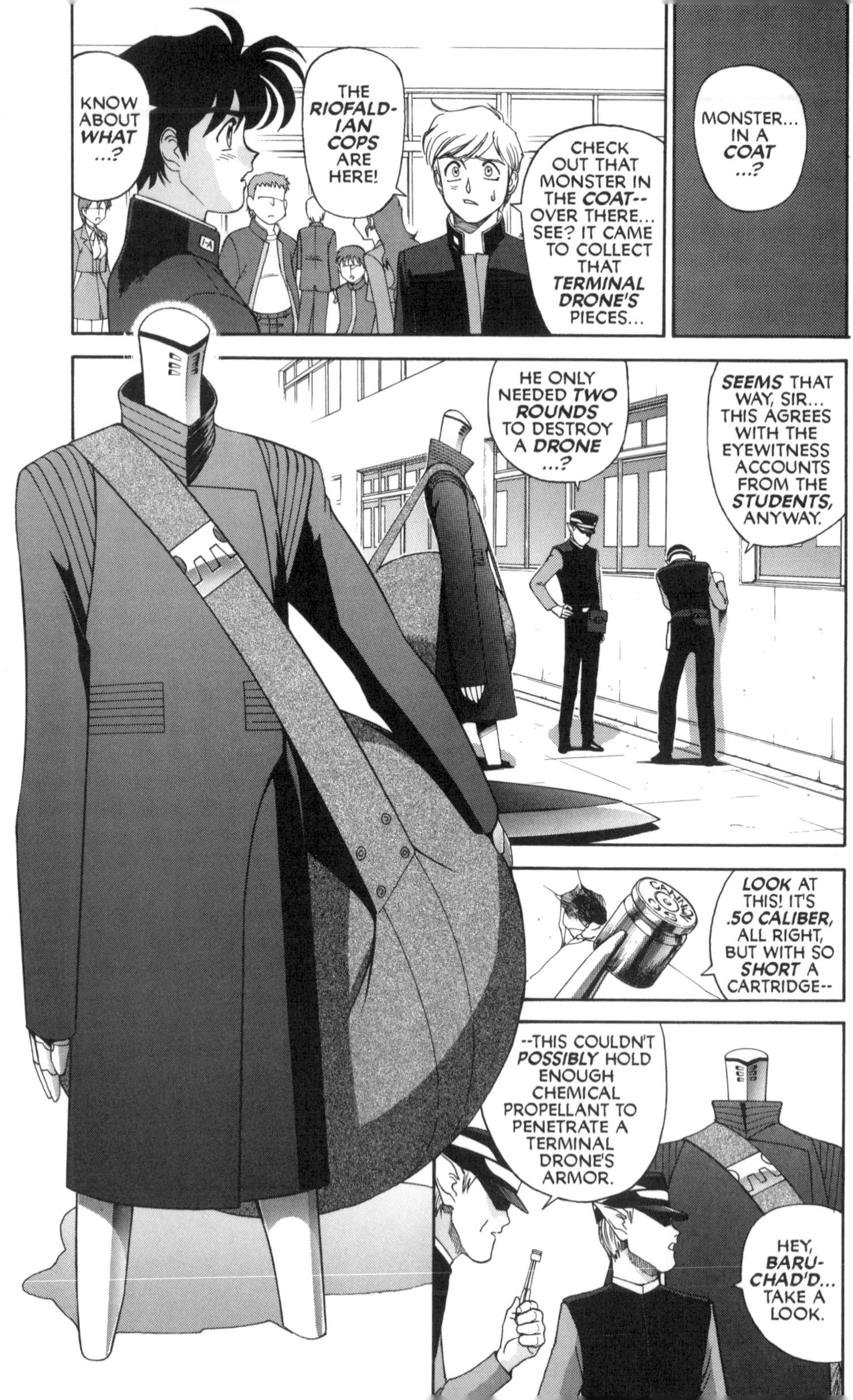

KNOW ABOUT *WHAT* ...?
THE *RIOFALDIAN COPS* ARE HERE!
CHECK OUT THAT MONSTER IN THE *COAT*-- OVER THERE... SEE? IT CAME TO COLLECT THAT *TERMINAL DRONE'S* PIECES...
MONSTER... IN A *COAT* ...?
HE ONLY NEEDED *TWO ROUNDS* TO DESTROY A *DRONE* ...?
SEEMS THAT WAY, SIR... THIS AGREES WITH THE EYEWITNESS ACCOUNTS FROM THE *STUDENTS,* ANYWAY.
LOOK AT THIS! IT'S *.50 CALIBER,* ALL RIGHT, BUT WITH SO *SHORT* A CARTRIDGE--
--THIS COULDN'T *POSSIBLY* HOLD ENOUGH CHEMICAL PROPELLANT TO PENETRATE A TERMINAL DRONE'S ARMOR.
HEY, *BARUCHAD'D*... TAKE A LOOK.

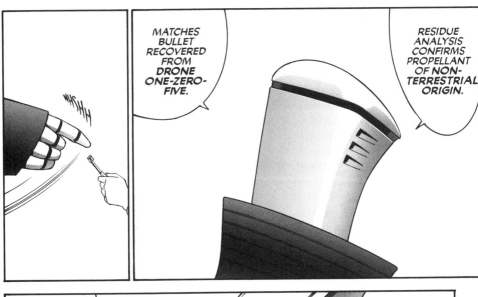

MATCHES BULLET RECOVERED FROM *DRONE ONE-ZERO-FIVE.*

RESIDUE ANALYSIS CONFIRMS PROPELLANT OF *NON-TERRESTRIAL* ORIGIN.

EJECTOR *COMPRESSION MARKS* SUGGEST A *HUMAN* COULD NOT FIRE THIS WEAPON.

VREEE

ESTIMATED RECOIL--OVER *TEN TIMES GREATER* THAN TERRESTRIAL .50 CALIBER ACTION EXPRESS PISTOL ROUND.

YEAH... EVEN THE *EJECTED CASINGS* WERE DRIVEN INTO *CONCRETE...*

SO OUR MAN IN BLACK MUST BE A *CYBORG* OR AN *ANDROID,* THEN...OR IS HE WEARING A *POWER-SUIT...?*

THAT'S ONE *BIG* MOTHER...!

*YEAH...*A RIOFALDIAN *DRONE TROOPER,* THEY SAID. AND THE PRINCIPAL SAYS, "OBEY HIM, OR *ELSE"...!*

AND CHECK OUT THAT *BAG...* HE'S CARRYING THE *"BLACK EIGHTBALL"* PART OF THE DRONE IN IT...!

SAY, WHAT HAPPENED TO *MISS KIN'BA...?*

BEATS *ME...* I HAVEN'T SEEN HER SINCE WE WERE SENT DOWN TO THE *SHELTER.*

HEY! YOU *STUDENTS!* GET BACK TO CLASS!

WHTT

OUR TOP PRIORITY IS THE *UNIDENTIFIED COMBATANT.*

WE'LL RUN CHECKS ON EVERYONE... *TEACHERS,* TOO.

I WILL ASSIST.

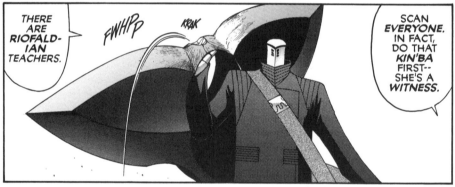

THERE ARE *RIOFALDIAN* TEACHERS.

FWHPP

KRAK

SCAN *EVERYONE.* IN FACT, DO THAT *KIN'BA* FIRST-- SHE'S A *WITNESS.*

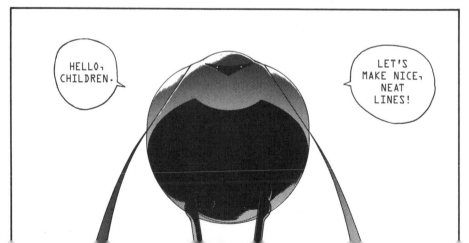

HELLO, CHILDREN.

LET'S MAKE NICE, NEAT LINES!

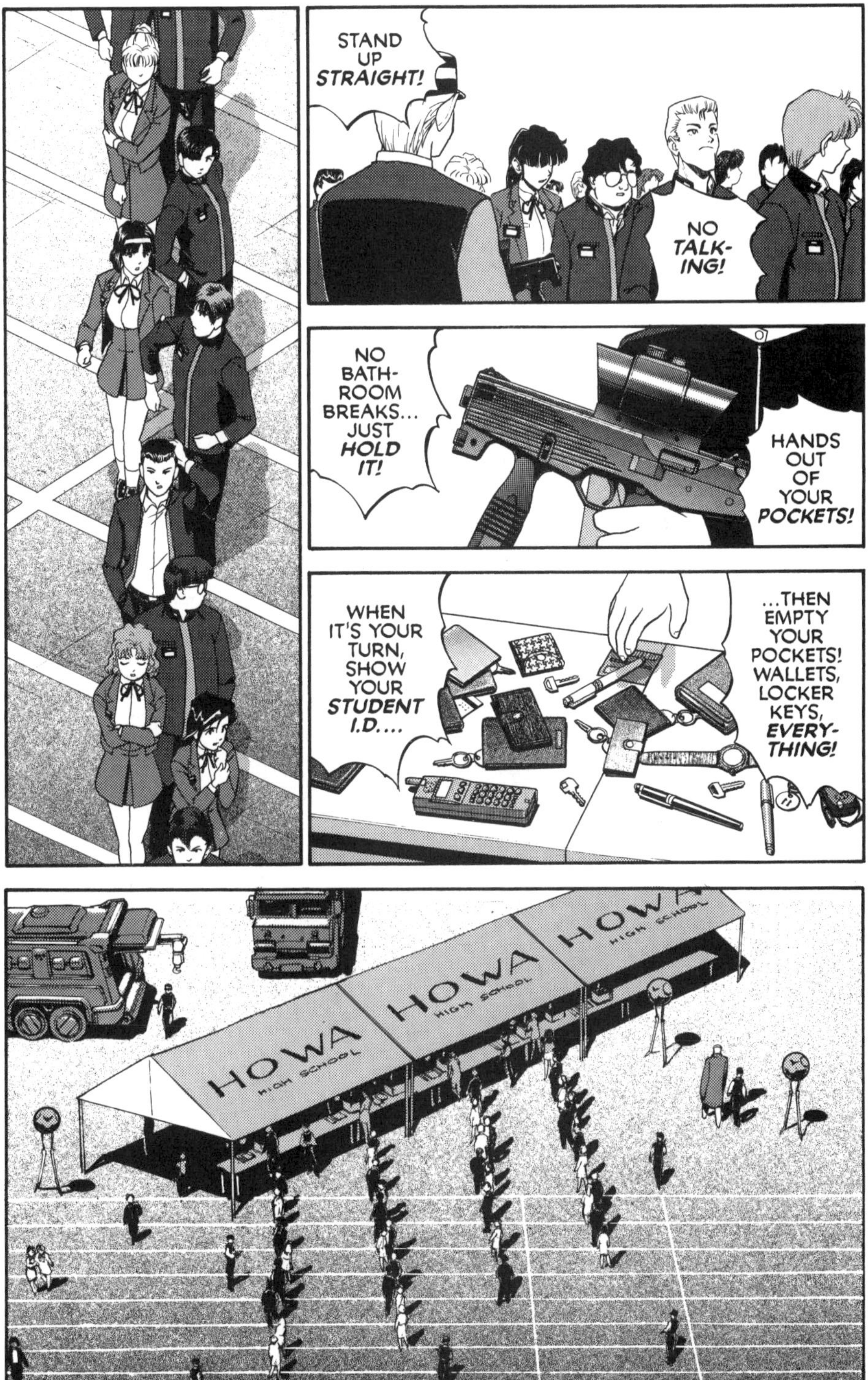
STAND UP *STRAIGHT!*
NO *TALKING!*
NO BATHROOM BREAKS... JUST *HOLD IT!*
HANDS OUT OF YOUR *POCKETS!*
WHEN IT'S YOUR TURN, SHOW YOUR *STUDENT I.D....*
...THEN EMPTY YOUR POCKETS! WALLETS, LOCKER KEYS, *EVERYTHING!*
HOWA HIGH SCHOOL
HOWA HIGH SCHOOL
HOWA HIGH SCHOOL

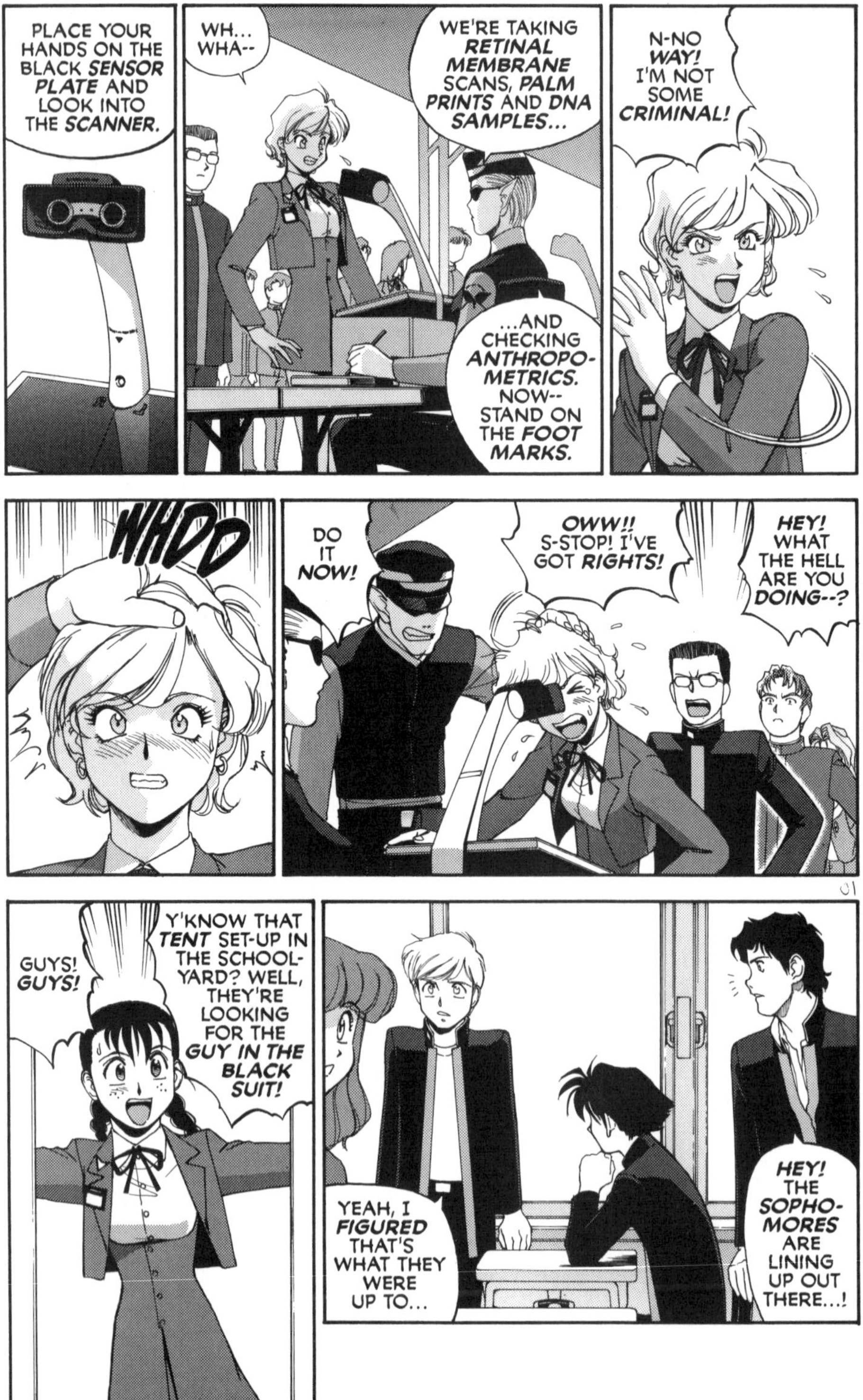
PLACE YOUR HANDS ON THE BLACK SENSOR PLATE AND LOOK INTO THE SCANNER.
WH... WHA--
WE'RE TAKING RETINAL MEMBRANE SCANS, PALM PRINTS AND DNA SAMPLES...
...AND CHECKING ANTHROPO-METRICS. NOW-- STAND ON THE FOOT MARKS.
N-NO WAY! I'M NOT SOME CRIMINAL!
WHDD
DO IT NOW!
OWW!! S-STOP! I'VE GOT RIGHTS!
HEY! WHAT THE HELL ARE YOU DOING--?
GUYS! GUYS!
Y'KNOW THAT TENT SET-UP IN THE SCHOOL-YARD? WELL, THEY'RE LOOKING FOR THE GUY IN THE BLACK SUIT!
YEAH, I FIGURED THAT'S WHAT THEY WERE UP TO...
HEY! THE SOPHO-MORES ARE LINING UP OUT THERE...!

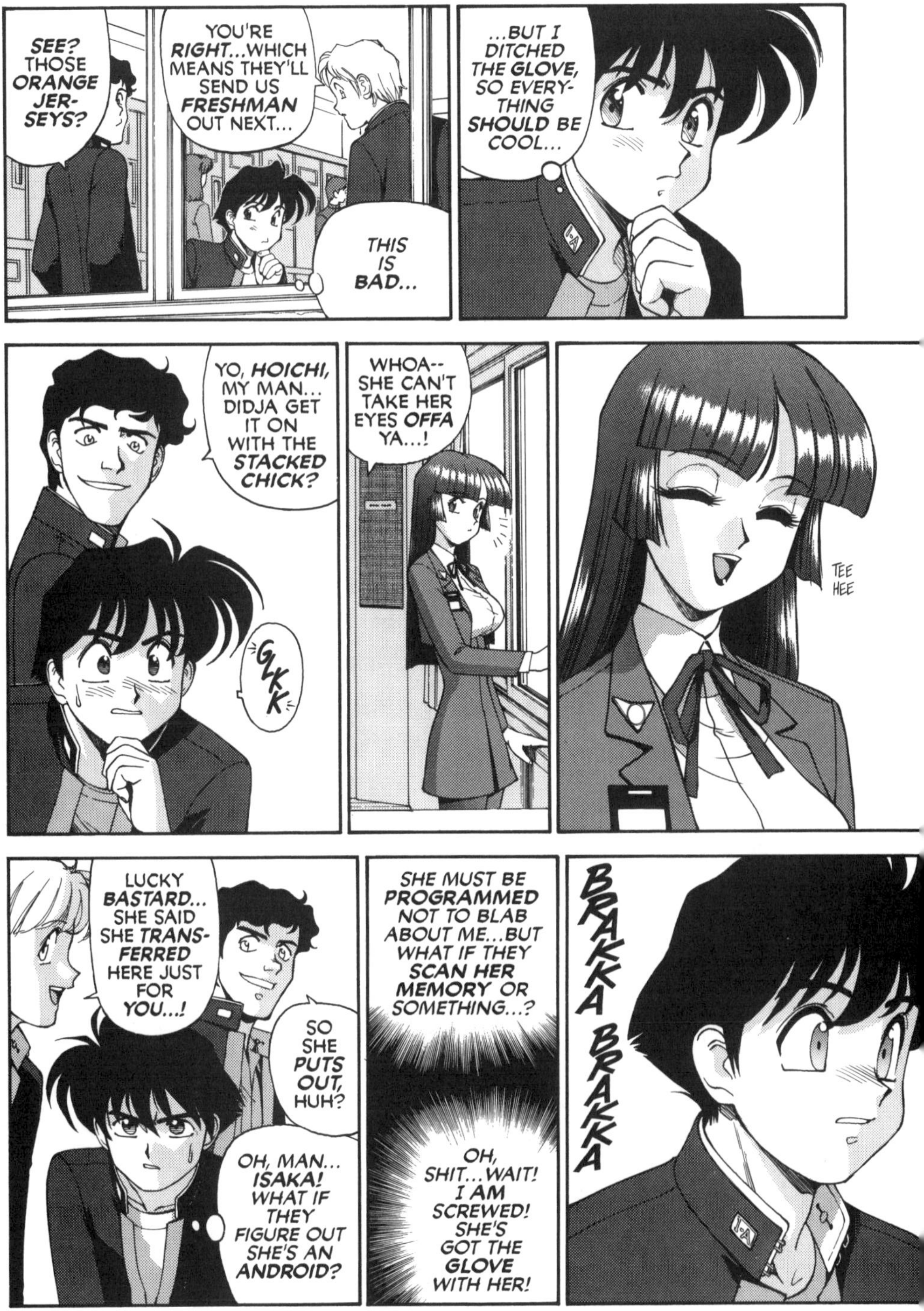
SEE? THOSE ORANGE JERSEYS?
YOU'RE RIGHT...WHICH MEANS THEY'LL SEND US FRESHMAN OUT NEXT...
THIS IS BAD...
...BUT I DITCHED THE GLOVE, SO EVERYTHING SHOULD BE COOL...
YO, HOICHI, MY MAN... DIDJA GET IT ON WITH THE STACKED CHICK?
GLKK
WHOA-- SHE CAN'T TAKE HER EYES OFFA YA...!
TEE HEE
LUCKY BASTARD... SHE SAID SHE TRANSFERRED HERE JUST FOR YOU...!
SO SHE PUTS OUT, HUH?
OH, MAN... ISAKA! WHAT IF THEY FIGURE OUT SHE'S AN ANDROID?
SHE MUST BE PROGRAMMED NOT TO BLAB ABOUT ME...BUT WHAT IF THEY SCAN HER MEMORY OR SOMETHING...?
OH, SHIT...WAIT! I AM SCREWED! SHE'S GOT THE GLOVE WITH HER!
BRAKKA BRAKKA

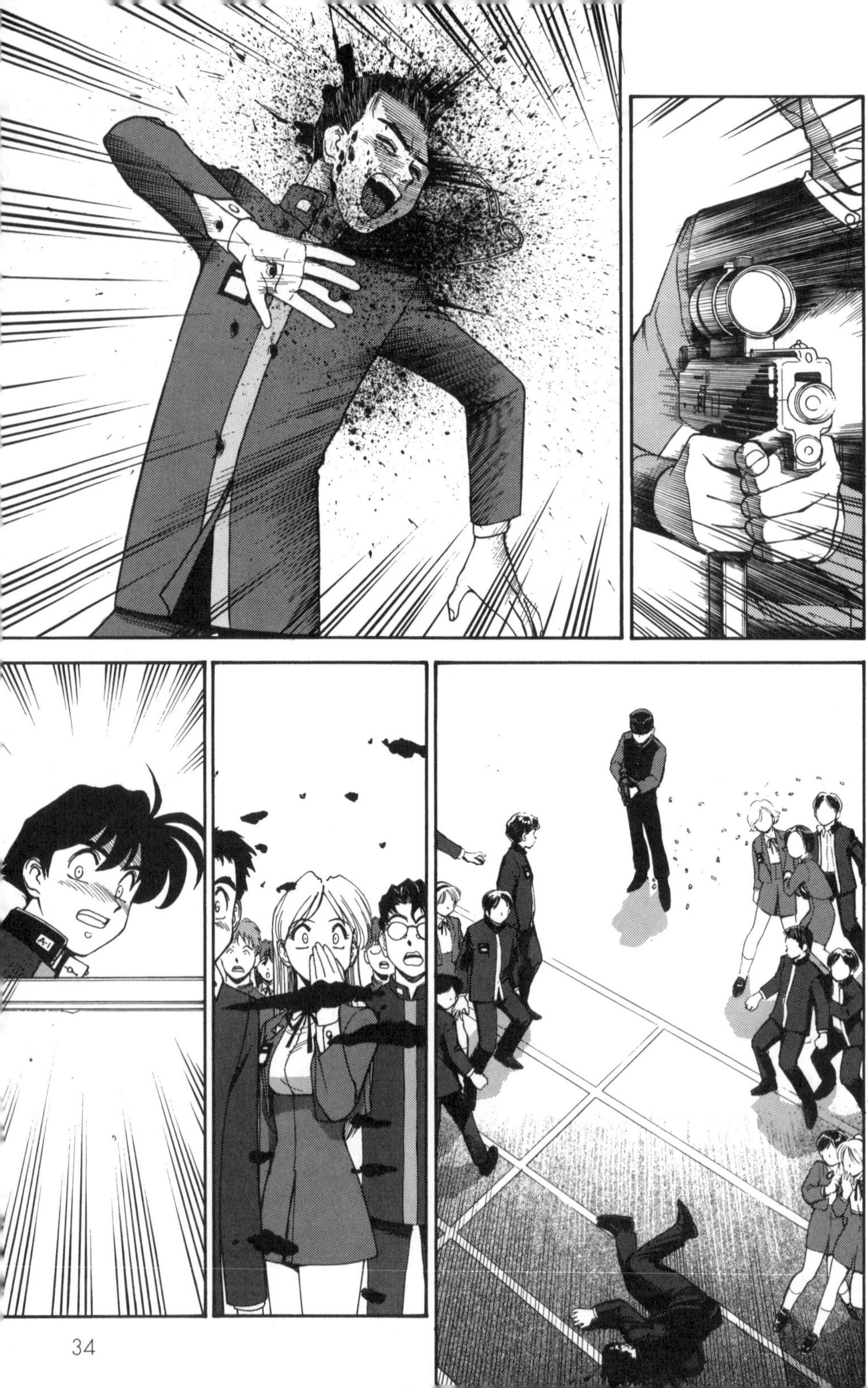
A-1

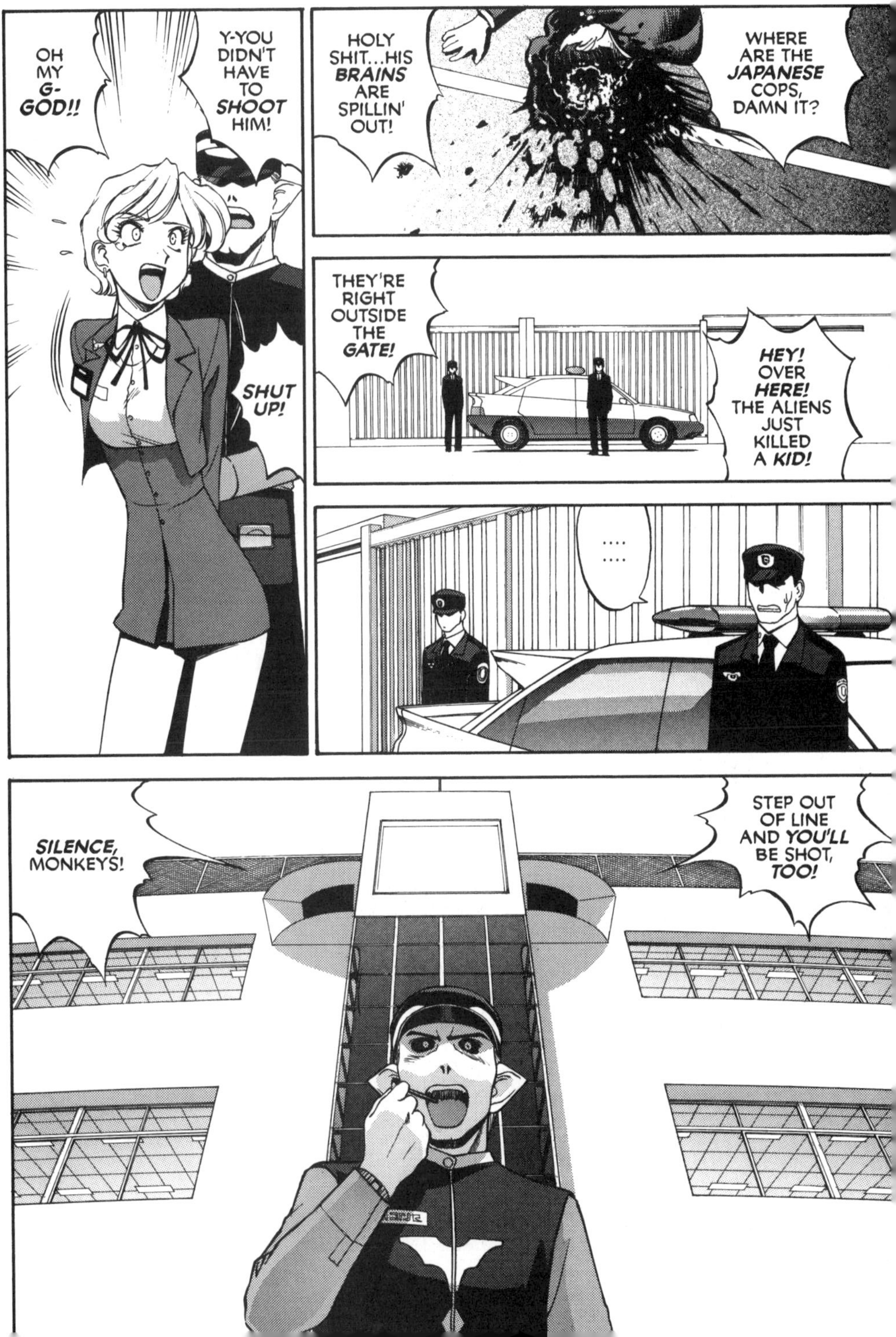
OH MY G-GOD!!
Y-YOU DIDN'T HAVE TO SHOOT HIM!
SHUT UP!
HOLY SHIT...HIS BRAINS ARE SPILLIN' OUT!
WHERE ARE THE JAPANESE COPS, DAMN IT?
THEY'RE RIGHT OUTSIDE THE GATE!
HEY! OVER HERE! THE ALIENS JUST KILLED A KID!
....
....
SILENCE, MONKEYS!
STEP OUT OF LINE AND YOU'LL BE SHOT, TOO!

AND DON'T BOTHER TRYING TO APPEAL TO THE TOKYO METROPOLITAN POLICE...THEY'RE *UNDER OUR COMMAND*... AS ARE *ALL OF YOU.*

UNDER-STAND THIS-- *YOU HAVE NO RIGHTS!*

WE'RE *ALLOWING* YOU TO LIVE! DO NOT *FORGET* IT!

I'M AUTHORIZED TO *TERMINATE* ANY HUMAN WHO OBSTRUCTS THE PEACEFUL EXECUTION OF OUR PUBLIC DUTIES!

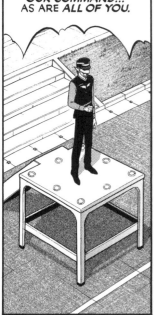

OBEY OUR *COMMANDS,* AND YOU WON'T GET *HURT!*

STOP ACTING LIKE *ANIMALS!* ACT LIKE *RIOFALDIANS*... AND *FOLLOW ORDERS!*

KRKK

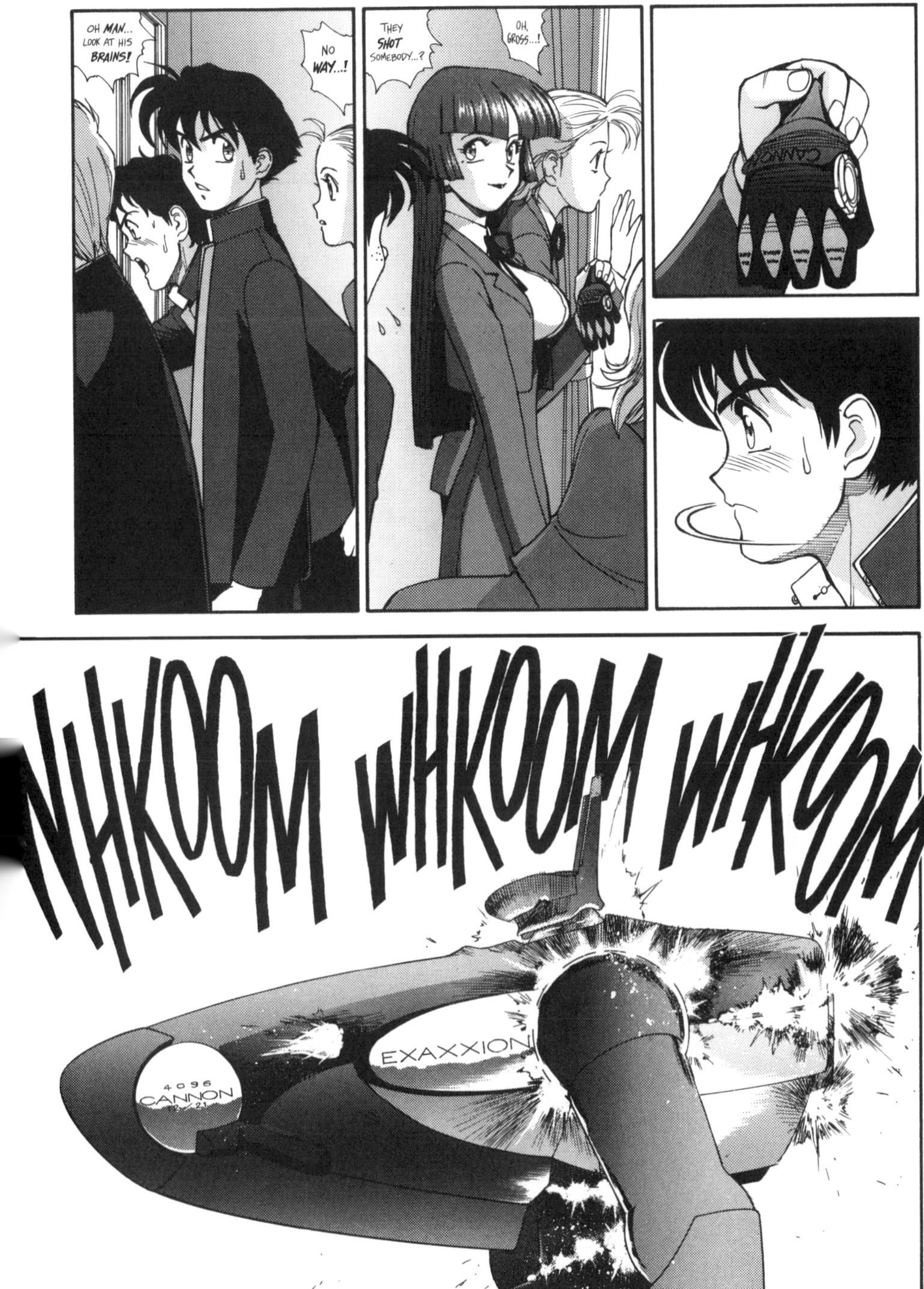
OH MAN... LOOK AT HIS BRAINS!
NO WAY...!
THEY SHOT SOMEBODY...?
OH, GROSS...!
CANNON
WHKOOM WHKOOM WHKOOM
EXAXXION
4096 CANNON

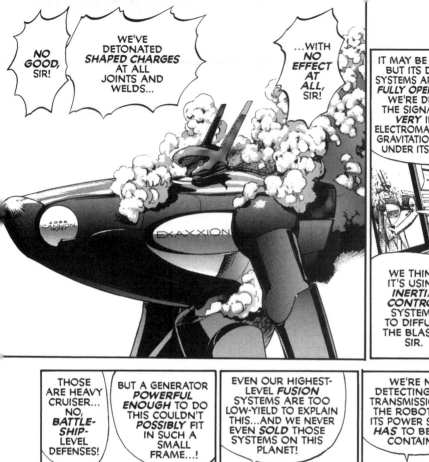

NO GOOD, SIR!

WE'VE DETONATED *SHAPED CHARGES* AT ALL JOINTS AND WELDS...

...WITH *NO EFFECT AT ALL,* SIR!

IT MAY BE *IMMOBILE,* BUT ITS DEFENSIVE SYSTEMS APPEAR TO BE *FULLY OPERATIONAL...* WE'RE DETECTING THE SIGNATURES OF *VERY* INTENSE ELECTROMAGNETIC AND GRAVITATIONAL FLUXES UNDER ITS ARMOR...!

WE THINK IT'S USING *INERTIA CONTROL* SYSTEMS TO DIFFUSE THE BLASTS, SIR.

THOSE ARE HEAVY CRUISER... NO, *BATTLE-SHIP-* LEVEL DEFENSES!

BUT A GENERATOR *POWERFUL ENOUGH* TO DO THIS COULDN'T *POSSIBLY* FIT IN SUCH A SMALL FRAME...!

EVEN OUR HIGHEST-LEVEL *FUSION* SYSTEMS ARE TOO LOW-YIELD TO EXPLAIN THIS...AND WE NEVER EVEN *SOLD* THOSE SYSTEMS ON THIS PLANET!

AN *EXTERNAL* POWER SOURCE, THEN ...?

WE'RE NOT DETECTING *ANY* TRANSMISSIONS TO THE ROBOT, SIR... ITS POWER SOURCE *HAS* TO BE SELF-CONTAINED.

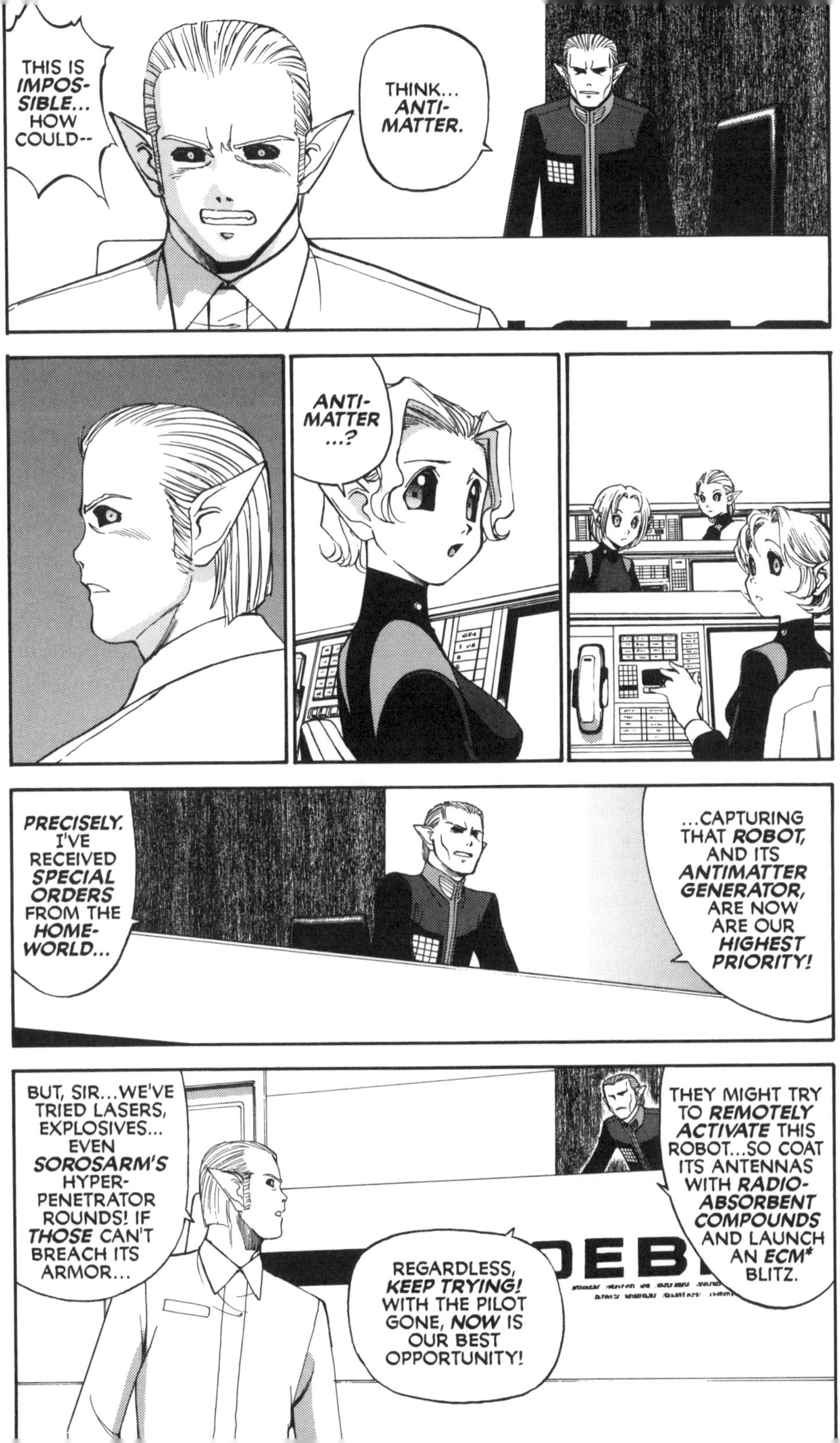
THIS IS IMPOSSIBLE... HOW COULD--
THINK... ANTI-MATTER.
ANTI-MATTER ...?
PRECISELY. I'VE RECEIVED SPECIAL ORDERS FROM THE HOME-WORLD...
...CAPTURING THAT ROBOT, AND ITS ANTIMATTER GENERATOR, ARE NOW ARE OUR HIGHEST PRIORITY!
BUT, SIR...WE'VE TRIED LASERS, EXPLOSIVES... EVEN SOROSARM'S HYPER-PENETRATOR ROUNDS! IF THOSE CAN'T BREACH ITS ARMOR...
REGARDLESS, KEEP TRYING! WITH THE PILOT GONE, NOW IS OUR BEST OPPORTUNITY!
THEY MIGHT TRY TO REMOTELY ACTIVATE THIS ROBOT...SO COAT ITS ANTENNAS WITH RADIO-ABSORBENT COMPOUNDS AND LAUNCH AN ECM* BLITZ.

*: ELECTRONIC COUNTERMEASURES

OF *COURSE,* SIR... WE'LL TRY *EVERY-THING,* BUT...

I *KNOW.*

IN THE MEAN-TIME, I'LL WORK A *DIFFERENT* ANGLE...

...IF THIS ROBOT IS PROTECTED BY HIGH-OUTPUT *GRAVITY* AND *INERTIA* CONTROL SYSTEMS, THE ONLY ANSWER IS *OVERWHELMING KINETIC ENERGY!*

I'VE DEPLOYED THE PERFECT *HEAVY-MASS WEAPON* TO ORBITAL BASE ONE.

IT SHIPS FOR JAPAN THE *MOMENT* IT'S READY...

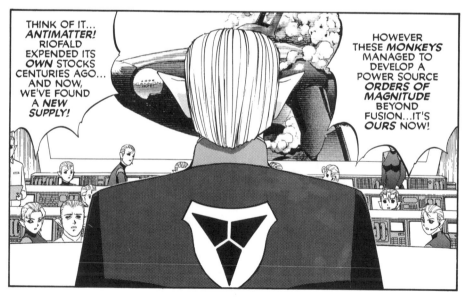

THINK OF IT... *ANTIMATTER!* RIOFALD EXPENDED ITS *OWN* STOCKS CENTURIES AGO... AND NOW, WE'VE FOUND A *NEW* SUPPLY!

HOWEVER THESE *MONKEYS* MANAGED TO DEVELOP A POWER SOURCE *ORDERS OF MAGNITUDE* BEYOND FUSION...IT'S *OURS* NOW!

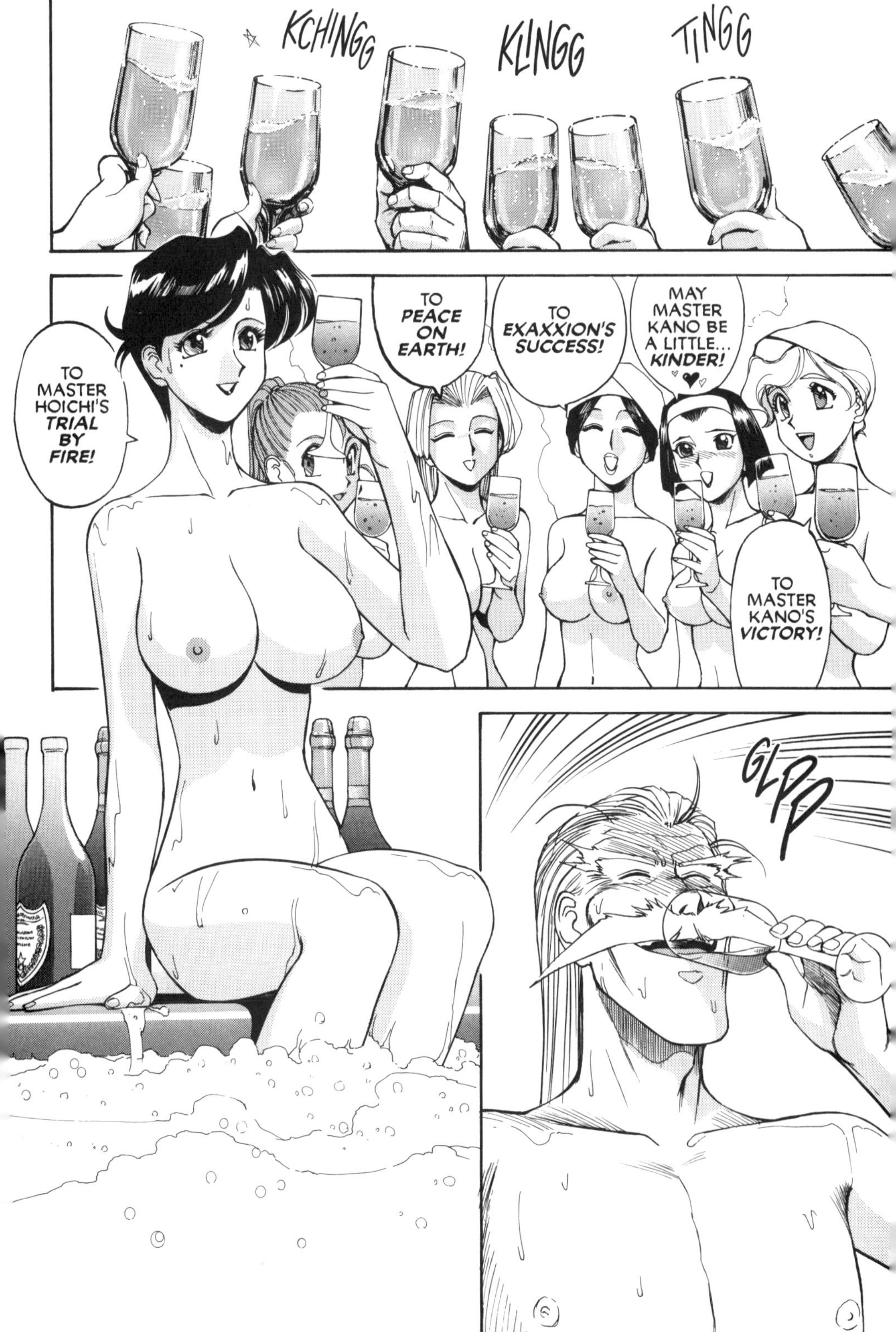
KCHINGG
KLINGG
TINGG
TO MASTER HOICHI'S TRIAL BY FIRE!
TO PEACE ON EARTH!
TO EXAXXION'S SUCCESS!
MAY MASTER KANO BE A LITTLE... KINDER!
TO MASTER KANO'S VICTORY!
GLPP

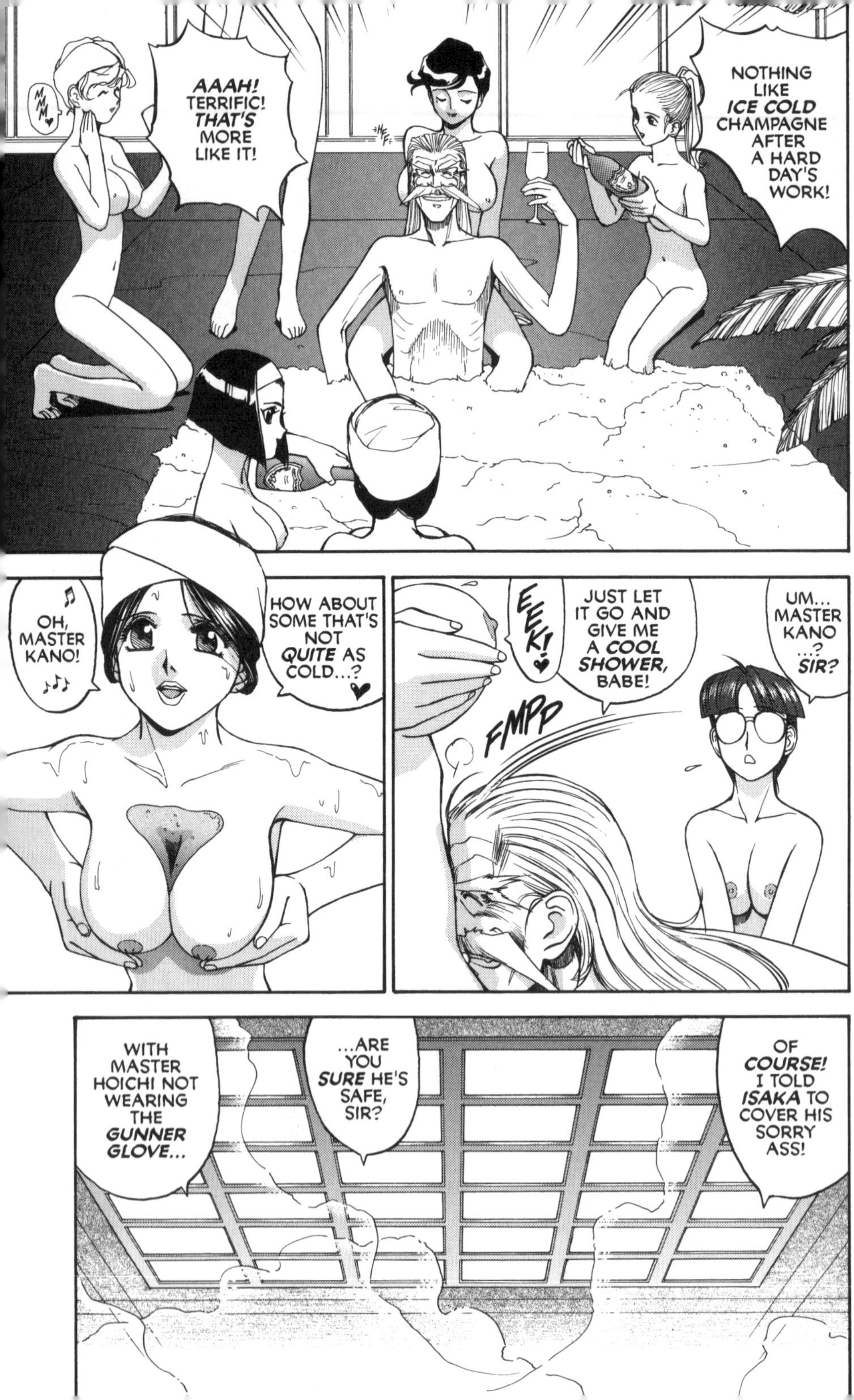
MMM ♥
AAAH! TERRIFIC! THAT'S MORE LIKE IT!
NOTHING LIKE ICE COLD CHAMPAGNE AFTER A HARD DAY'S WORK!
♪ OH, MASTER KANO! ♪♪
HOW ABOUT SOME THAT'S NOT QUITE AS COLD...? ♥
EEK! ♥
JUST LET IT GO AND GIVE ME A COOL SHOWER, BABE!
FMPP
UM... MASTER KANO ...? SIR?
WITH MASTER HOICHI NOT WEARING THE GUNNER GLOVE...
...ARE YOU SURE HE'S SAFE, SIR?
OF COURSE! I TOLD ISAKA TO COVER HIS SORRY ASS!

BINGG ♪ BONGG ♪

LET'S FOLLOW OUR RIOFALDIAN FRIENDS TO A PEACEFUL SOCIETY! A MESSAGE FROM THE PRIME MINISTER'S OFFICE

ATTENTION ALL *FRESHMEN!* LINE UP IN FRONT OF THE SCHOOL-YARD TENTS IMMEDI-ATELY!

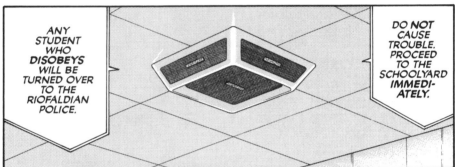

ANY STUDENT WHO DISOBEYS WILL BE TURNED OVER TO THE RIOFALDIAN POLICE.

DO *NOT* CAUSE TROUBLE. PROCEED TO THE SCHOOLYARD IMMEDI-ATELY.

OH, HOICHI ...?

ISAKA ...?

43

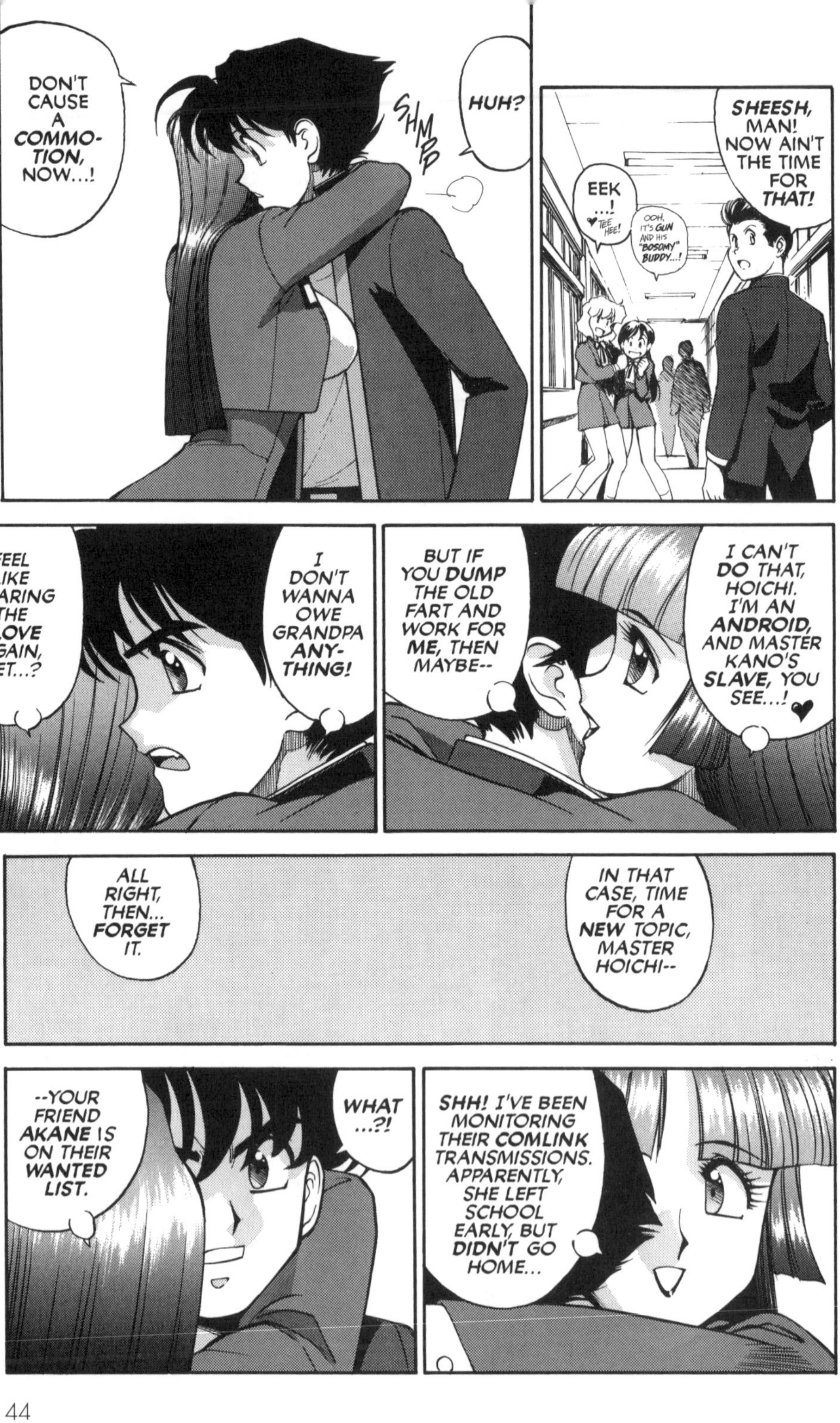
DON'T CAUSE A COMMOTION, NOW...!
SHMPP
HUH?
EEK...!
TEE HEE!
OOH, IT'S GUN AND HIS "BOSOMY" BUDDY...!
SHEESH, MAN! NOW AIN'T THE TIME FOR THAT!
FEEL LIKE WEARING THE GLOVE AGAIN, YET...?
I DON'T WANNA OWE GRANDPA ANYTHING!
BUT IF YOU DUMP THE OLD FART AND WORK FOR ME, THEN MAYBE--
I CAN'T DO THAT, HOICHI. I'M AN ANDROID, AND MASTER KANO'S SLAVE, YOU SEE...!
ALL RIGHT, THEN... FORGET IT.
IN THAT CASE, TIME FOR A NEW TOPIC, MASTER HOICHI--
--YOUR FRIEND AKANE IS ON THEIR WANTED LIST.
WHAT...?!
SHH! I'VE BEEN MONITORING THEIR COMLINK TRANSMISSIONS. APPARENTLY, SHE LEFT SCHOOL EARLY, BUT DIDN'T GO HOME...

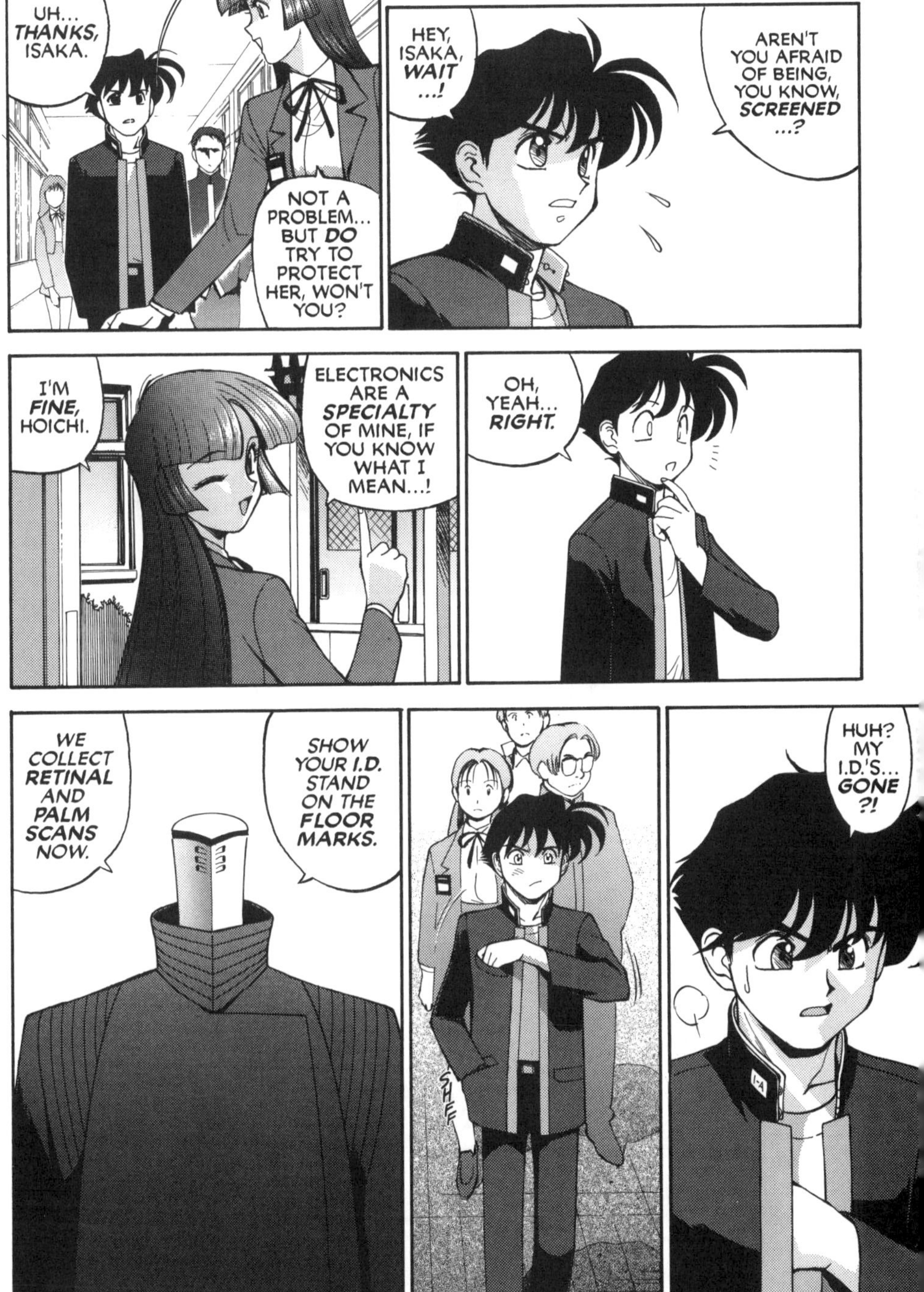
UH... THANKS, ISAKA.
NOT A PROBLEM... BUT DO TRY TO PROTECT HER, WON'T YOU?
HEY, ISAKA, WAIT ...!
AREN'T YOU AFRAID OF BEING, YOU KNOW, SCREENED ...?
I'M FINE, HOICHI.
ELECTRONICS ARE A SPECIALTY OF MINE, IF YOU KNOW WHAT I MEAN...!
OH, YEAH... RIGHT.
WE COLLECT RETINAL AND PALM SCANS NOW.
SHOW YOUR I.D. STAND ON THE FLOOR MARKS.
SHFF
HUH? MY I.D.'S... GONE ?!

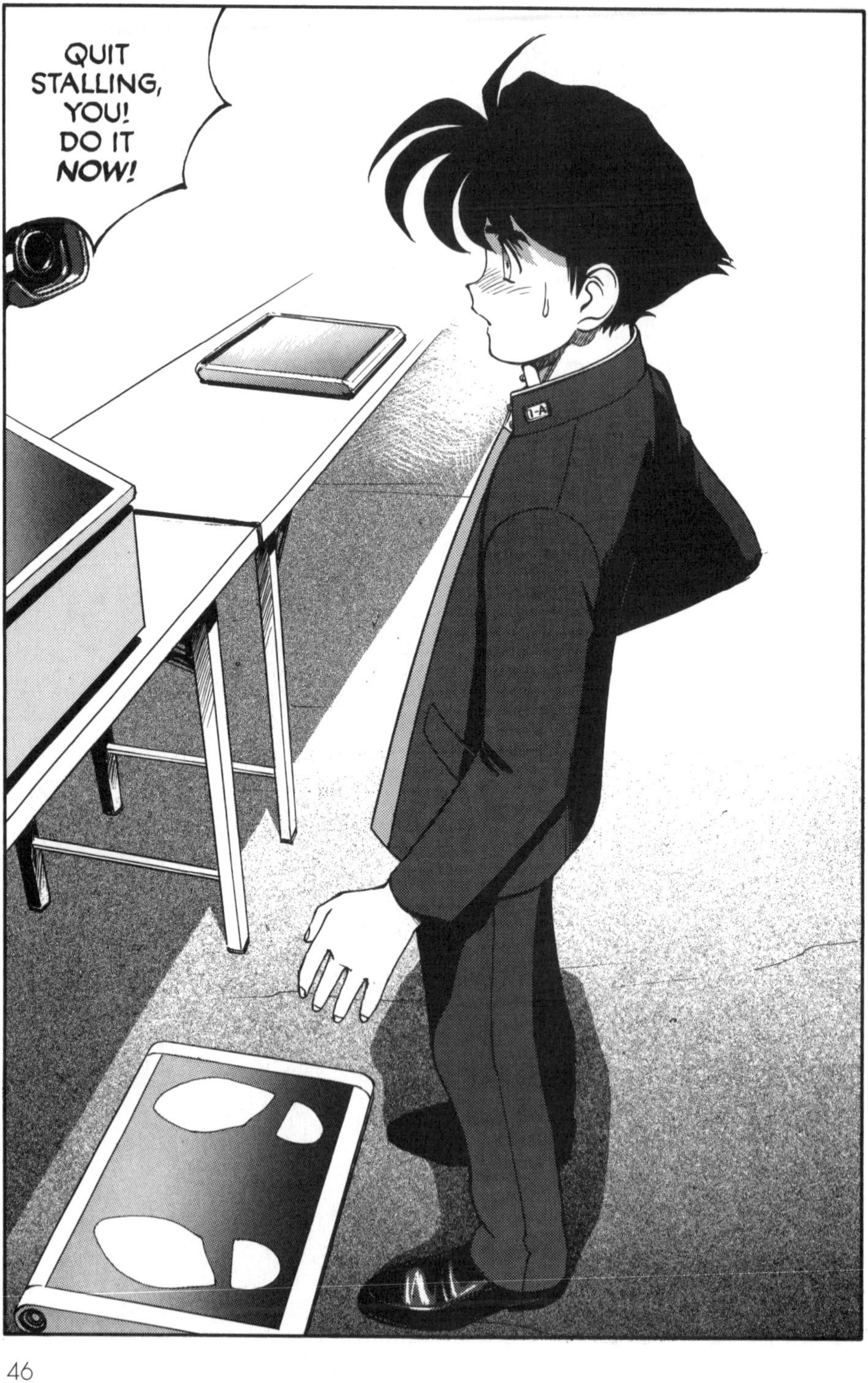
QUIT STALLING, YOU! DO IT NOW!
1-A

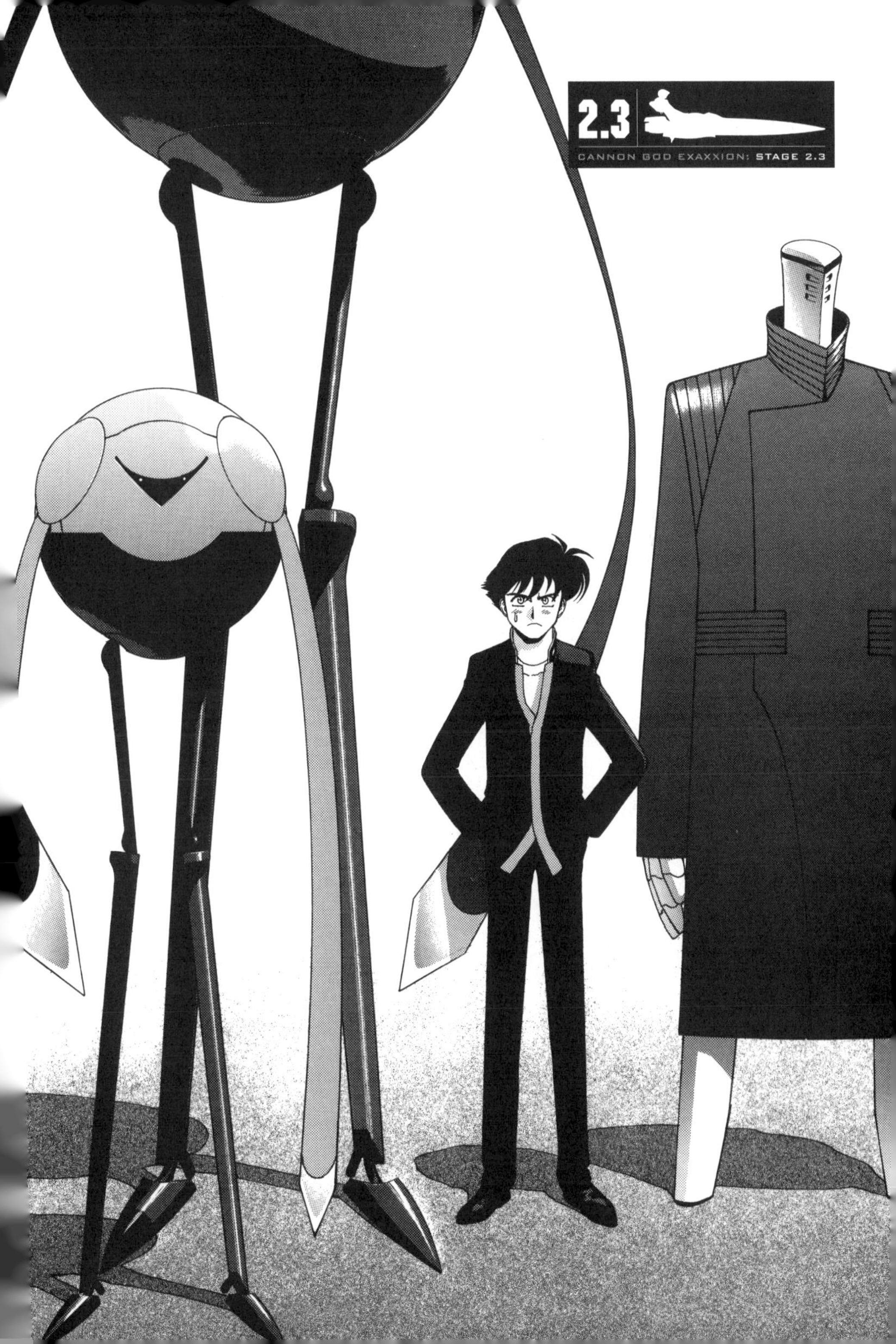
2.3
CANNON GOD EXAXXION: STAGE 2.3

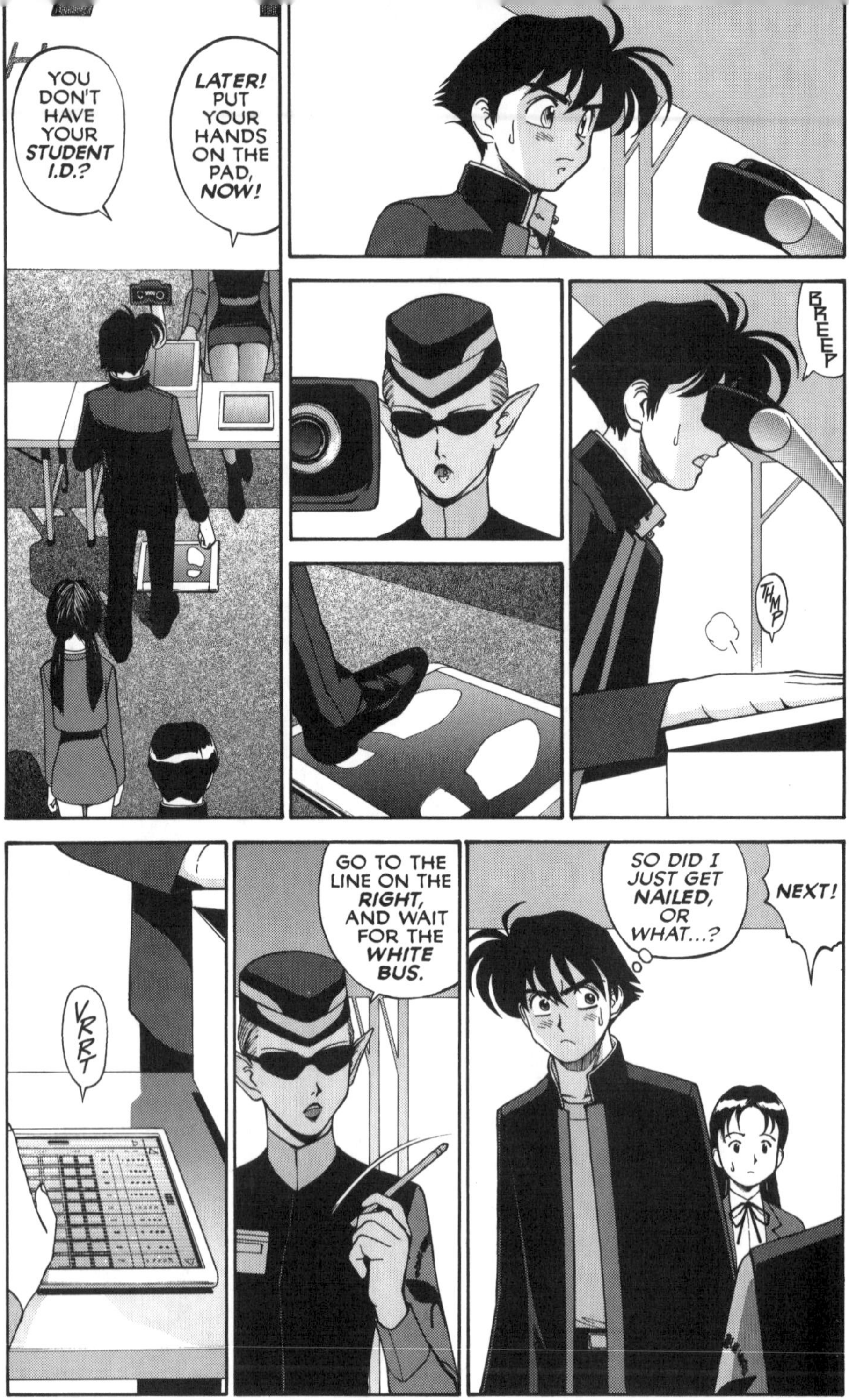
YOU DON'T HAVE YOUR STUDENT I.D.?
LATER! PUT YOUR HANDS ON THE PAD, NOW!
BREEP
THMP
VRRT
GO TO THE LINE ON THE RIGHT, AND WAIT FOR THE WHITE BUS.
SO DID I JUST GET NAILED, OR WHAT...?
NEXT!

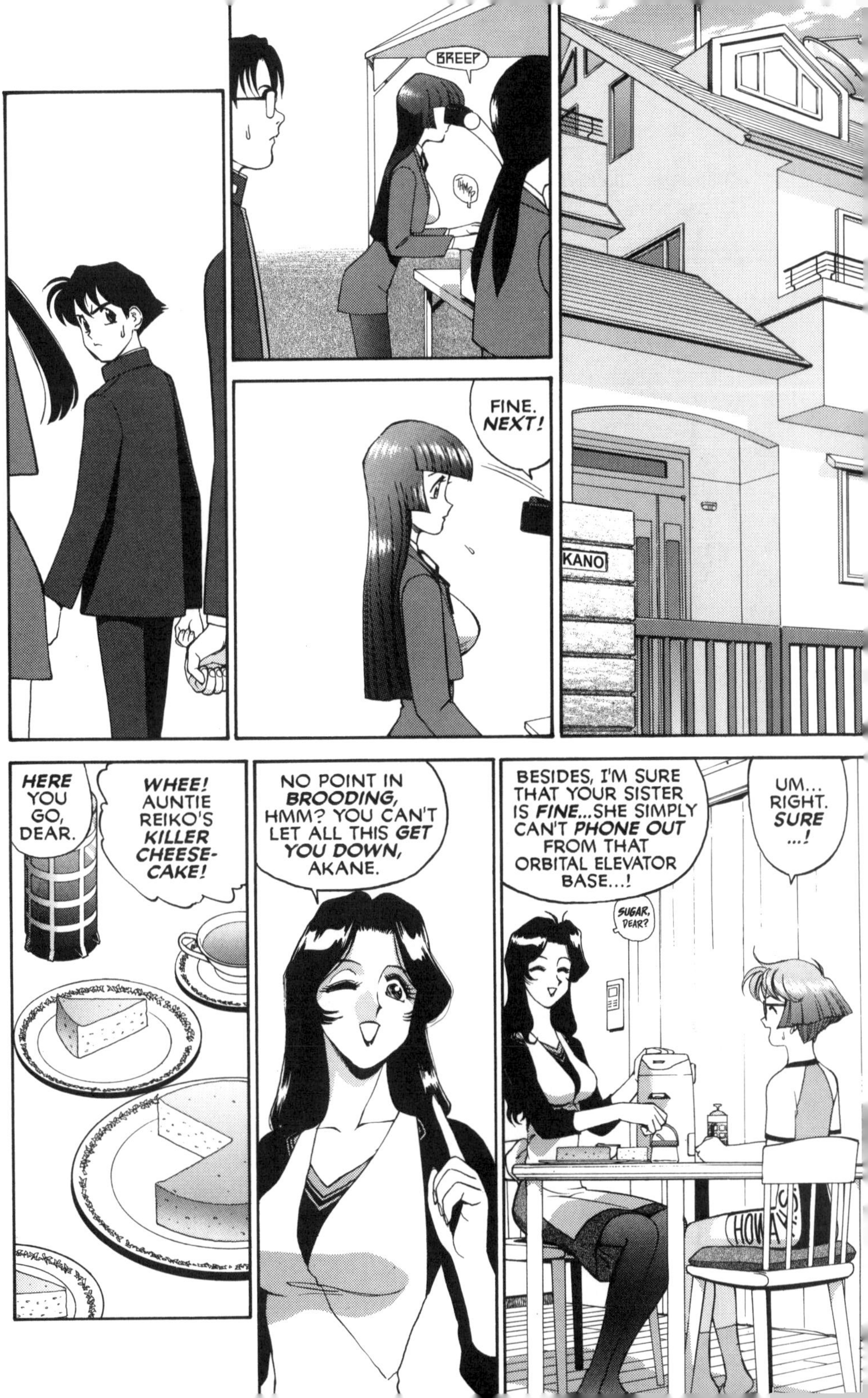
BREEP
THMP
FINE. NEXT!
KANO
HERE YOU GO, DEAR.
WHEE! AUNTIE REIKO'S KILLER CHEESE-CAKE!
NO POINT IN BROODING, HMM? YOU CAN'T LET ALL THIS GET YOU DOWN, AKANE.
BESIDES, I'M SURE THAT YOUR SISTER IS FINE...SHE SIMPLY CAN'T PHONE OUT FROM THAT ORBITAL ELEVATOR BASE...!
SUGAR, DEAR?
UM... RIGHT. SURE ...!

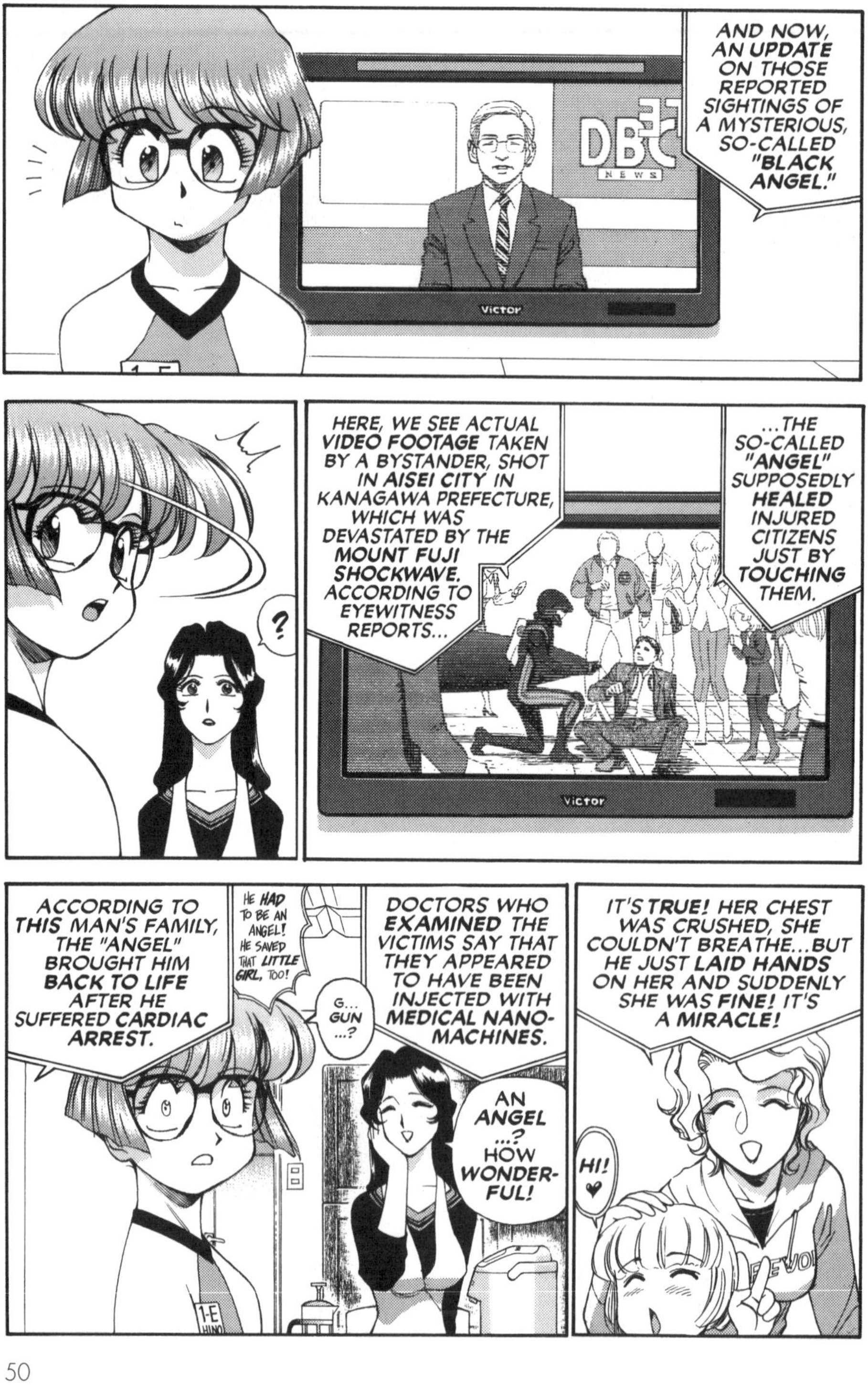

AND NOW, AN UPDATE ON THOSE REPORTED SIGHTINGS OF A MYSTERIOUS, SO-CALLED "BLACK ANGEL."
?
HERE, WE SEE ACTUAL VIDEO FOOTAGE TAKEN BY A BYSTANDER, SHOT IN AISEI CITY IN KANAGAWA PREFECTURE, WHICH WAS DEVASTATED BY THE MOUNT FUJI SHOCKWAVE. ACCORDING TO EYEWITNESS REPORTS...
...THE SO-CALLED "ANGEL" SUPPOSEDLY HEALED INJURED CITIZENS JUST BY TOUCHING THEM.
ACCORDING TO THIS MAN'S FAMILY, THE "ANGEL" BROUGHT HIM BACK TO LIFE AFTER HE SUFFERED CARDIAC ARREST.
HE HAD TO BE AN ANGEL! HE SAVED THAT LITTLE GIRL, TOO!
G... GUN ...?
DOCTORS WHO EXAMINED THE VICTIMS SAY THAT THEY APPEARED TO HAVE BEEN INJECTED WITH MEDICAL NANO-MACHINES.
AN ANGEL ...? HOW WONDERFUL!
IT'S TRUE! HER CHEST WAS CRUSHED, SHE COULDN'T BREATHE...BUT HE JUST LAID HANDS ON HER AND SUDDENLY SHE WAS FINE! IT'S A MIRACLE!
HI! ♥

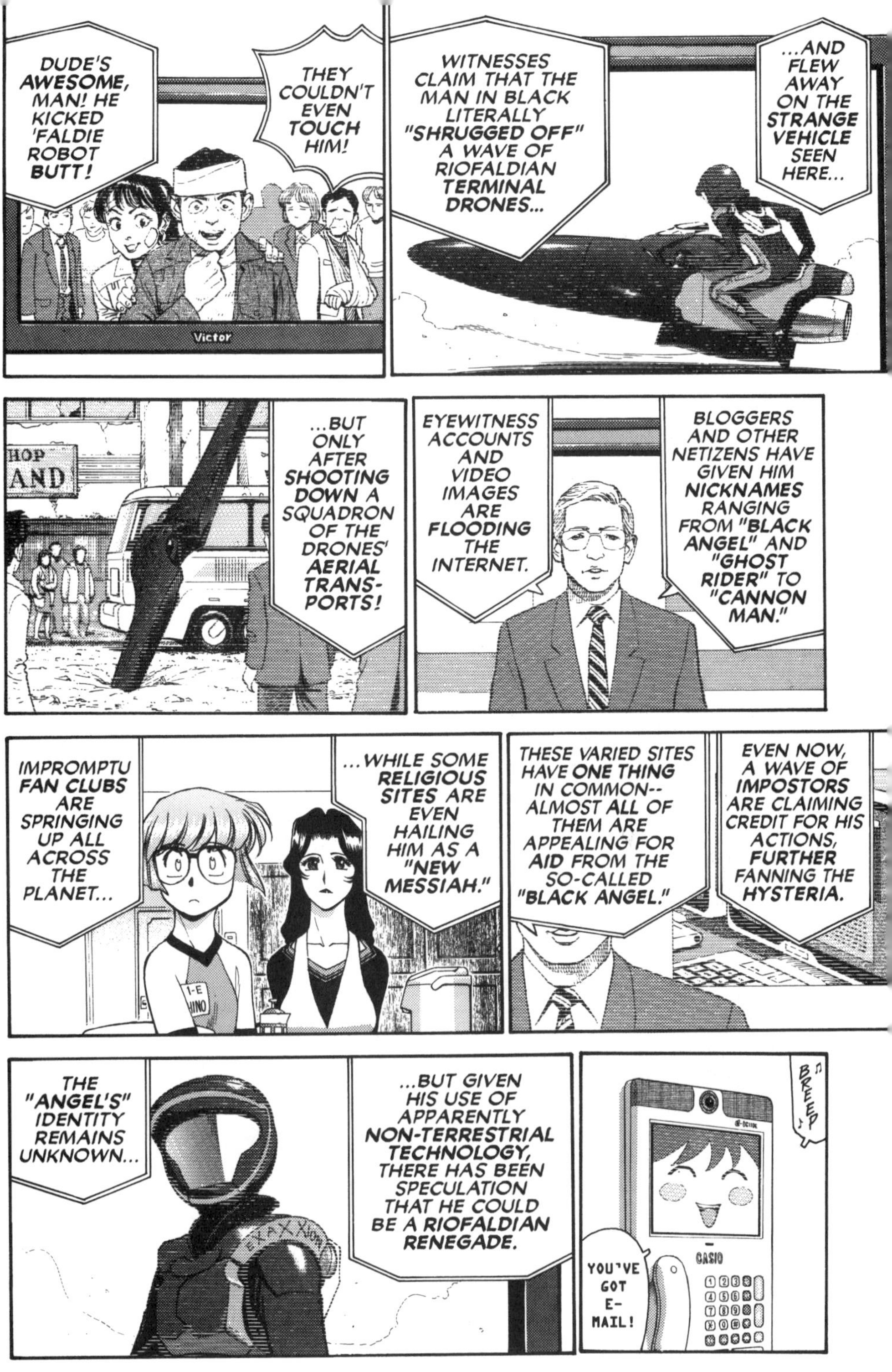
DUDE'S AWESOME, MAN! HE KICKED 'FALDIE ROBOT BUTT!
THEY COULDN'T EVEN TOUCH HIM!
Victor
WITNESSES CLAIM THAT THE MAN IN BLACK LITERALLY "SHRUGGED OFF" A WAVE OF RIOFALDIAN TERMINAL DRONES...
...AND FLEW AWAY ON THE STRANGE VEHICLE SEEN HERE...
...BUT ONLY AFTER SHOOTING DOWN A SQUADRON OF THE DRONES' AERIAL TRANSPORTS!
EYEWITNESS ACCOUNTS AND VIDEO IMAGES ARE FLOODING THE INTERNET.
BLOGGERS AND OTHER NETIZENS HAVE GIVEN HIM NICKNAMES RANGING FROM "BLACK ANGEL" AND "GHOST RIDER" TO "CANNON MAN."
IMPROMPTU FAN CLUBS ARE SPRINGING UP ALL ACROSS THE PLANET...
...WHILE SOME RELIGIOUS SITES ARE EVEN HAILING HIM AS A "NEW MESSIAH."
THESE VARIED SITES HAVE ONE THING IN COMMON-- ALMOST ALL OF THEM ARE APPEALING FOR AID FROM THE SO-CALLED "BLACK ANGEL."
EVEN NOW, A WAVE OF IMPOSTORS ARE CLAIMING CREDIT FOR HIS ACTIONS, FURTHER FANNING THE HYSTERIA.
THE "ANGEL'S" IDENTITY REMAINS UNKNOWN...
...BUT GIVEN HIS USE OF APPARENTLY NON-TERRESTRIAL TECHNOLOGY, THERE HAS BEEN SPECULATION THAT HE COULD BE A RIOFALDIAN RENEGADE.
BREEP♪
CASIO
YOU'VE GOT E-MAIL!

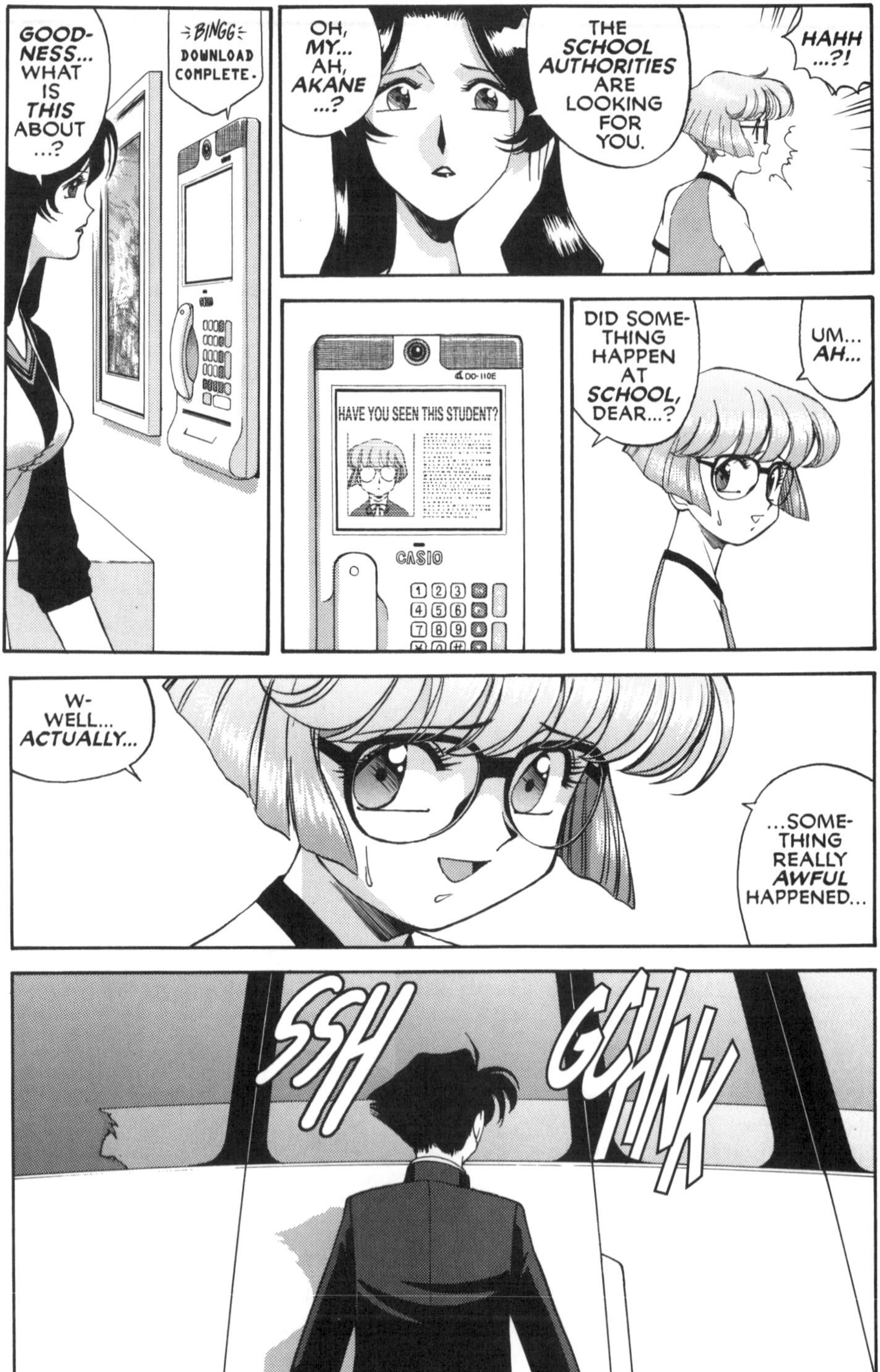
GOOD-NESS... WHAT IS THIS ABOUT...?
BINGG
DOWNLOAD COMPLETE.
OH, MY... AH, AKANE...?
THE SCHOOL AUTHORITIES ARE LOOKING FOR YOU.
HAHH...?!
DO-110E
HAVE YOU SEEN THIS STUDENT?
CASIO
DID SOME-THING HAPPEN AT SCHOOL, DEAR...?
UM... AH...
W-WELL... ACTUALLY...
...SOME-THING REALLY AWFUL HAPPENED...
SSH
GCHINK

STAY IN LINE! ANOTHER BUS IS ON THE WAY!
VRRMBB
BRRMBB
HOW MANY MATCHES DID WE GET?
TOO DAMN MANY... WE ONLY BROUGHT ONE BUS.
37, SIR.
SORRY, SIR, BUT WE COULDN'T RETRIEVE ENOUGH VIDEO FROM DRONE 105 TO REFINE THE PARAMETERS ANY FURTHER.
BUT IF WE FOLLOW ORDERS AND TERMINATE EVERYONE WHO MATCHES THE APPROXIMATE BODY TYPE, THEN WE'LL HAVE TO--
ORDERS ARE ORDERS!
JUST KEEP THE BODIES OUT OF SIGHT UNTIL WE'RE FINISHED HERE.

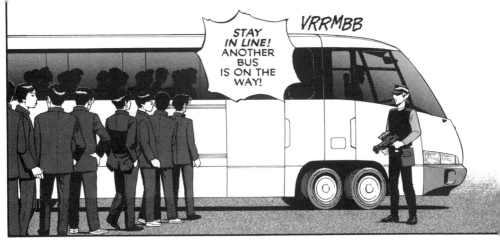

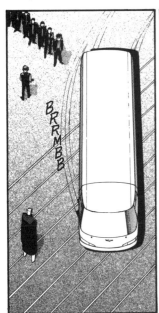

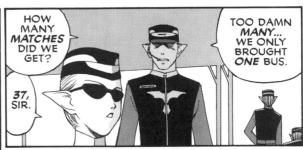

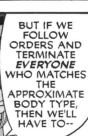

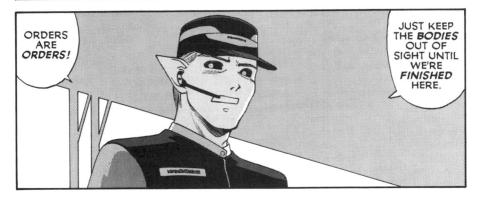

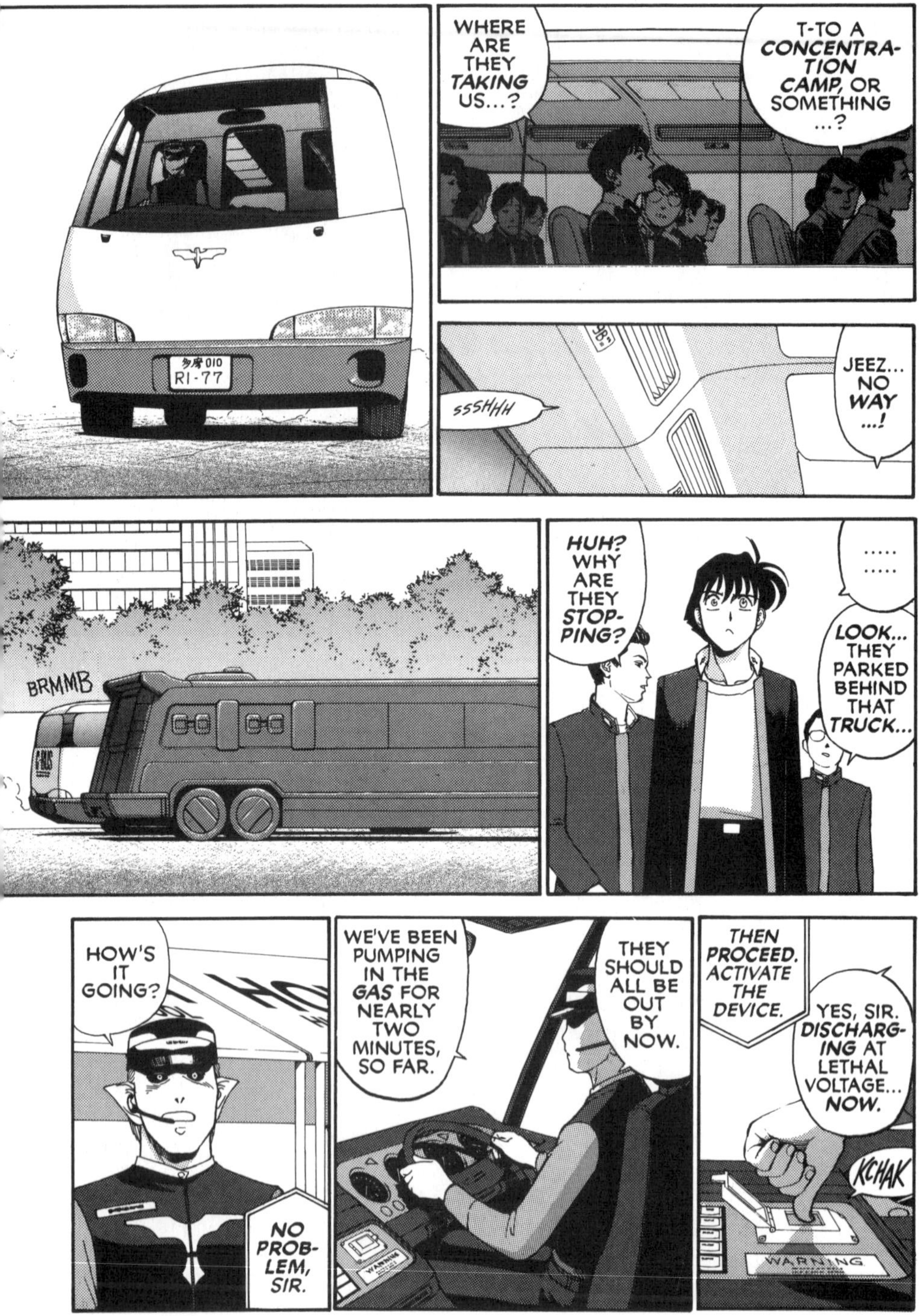
多摩010
RI-77
WHERE ARE THEY TAKING US...?
T-TO A CONCENTRATION CAMP, OR SOMETHING ...?
SSSHHH
JEEZ... NO WAY ...!
BRMMB
HUH? WHY ARE THEY STOPPING?
.....
.....
LOOK... THEY PARKED BEHIND THAT TRUCK...
HOW'S IT GOING?
NO PROBLEM, SIR.
WE'VE BEEN PUMPING IN THE GAS FOR NEARLY TWO MINUTES, SO FAR.
THEY SHOULD ALL BE OUT BY NOW.
THEN PROCEED. ACTIVATE THE DEVICE.
YES, SIR. DISCHARGING AT LETHAL VOLTAGE... NOW.
KCHAK
WARNING
WARNING

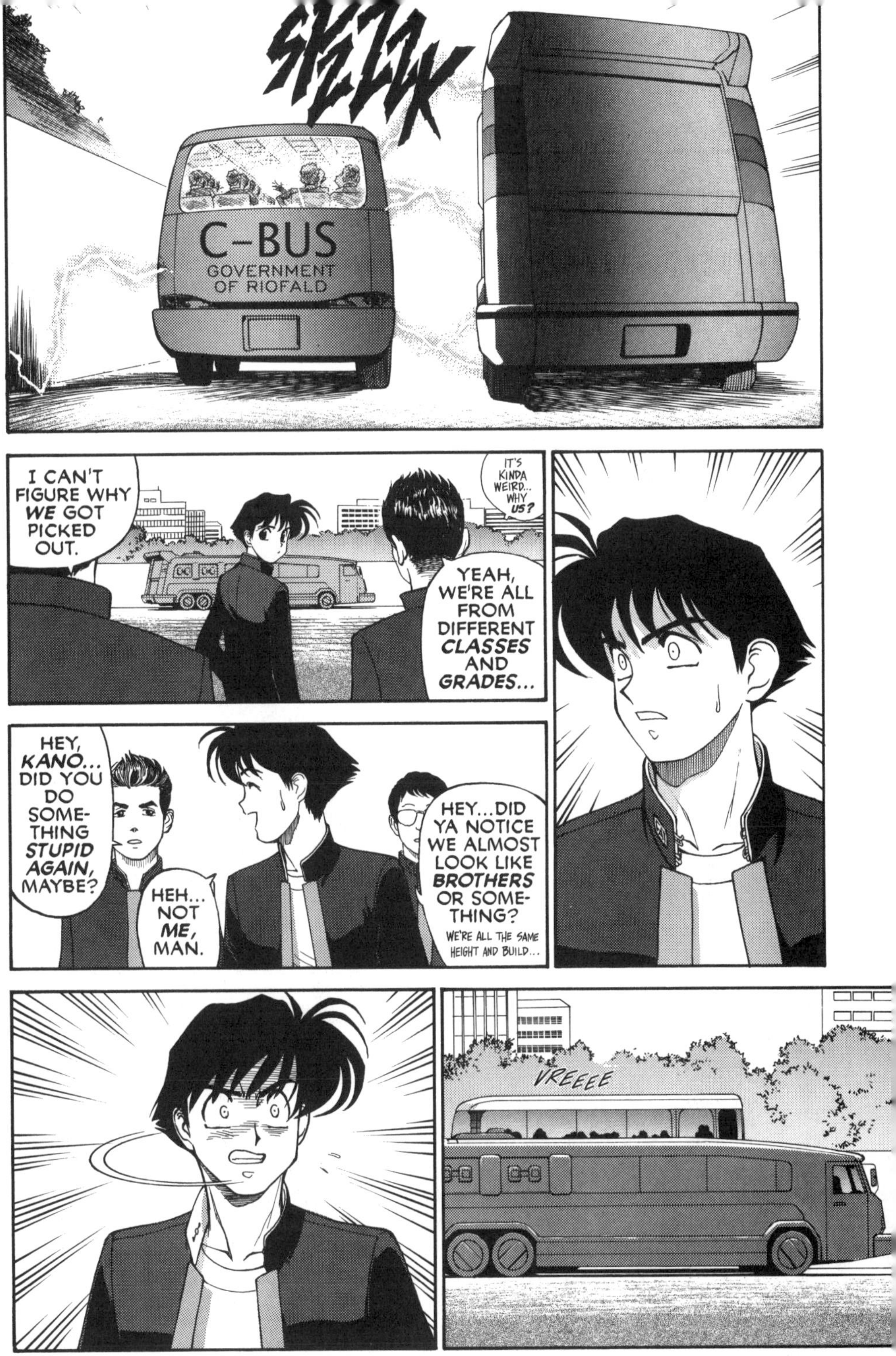
SKZZZK
C-BUS
GOVERNMENT OF RIOFALD
I CAN'T FIGURE WHY WE GOT PICKED OUT.
IT'S KINDA WEIRD... WHY US?
YEAH, WE'RE ALL FROM DIFFERENT CLASSES AND GRADES...
HEY, KANO... DID YOU DO SOME-THING STUPID AGAIN, MAYBE?
HEH... NOT ME, MAN.
HEY...DID YA NOTICE WE ALMOST LOOK LIKE BROTHERS OR SOME-THING?
WE'RE ALL THE SAME HEIGHT AND BUILD...
VREEEE

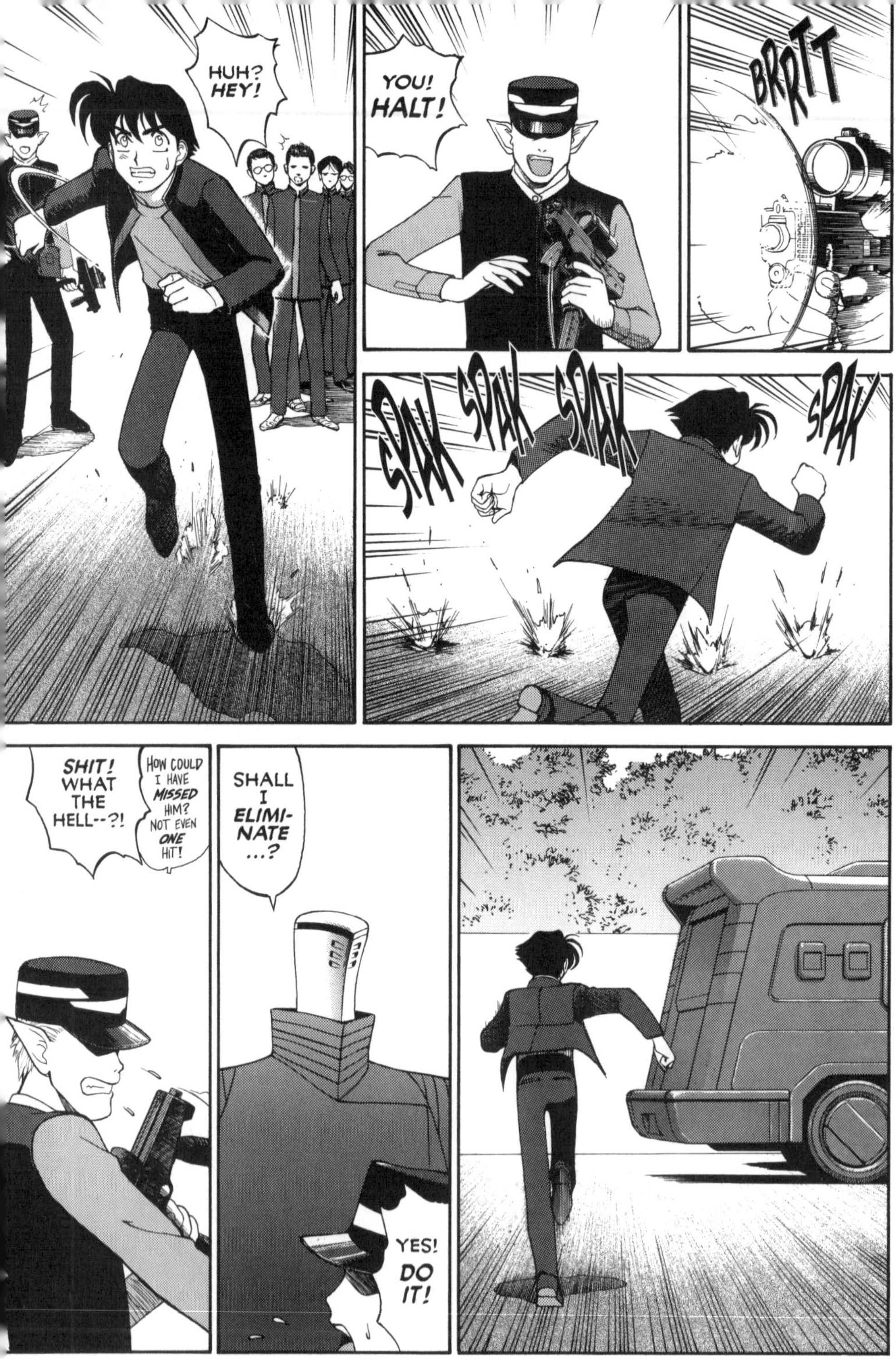
HUH? HEY!
YOU! HALT!
BRRTT
SPAK SPAK SPAK SPAK
SHIT! WHAT THE HELL--?!
HOW COULD I HAVE MISSED HIM? NOT EVEN ONE HIT!
SHALL I ELIMINATE ...?
YES! DO IT!

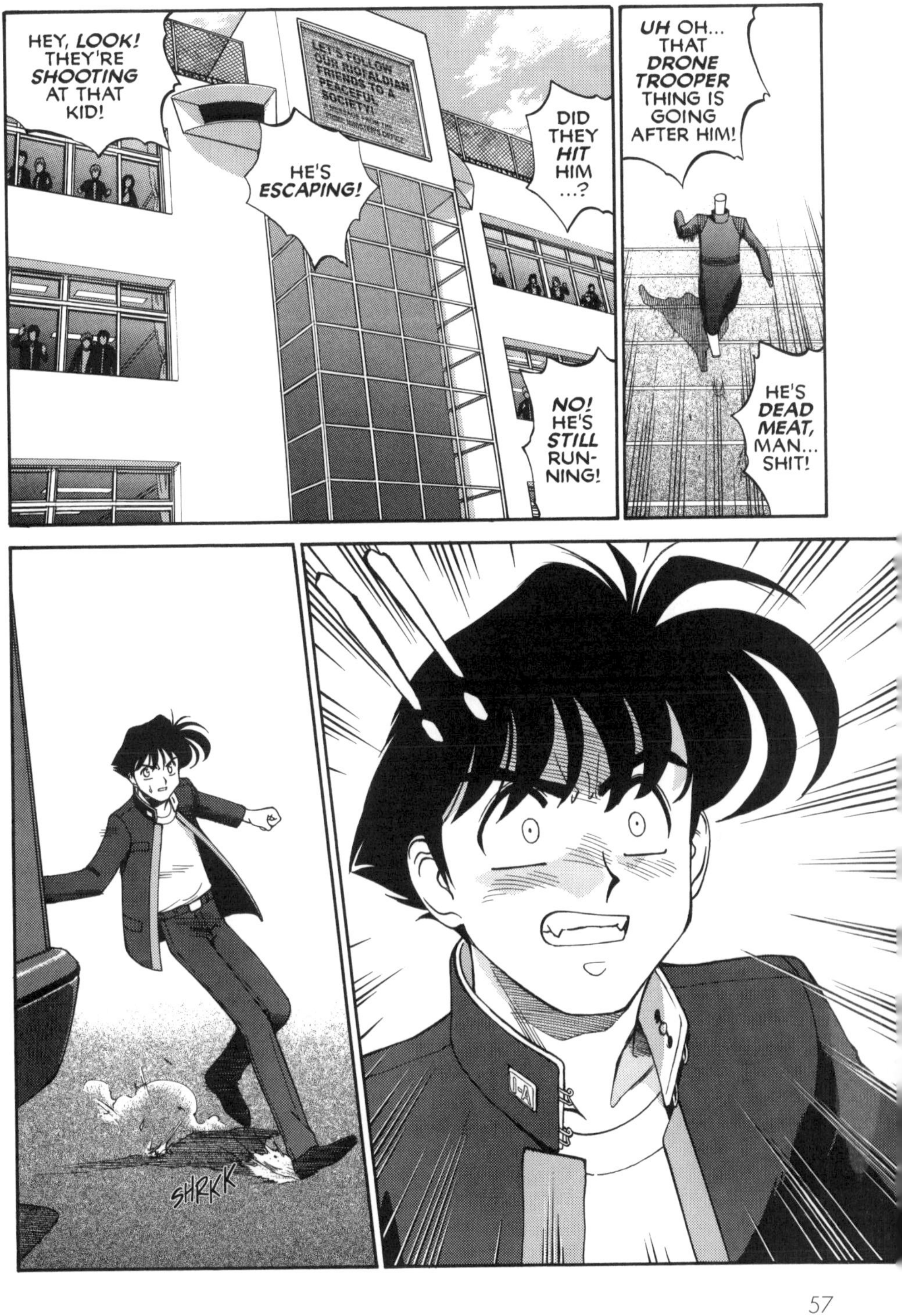
HEY, *LOOK!* THEY'RE *SHOOTING* AT THAT KID!
LET'S FOLLOW OUR RIOFALDIAN FRIENDS TO A PEACEFUL SOCIETY!
HE'S *ESCAPING!*
DID THEY *HIT* HIM ...?
NO! HE'S *STILL* RUN-NING!
UH OH... THAT *DRONE TROOPER* THING IS GOING AFTER HIM!
HE'S *DEAD MEAT,* MAN... SHIT!
SHRKK

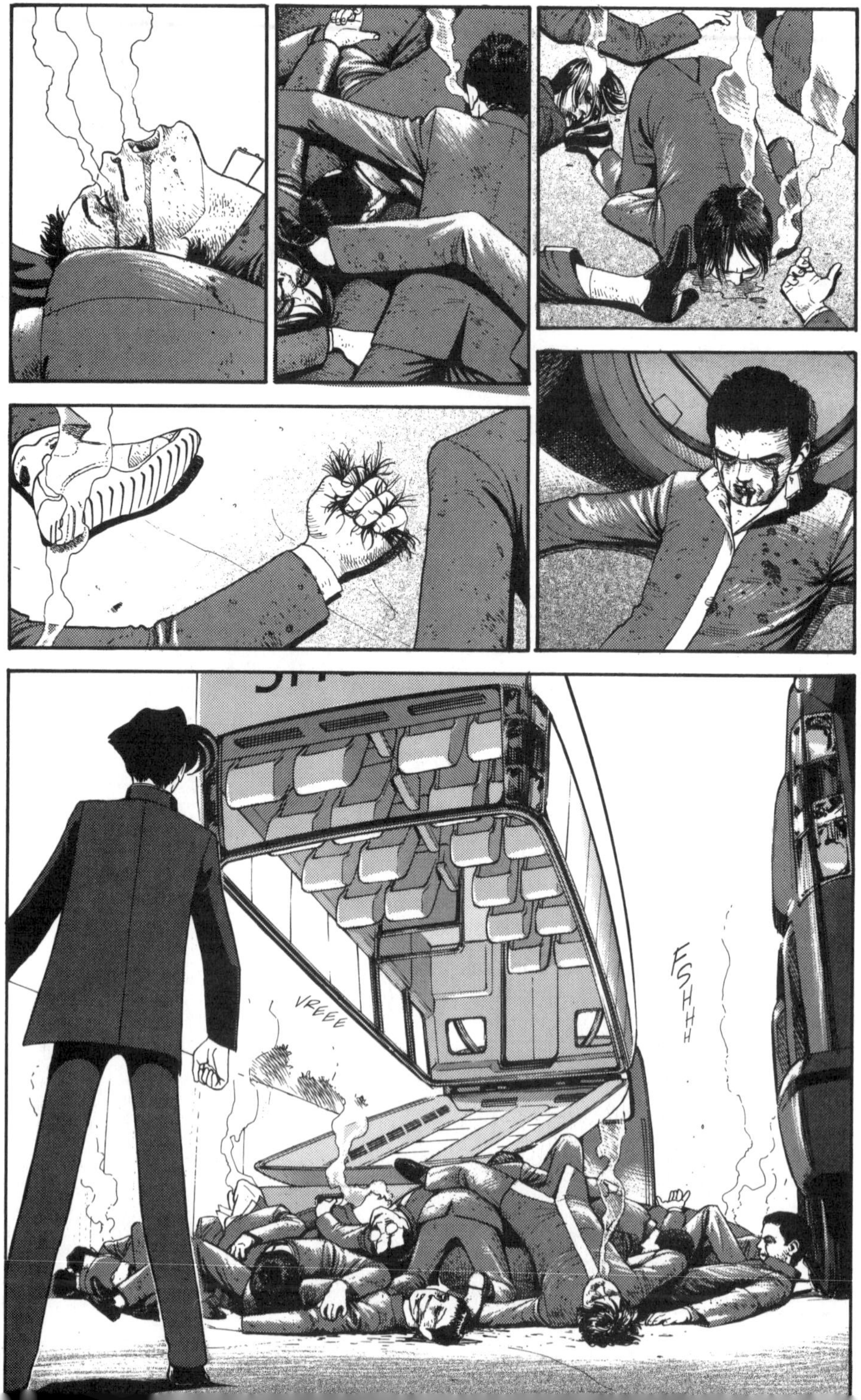
VREEE
FSHHH

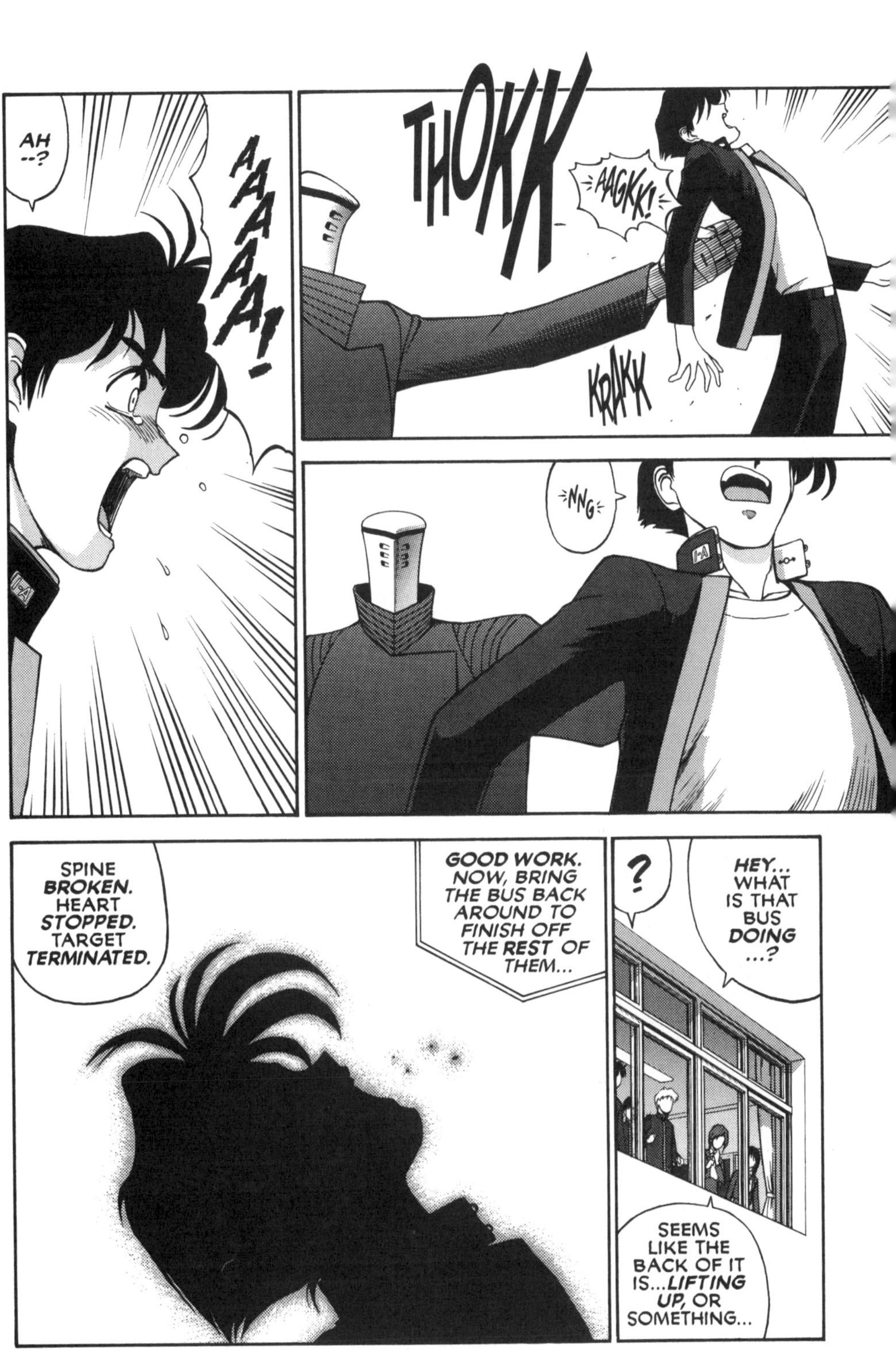
AH --?
AAAAAA!
THOKK
AAGKK!
KRAKK
NNG
SPINE BROKEN. HEART STOPPED. TARGET TERMINATED.
GOOD WORK. NOW, BRING THE BUS BACK AROUND TO FINISH OFF THE REST OF THEM...
?
HEY... WHAT IS THAT BUS DOING ...?
SEEMS LIKE THE BACK OF IT IS...LIFTING UP, OR SOMETHING...

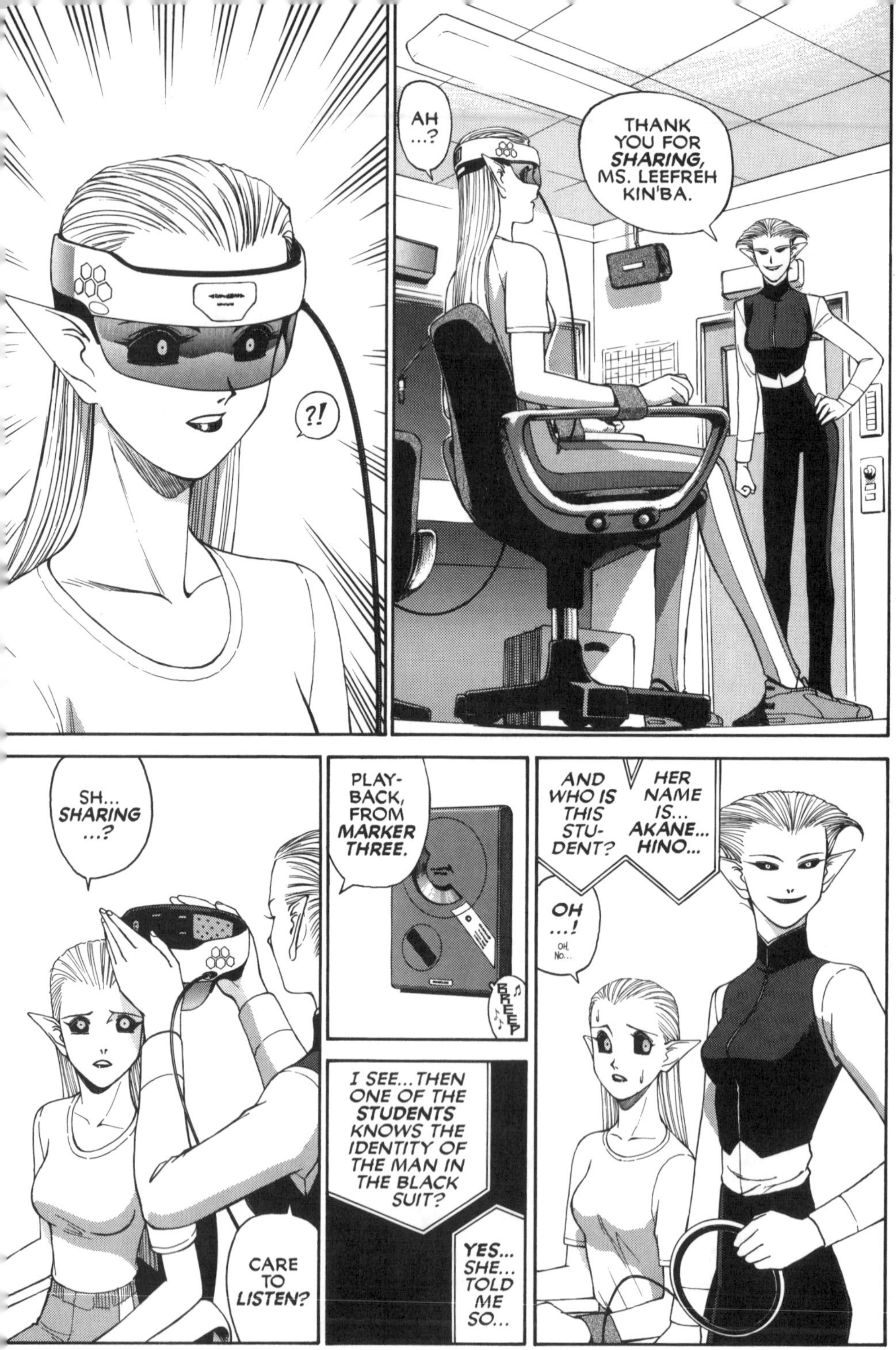
?!
AH ...?
THANK YOU FOR SHARING, MS. LEEFREH KIN'BA.
SH... SHARING ...?
CARE TO LISTEN?
PLAY-BACK, FROM MARKER THREE.
BREEP
I SEE...THEN ONE OF THE STUDENTS KNOWS THE IDENTITY OF THE MAN IN THE BLACK SUIT?
YES... SHE... TOLD ME SO...
AND WHO IS THIS STU-DENT?
HER NAME IS... AKANE... HINO...
OH ...!
OH, NO...

WHICH CLASS IS SHE IN?

...FRESH-MAN ...IN CLASS E...

STOP!

BEEP

SO...*AKANE HINO*, HMM? THAT'S THE GIRL WHO'S MYSTERIOUSLY *GONE MISSING* FROM SCHOOL, AS I RECALL...!

WELL. ONCE WE FIND HER, SHE'LL BE *CERTAIN* TO CLEAR UP ANY *NUMBER* OF MYSTERIES FOR US.

THIS WORKS ON *HUMANS*, TOO...

NO! *STOP* IT!

I'M... I'M NOT *OPPOSED* TO OUR *COLONIZATION* POLICIES... BUT...

PLEASE... DON'T HURT MY *STUDENTS*!

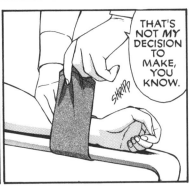

THAT'S NOT *MY* DECISION TO MAKE, YOU KNOW.

SHRIP

BUT LOOK AT EARTH'S *HISTORY*...AND *OUR* HISTORY, AS WELL. IN TIME, POPULATIONS *ALWAYS* RISE UP AGAINST COLONIALISM...!

WE'RE GOING TO NEED THE HUMANS' *GOOD WILL* TO HELP SUPPRESS THESE UPRISINGS!

WE NEED TO HAVE THE MORAL COURAGE TO *REJECT* GOVERNING THEM BY TERROR!

A PRETTY *SERMON*... BUT IT COMES A *BIT* TOO LATE, I'M AFRAID.

WE JUST *EXECUTED* THIRTY-SEVEN OF "YOUR" STUDENTS.

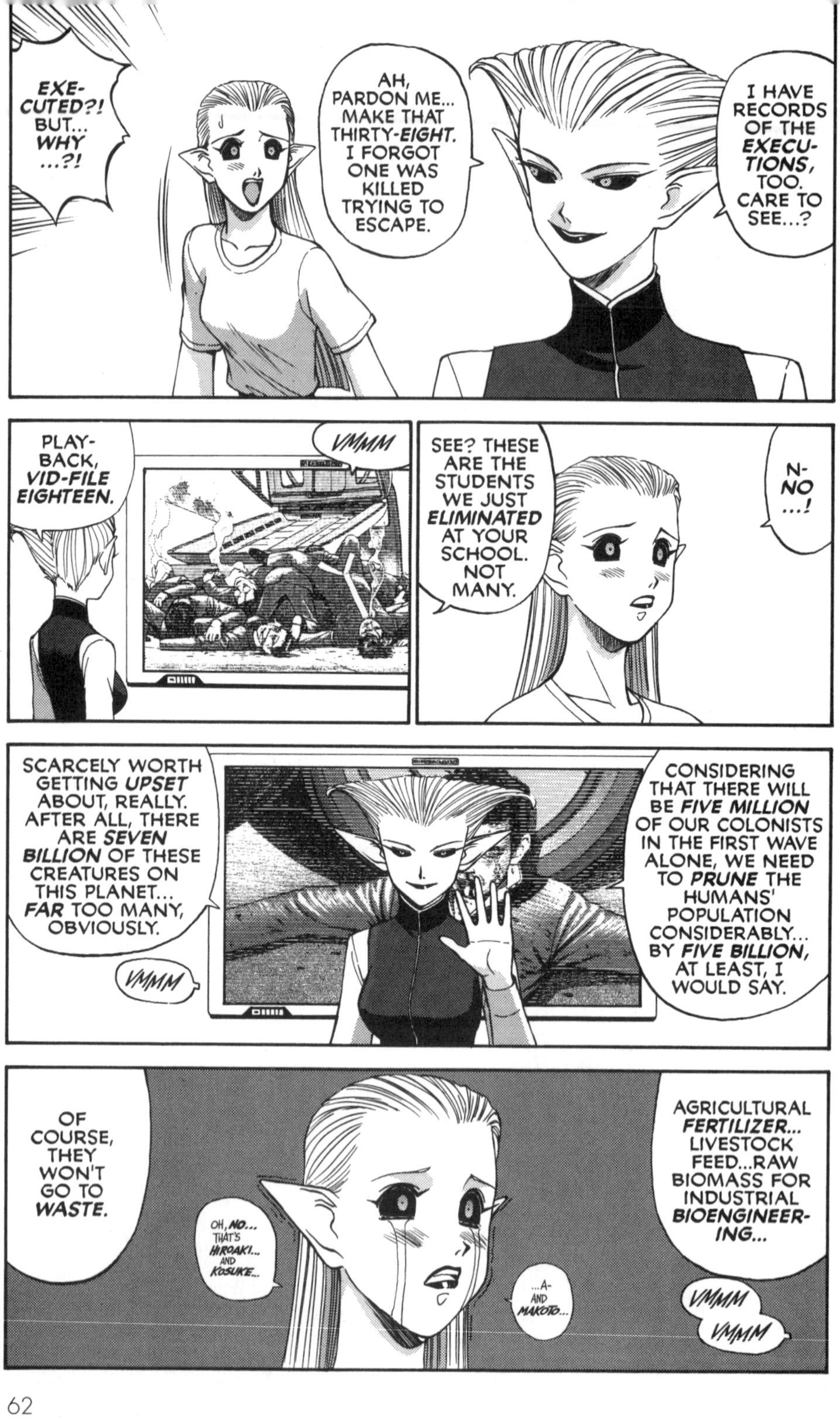
EXECUTED?! BUT... WHY ...?!
AH, PARDON ME... MAKE THAT THIRTY-EIGHT. I FORGOT ONE WAS KILLED TRYING TO ESCAPE.
I HAVE RECORDS OF THE EXECUTIONS, TOO. CARE TO SEE...?
PLAYBACK, VID-FILE EIGHTEEN.
VMMM
SEE? THESE ARE THE STUDENTS WE JUST ELIMINATED AT YOUR SCHOOL. NOT MANY.
N-NO ...!
SCARCELY WORTH GETTING UPSET ABOUT, REALLY. AFTER ALL, THERE ARE SEVEN BILLION OF THESE CREATURES ON THIS PLANET... FAR TOO MANY, OBVIOUSLY.
VMMM
CONSIDERING THAT THERE WILL BE FIVE MILLION OF OUR COLONISTS IN THE FIRST WAVE ALONE, WE NEED TO PRUNE THE HUMANS' POPULATION CONSIDERABLY... BY FIVE BILLION, AT LEAST, I WOULD SAY.
OF COURSE, THEY WON'T GO TO WASTE.
OH, NO... THAT'S HIROAKI... AND KOSUKE...
...A- AND MAKOTO...
AGRICULTURAL FERTILIZER... LIVESTOCK FEED...RAW BIOMASS FOR INDUSTRIAL BIOENGINEERING...
VMMM
VMMM

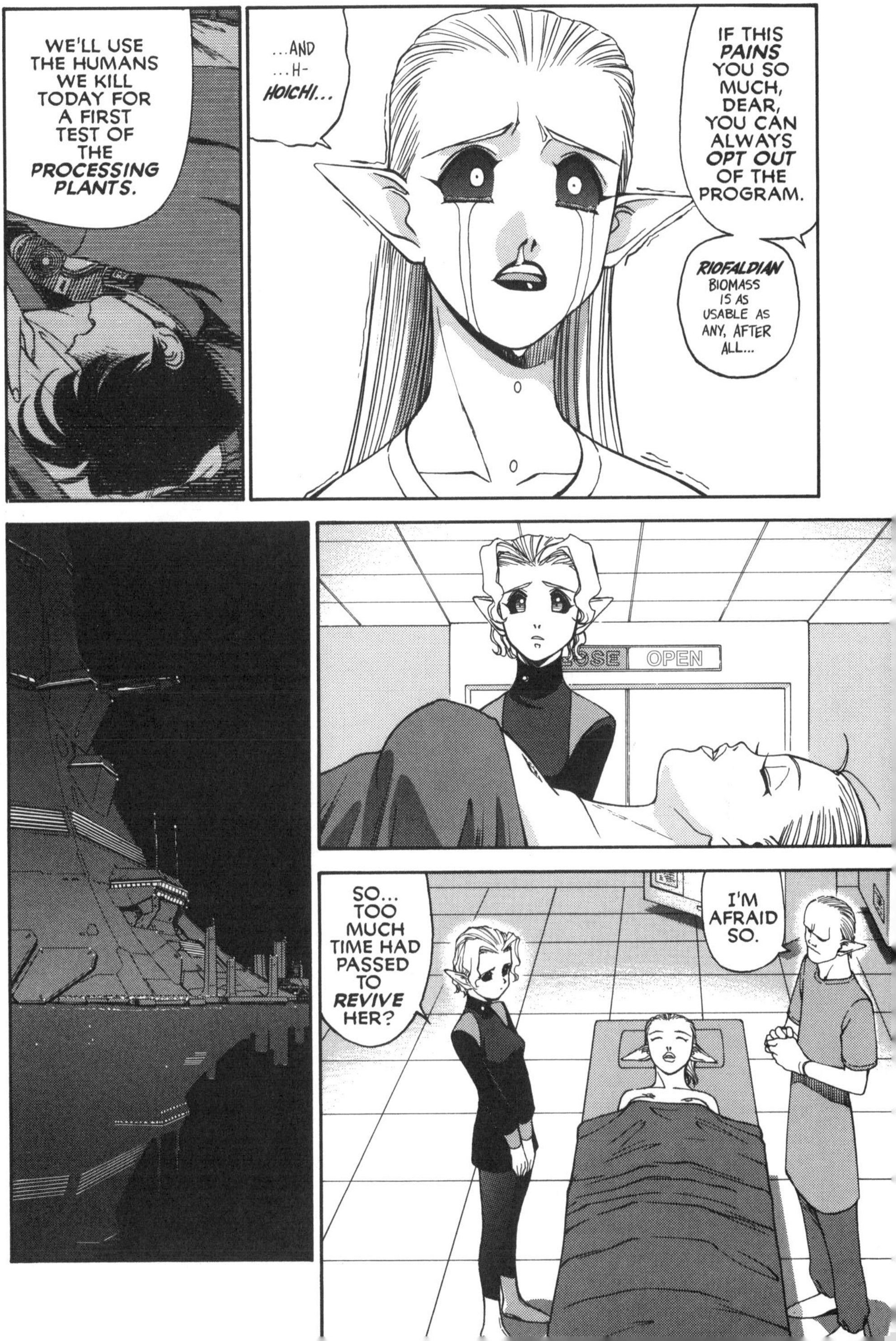
WE'LL USE THE HUMANS WE KILL TODAY FOR A FIRST TEST OF THE *PROCESSING PLANTS.*
...AND ...H- *HOICHI...*
IF THIS *PAINS* YOU SO MUCH, DEAR, YOU CAN ALWAYS *OPT OUT* OF THE PROGRAM.
RIOFALDIAN BIOMASS IS AS USABLE AS ANY, AFTER ALL...
OPEN
SO... TOO MUCH TIME HAD PASSED TO *REVIVE* HER?
I'M AFRAID SO.

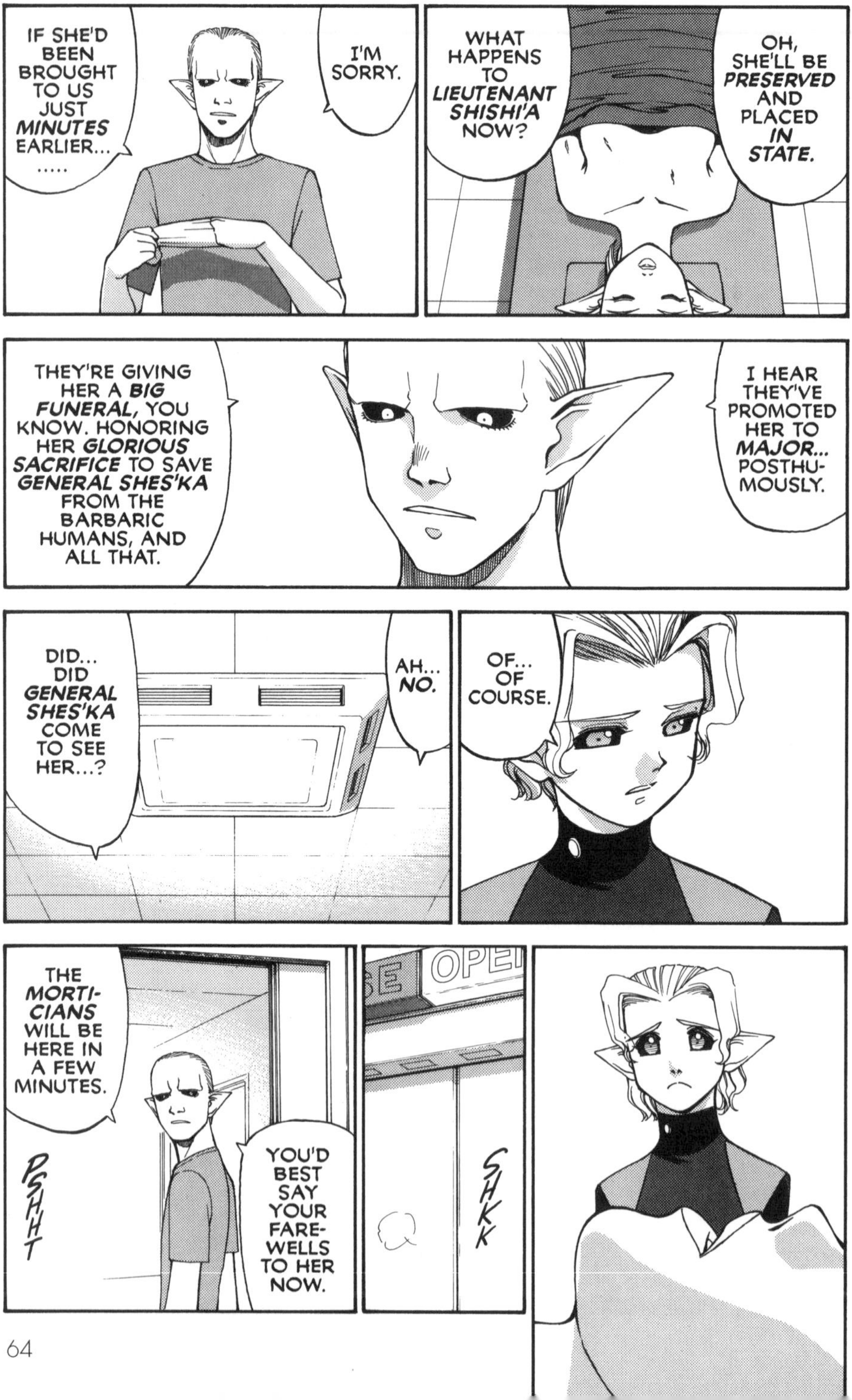

IF SHE'D BEEN BROUGHT TO US JUST *MINUTES* EARLIER... .....
I'M SORRY.
WHAT HAPPENS TO *LIEUTENANT SHISHI'A* NOW?
OH, SHE'LL BE *PRESERVED* AND PLACED *IN STATE.*
THEY'RE GIVING HER A *BIG FUNERAL,* YOU KNOW. HONORING HER *GLORIOUS SACRIFICE* TO SAVE *GENERAL SHES'KA* FROM THE BARBARIC HUMANS, AND ALL THAT.
I HEAR THEY'VE PROMOTED HER TO *MAJOR...* POSTHU-MOUSLY.
DID... DID *GENERAL SHES'KA* COME TO SEE HER...?
AH... *NO.*
OF... OF COURSE.
THE *MORTI-CIANS* WILL BE HERE IN A FEW MINUTES.
YOU'D BEST SAY YOUR FARE-WELLS TO HER NOW.
PSHHT
OPE
SHKK

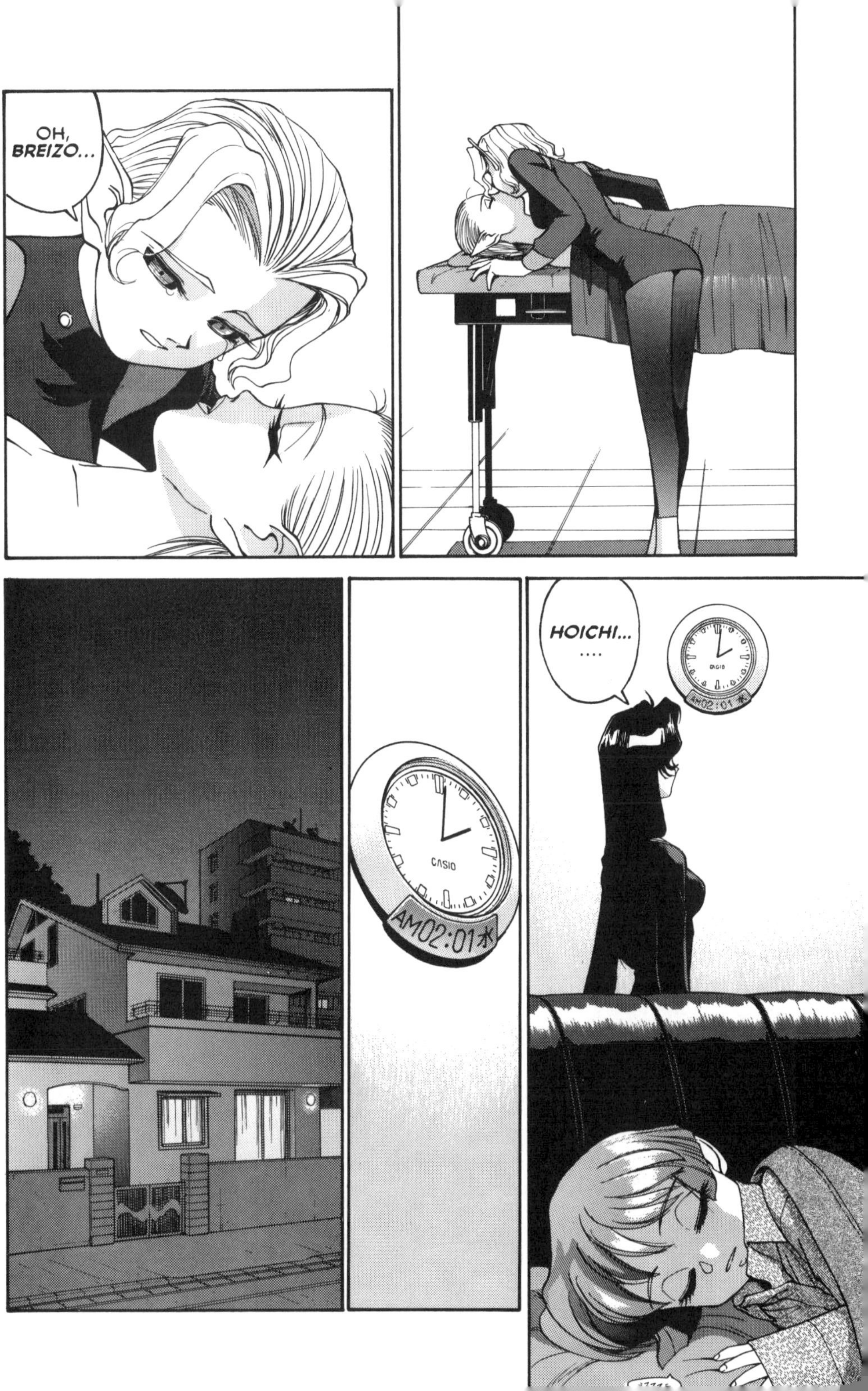
OH, BREIZO...
CASIO
AM02:01水
HOICHI...
....
CASIO
AM02:01水

OWW...! DAMN... I REALLY HURT...
BODY FEELS ALL... STIFF...
HUH? I'M... ALIVE ...?
BUT WHY...? I WASN'T WEARING THE GUNNER SUIT...!
DID THE DAMN ALIENS SCREW UP SOME-HOW...?
OR... MAYBE I STILL GOT SOME NANO-MACHINES IN ME...?
JEEZUZ! WHAT'S THAT SMELL ...?
AND WHERE THE HELL AM I...?

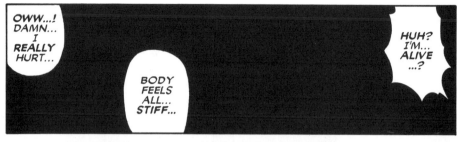

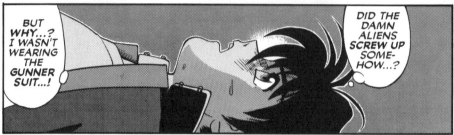

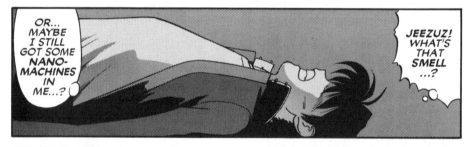

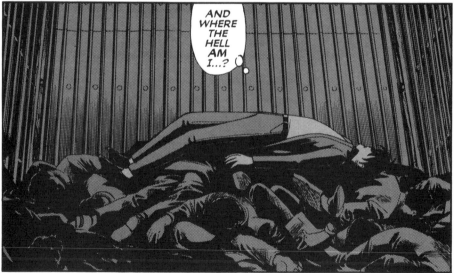

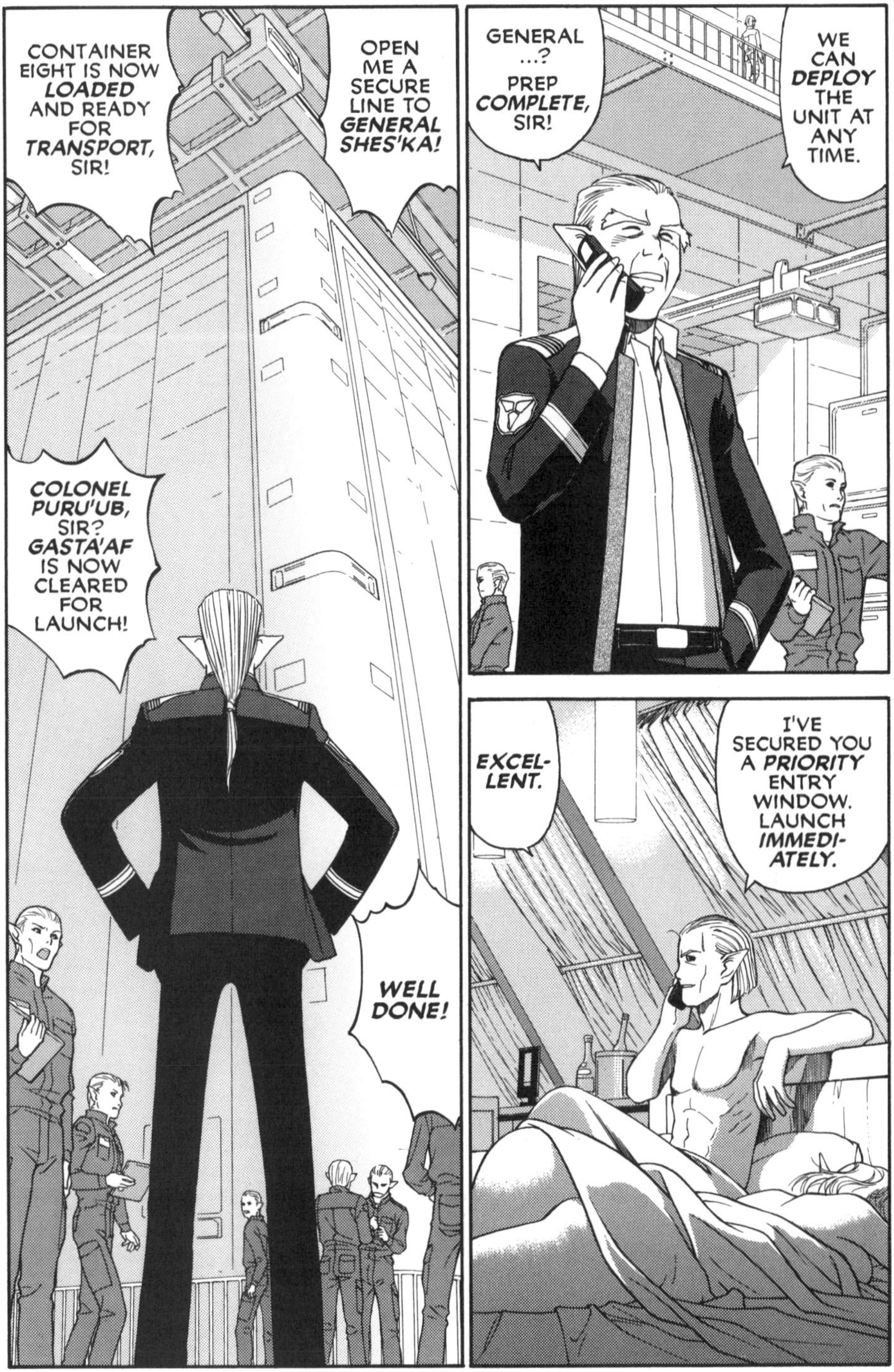
CONTAINER EIGHT IS NOW LOADED AND READY FOR TRANSPORT, SIR!
OPEN ME A SECURE LINE TO GENERAL SHES'KA!
COLONEL PURU'UB, SIR? GASTA'AF IS NOW CLEARED FOR LAUNCH!
WELL DONE!
GENERAL ...? PREP COMPLETE, SIR!
WE CAN DEPLOY THE UNIT AT ANY TIME.
EXCEL-LENT.
I'VE SECURED YOU A PRIORITY ENTRY WINDOW. LAUNCH IMMEDI-ATELY.

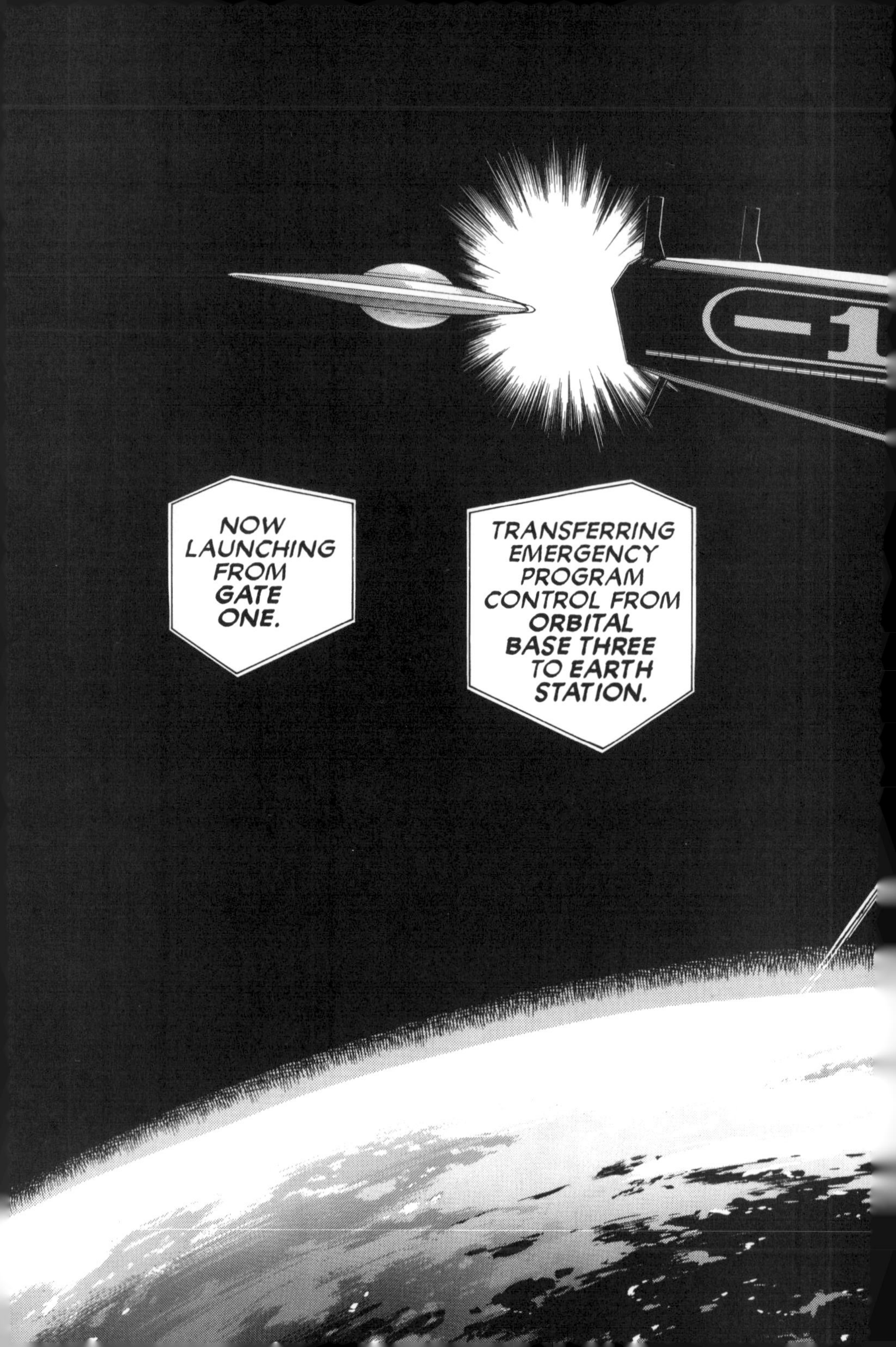
NOW LAUNCHING FROM GATE ONE.
TRANSFERRING EMERGENCY PROGRAM CONTROL FROM ORBITAL BASE THREE TO EARTH STATION.
-1

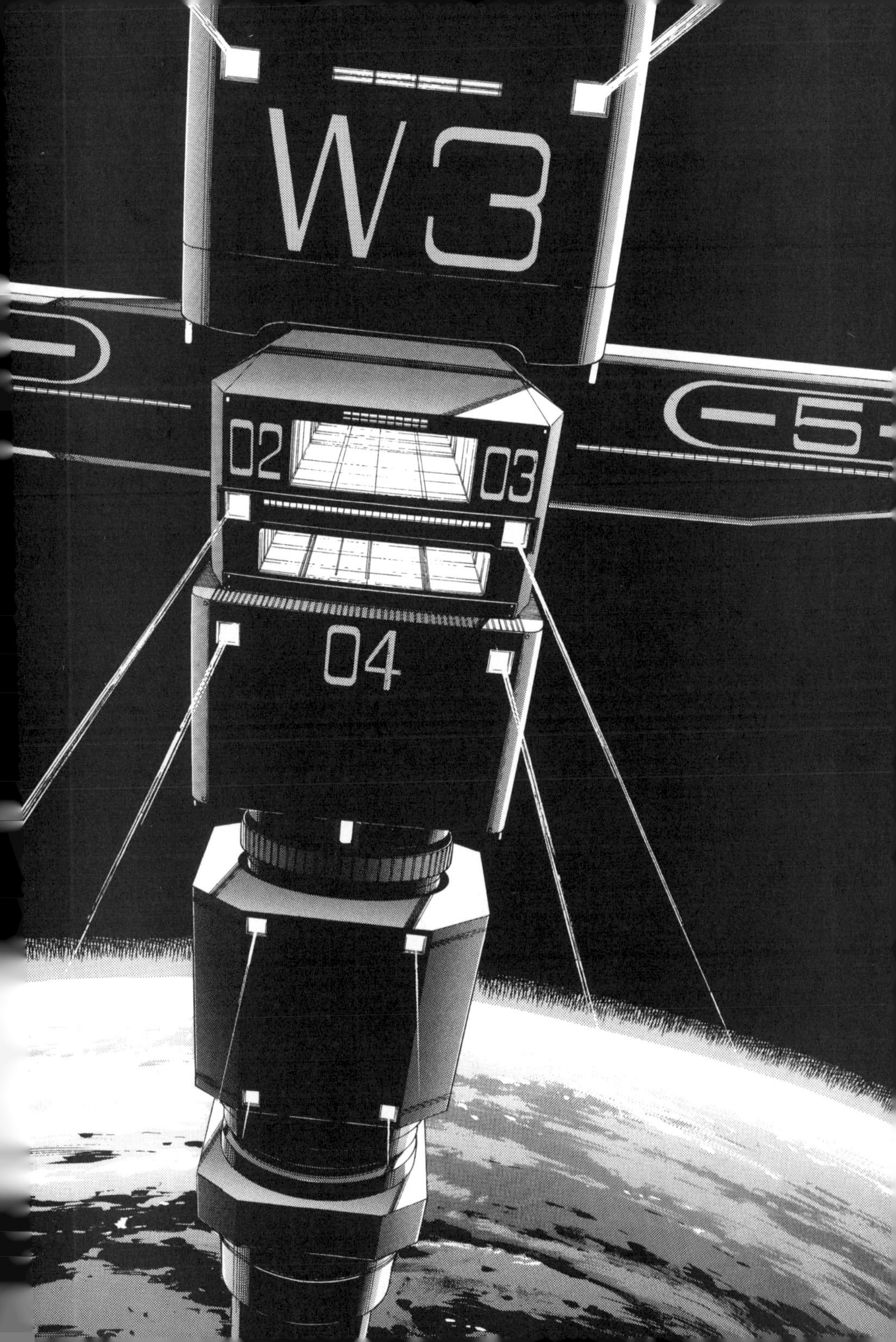
W3
02
03
04
5

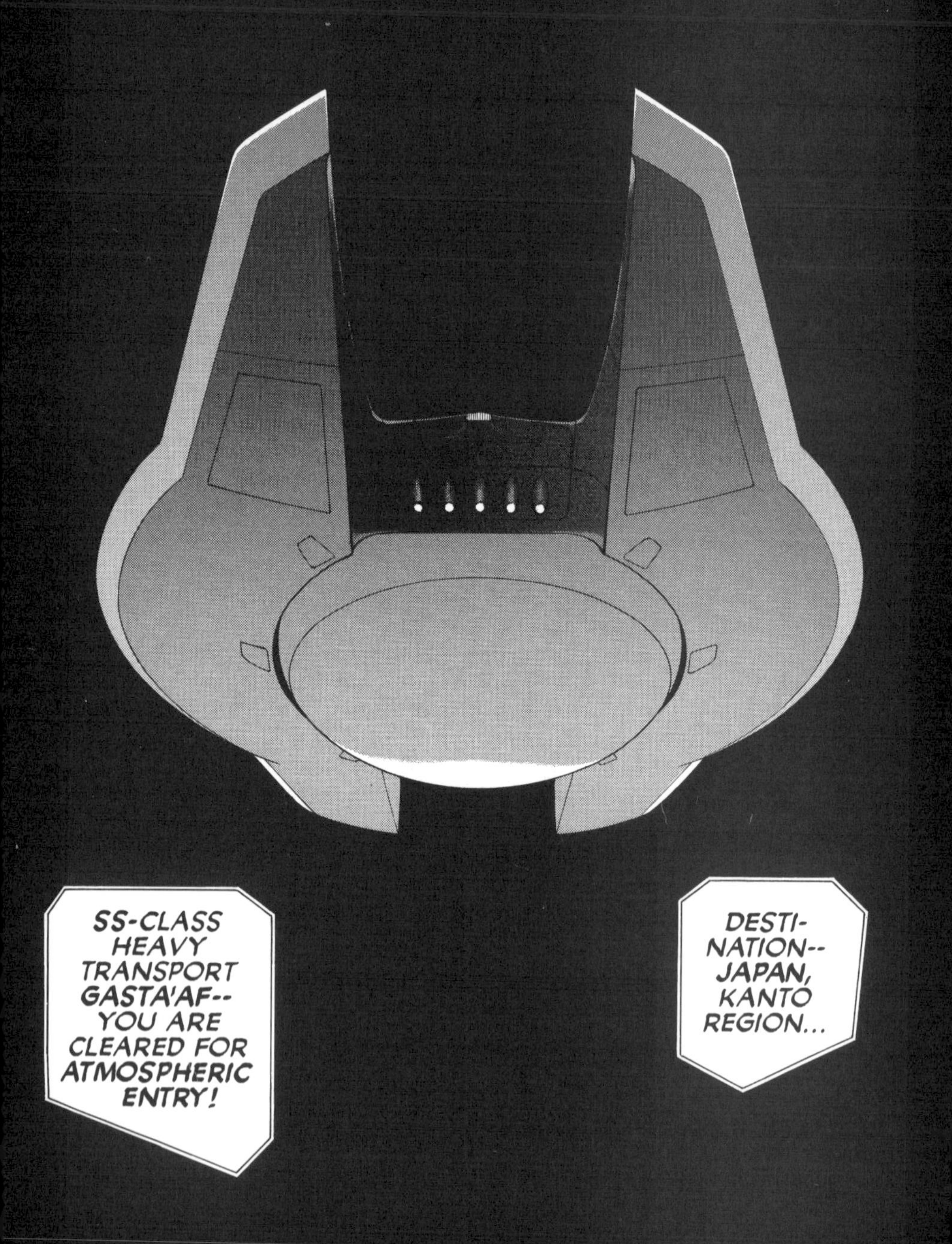
SS-CLASS HEAVY TRANSPORT GASTA'AF-- YOU ARE CLEARED FOR ATMOSPHERIC ENTRY!
DESTI-NATION-- JAPAN, KANTO REGION...

2.4

CANNON GOD EXAXXION: **STAGE 2.4**

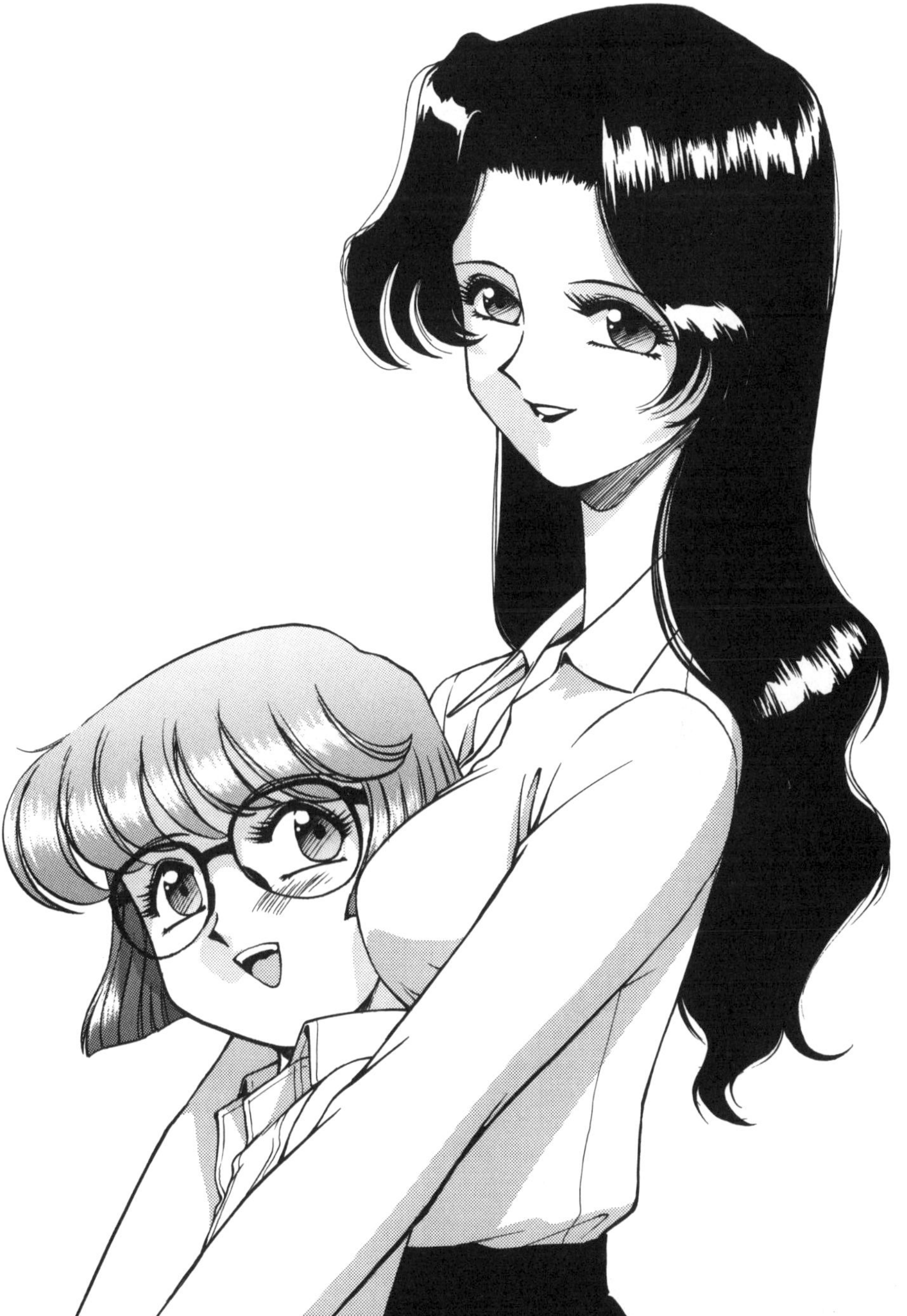

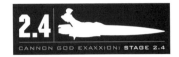

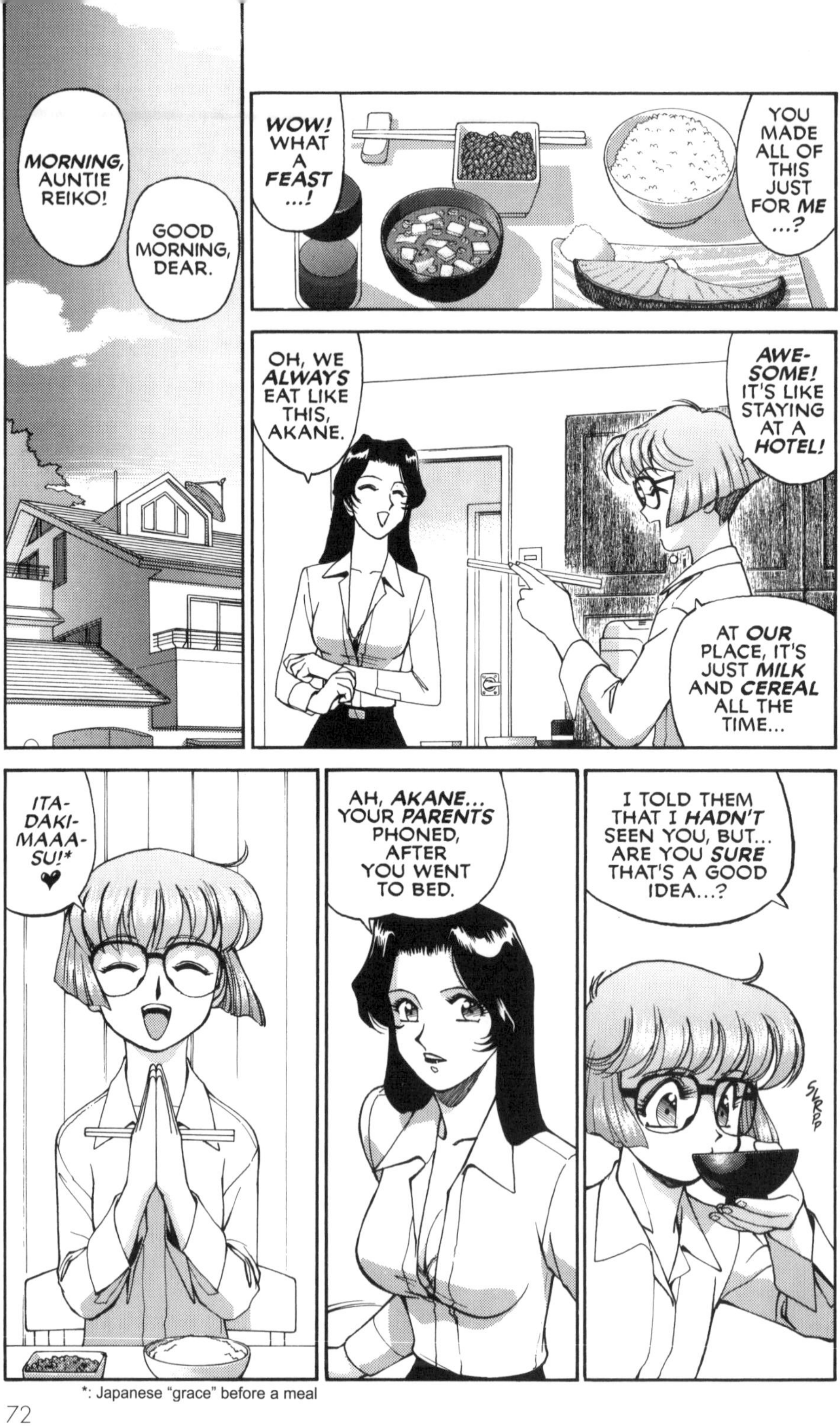
MORNING, AUNTIE REIKO!
GOOD MORNING, DEAR.
WOW! WHAT A FEAST ...!
YOU MADE ALL OF THIS JUST FOR ME ...?
OH, WE ALWAYS EAT LIKE THIS, AKANE.
AWE-SOME! IT'S LIKE STAYING AT A HOTEL!
AT OUR PLACE, IT'S JUST MILK AND CEREAL ALL THE TIME...
ITA-DAKI-MAAA-SU!* ♥
AH, AKANE... YOUR PARENTS PHONED, AFTER YOU WENT TO BED.
I TOLD THEM THAT I HADN'T SEEN YOU, BUT... ARE YOU SURE THAT'S A GOOD IDEA...?
SLRPP

*: Japanese "grace" before a meal

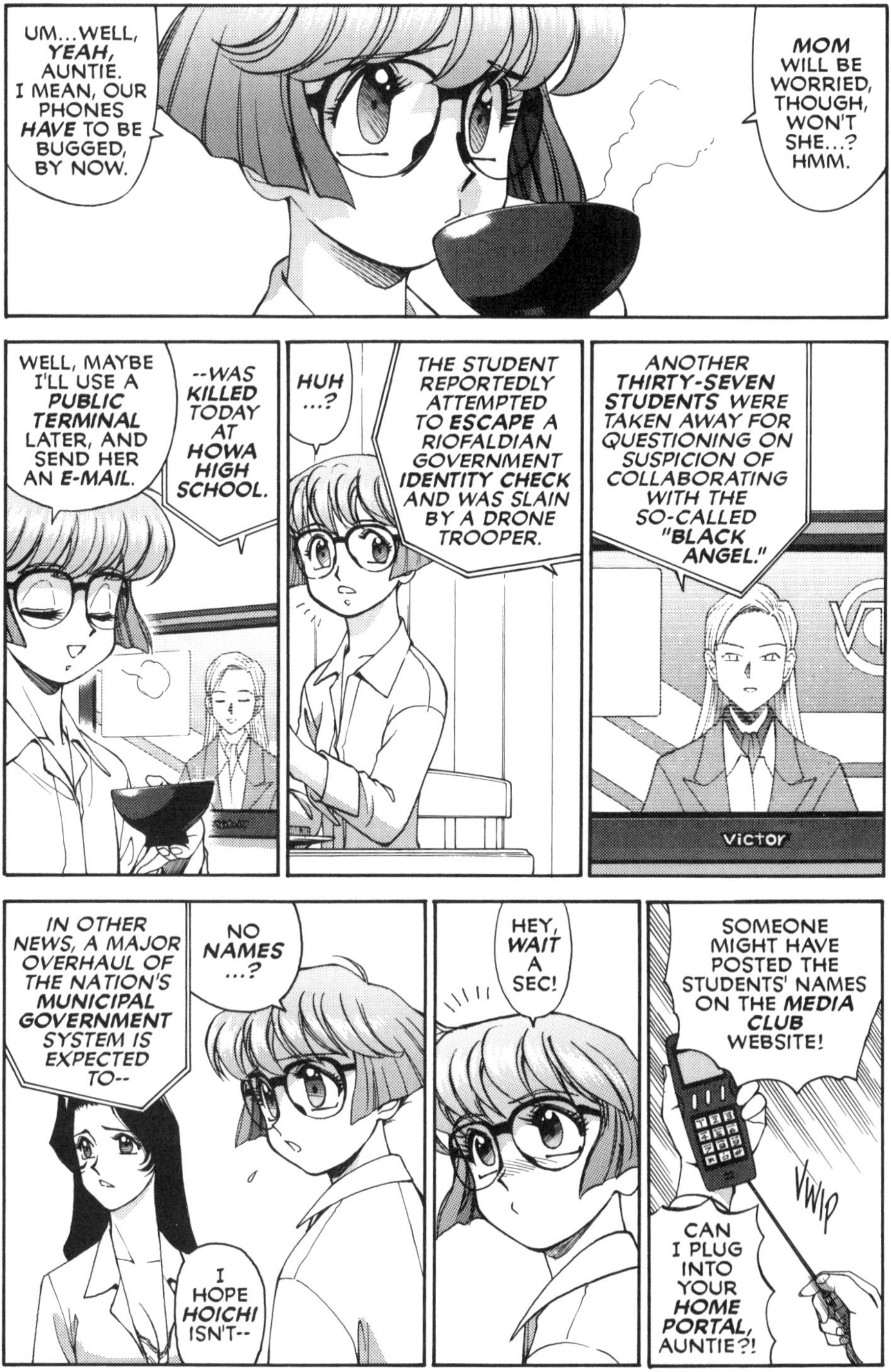
UM...WELL, YEAH, AUNTIE. I MEAN, OUR PHONES HAVE TO BE BUGGED, BY NOW.
MOM WILL BE WORRIED, THOUGH, WON'T SHE...? HMM.
WELL, MAYBE I'LL USE A PUBLIC TERMINAL LATER, AND SEND HER AN E-MAIL.
--WAS KILLED TODAY AT HOWA HIGH SCHOOL.
HUH ...?
THE STUDENT REPORTEDLY ATTEMPTED TO ESCAPE A RIOFALDIAN GOVERNMENT IDENTITY CHECK AND WAS SLAIN BY A DRONE TROOPER.
ANOTHER THIRTY-SEVEN STUDENTS WERE TAKEN AWAY FOR QUESTIONING ON SUSPICION OF COLLABORATING WITH THE SO-CALLED "BLACK ANGEL."
victor
IN OTHER NEWS, A MAJOR OVERHAUL OF THE NATION'S MUNICIPAL GOVERNMENT SYSTEM IS EXPECTED TO--
NO NAMES ...?
I HOPE HOICHI ISN'T--
HEY, WAIT A SEC!
SOMEONE MIGHT HAVE POSTED THE STUDENTS' NAMES ON THE MEDIA CLUB WEBSITE!
VWIP
CAN I PLUG INTO YOUR HOME PORTAL, AUNTIE?!

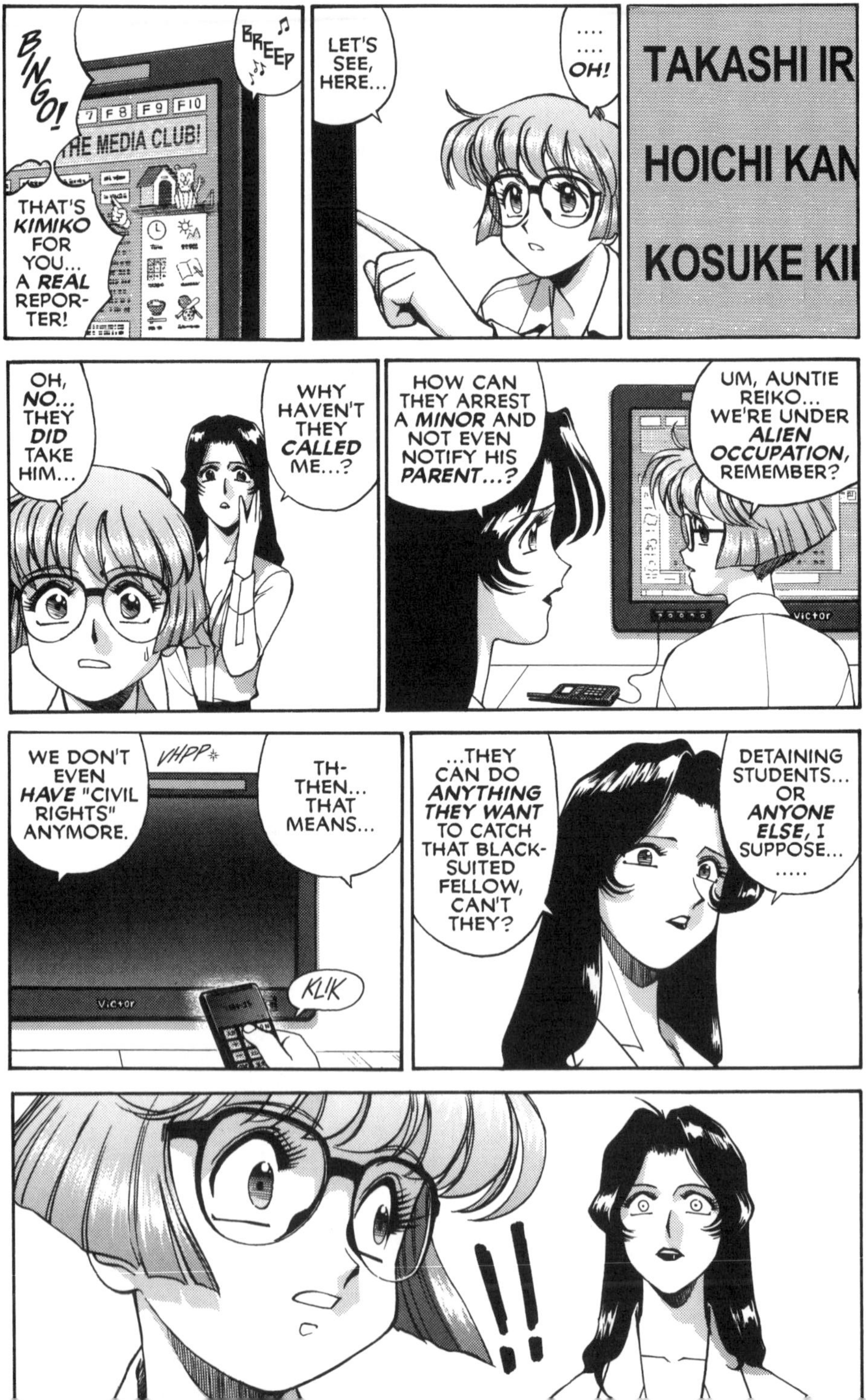
BINGO!
BREEP
THE MEDIA CLUB!
F7 F8 F9 F10
THAT'S KIMIKO FOR YOU... A REAL REPORTER!
LET'S SEE, HERE...
.... OH!
TAKASHI IR
HOICHI KAN
KOSUKE KI
OH, NO... THEY DID TAKE HIM...
WHY HAVEN'T THEY CALLED ME...?
HOW CAN THEY ARREST A MINOR AND NOT EVEN NOTIFY HIS PARENT...?
UM, AUNTIE REIKO... WE'RE UNDER ALIEN OCCUPATION, REMEMBER?
victor
WE DON'T EVEN HAVE "CIVIL RIGHTS" ANYMORE.
VHPP
TH-THEN... THAT MEANS...
KLIK
Victor
...THEY CAN DO ANYTHING THEY WANT TO CATCH THAT BLACK-SUITED FELLOW, CAN'T THEY?
DETAINING STUDENTS... OR ANYONE ELSE, I SUPPOSE... .....
!!

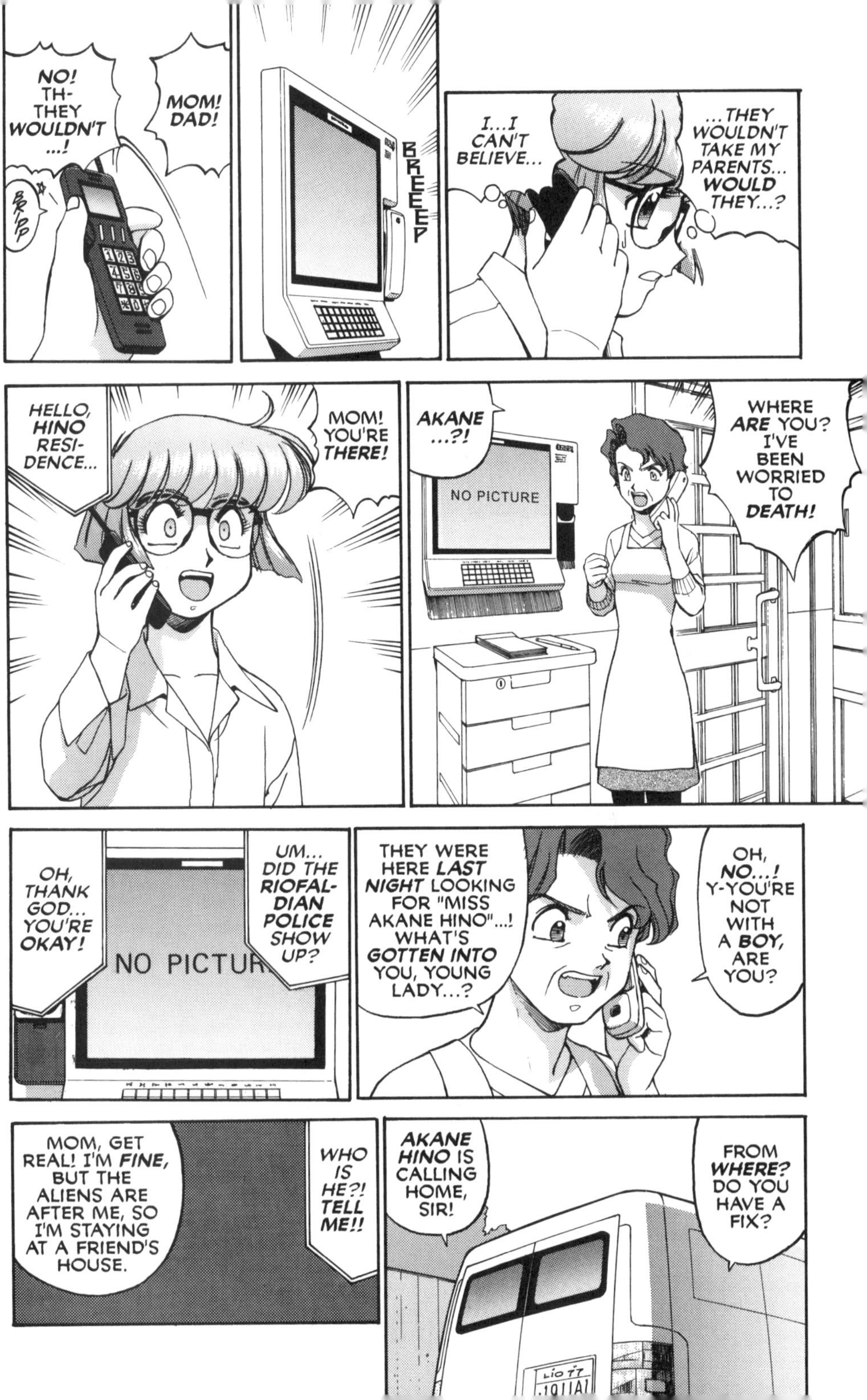
NO! TH- THEY WOULDN'T ...!
MOM! DAD!
BRIPP
BREEEP
I...I CAN'T BELIEVE...
...THEY WOULDN'T TAKE MY PARENTS... WOULD THEY...?
HELLO, HINO RESI- DENCE...
MOM! YOU'RE THERE!
AKANE ...?!
NO PICTURE
WHERE ARE YOU? I'VE BEEN WORRIED TO DEATH!
OH, THANK GOD... YOU'RE OKAY!
NO PICTUR
UM... DID THE RIOFAL- DIAN POLICE SHOW UP?
THEY WERE HERE LAST NIGHT LOOKING FOR "MISS AKANE HINO"...! WHAT'S GOTTEN INTO YOU, YOUNG LADY...?
OH, NO...! Y-YOU'RE NOT WITH A BOY, ARE YOU?
MOM, GET REAL! I'M FINE, BUT THE ALIENS ARE AFTER ME, SO I'M STAYING AT A FRIEND'S HOUSE.
WHO IS HE?! TELL ME!!
AKANE HINO IS CALLING HOME, SIR!
FROM WHERE? DO YOU HAVE A FIX?

SHE'S ON AN *M-CLASS CELL PHONE*, SO I CAN'T TRIANGULATE. THE CLOSEST RELAY IS THE MUSASHINO CITY *N2* TOWER.

IF THE PHONE IS USING *N2*, SHE MUST BE WITHIN 500 YARDS!

COMPILE A LIST OF HER *CLASS-MATES* AND *KNOWN ASSOCI-ATES*.

IF ANY OF THEM LIVE IN THE AREA, SEND A *SEARCH UNIT*!

WE'RE THE *BEST* OF *FRIENDS*...!

RMMMBB

BEST FRIENDS! MAGAZINE

PSHNNNK

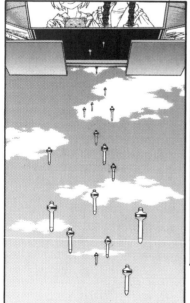

FWSHH

COFFEE

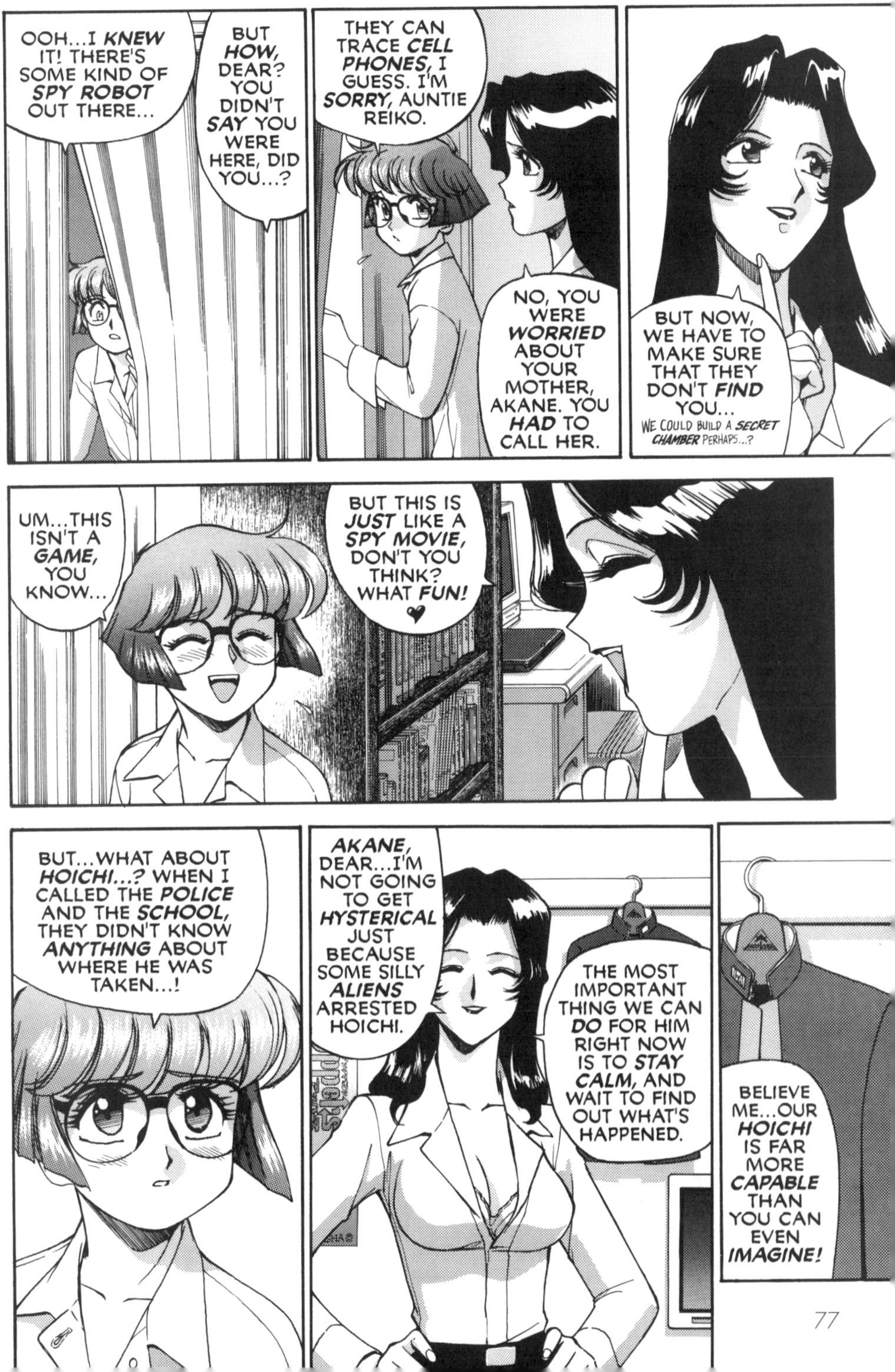

OOH...I KNEW IT! THERE'S SOME KIND OF SPY ROBOT OUT THERE...
BUT HOW, DEAR? YOU DIDN'T SAY YOU WERE HERE, DID YOU...?
THEY CAN TRACE CELL PHONES, I GUESS. I'M SORRY, AUNTIE REIKO.
NO, YOU WERE WORRIED ABOUT YOUR MOTHER, AKANE. YOU HAD TO CALL HER.
BUT NOW, WE HAVE TO MAKE SURE THAT THEY DON'T FIND YOU...
WE COULD BUILD A SECRET CHAMBER PERHAPS...?
UM...THIS ISN'T A GAME, YOU KNOW...
BUT THIS IS JUST LIKE A SPY MOVIE, DON'T YOU THINK? WHAT FUN! ♥
BUT...WHAT ABOUT HOICHI...? WHEN I CALLED THE POLICE AND THE SCHOOL, THEY DIDN'T KNOW ANYTHING ABOUT WHERE HE WAS TAKEN...!
AKANE, DEAR...I'M NOT GOING TO GET HYSTERICAL JUST BECAUSE SOME SILLY ALIENS ARRESTED HOICHI.
THE MOST IMPORTANT THING WE CAN DO FOR HIM RIGHT NOW IS TO STAY CALM, AND WAIT TO FIND OUT WHAT'S HAPPENED.
BELIEVE ME...OUR HOICHI IS FAR MORE CAPABLE THAN YOU CAN EVEN IMAGINE!

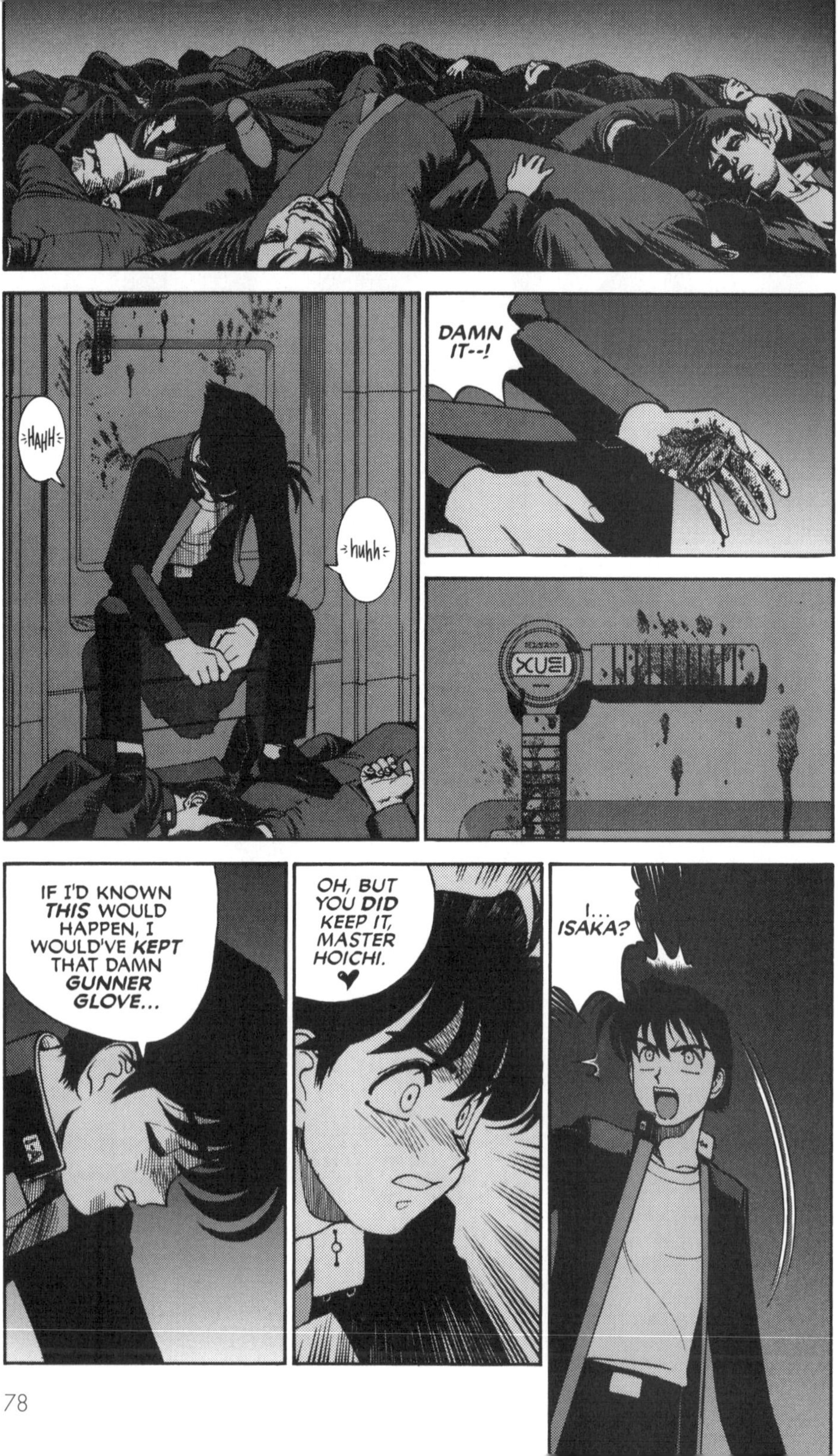
HAHH
huhh
DAMN IT--!
IF I'D KNOWN THIS WOULD HAPPEN, I WOULD'VE KEPT THAT DAMN GUNNER GLOVE...
OH, BUT YOU DID KEEP IT, MASTER HOICHI. ♥
I... ISAKA?

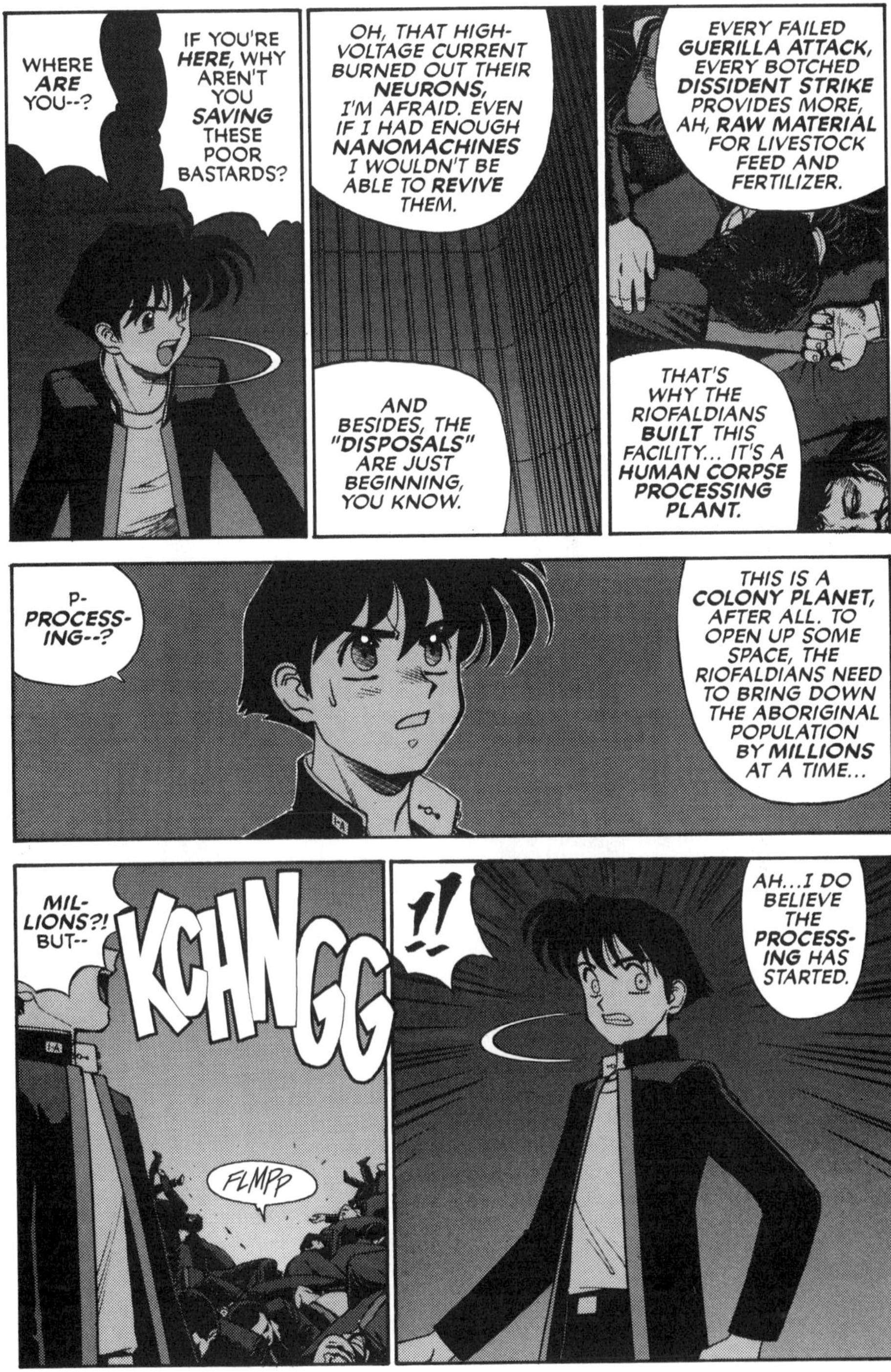
WHERE ARE YOU--?
IF YOU'RE HERE, WHY AREN'T YOU SAVING THESE POOR BASTARDS?
OH, THAT HIGH-VOLTAGE CURRENT BURNED OUT THEIR NEURONS, I'M AFRAID. EVEN IF I HAD ENOUGH NANOMACHINES I WOULDN'T BE ABLE TO REVIVE THEM.
AND BESIDES, THE "DISPOSALS" ARE JUST BEGINNING, YOU KNOW.
EVERY FAILED GUERILLA ATTACK, EVERY BOTCHED DISSIDENT STRIKE PROVIDES MORE, AH, RAW MATERIAL FOR LIVESTOCK FEED AND FERTILIZER.
THAT'S WHY THE RIOFALDIANS BUILT THIS FACILITY... IT'S A HUMAN CORPSE PROCESSING PLANT.
P-PROCESS-ING--?
THIS IS A COLONY PLANET, AFTER ALL. TO OPEN UP SOME SPACE, THE RIOFALDIANS NEED TO BRING DOWN THE ABORIGINAL POPULATION BY MILLIONS AT A TIME...
MIL-LIONS?! BUT--
KCHNGG
FLMPP
!!
AH...I DO BELIEVE THE PROCESS-ING HAS STARTED.

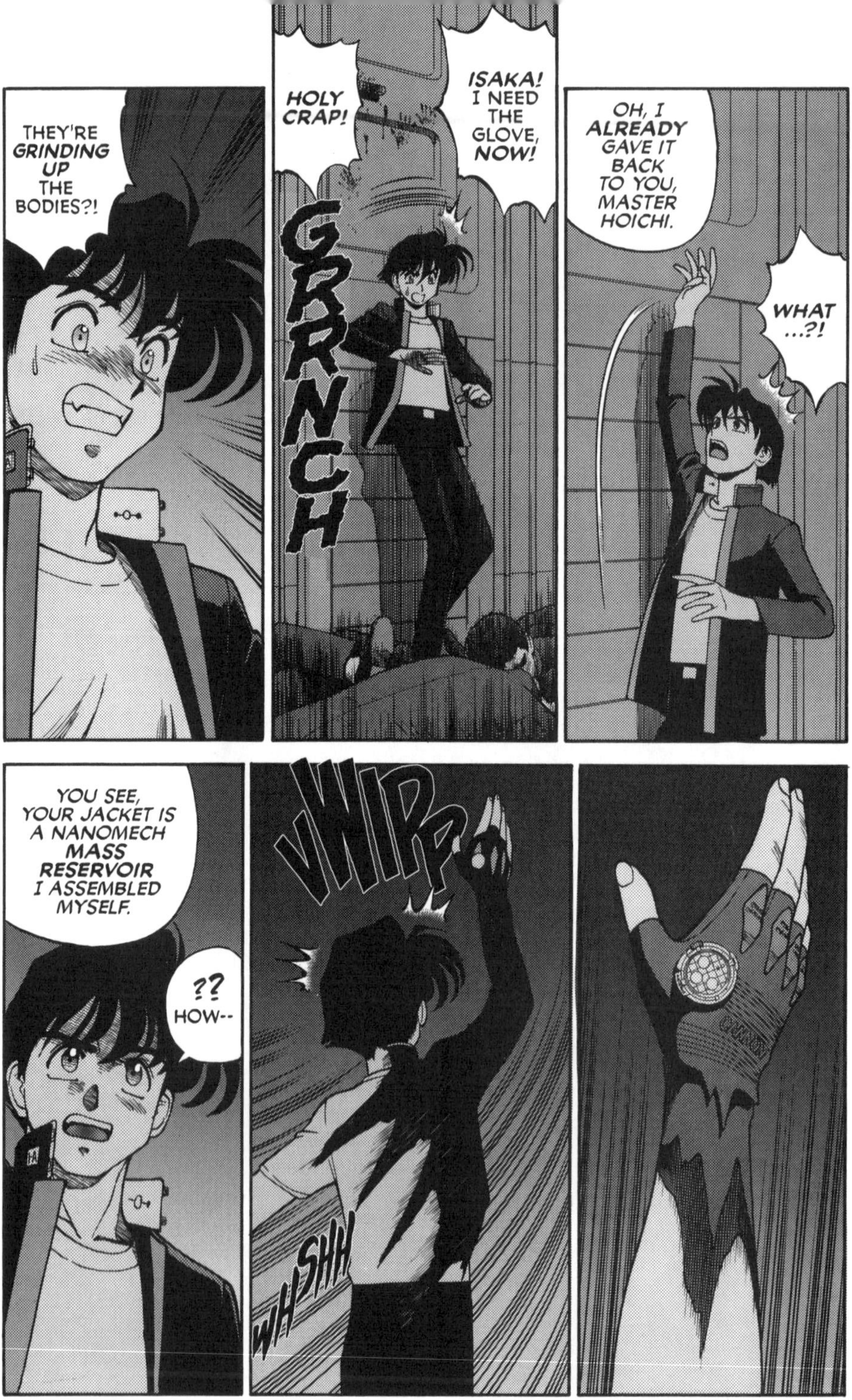
THEY'RE GRINDING UP THE BODIES?!
HOLY CRAP!
ISAKA! I NEED THE GLOVE, NOW!
GRRNCH
OH, I ALREADY GAVE IT BACK TO YOU, MASTER HOICHI.
WHAT ...?!
YOU SEE, YOUR JACKET IS A NANOMECH MASS RESERVOIR I ASSEMBLED MYSELF.
?? HOW--
VWIRR
WHSHH

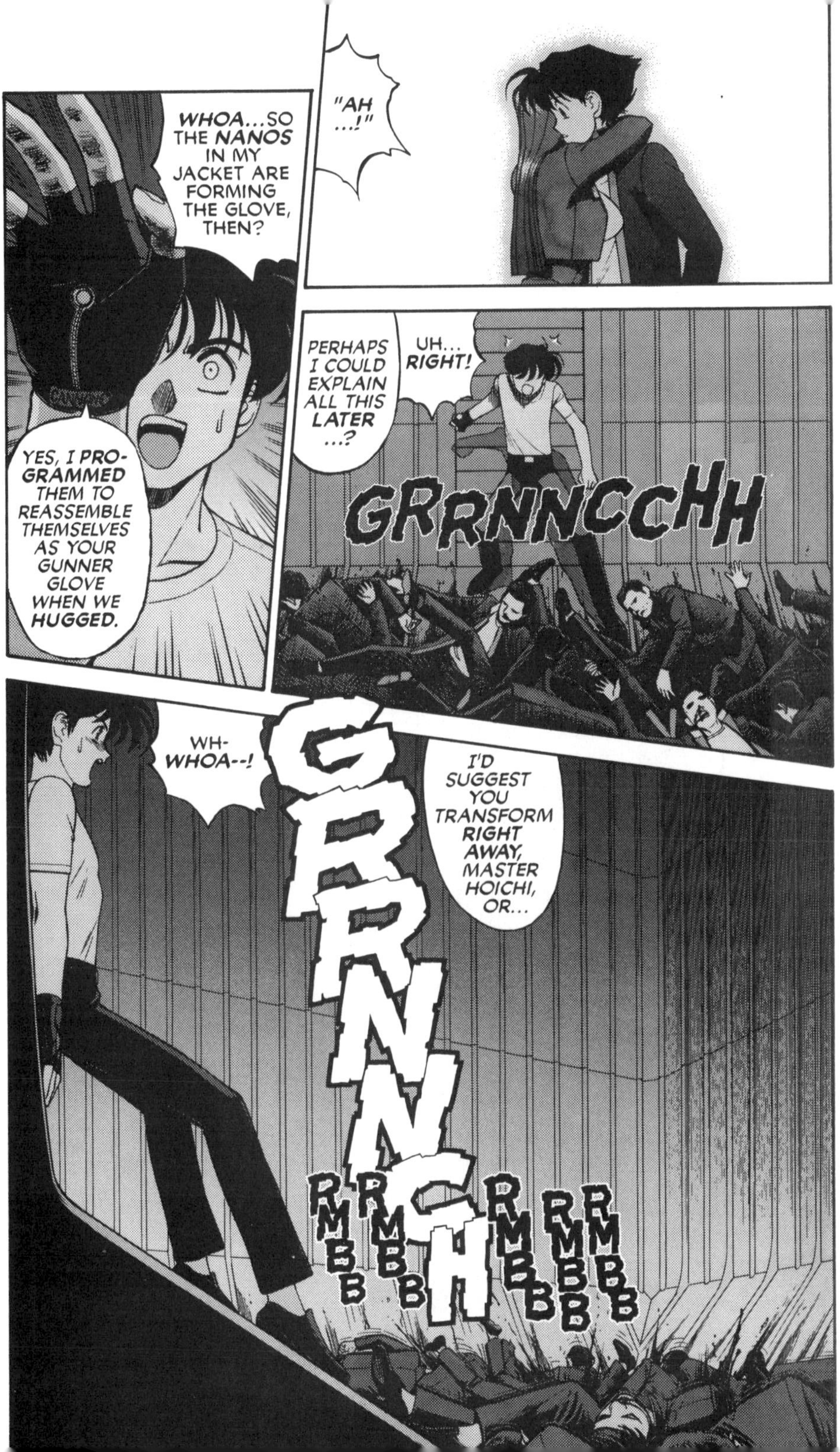
WHOA...SO THE NANOS IN MY JACKET ARE FORMING THE GLOVE, THEN?
YES, I PRO-GRAMMED THEM TO REASSEMBLE THEMSELVES AS YOUR GUNNER GLOVE WHEN WE HUGGED.
"AH ...!"
PERHAPS I COULD EXPLAIN ALL THIS LATER ...?
UH... RIGHT!
GRRNNCCHH
WH- WHOA--!
GRRNNCH
I'D SUGGEST YOU TRANSFORM RIGHT AWAY, MASTER HOICHI, OR...
RMBB RMBB RMBB RMBB RMBB

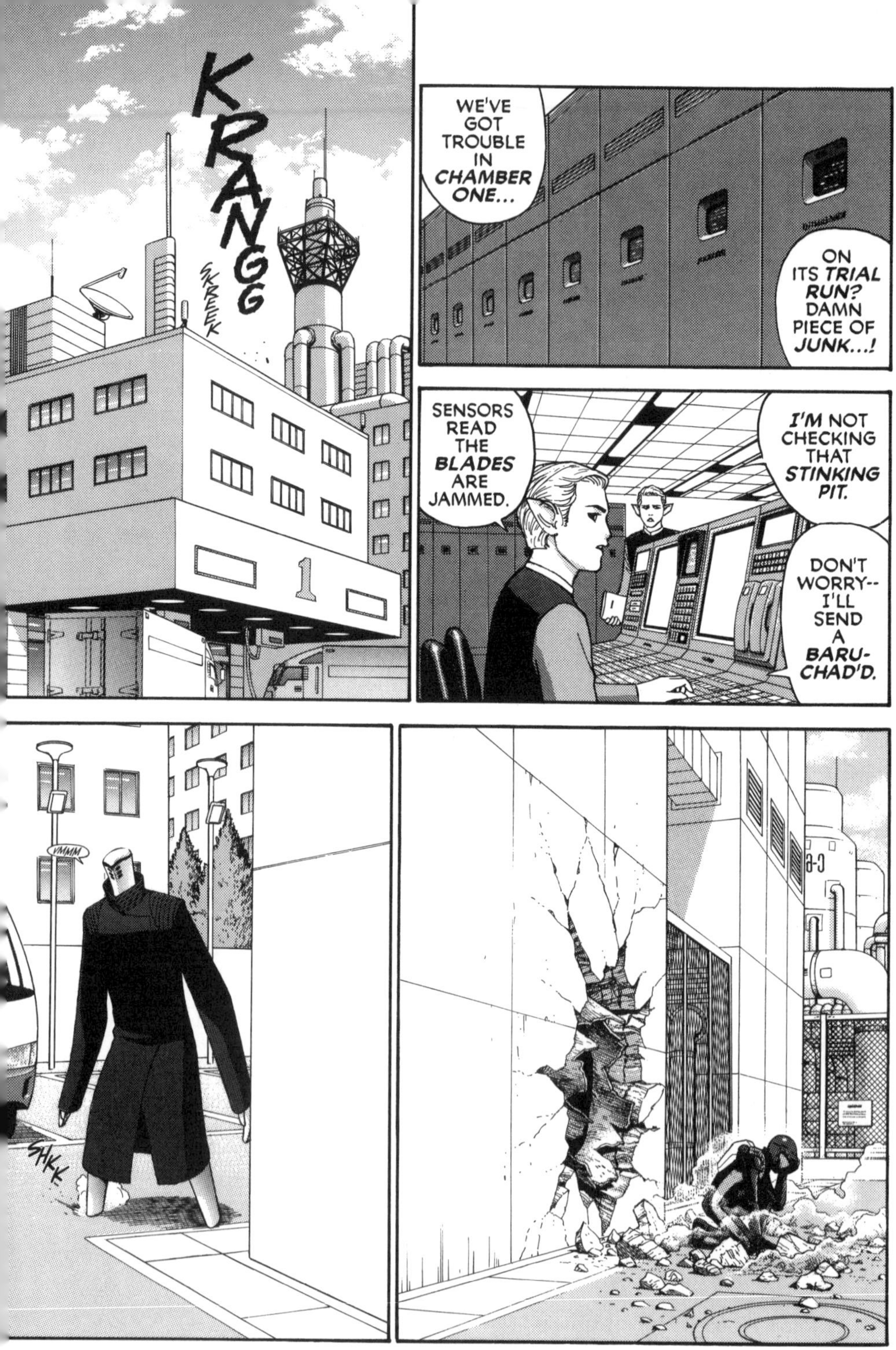
KRANGG
SKREEK
WE'VE GOT TROUBLE IN *CHAMBER ONE*...
ON ITS *TRIAL RUN?* DAMN PIECE OF *JUNK*...!
SENSORS READ THE *BLADES* ARE JAMMED.
I'M NOT CHECKING THAT *STINKING PIT.*
DON'T WORRY-- I'LL SEND A *BARU-CHAD'D.*
VMMM
SHKK

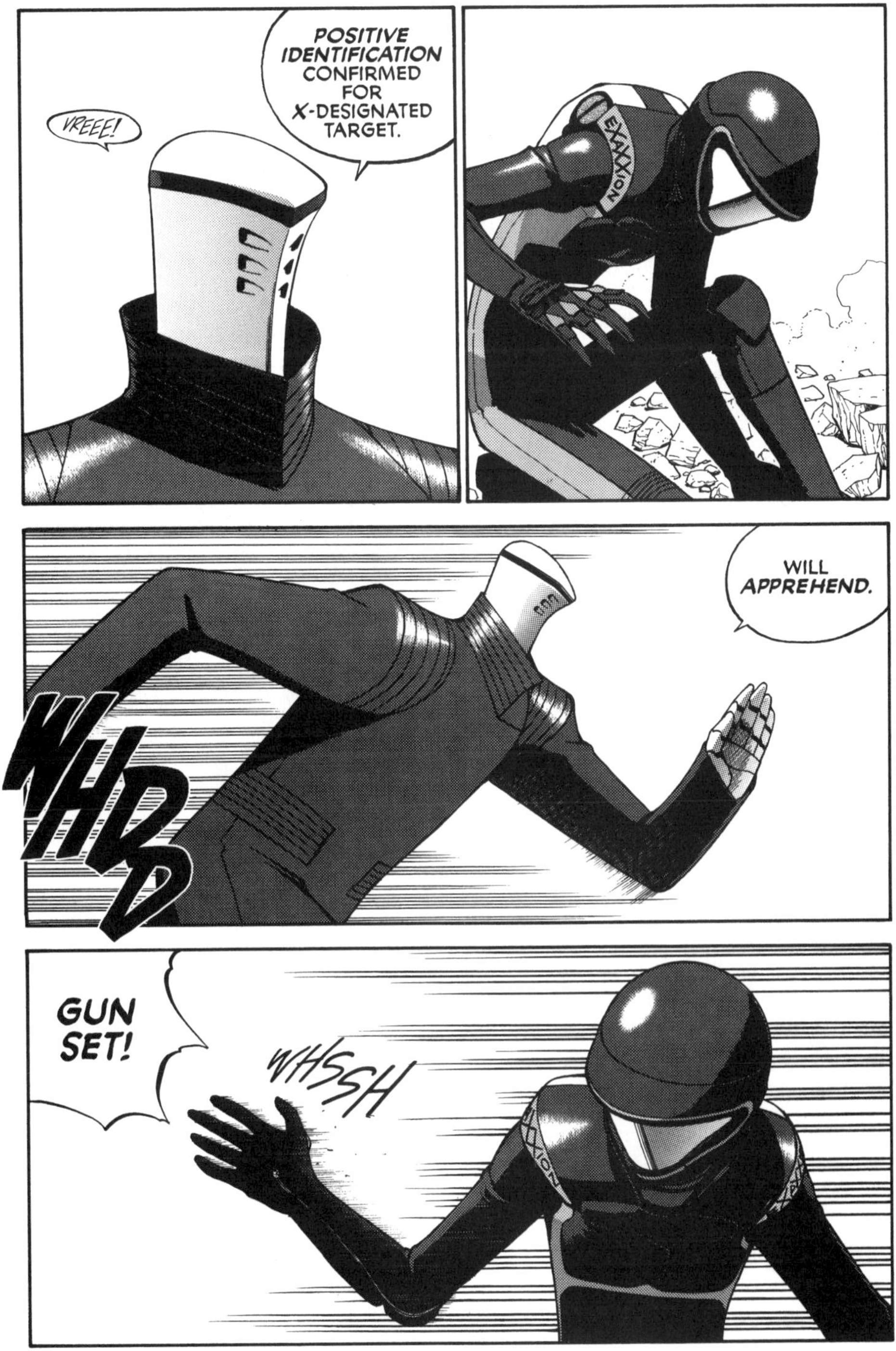
VREEE!
POSITIVE IDENTIFICATION CONFIRMED FOR X-DESIGNATED TARGET.
EXAXXION
WILL APPREHEND.
WHDD
GUN SET!
WHSSH
EXAXXION

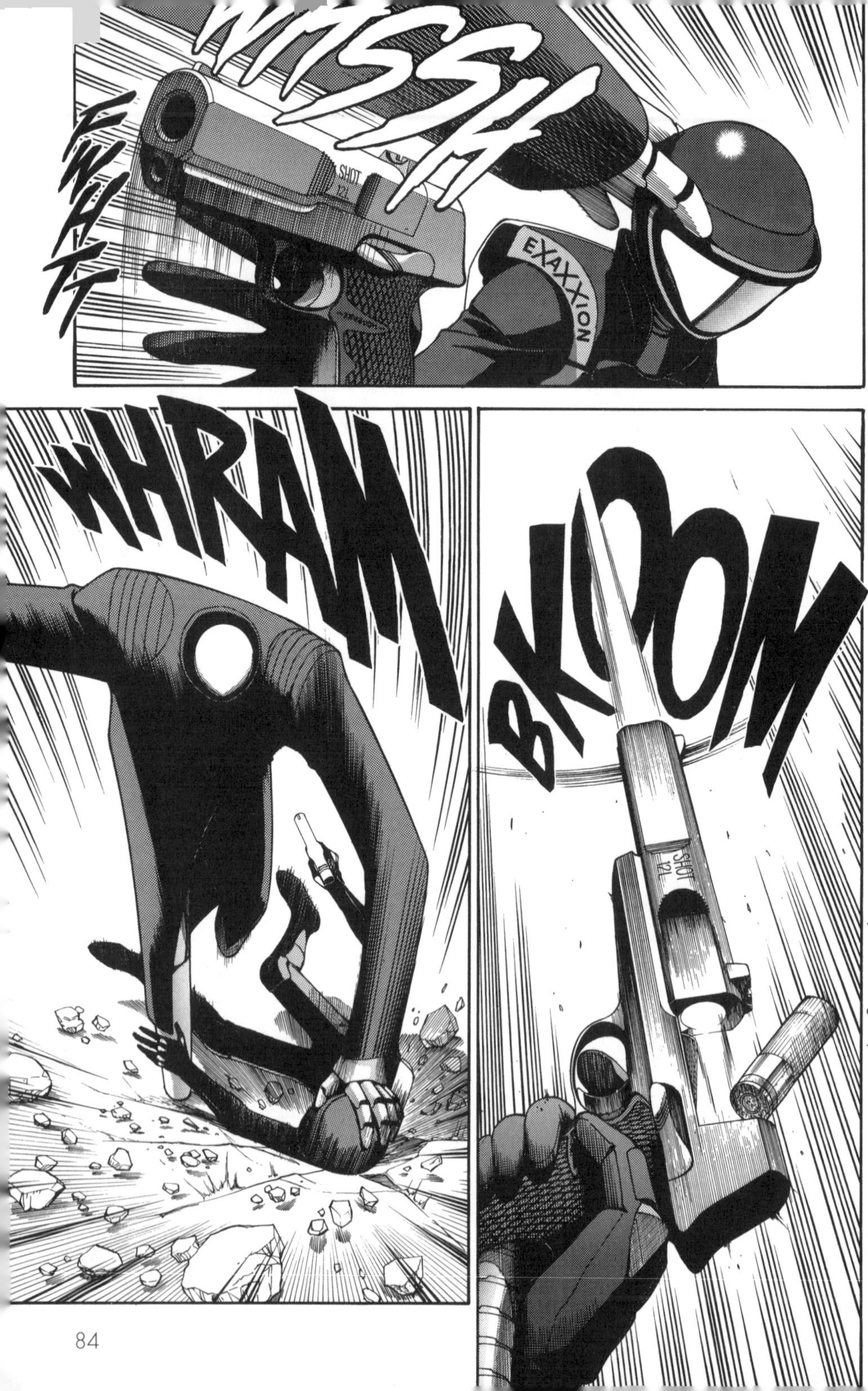
FWHTT
WHSSH
SHOT 12L
EXAXXION
WHRAM
BKOOM
SHOT 12L

This pistol uses a gas-operated "blow-forward" mechanism.

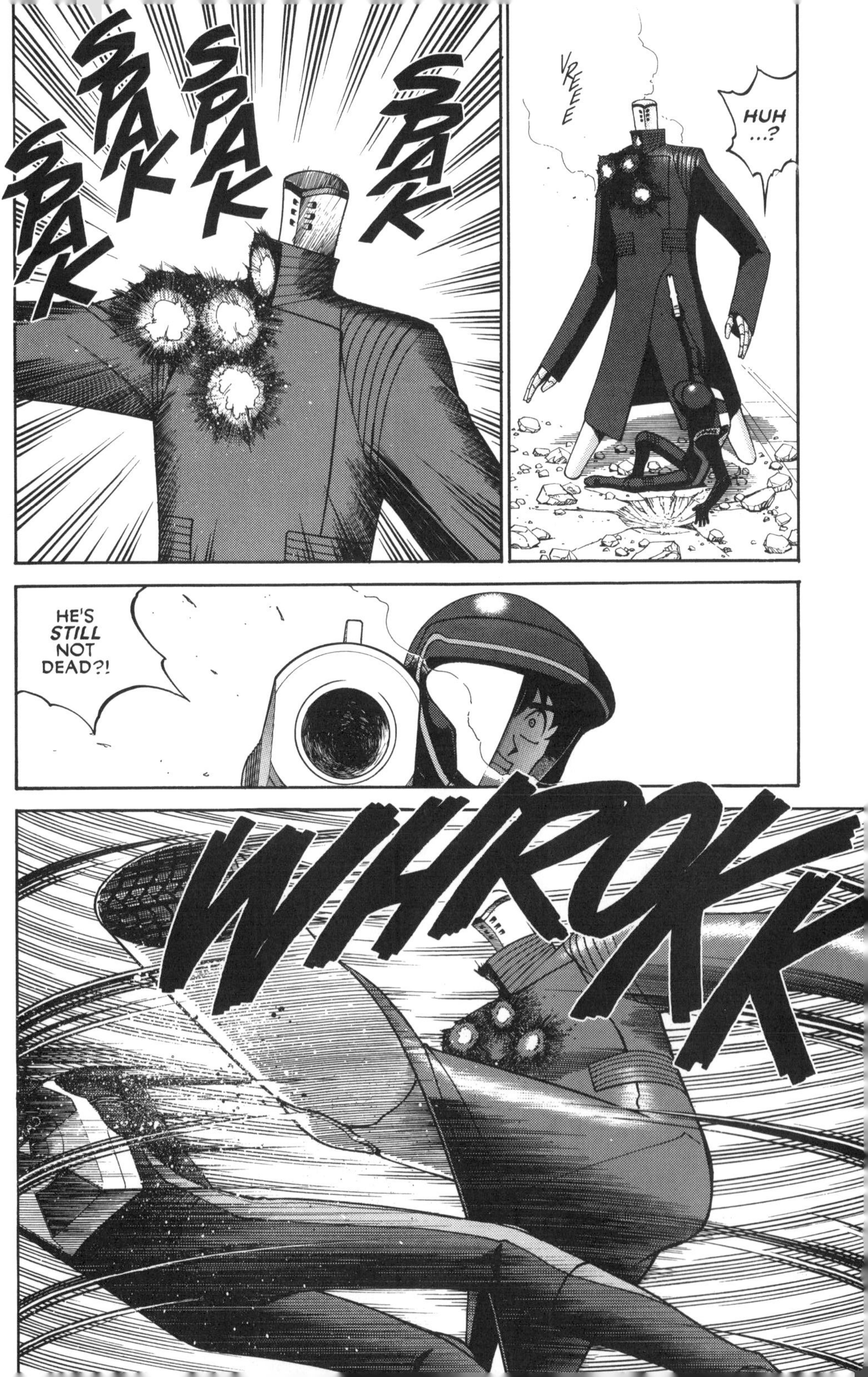
SPAK
SPAK
SPAK
SPAK
VREEE
HUH ...?
HE'S *STILL* NOT DEAD?!
WHROKK

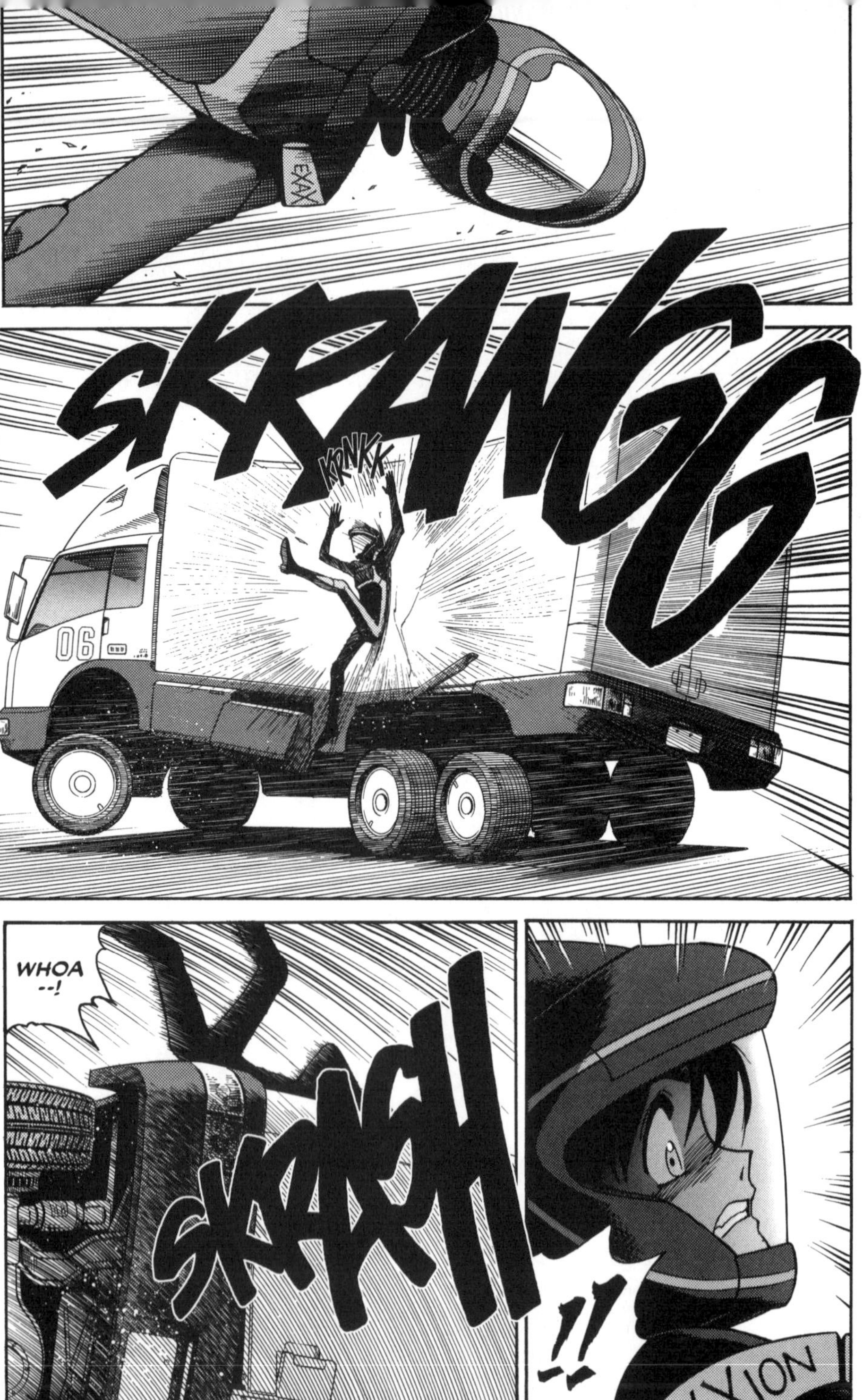
SKRANGG
KRNKK
WDD
WHOA --!
SKRASH
!!
XION

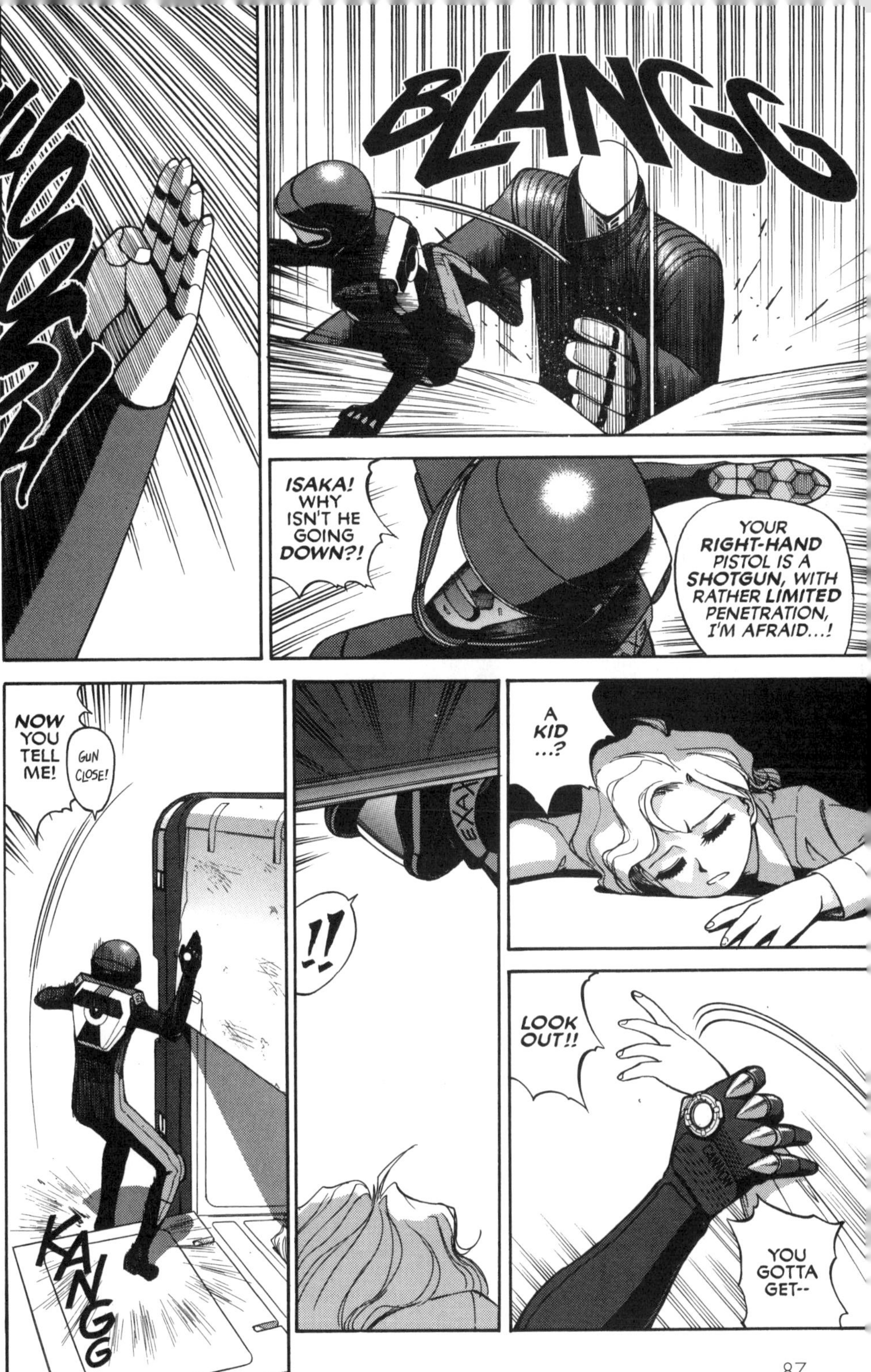
WHOOSH
BLANGG
ISAKA! WHY ISN'T HE GOING DOWN?!
YOUR RIGHT-HAND PISTOL IS A SHOTGUN, WITH RATHER LIMITED PENETRATION, I'M AFRAID...!
NOW YOU TELL ME!
GUN CLOSE!
KANGG
!!
A KID ...?
LOOK OUT!!
YOU GOTTA GET--

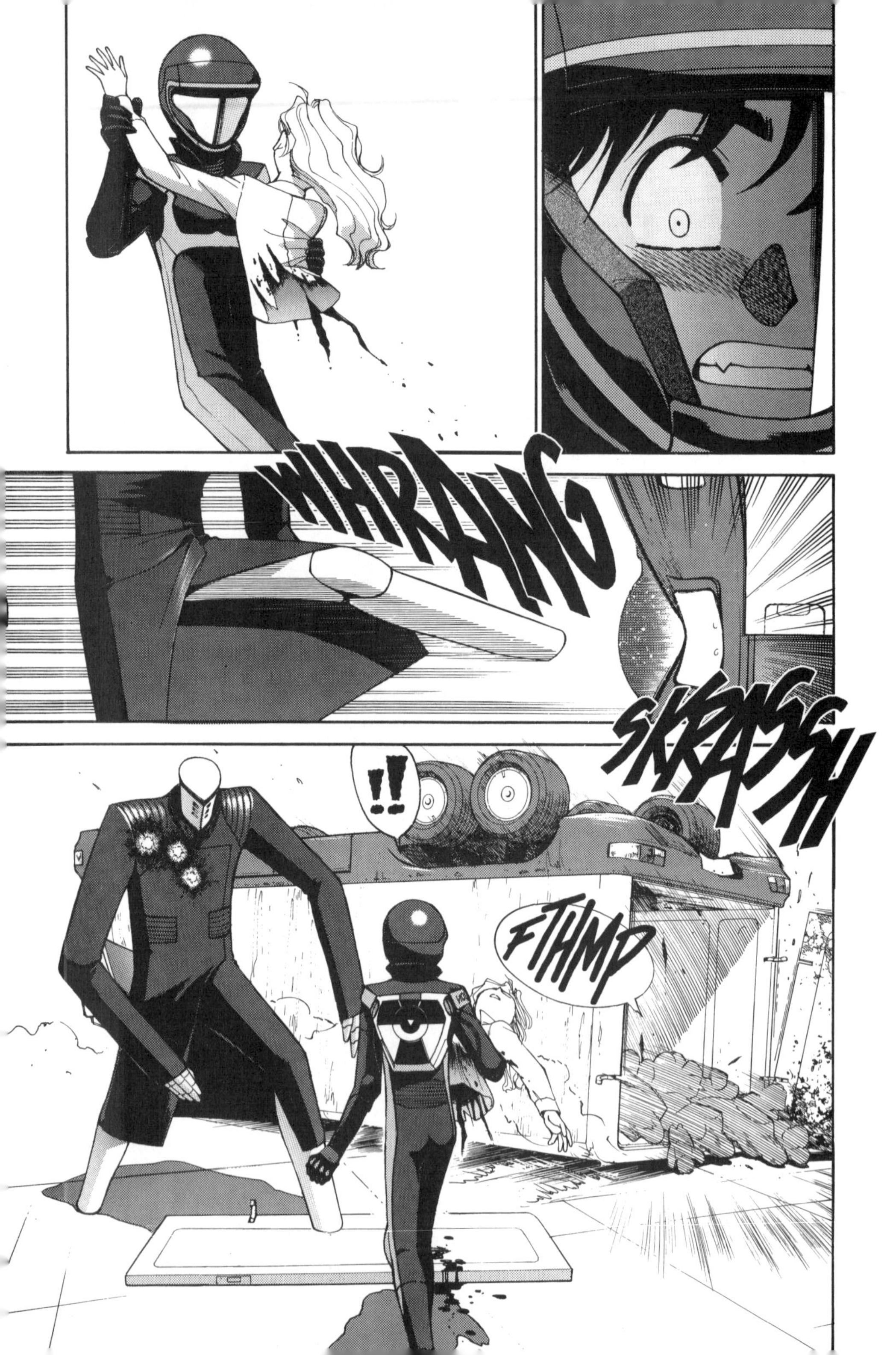
WHRANG
SKRASSH
!!
FTHMP

AH...!
AAA!

HRAAAAA!

GUN
SET!

KCHAK

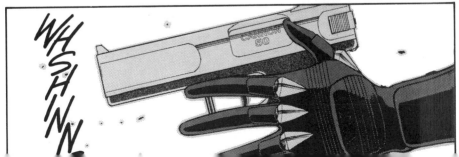

WHSHINN...

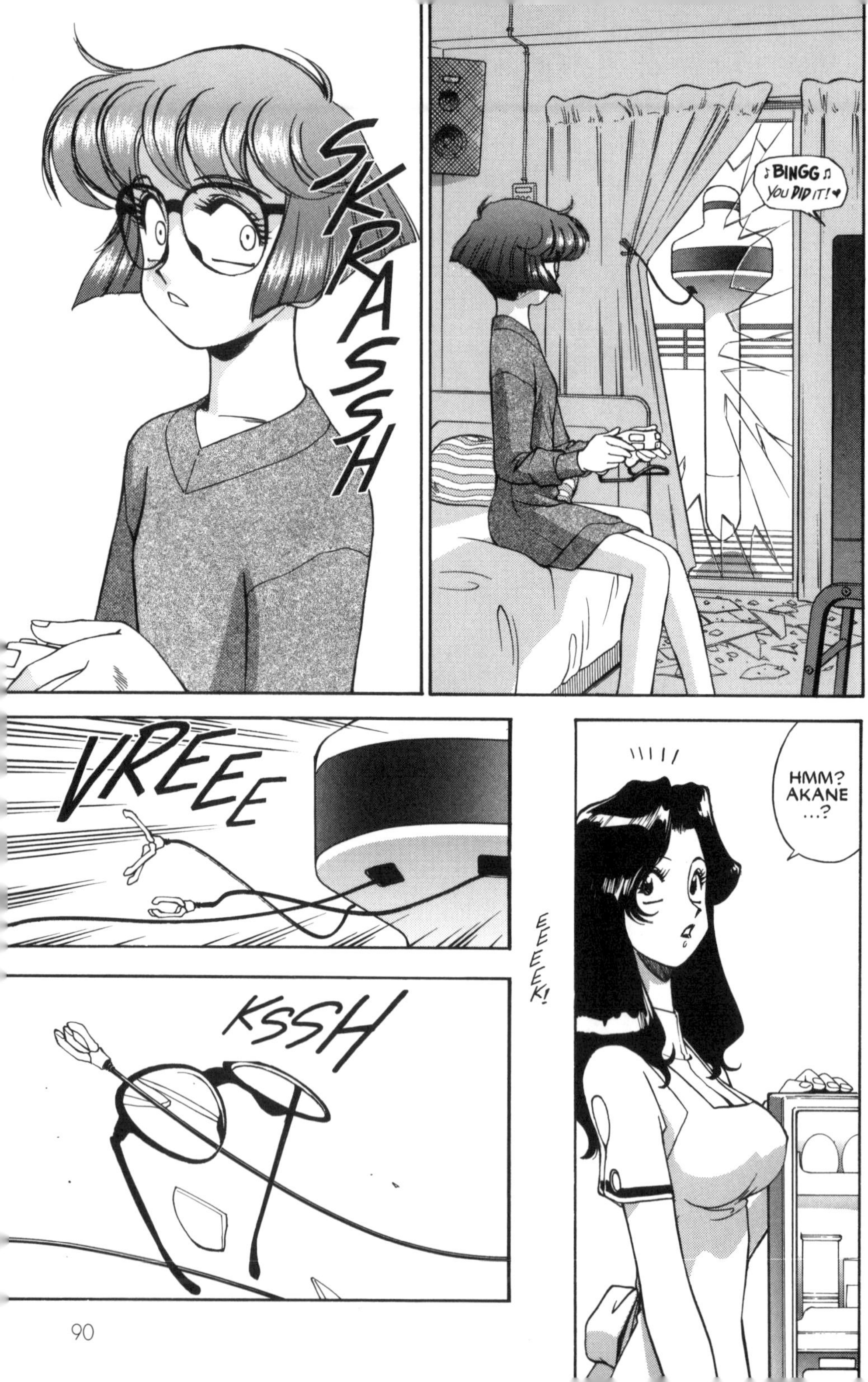
SKRASSH
♪ BINGG ♫ YOU DID IT! ♥
VREEE
KSSH
EEEEK!
HMM? AKANE ...?

2.5

CANNON GOD EXAXXION: **STAGE 2.5**

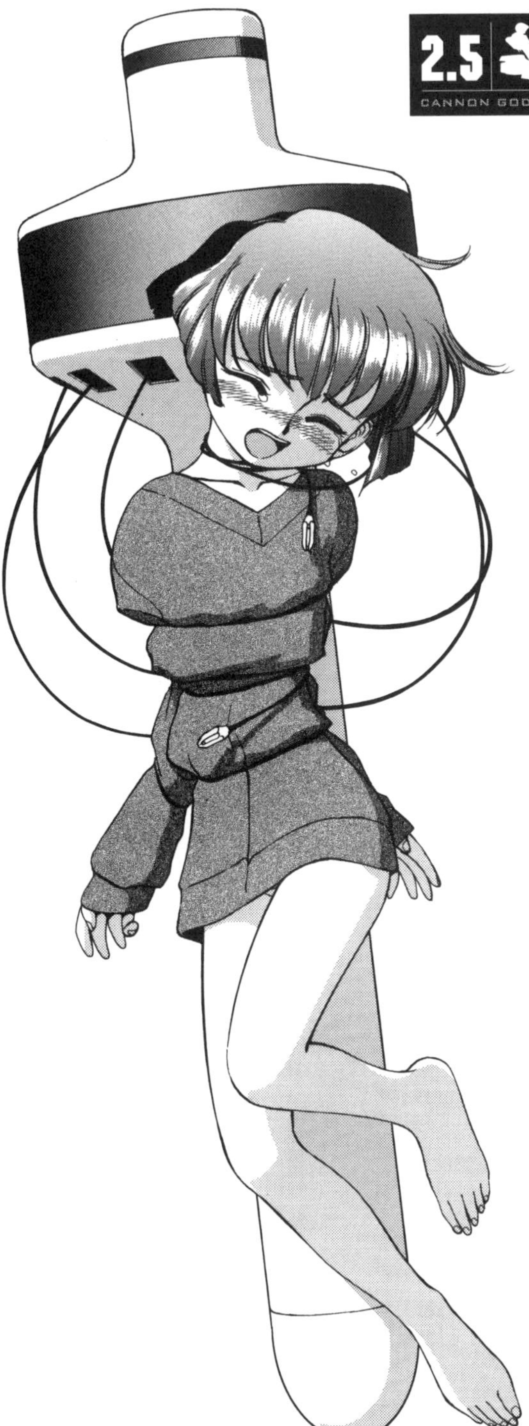

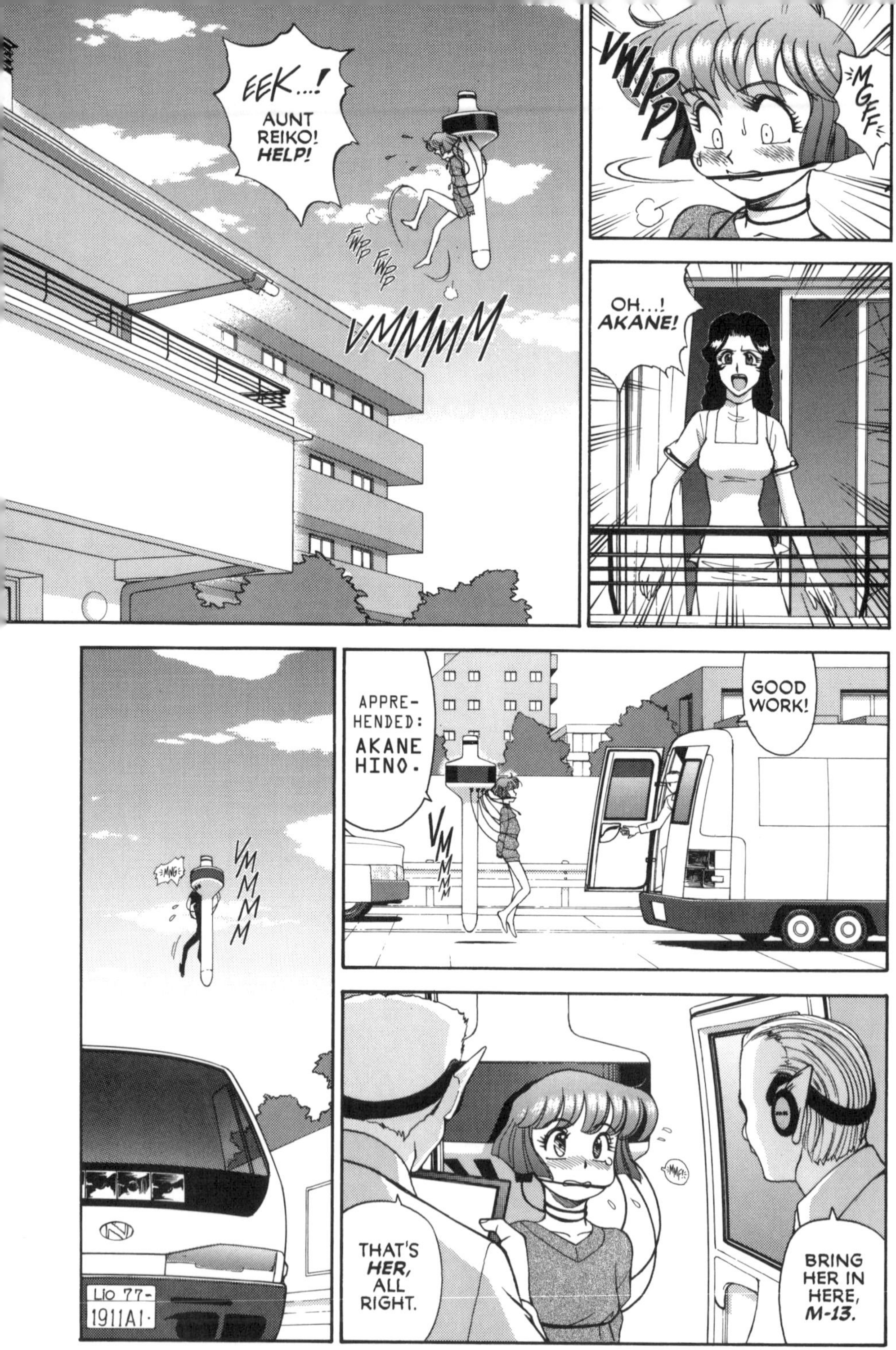
EEK...! AUNT REIKO! HELP!
FWPP FWPP
VMMMMM
VWIPP
MGFF
OH...! AKANE!
MNG
VMMMMM
APPRE-HENDED: AKANE HINO.
VMMMM
GOOD WORK!
Lio 77-
1911A1·
THAT'S HER, ALL RIGHT.
MMF
BRING HER IN HERE, M-13.

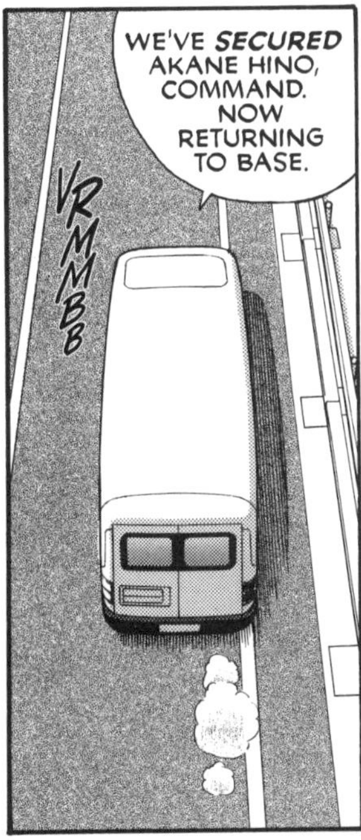
WE'VE *SECURED* AKANE HINO, COMMAND. NOW RETURNING TO BASE.
VRMMBB

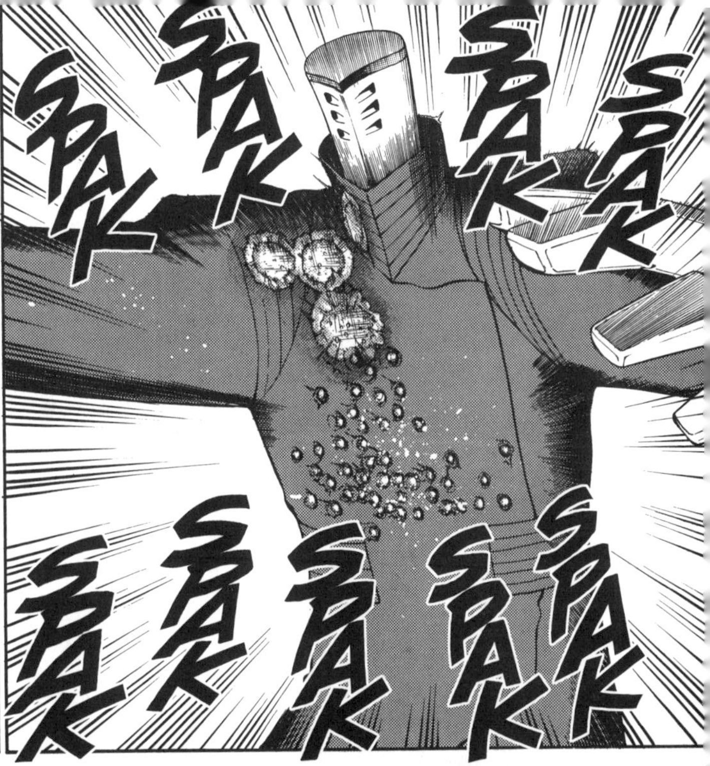
SPAK
SPAK
SPAK
SPAK
SPAK
SPAK
SPAK
SPAK
SPAK

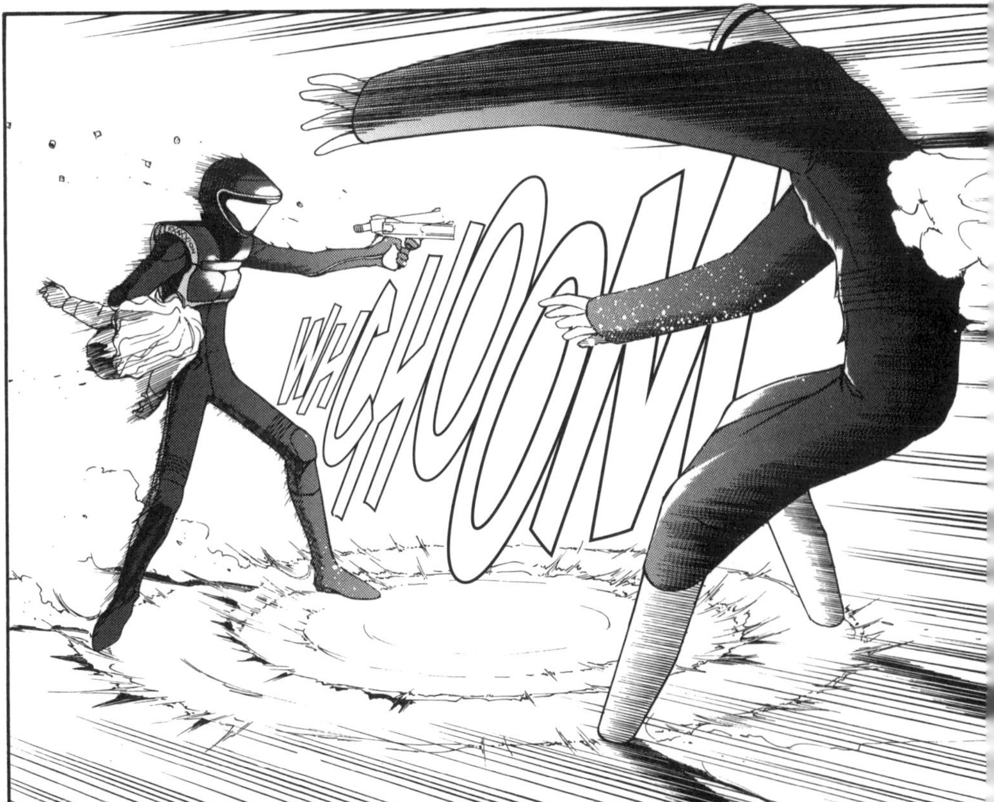
WHCHOOM

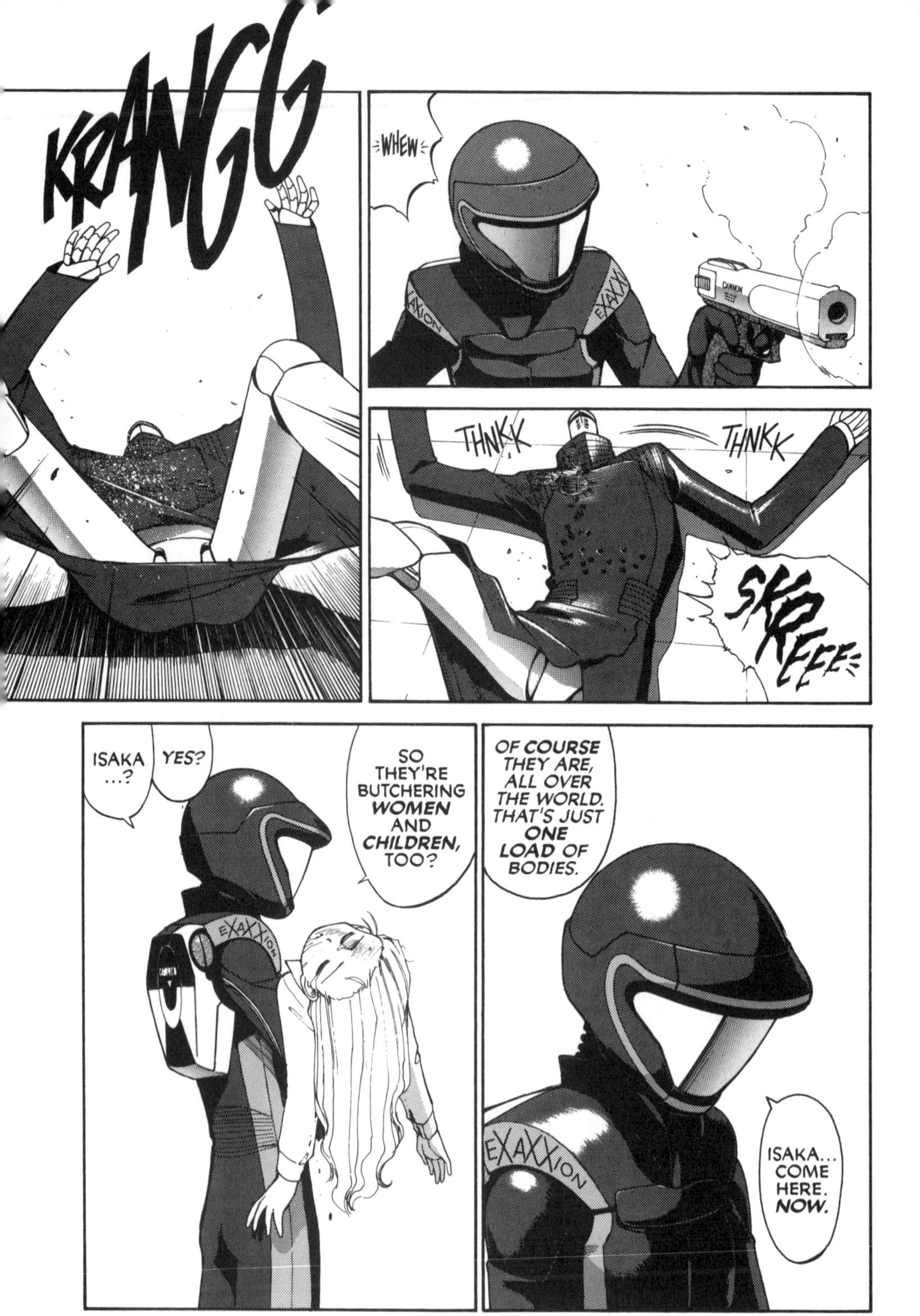
KRANGG
WHEW
CANNON
THNKK
THNKK
SKREEE
ISAKA ...?
YES?
SO THEY'RE BUTCHERING **WOMEN** AND **CHILDREN,** TOO?
OF **COURSE** THEY ARE, ALL OVER THE WORLD. THAT'S JUST **ONE LOAD** OF BODIES.
EXAXXION
ISAKA... COME HERE. **NOW.**

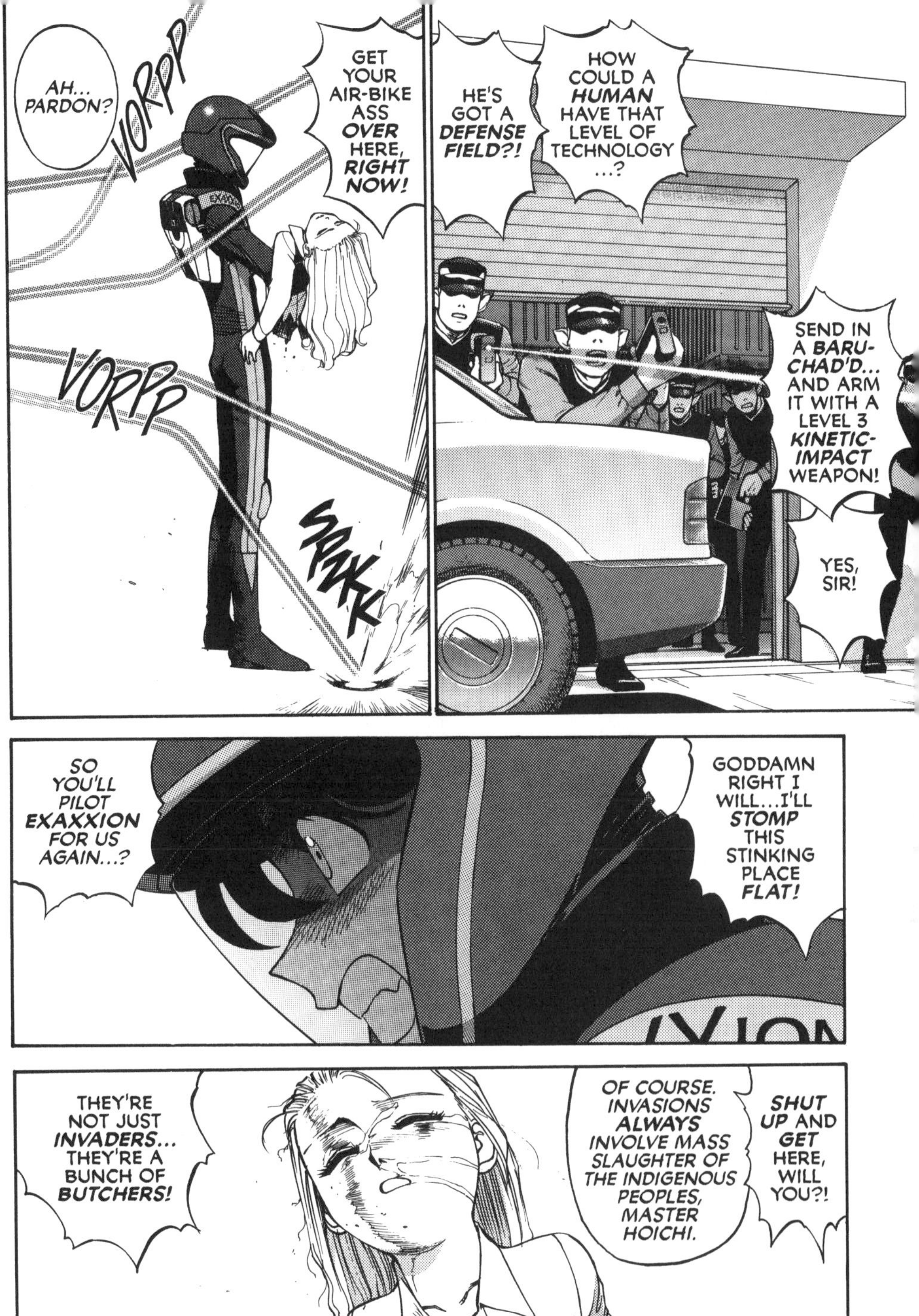
AH... PARDON?
VORPP
GET YOUR AIR-BIKE ASS **OVER** HERE, **RIGHT NOW!**
VORPP
SPAKK
HE'S GOT A **DEFENSE FIELD?!**
HOW COULD A **HUMAN** HAVE THAT LEVEL OF TECHNOLOGY ...?
SEND IN A **BARU-CHAD'D...** AND ARM IT WITH A LEVEL 3 **KINETIC-IMPACT** WEAPON!
YES, SIR!
SO YOU'LL PILOT **EXAXXION** FOR US AGAIN...?
GODDAMN RIGHT I WILL...I'LL **STOMP** THIS STINKING PLACE **FLAT!**
XION
THEY'RE NOT JUST **INVADERS...** THEY'RE A BUNCH OF **BUTCHERS!**
OF COURSE. INVASIONS **ALWAYS** INVOLVE MASS SLAUGHTER OF THE INDIGENOUS PEOPLES, MASTER HOICHI.
SHUT UP AND **GET** HERE, WILL YOU?!

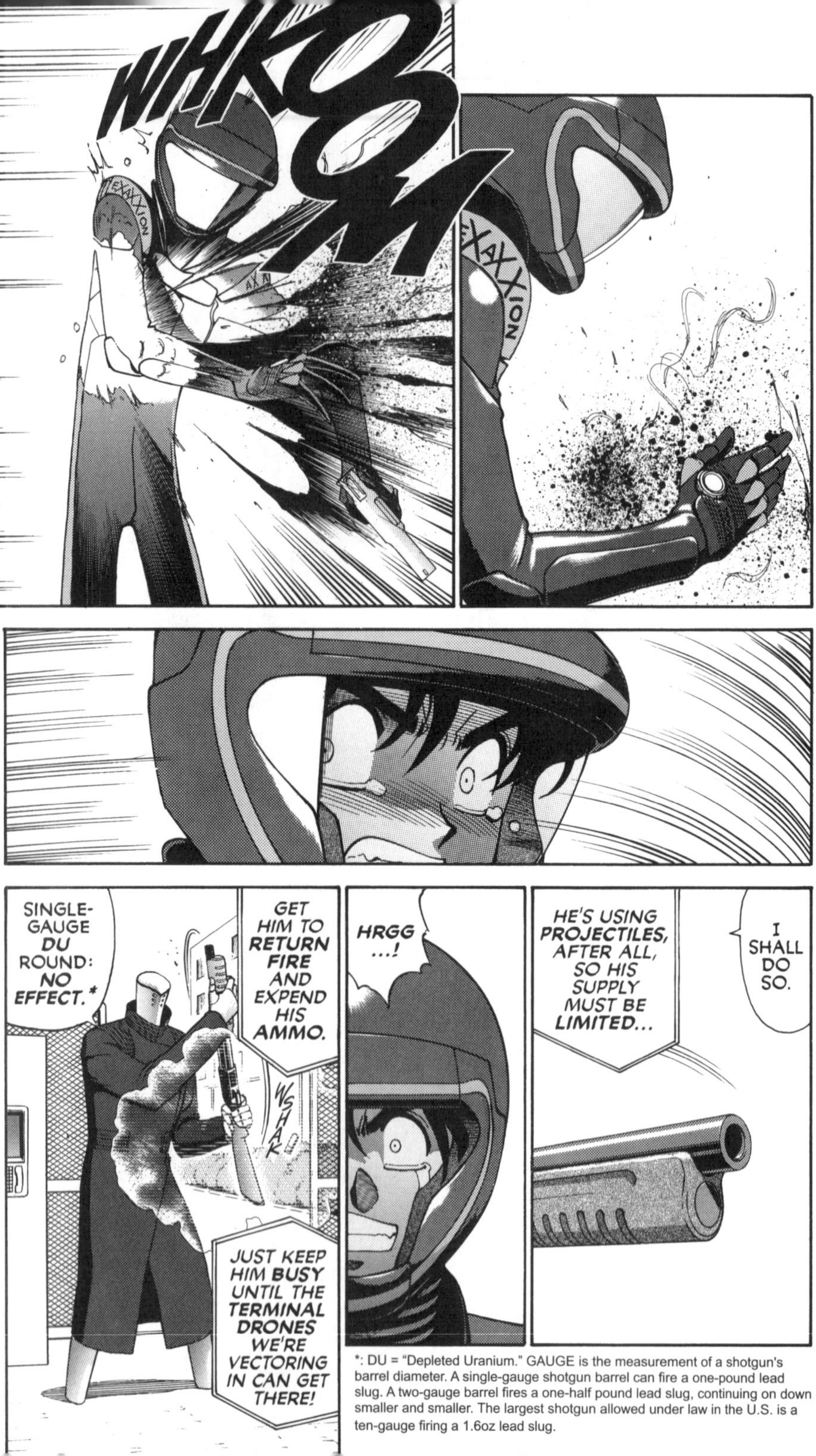
WHKOOM
SINGLE-GAUGE DU ROUND: NO EFFECT.*
GET HIM TO RETURN FIRE AND EXPEND HIS AMMO.
WSHAK
JUST KEEP HIM BUSY UNTIL THE TERMINAL DRONES WE'RE VECTORING IN CAN GET THERE!
HRGG ...!
HE'S USING PROJECTILES, AFTER ALL, SO HIS SUPPLY MUST BE LIMITED...
I SHALL DO SO.

*: DU = "Depleted Uranium." GAUGE is the measurement of a shotgun's barrel diameter. A single-gauge shotgun barrel can fire a one-pound lead slug. A two-gauge barrel fires a one-half pound lead slug, continuing on down smaller and smaller. The largest shotgun allowed under law in the U.S. is a ten-gauge firing a 1.6oz lead slug.

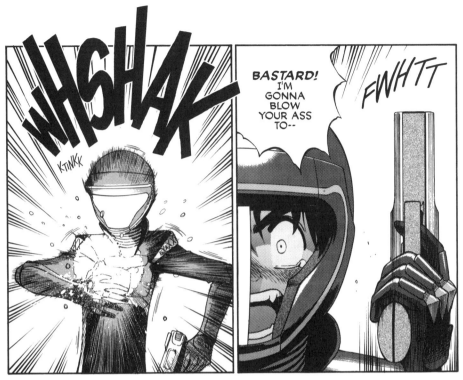

WHSHAK

KTINKK

BASTARD! I'M GONNA BLOW YOUR ASS TO--

FWHTT

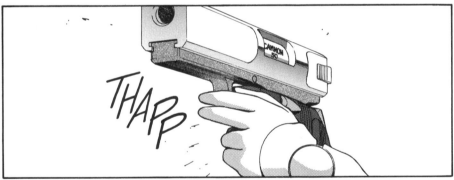

THAPP

!

DON'T EVEN WASTE YOUR AMMO ON THEM.

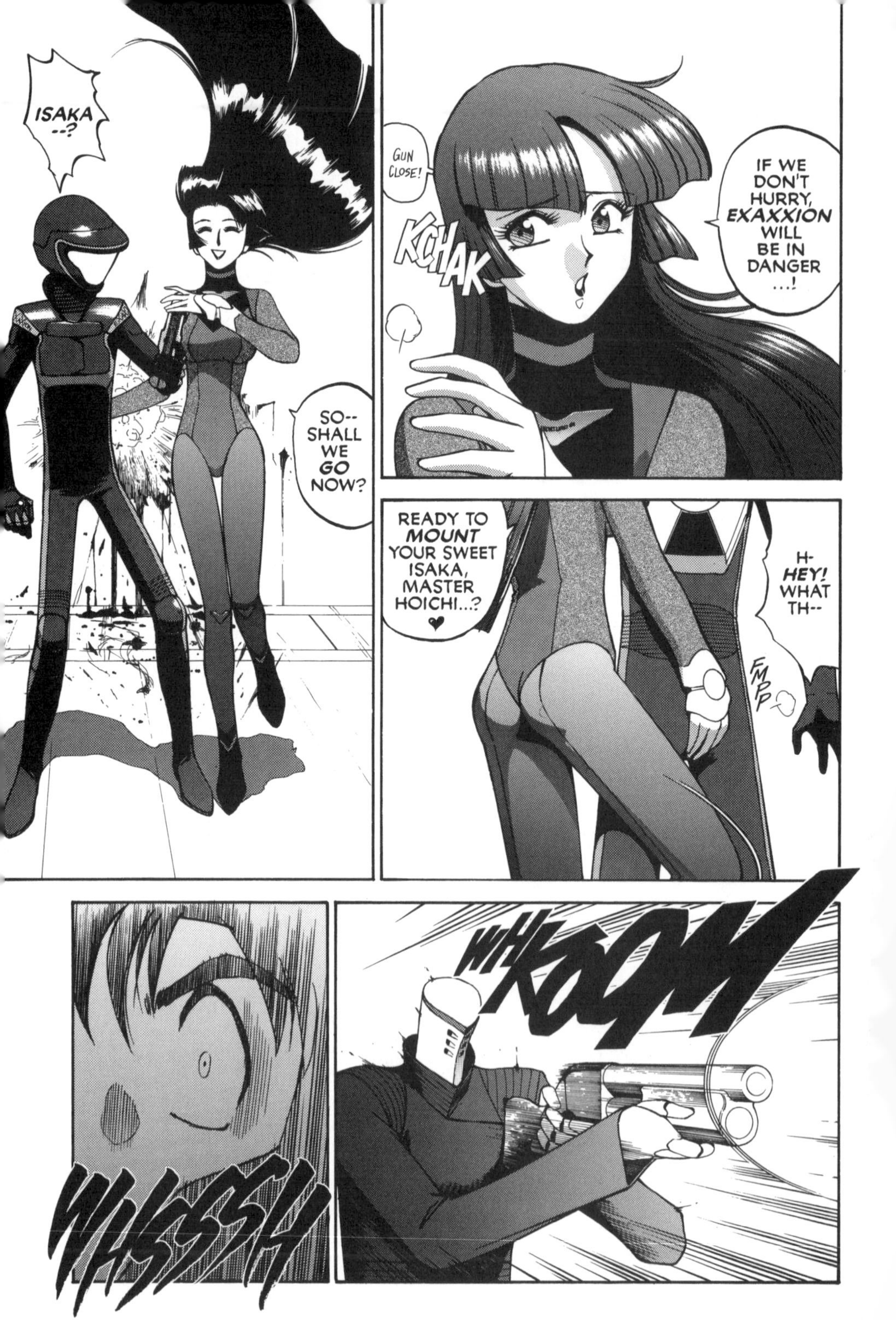
ISAKA --?
SO-- SHALL WE *GO* NOW?
GUN CLOSE!
KCHAK
IF WE DON'T HURRY, ***EXAXXION*** WILL BE IN DANGER ...!
READY TO ***MOUNT*** YOUR SWEET ISAKA, MASTER HOICHI...? ❤
H- ***HEY!*** WHAT TH--
FMPP
WHSSSH
WHKOOM

SPRAKK

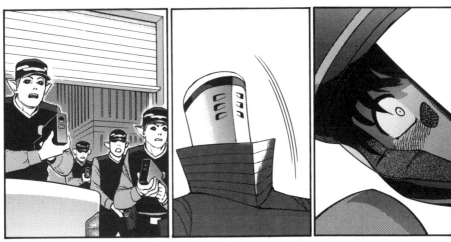

UUWPAAA!

ISAKA! *WAIT*, DAMN IT!

PSHTT

LET ME KILL *ONE* OF 'EM, AT LEAST!

LOOKING TO *VENT* ON SOME ALIEN *CANNON FODDER*, MMM...?

SORRY! RIGHT NOW, IT'S *FAR* MORE IMPORTANT THAT WE GET YOU TO *EXAXXION*.

AND SO... *AWAY* WE GO!

H-HEY! *WAIT*--!

SHWIPP

FHWSSSHH

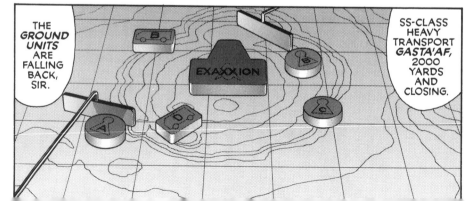

THE *GROUND UNITS* ARE FALLING BACK, SIR.

SS-CLASS HEAVY TRANSPORT *GASTA'AF*, 2000 YARDS AND CLOSING.

EXAXXION

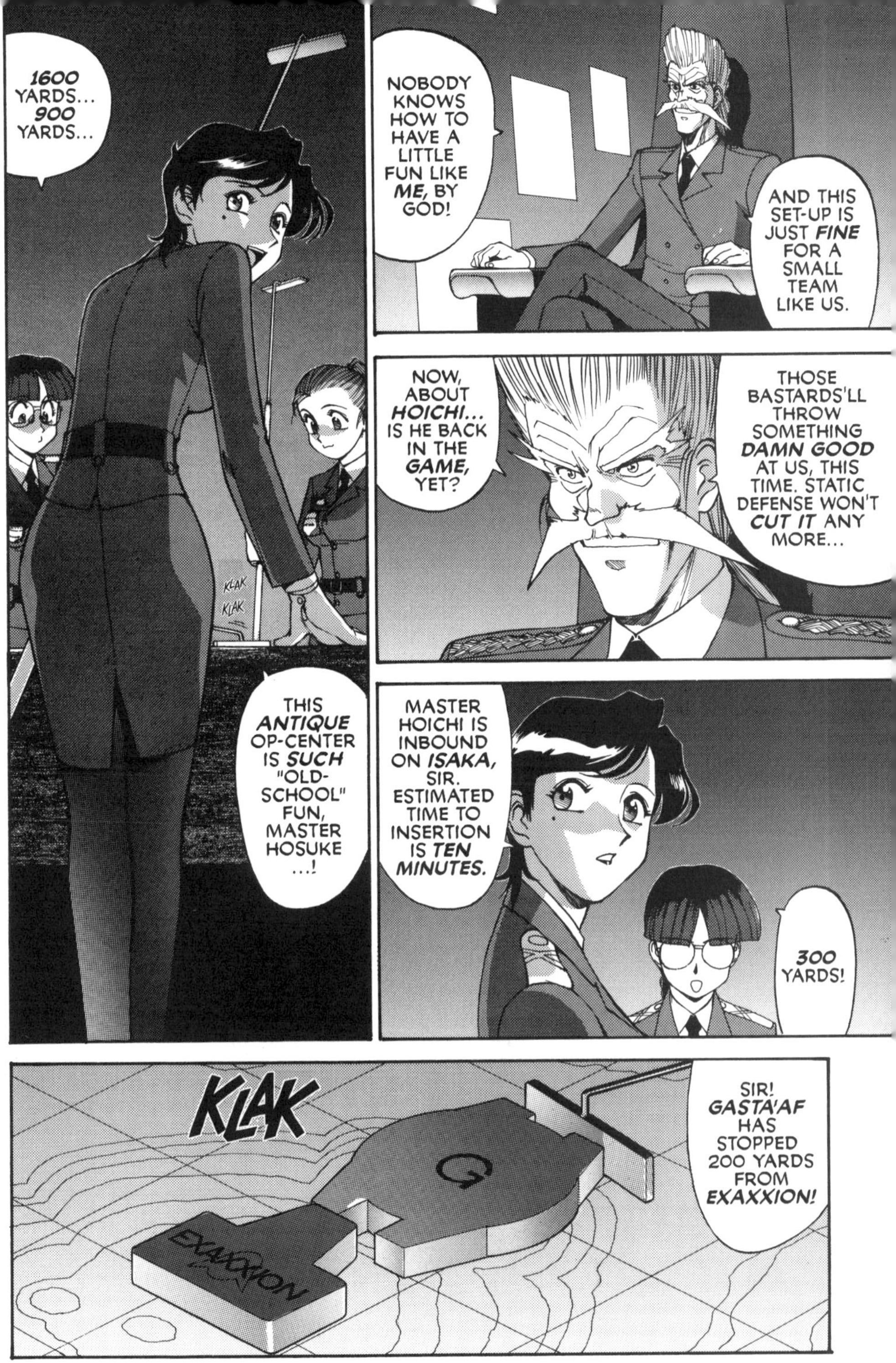

1600 YARDS... 900 YARDS...
KLAK KLAK
THIS ANTIQUE OP-CENTER IS SUCH "OLD-SCHOOL" FUN, MASTER HOSUKE ...!
NOBODY KNOWS HOW TO HAVE A LITTLE FUN LIKE ME, BY GOD!
AND THIS SET-UP IS JUST FINE FOR A SMALL TEAM LIKE US.
NOW, ABOUT HOICHI... IS HE BACK IN THE GAME, YET?
THOSE BASTARDS'LL THROW SOMETHING DAMN GOOD AT US, THIS TIME. STATIC DEFENSE WON'T CUT IT ANY MORE...
MASTER HOICHI IS INBOUND ON ISAKA, SIR. ESTIMATED TIME TO INSERTION IS TEN MINUTES.
300 YARDS!
KLAK
EXAXXION
SIR! GASTA'AF HAS STOPPED 200 YARDS FROM EXAXXION!

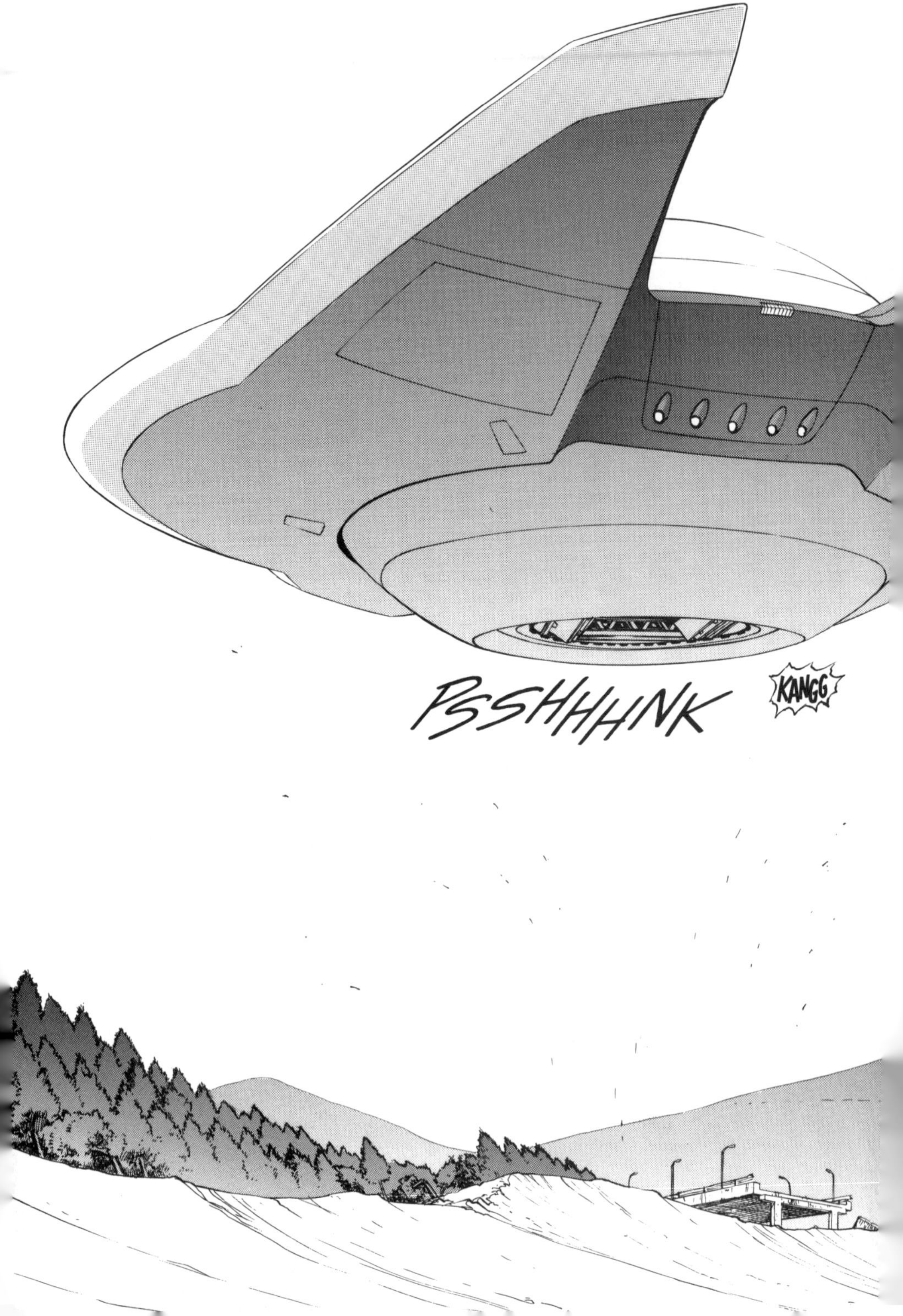
PSSHHHNK
KANGG

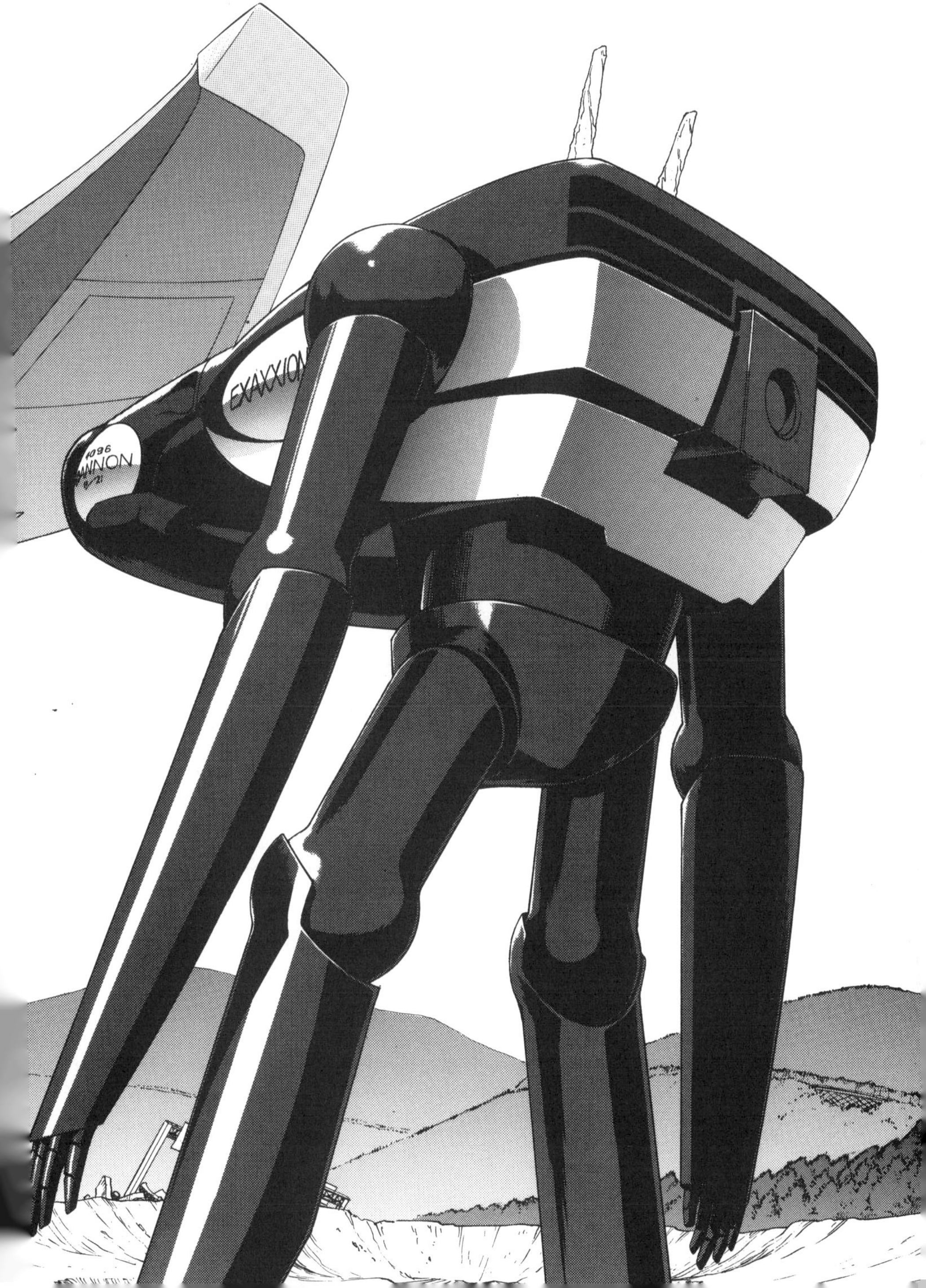
EXAXXION
4096
ANNON

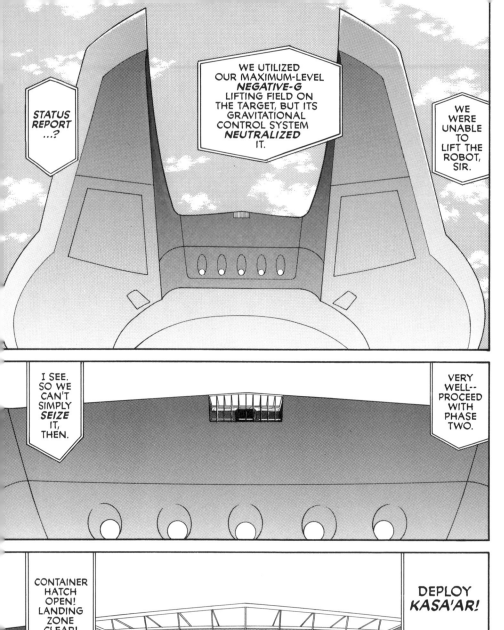

STATUS REPORT...?

WE UTILIZED OUR MAXIMUM-LEVEL *NEGATIVE-G* LIFTING FIELD ON THE TARGET, BUT ITS GRAVITATIONAL CONTROL SYSTEM *NEUTRALIZED* IT.

WE WERE UNABLE TO LIFT THE ROBOT, SIR.

I SEE. SO WE CAN'T SIMPLY *SEIZE* IT, THEN.

VERY WELL-- PROCEED WITH PHASE TWO.

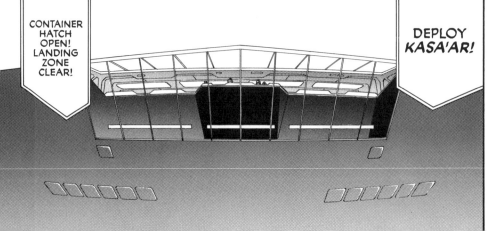

CONTAINER HATCH OPEN! LANDING ZONE CLEAR!

DEPLOY *KASA'AR!*

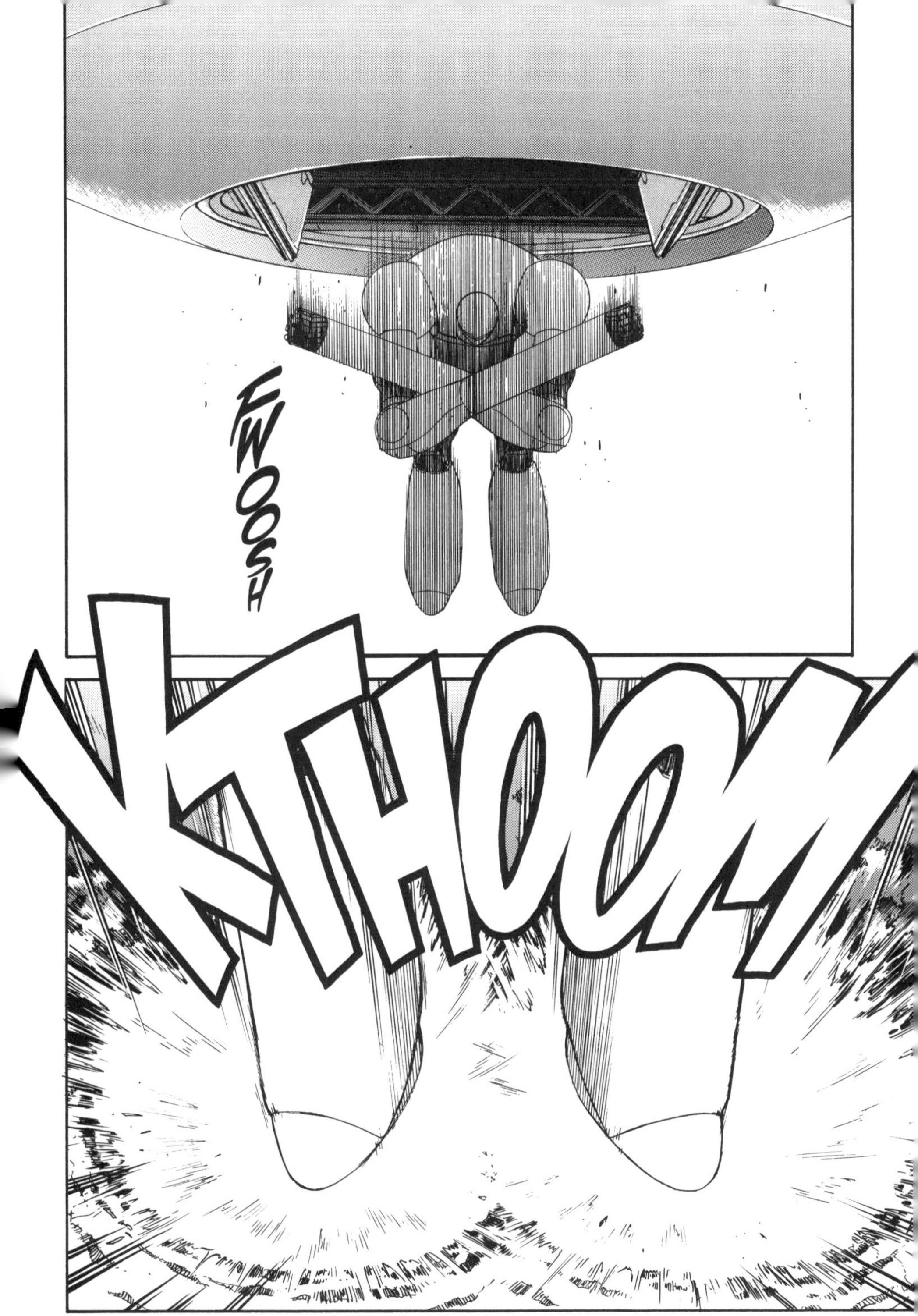
FWOOSH
KTHOOM

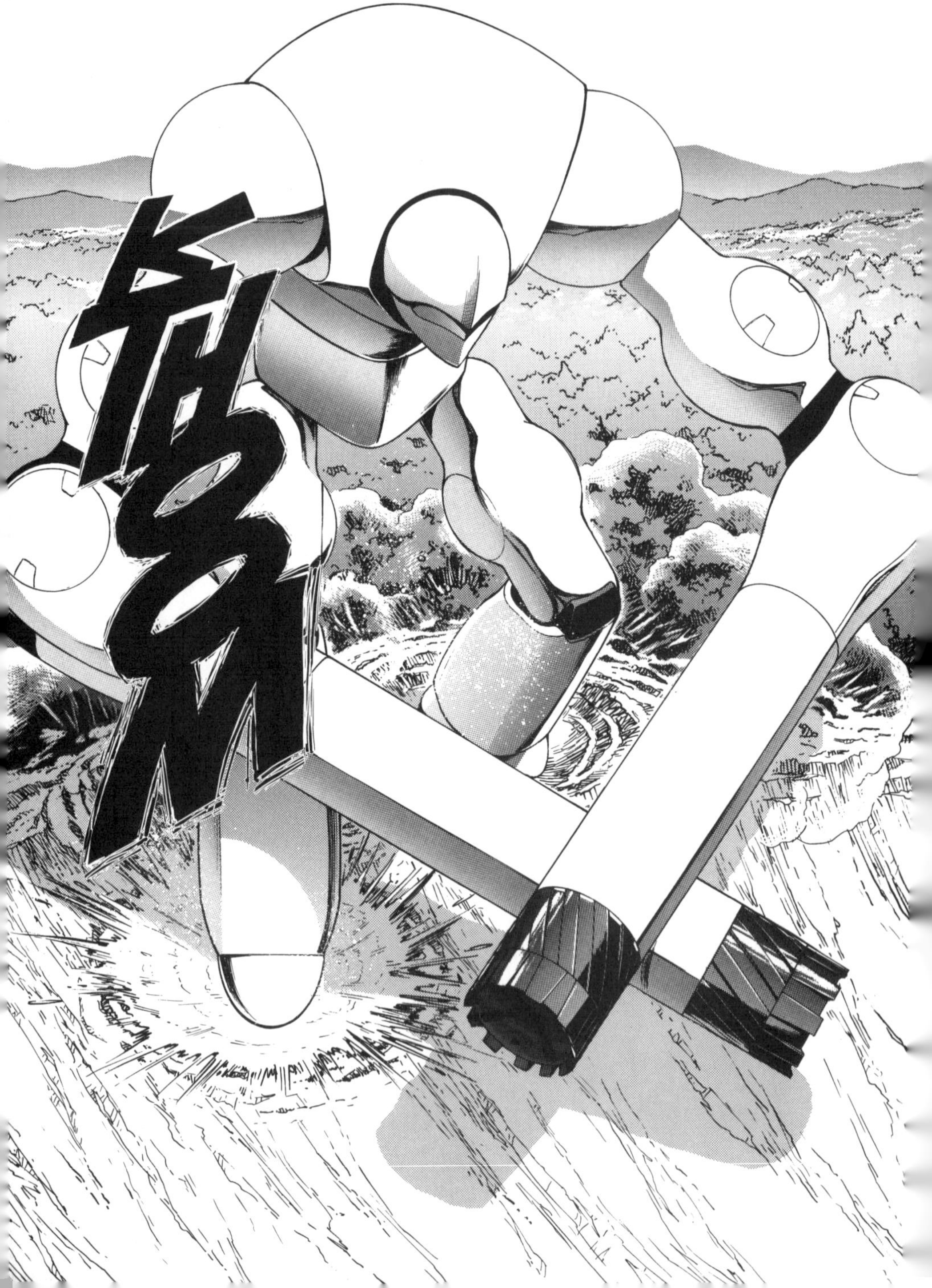

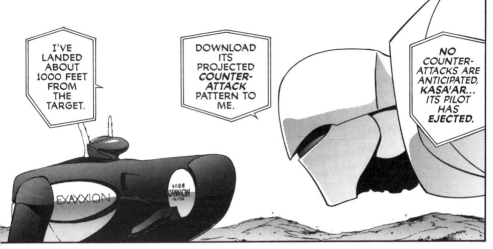

I'VE LANDED ABOUT 1000 FEET FROM THE TARGET.
DOWNLOAD ITS PROJECTED COUNTER-ATTACK PATTERN TO ME.
NO COUNTER-ATTACKS ARE ANTICIPATED, KASA'AR... ITS PILOT HAS EJECTED.
EXAXXION
4098 CANNON
CAN IT BE REMOTELY PILOTED?
NEGATIVE. WE'VE COATED ALL ANTENNAE WITH ELECTRO-MAGNETIC ABSORBENTS.
IT'S UNDER A FULL-SCALE ECM BLACK-OUT.*
WHICH LEAVES THE POSSIBILITY OF AN A.I., THEN...
AN ARTIFICIAL INTELLIGENCE WOULD BE NO MATCH FOR YOU, MAJOR AN'VIRU!
OF COURSE NOT, BOYS. FOR YOU, I'LL TAKE IT OUT WITH A SINGLE STRIKE!
JUST WATCH FOR CHANGES IN THE XXX UNIT'S RESPONSE.
OUR SCANS SHOW THE ANTI-MATTER GENERATOR IS MOUNTED IN THE ROBOT'S BACK.
DON'T DAMAGE IT OR WE'RE ALL HISTORY!
DON'T YOU WORRY.
THOOM

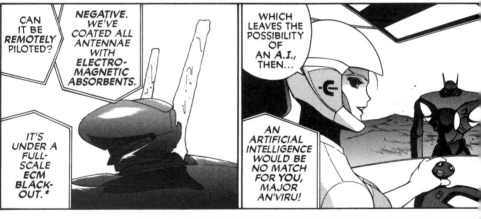

*ECM: Electronic Counter-Measures, generally used against electronic weaponry such as radar. Used here to block all radio frequency communications.

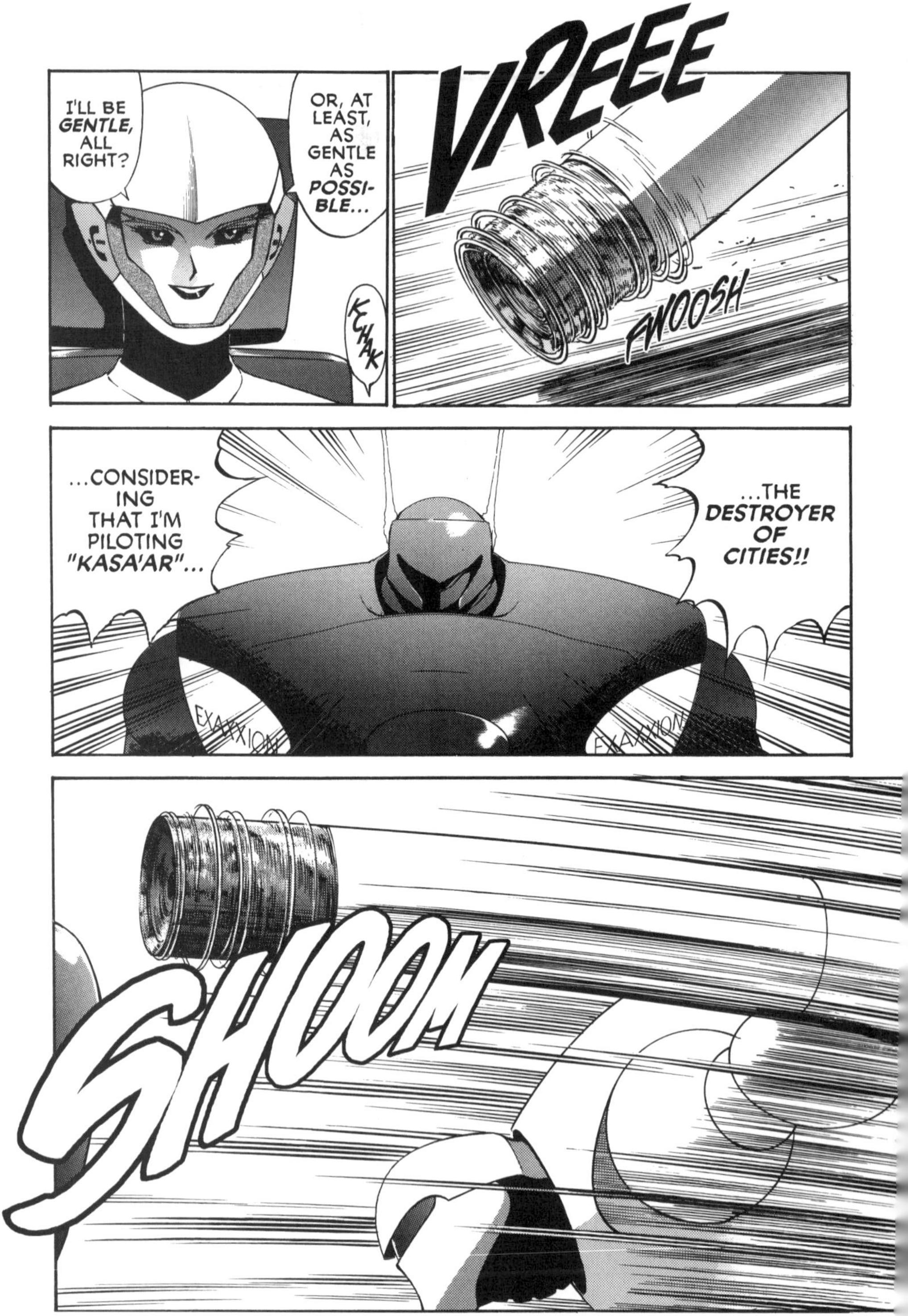
I'LL BE GENTLE, ALL RIGHT?
OR, AT LEAST, AS GENTLE AS POSSIBLE...
KCHAK
VREEE
FWOOSH
...CONSIDERING THAT I'M PILOTING "KASA'AR"...
...THE DESTROYER OF CITIES!!
EXAXXION
EXAXXION
SHOOM

2.6

CANNON GOD EXAXXION: STAGE 2.6

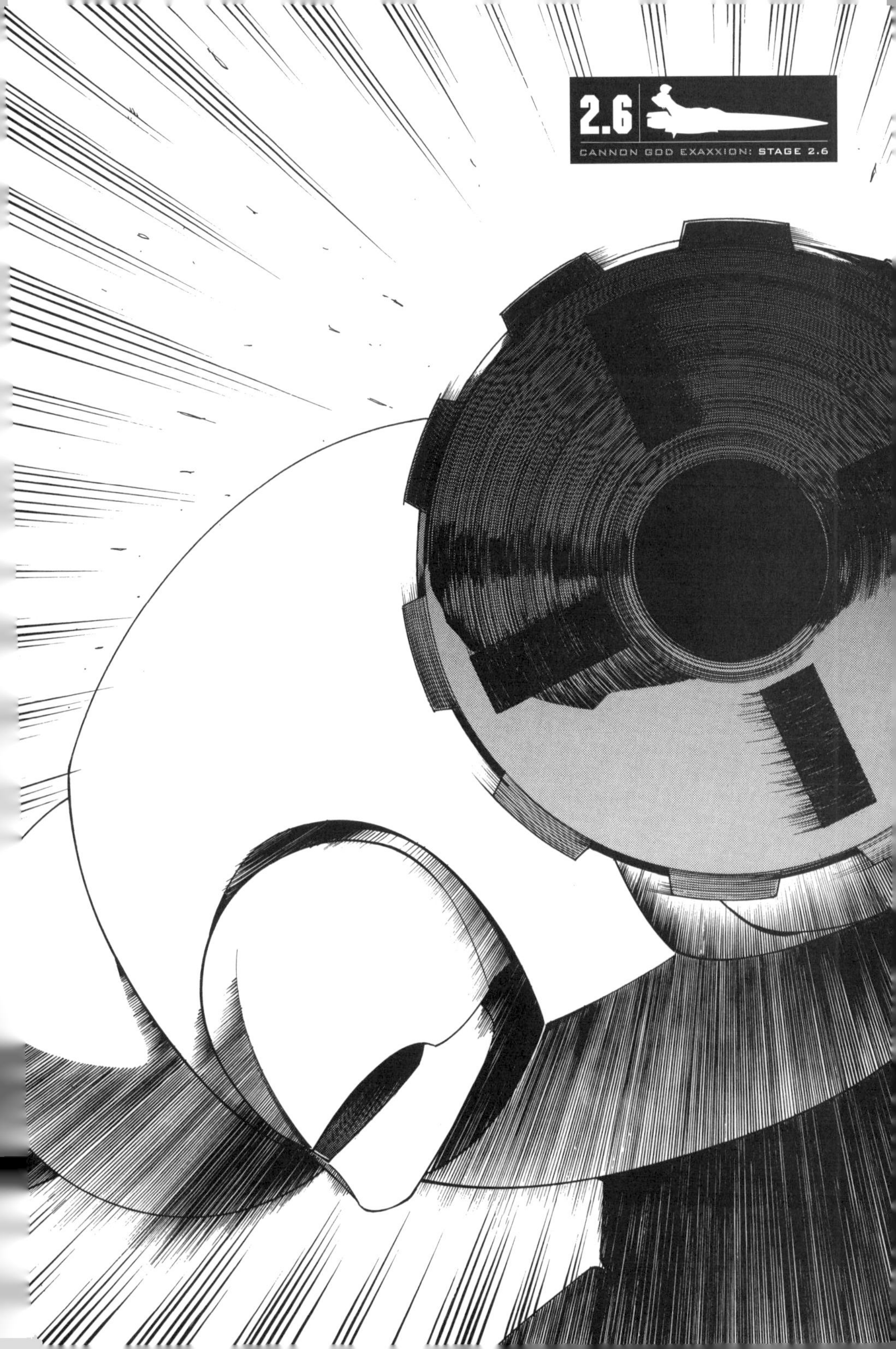

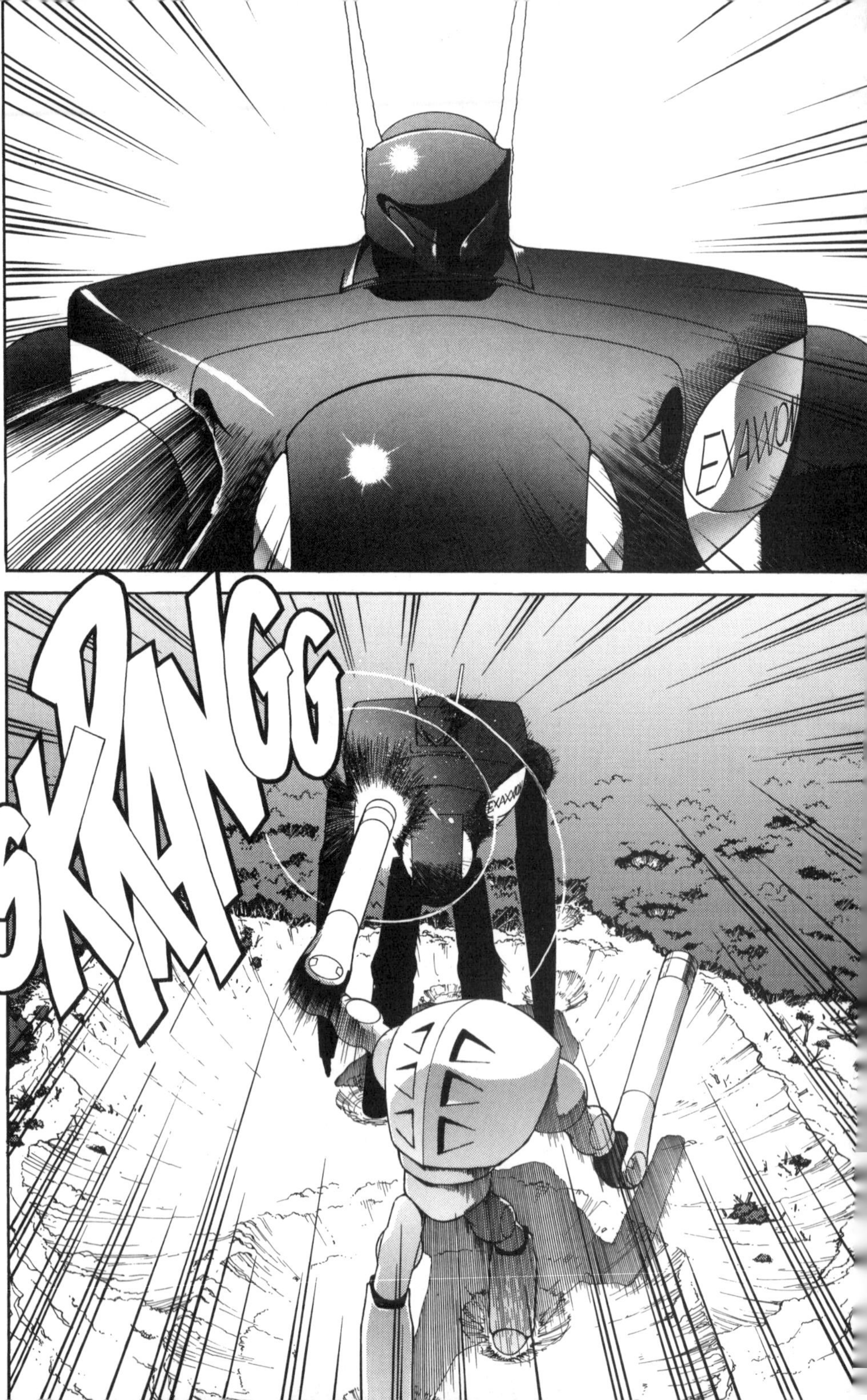
EXAXXION
SKRANGG
EXAXXION

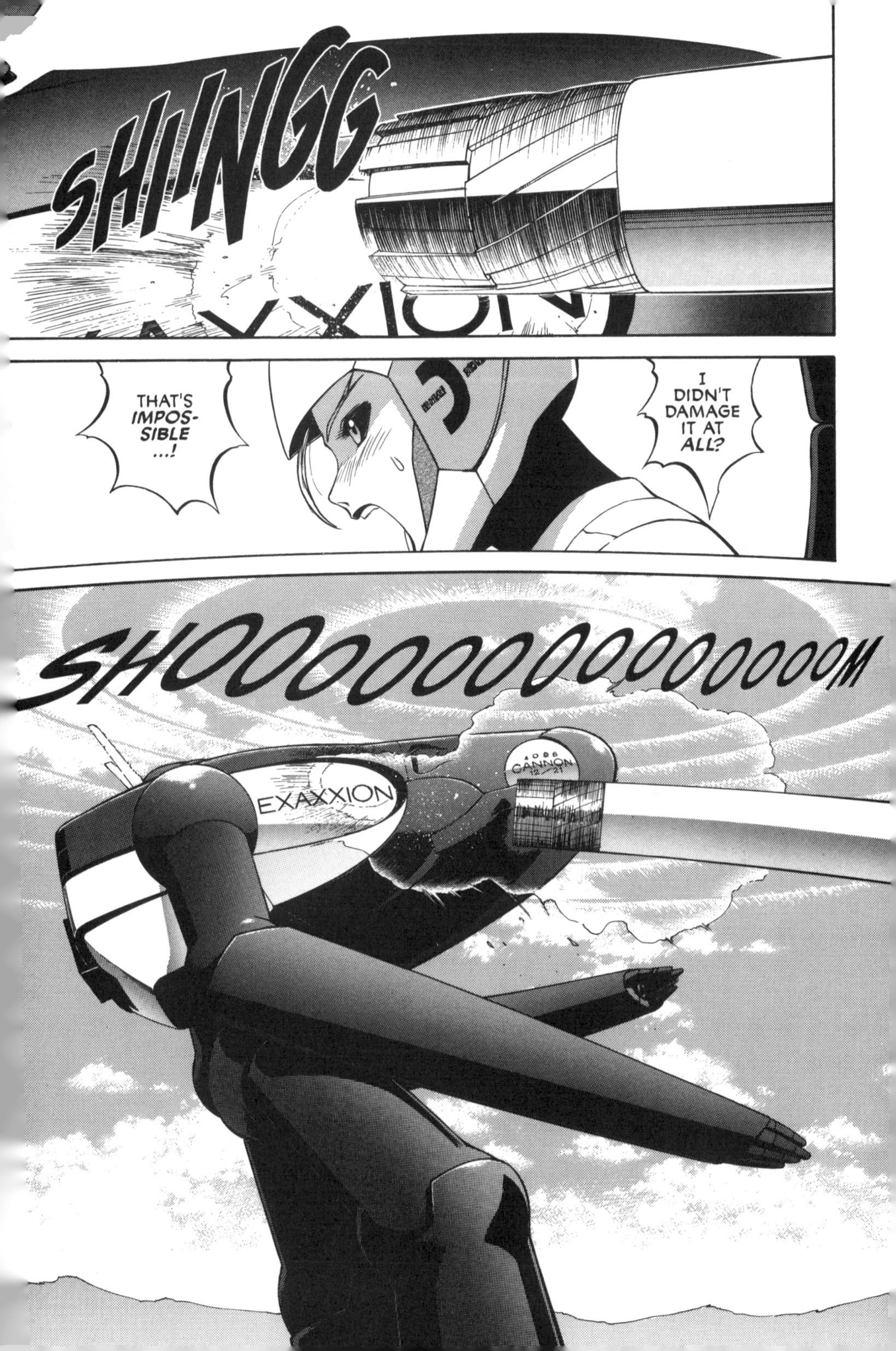
SHIINGG
THAT'S *IMPOSSIBLE* ...!
I DIDN'T DAMAGE IT AT *ALL?*
SHOOOOOOOOOOOOOM
EXAXXION
CANNON 12/21

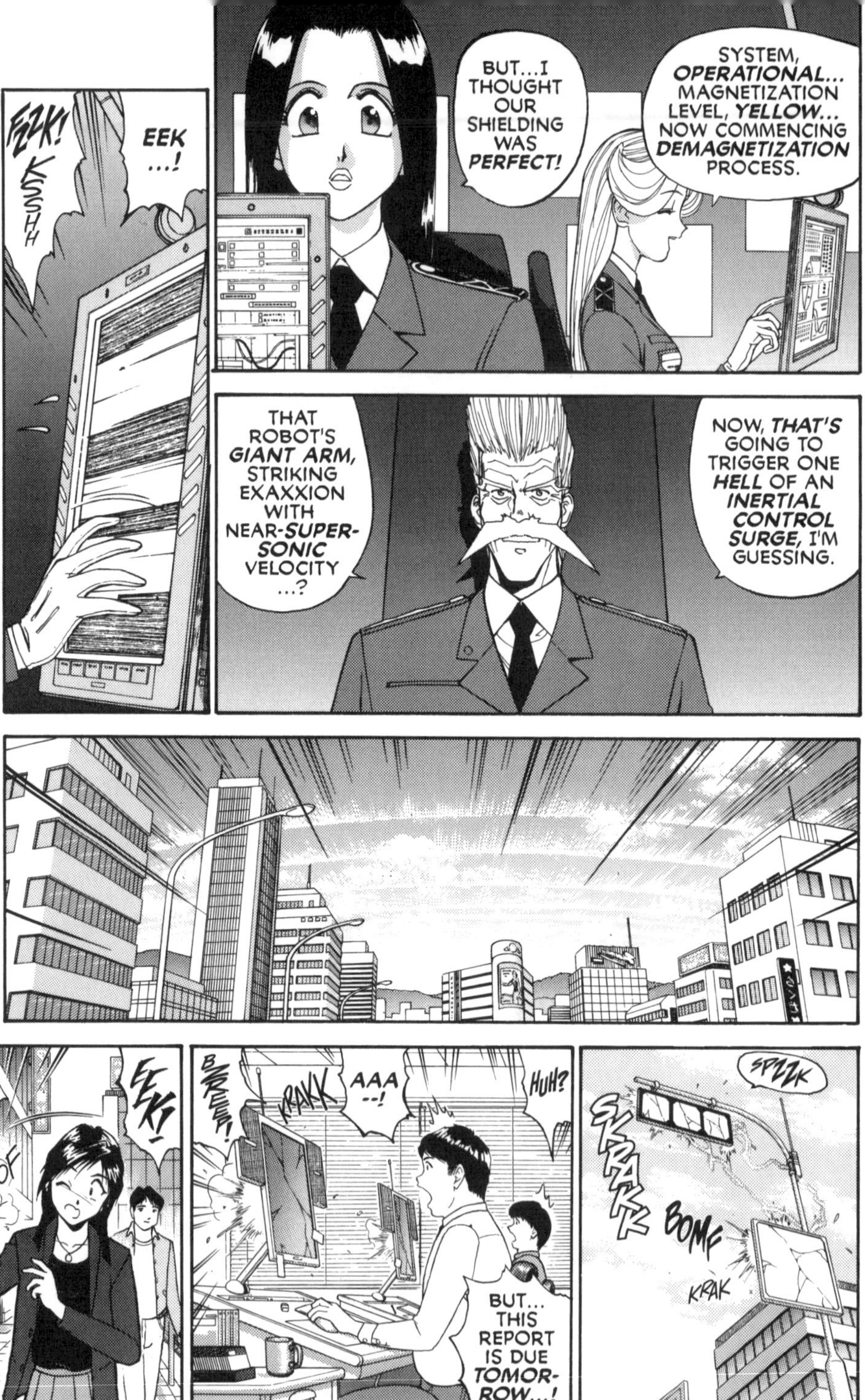
FZZK!
KSSHH
EEK ...!
BUT...I THOUGHT OUR SHIELDING WAS PERFECT!
SYSTEM, OPERATIONAL... MAGNETIZATION LEVEL, YELLOW... NOW COMMENCING DEMAGNETIZATION PROCESS.
THAT ROBOT'S GIANT ARM, STRIKING EXAXXION WITH NEAR-SUPER-SONIC VELOCITY ...?
NOW, THAT'S GOING TO TRIGGER ONE HELL OF AN INERTIAL CONTROL SURGE, I'M GUESSING.
SPZZK
POF
EEK!
KRAKK
AAA --!
HUH?
BUT... THIS REPORT IS DUE TOMOR-ROW...!
SPZZK
SKRAKK
BOMF
KRAK

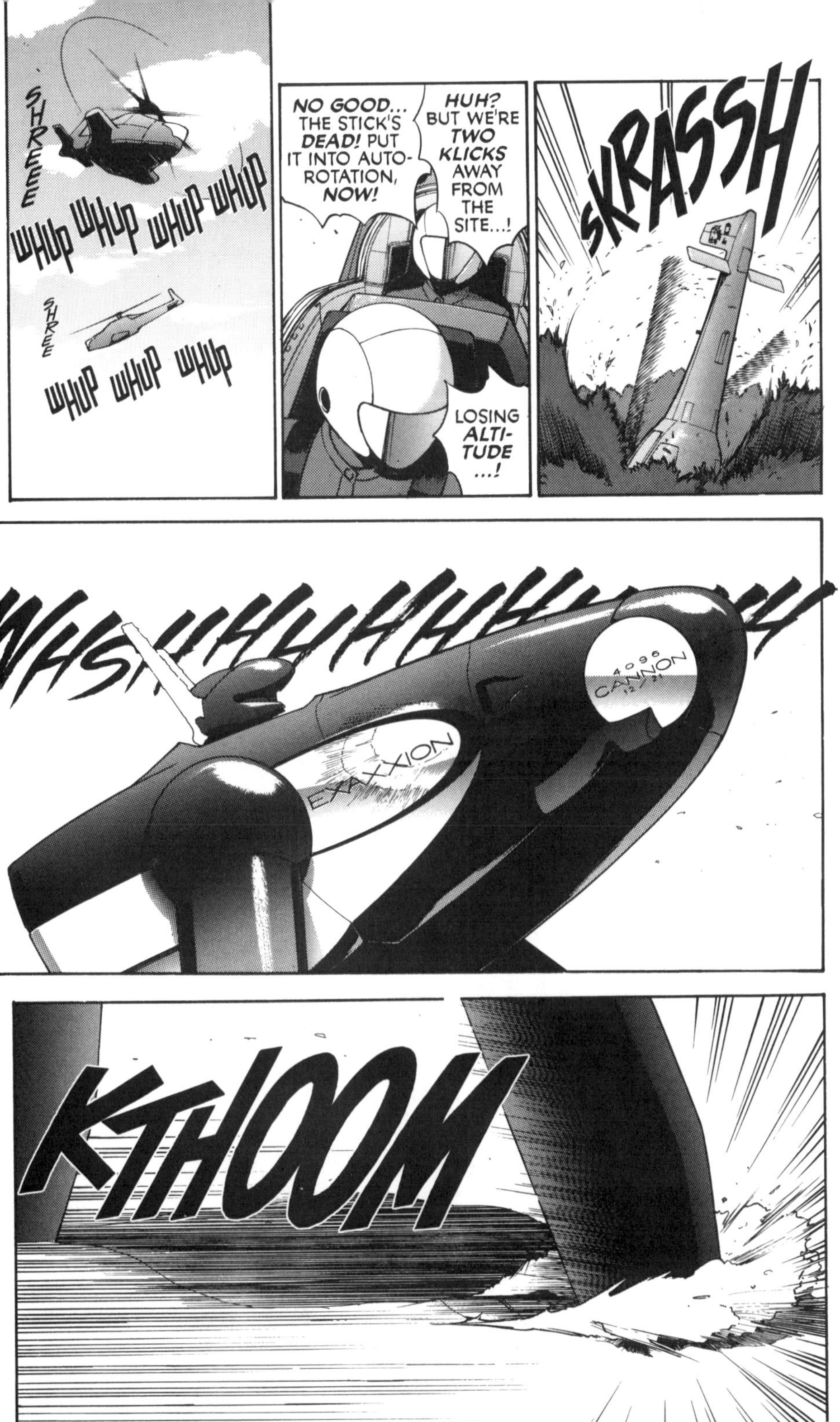
SHREEE
WHUP WHUP WHUP WHUP
SHREE
WHUP WHUP WHUP
NO GOOD... THE STICK'S DEAD! PUT IT INTO AUTO-ROTATION, NOW!
HUH? BUT WE'RE TWO KLICKS AWAY FROM THE SITE...!
LOSING ALTITUDE...!
SKRASSH
WHSHHHHHHHHHH
CANNON
KTHOOM

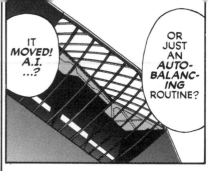

IT *MOVED!* A.I. ...?

OR JUST AN *AUTO-BALANC-ING* ROUTINE?

INCREDIBLE... KASA'AR'S STRIKE BARELY *STAG-GERED* IT...!

OUR SCANS INDICATE THAT THE ENEMY'S ARMOR REMAINS *INTACT,* SIR.

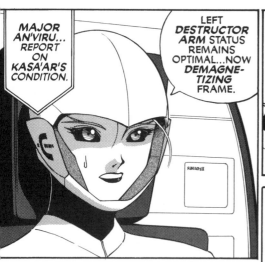

MAJOR AN'VIRU... REPORT ON KASA'AR'S CONDITION.

LEFT *DESTRUCTOR ARM* STATUS REMAINS OPTIMAL...NOW *DEMAGNE-TIZING* FRAME.

THAT MONSTER'S *POWER OUTPUT* MUST BE PRACTICALLY *OFF THE SCALE...*

IS IT BEING RUN BY A *COMBAT A.I.?*

BUT...THAT ROBOT LOOKS VIRTUALLY *UNTOUCHED...* AFTER A *127,000 TON STRIKE...!*

WE'VE ONLY SEEN *AUTO-BALANCING,* SO FAR. NO SIGN OF--

THEN I'LL USE *THRUST-ASSISTED STRIKE* MODE ON IT!

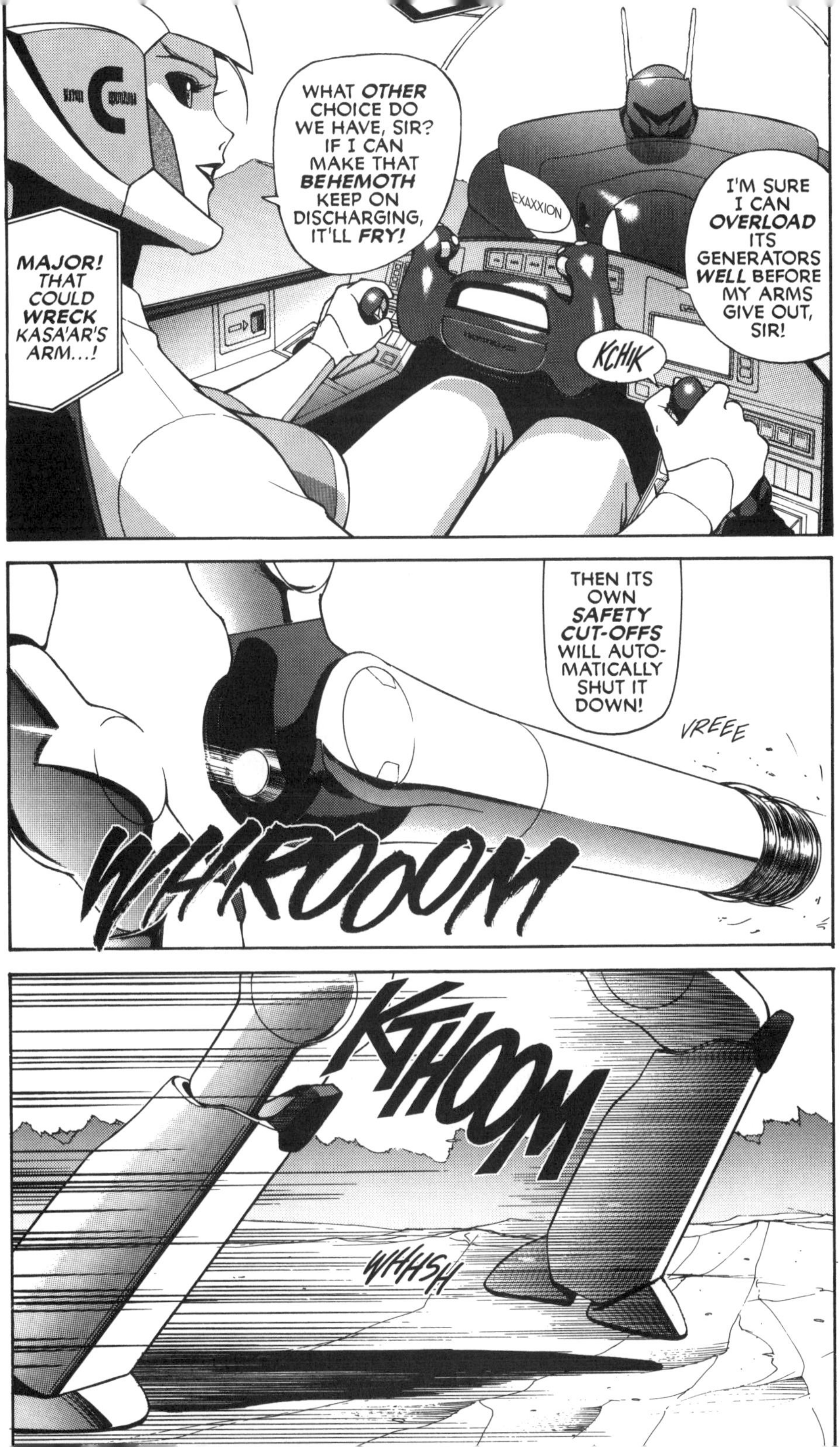
MAJOR! THAT COULD WRECK KASA'AR'S ARM...!
WHAT OTHER CHOICE DO WE HAVE, SIR? IF I CAN MAKE THAT BEHEMOTH KEEP ON DISCHARGING, IT'LL FRY!
EXAXXION
I'M SURE I CAN OVERLOAD ITS GENERATORS WELL BEFORE MY ARMS GIVE OUT, SIR!
KCHIK
THEN ITS OWN SAFETY CUT-OFFS WILL AUTO-MATICALLY SHUT IT DOWN!
VREEE
WHROOOM
KTHOOM
WHHSH

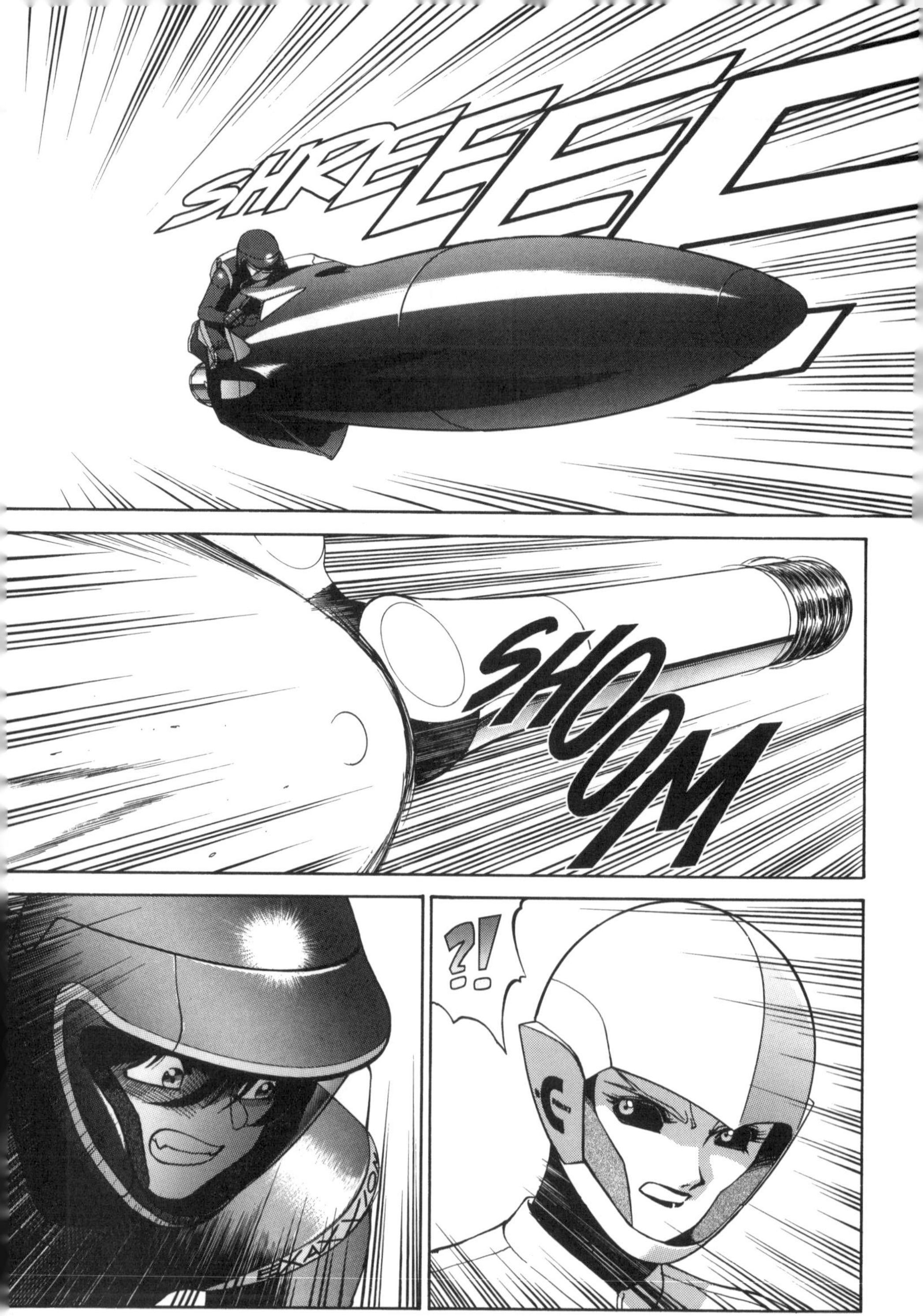
SHREEEK
SHOOM
?!

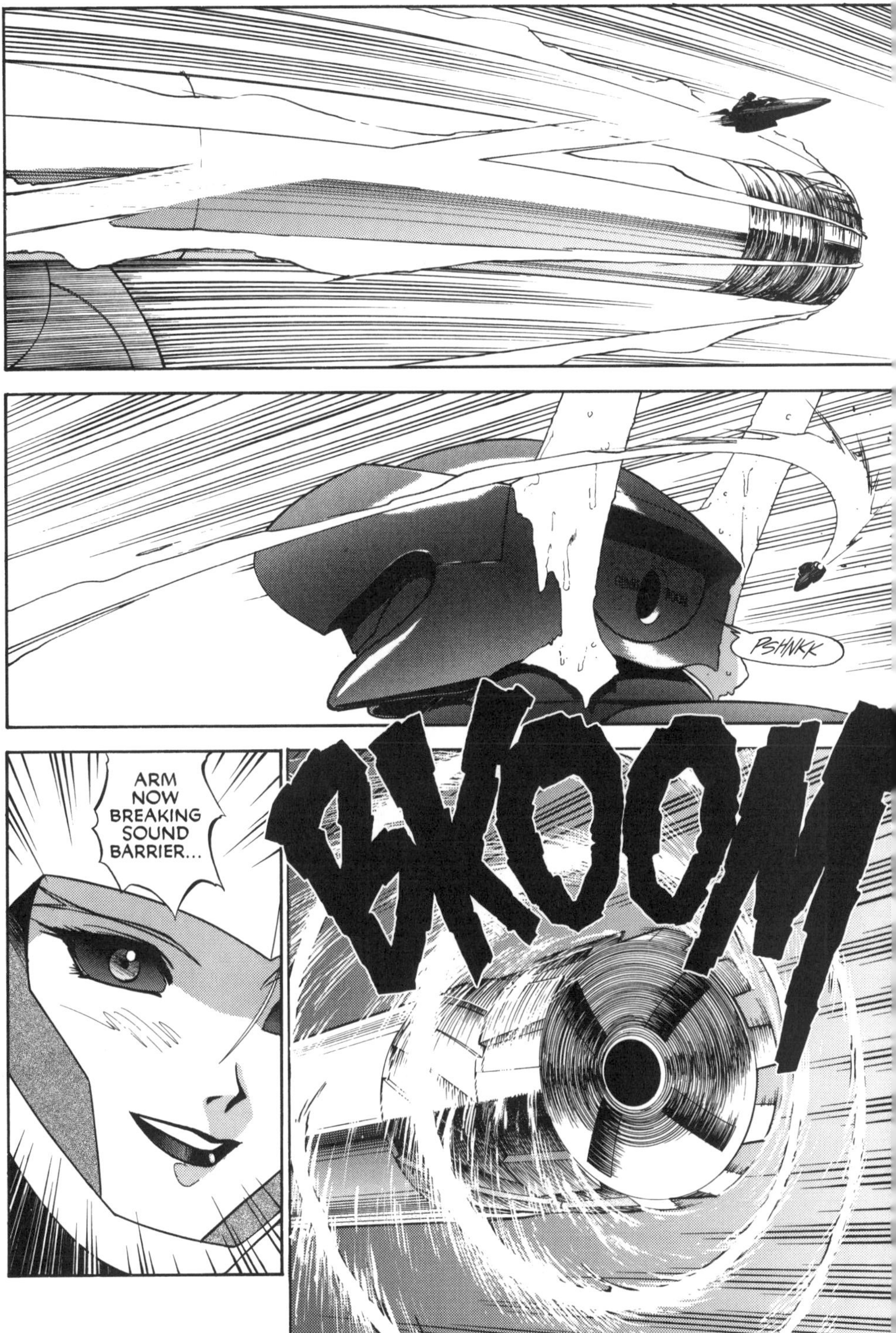
PSHNKK
ARM NOW BREAKING SOUND BARRIER...
BKOOM

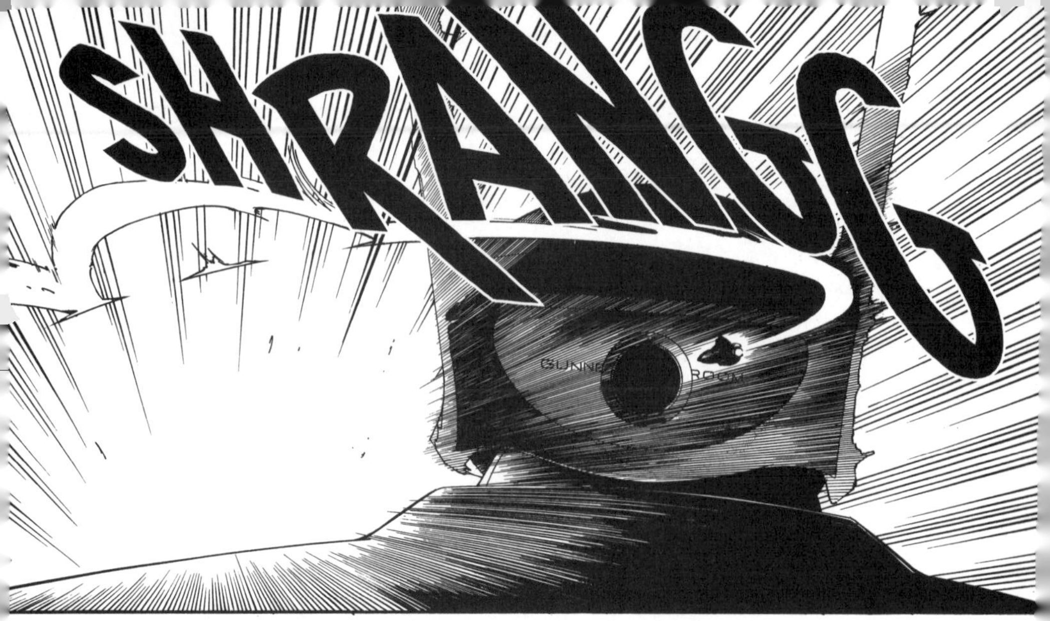
SHRANGG

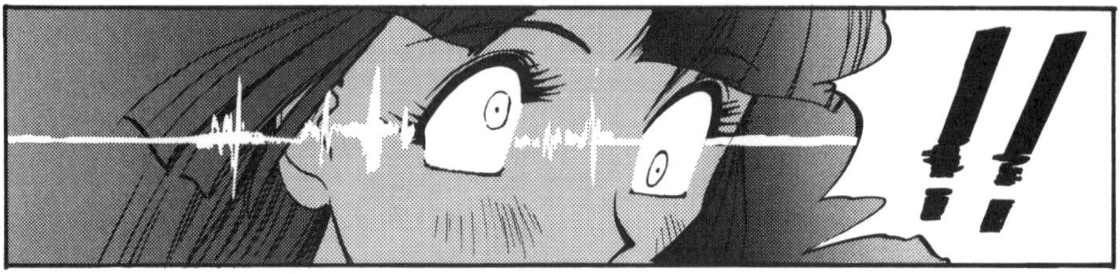
!!

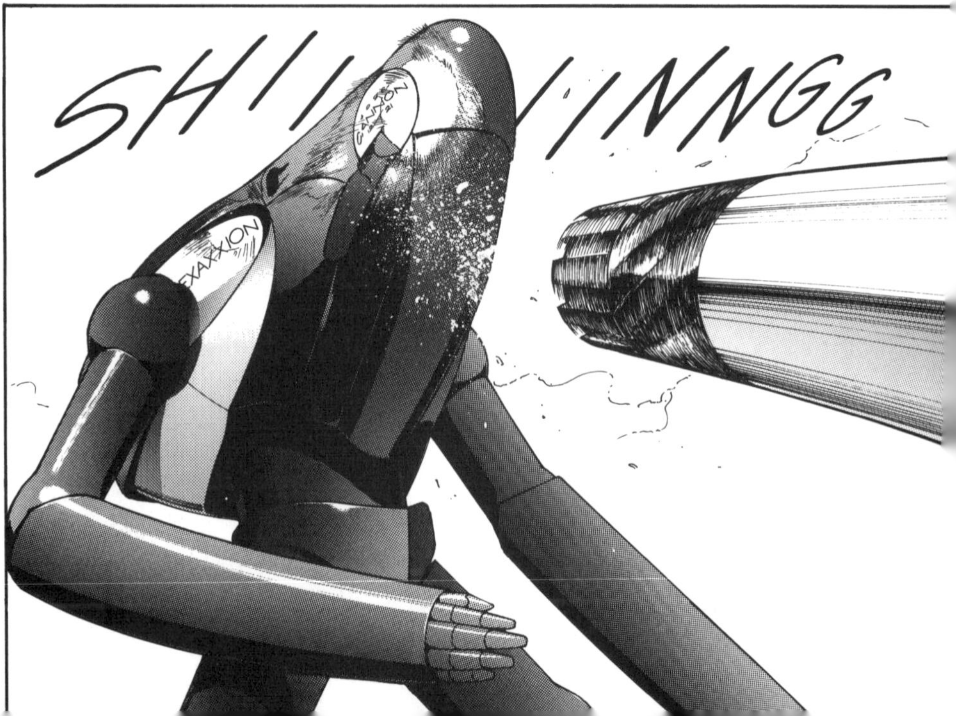
SHIIIIINNGG
EXAXXION

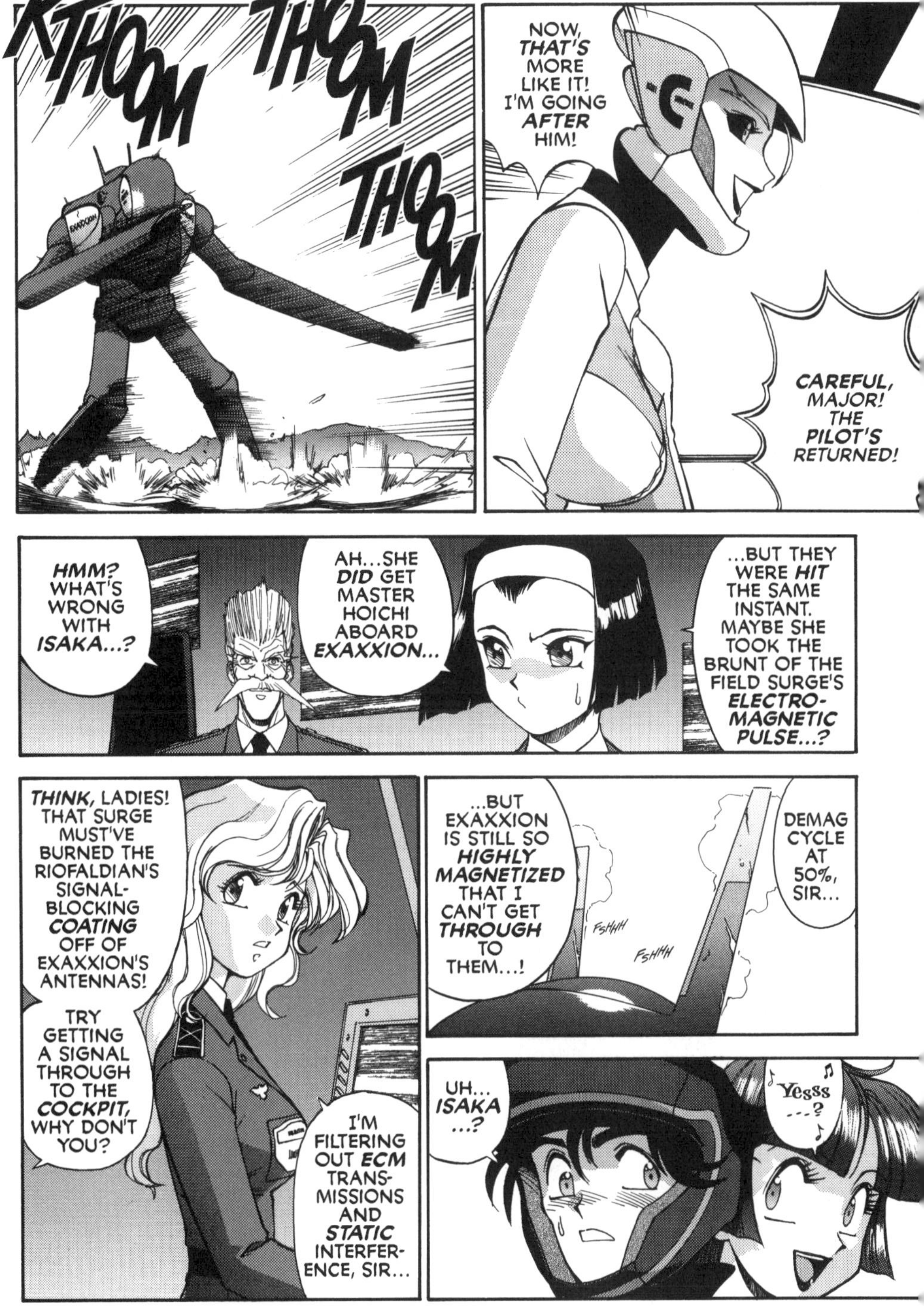
KTHOOM
THOOM
THOOM
NOW, THAT'S MORE LIKE IT! I'M GOING AFTER HIM!
CAREFUL, MAJOR! THE PILOT'S RETURNED!
HMM? WHAT'S WRONG WITH ISAKA...?
AH...SHE DID GET MASTER HOICHI ABOARD EXAXXION...
...BUT THEY WERE HIT THE SAME INSTANT. MAYBE SHE TOOK THE BRUNT OF THE FIELD SURGE'S ELECTRO-MAGNETIC PULSE...?
THINK, LADIES! THAT SURGE MUST'VE BURNED THE RIOFALDIAN'S SIGNAL-BLOCKING COATING OFF OF EXAXXION'S ANTENNAS!
TRY GETTING A SIGNAL THROUGH TO THE COCKPIT, WHY DON'T YOU?
I'M FILTERING OUT ECM TRANS-MISSIONS AND STATIC INTERFER-ENCE, SIR...
...BUT EXAXXION IS STILL SO HIGHLY MAGNETIZED THAT I CAN'T GET THROUGH TO THEM...!
DEMAG CYCLE AT 50%, SIR...
FSHHH
FSHHH
UH... ISAKA...?
Yesss...?

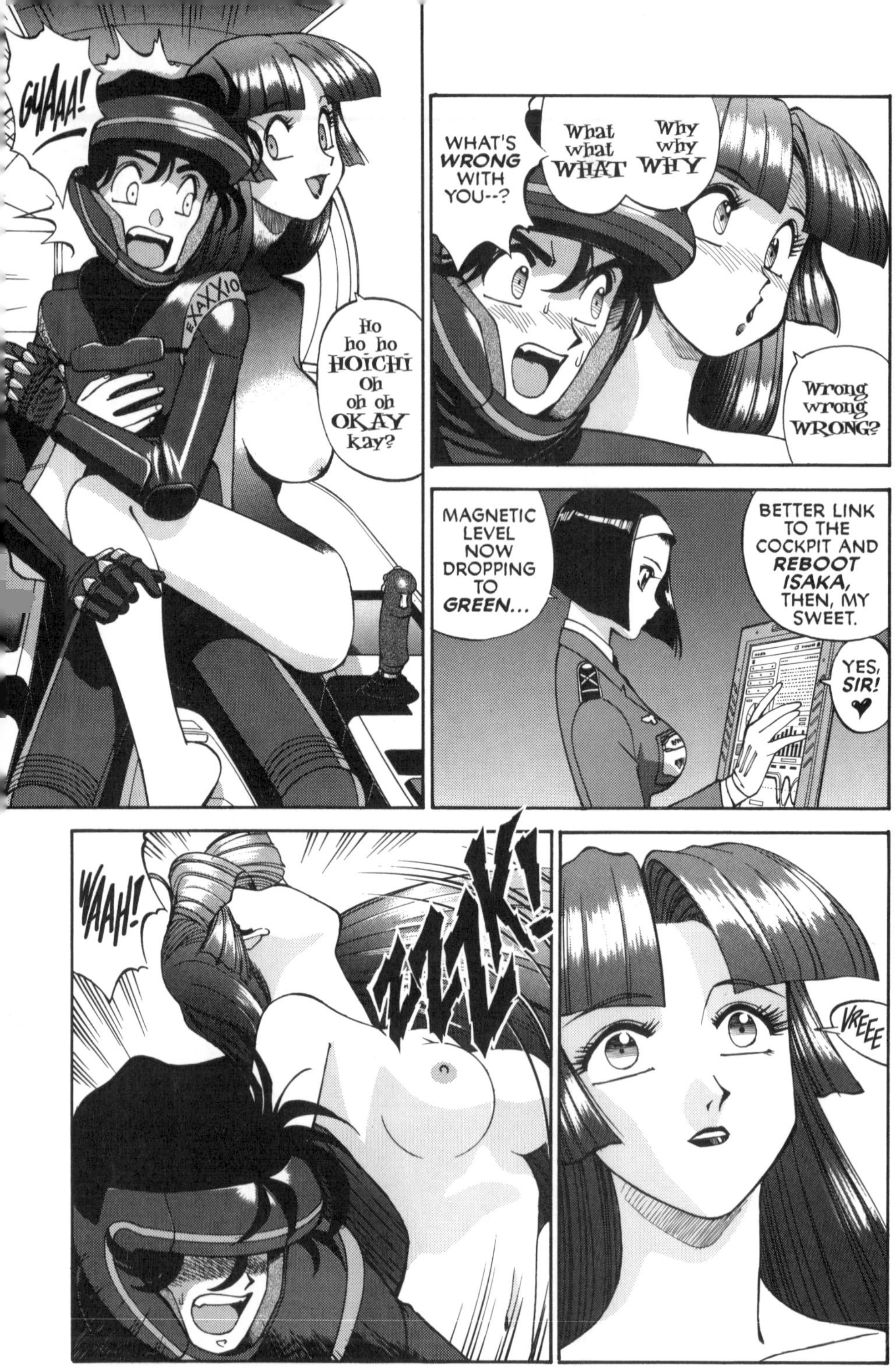
GYAAA!
Ho ho ho HOICHI Oh oh oh OKAY kay?
WHAT'S WRONG WITH YOU--?
What what WHAT
Why why WHY
Wrong wrong WRONG?
MAGNETIC LEVEL NOW DROPPING TO GREEN...
BETTER LINK TO THE COCKPIT AND REBOOT ISAKA, THEN, MY SWEET.
YES, SIR! ♥
WAAH!
VREEE

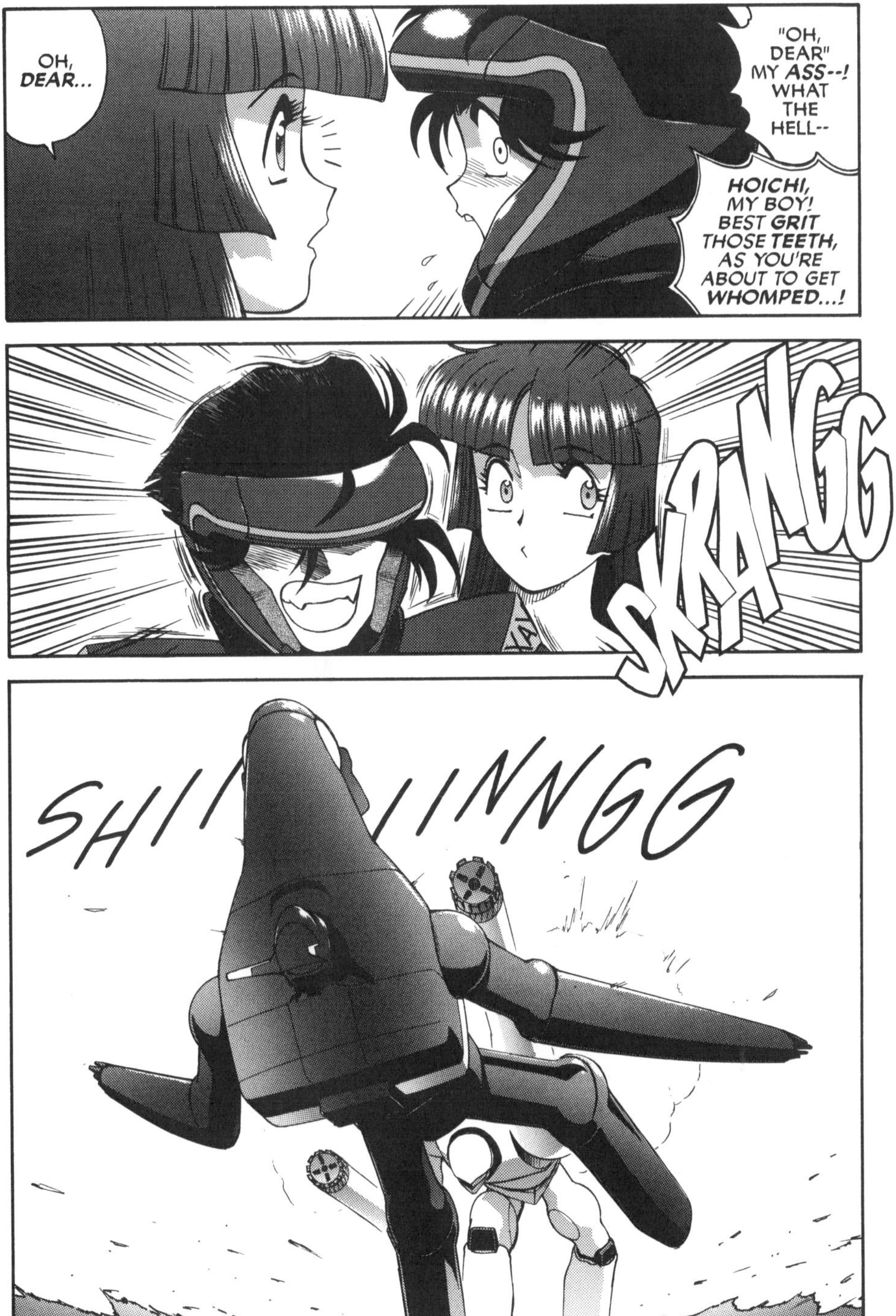
OH, DEAR...
"OH, DEAR" MY ASS--! WHAT THE HELL--
HOICHI, MY BOY! BEST GRIT THOSE TEETH, AS YOU'RE ABOUT TO GET WHOMPED...!
SKRANGG
SHIIIINNGG

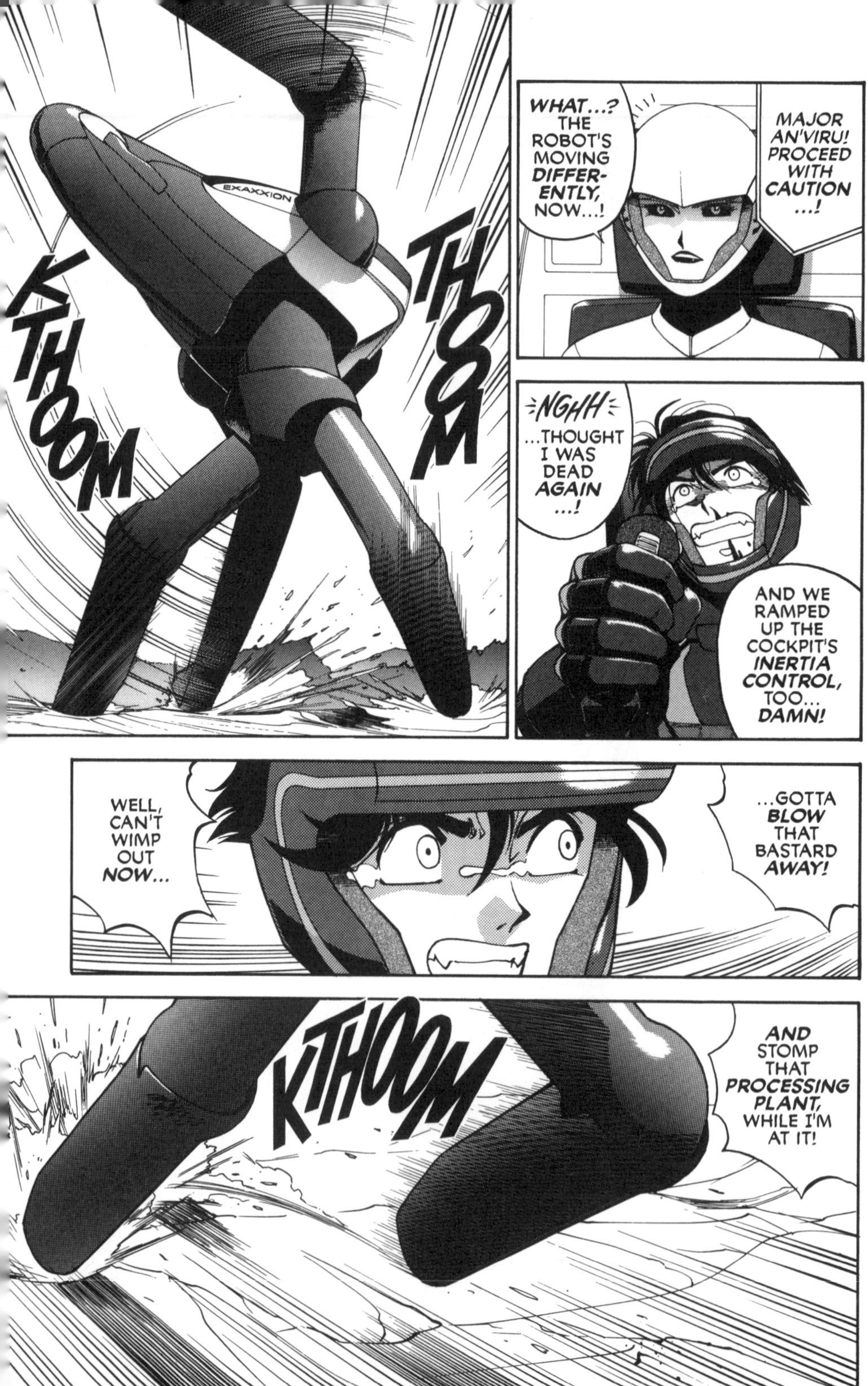
KTHOOM
EXAXXION
THOOM
WHAT...? THE ROBOT'S MOVING DIFFER- ENTLY, NOW...!
MAJOR AN'VIRU! PROCEED WITH CAUTION ...!
NGHH ...THOUGHT I WAS DEAD AGAIN ...!
AND WE RAMPED UP THE COCKPIT'S INERTIA CONTROL, TOO... DAMN!
WELL, CAN'T WIMP OUT NOW...
...GOTTA BLOW THAT BASTARD AWAY!
KTHOOM
AND STOMP THAT PROCESSING PLANT, WHILE I'M AT IT!

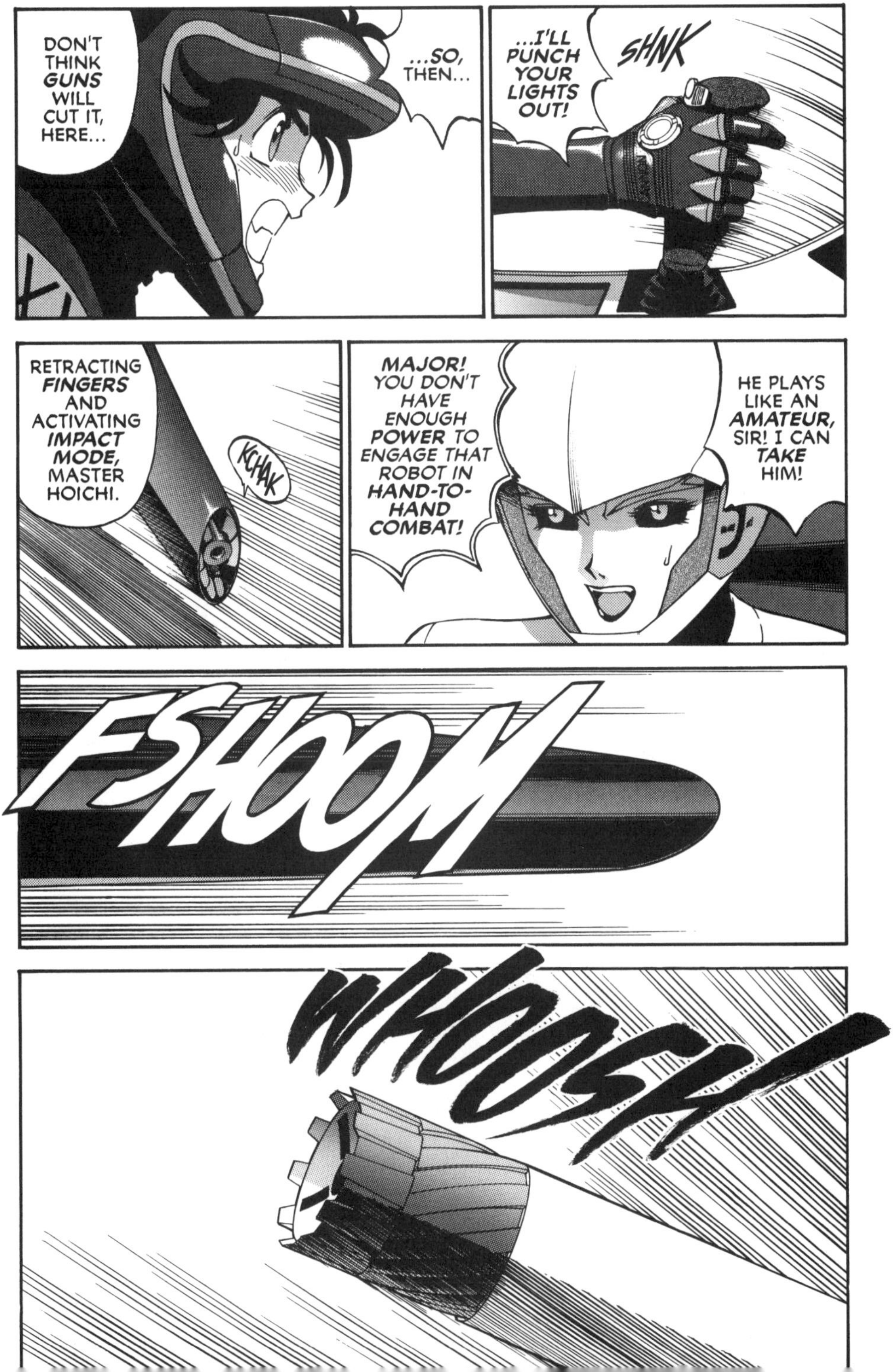
DON'T THINK GUNS WILL CUT IT, HERE...
...SO, THEN...
...I'LL PUNCH YOUR LIGHTS OUT!
SHNK
RETRACTING FINGERS AND ACTIVATING IMPACT MODE, MASTER HOICHI.
KCHAK
MAJOR! YOU DON'T HAVE ENOUGH POWER TO ENGAGE THAT ROBOT IN HAND-TO-HAND COMBAT!
HE PLAYS LIKE AN AMATEUR, SIR! I CAN TAKE HIM!
FSHOOM
WHOOSH!

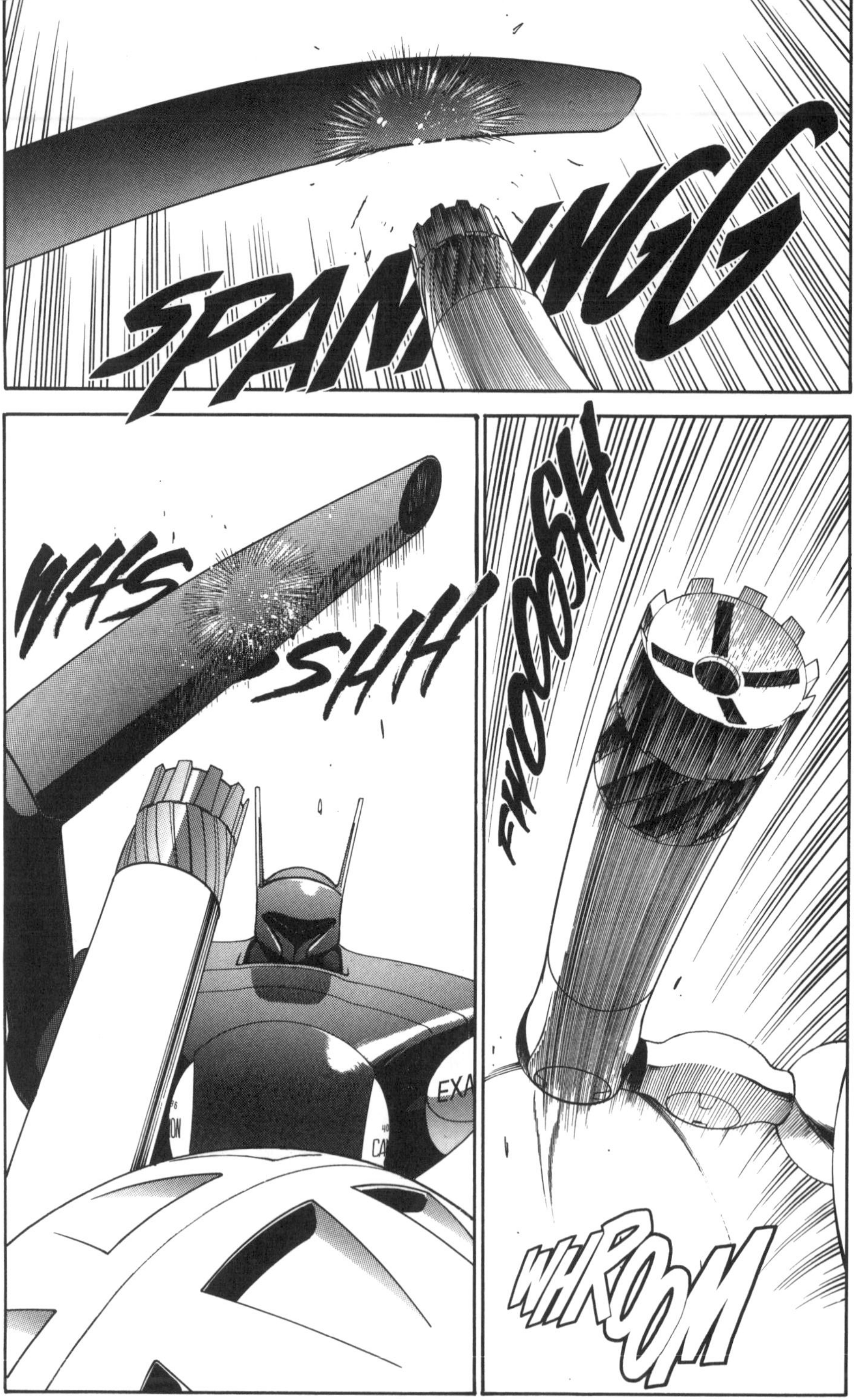
SPAN NGG
WHSSHH
FWOOOSH
WHROOM

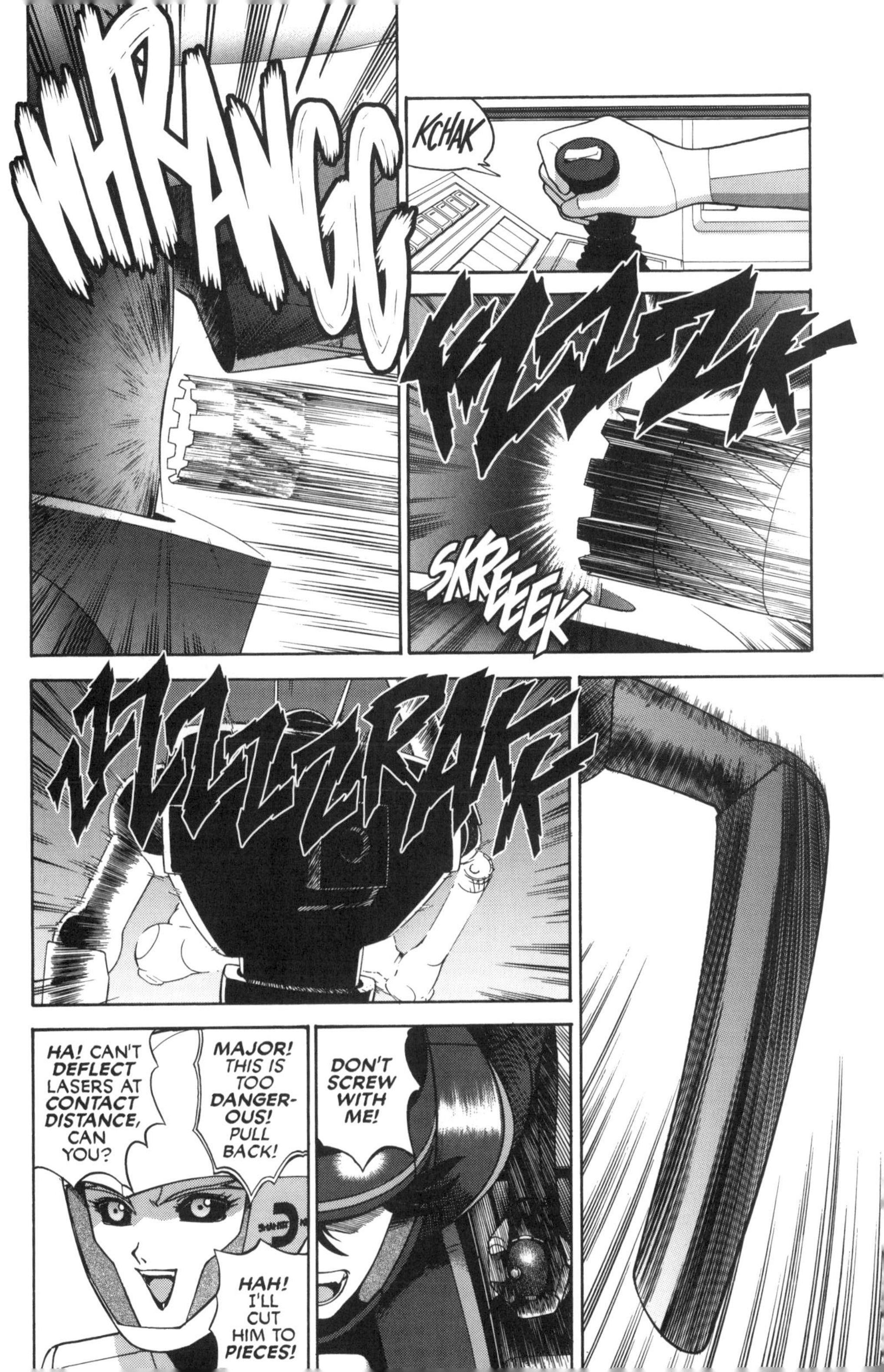
WHANGG
KCHAK
SKREEEK
HA! CAN'T **DEFLECT** LASERS AT **CONTACT DISTANCE**, CAN YOU?
MAJOR! THIS IS TOO **DANGER-OUS!** PULL BACK!
HAH! I'LL CUT HIM TO **PIECES!**
DON'T SCREW WITH ME!

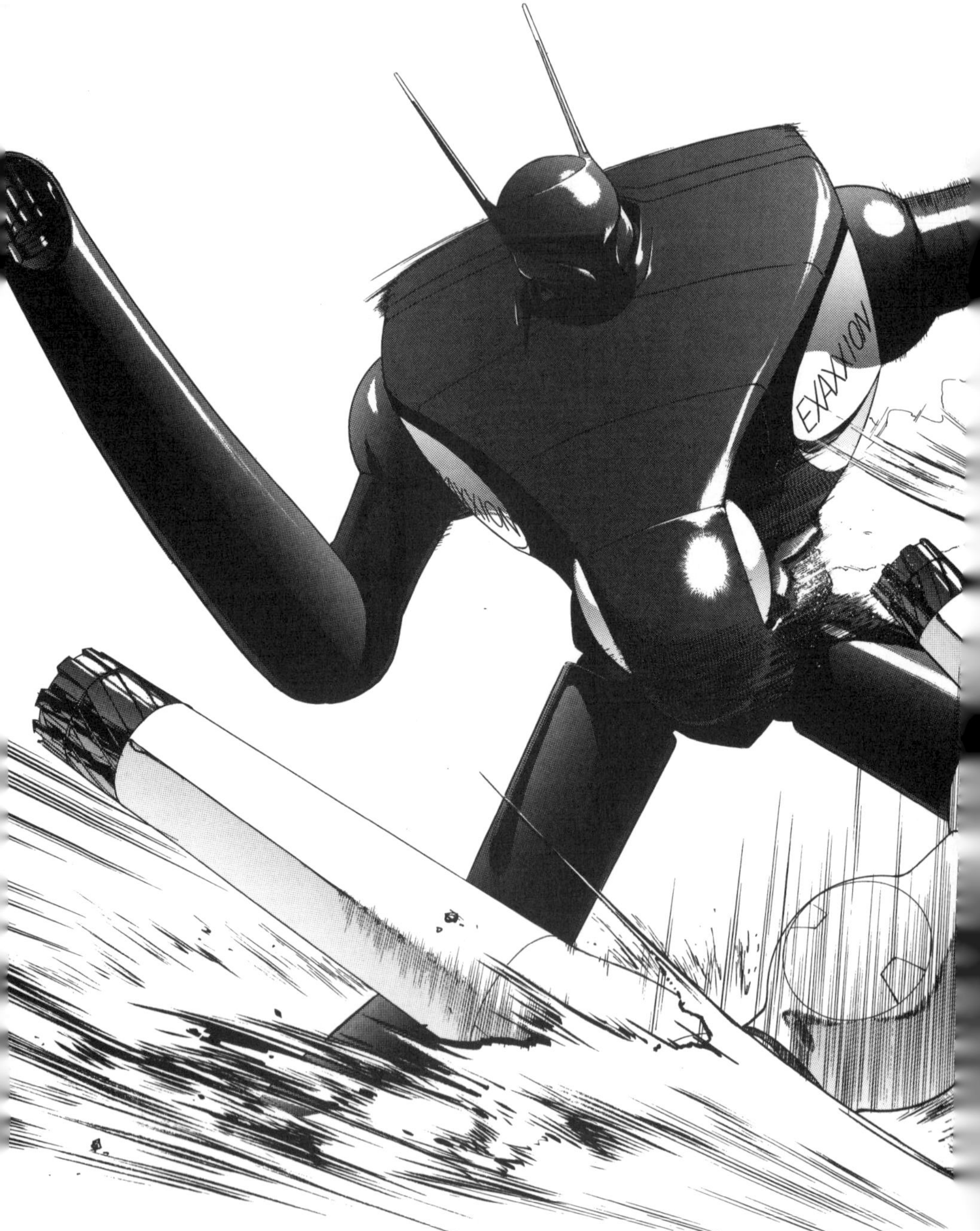
EXAXXION

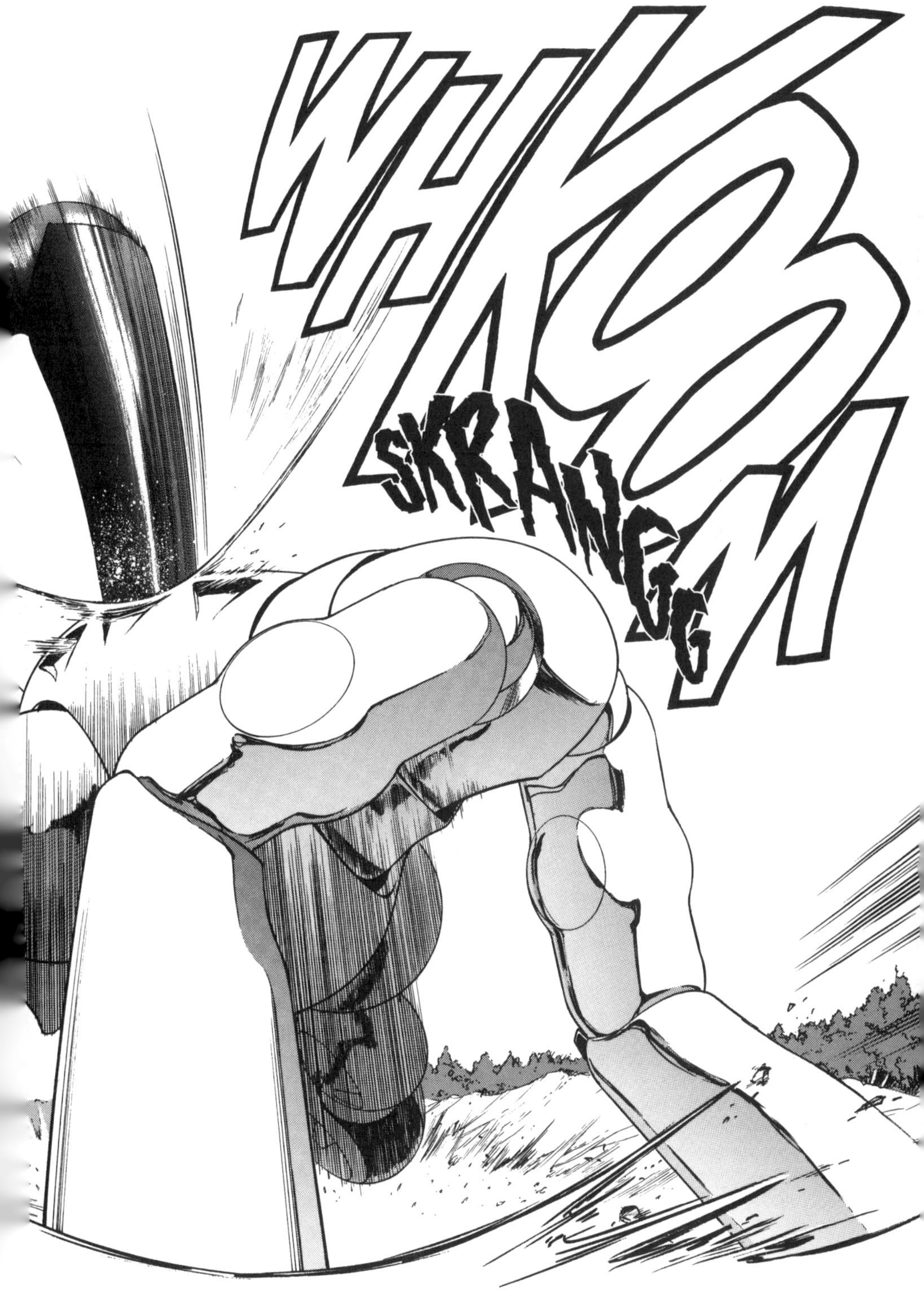
SKRANGG

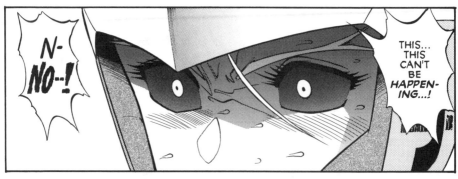

N-NO--!

THIS... THIS CAN'T BE HAPPENING...!

TOKYO OPERATIONS CENTER REPORTING TO **GENERAL SHES'KA** AT ELEVATOR BASE ONE.

S-CLASS INTERROGATION REPORT TO FOLLOW... REQUEST A SECURE LINE.

♪BREEP♪

SHES'KA, HERE... PROCEED.

SIR... WE'VE IDENTIFIED THE BLACK-SUITED RIDER...

2.7

CANNON GOD EXAXXION: STAGE 2.7

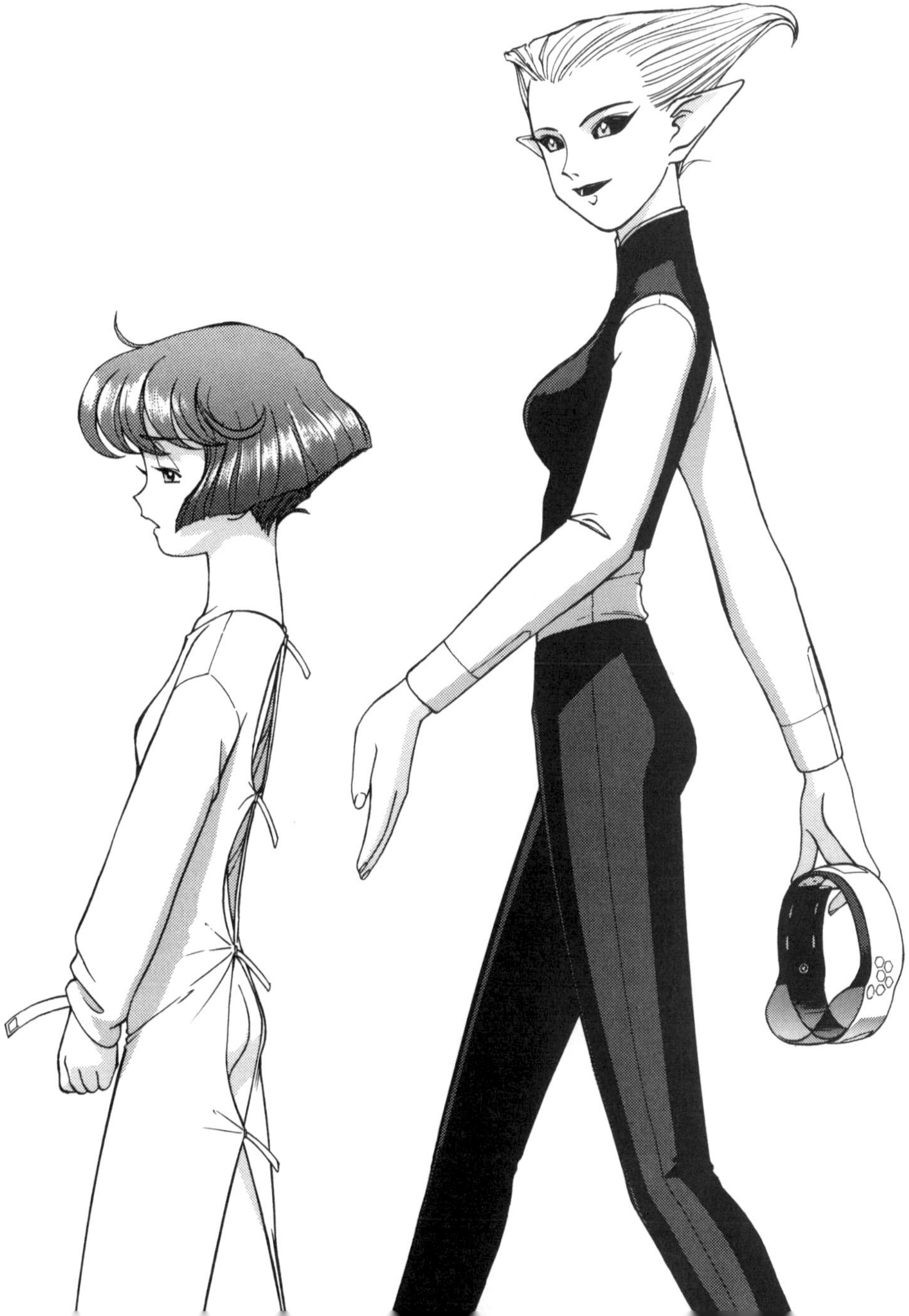

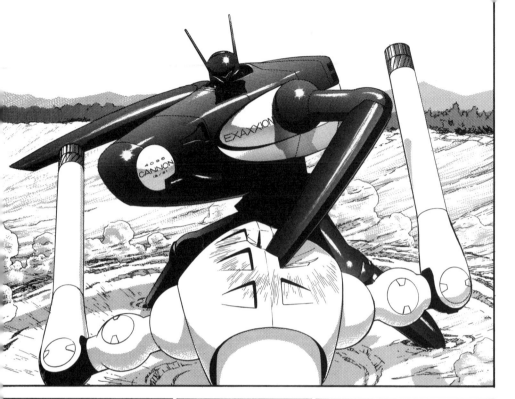

WE'VE **LOST** GENERATORS ONE, THREE, AND FOUR! KASA'AR'S PRIMARY **POWER CABLE** HAS BEEN SEVERED...NOW SWITCHING TO **BACK-UP** LINE!

GIVE ME AN **ANALYSIS** OF THAT STRIKE! **NOW!**

WE DETECTED **ZERO DECELERATION** AT IMPACT...!

KLIK KCHIK

HAHH? WHAT DOES **THAT** MEAN?

IT SEEMS TO BE USING **INERTIA CONTROL** IN **REVERSE**...NOT **NEGATING** MOMENTUM, BUT **AMPLIFYING** IT ENORMOUSLY!

YES! OF **COURSE!** USE IT **THAT** WAY, AND YOUR INERTIAL MASS AT IMPACT COULD BE MAGNIFIED TO **NEAR-INFINITE** LEVELS!

IS THAT **POSSIBLE** ...?

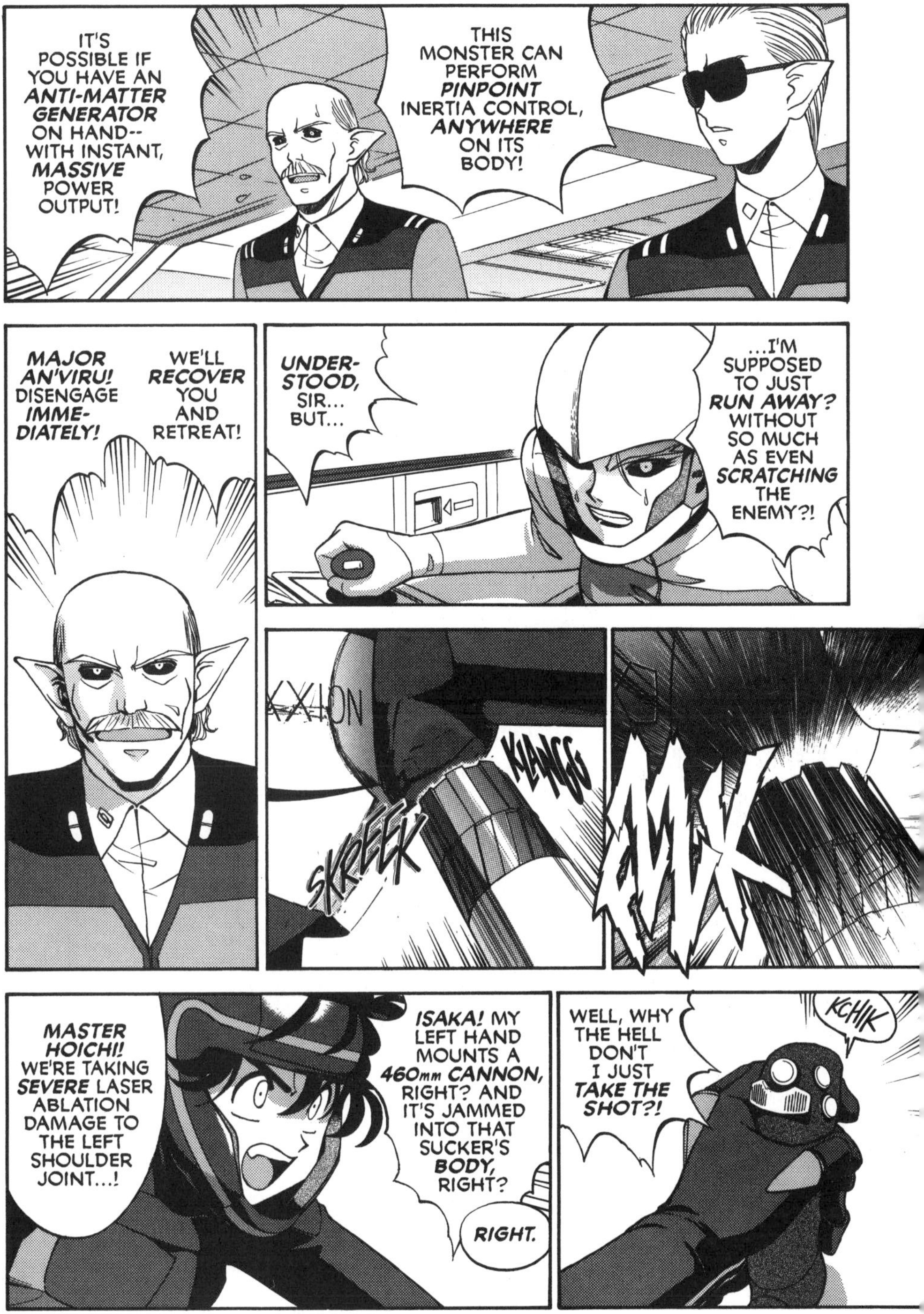
IT'S POSSIBLE IF YOU HAVE AN ANTI-MATTER GENERATOR ON HAND-- WITH INSTANT, MASSIVE POWER OUTPUT!
THIS MONSTER CAN PERFORM PINPOINT INERTIA CONTROL, ANYWHERE ON ITS BODY!
MAJOR AN'VIRU! DISENGAGE IMMEDIATELY!
WE'LL RECOVER YOU AND RETREAT!
UNDERSTOOD, SIR... BUT...
...I'M SUPPOSED TO JUST RUN AWAY? WITHOUT SO MUCH AS EVEN SCRATCHING THE ENEMY?!
KLANGG
SKREEEK
MASTER HOICHI! WE'RE TAKING SEVERE LASER ABLATION DAMAGE TO THE LEFT SHOULDER JOINT...!
ISAKA! MY LEFT HAND MOUNTS A 460mm CANNON, RIGHT? AND IT'S JAMMED INTO THAT SUCKER'S BODY, RIGHT?
RIGHT.
WELL, WHY THE HELL DON'T I JUST TAKE THE SHOT?!
KCHIK

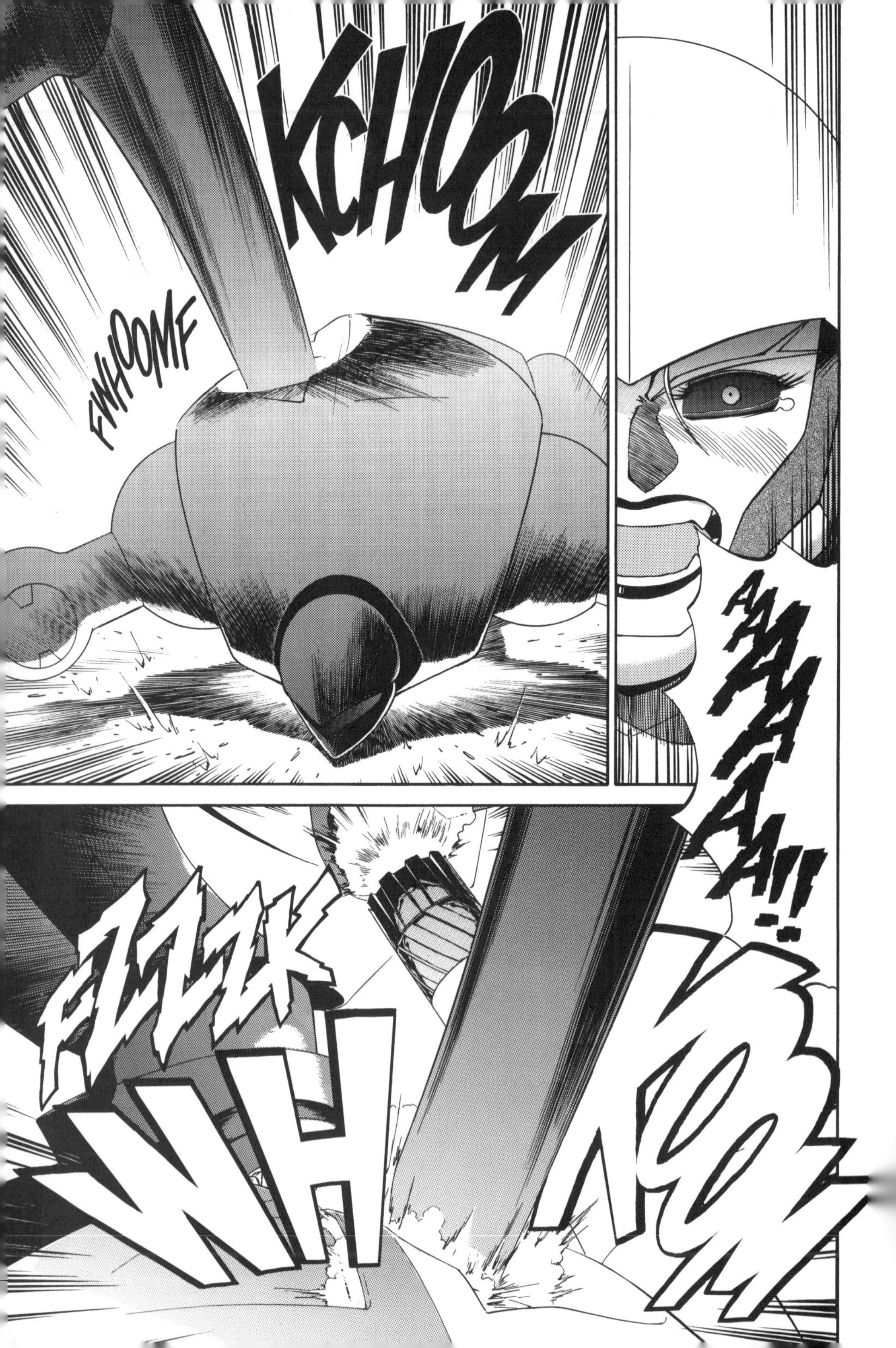
KCHOOM
FWHOOMF
AAAAAAAA!!
FZZZK
WHAOOM

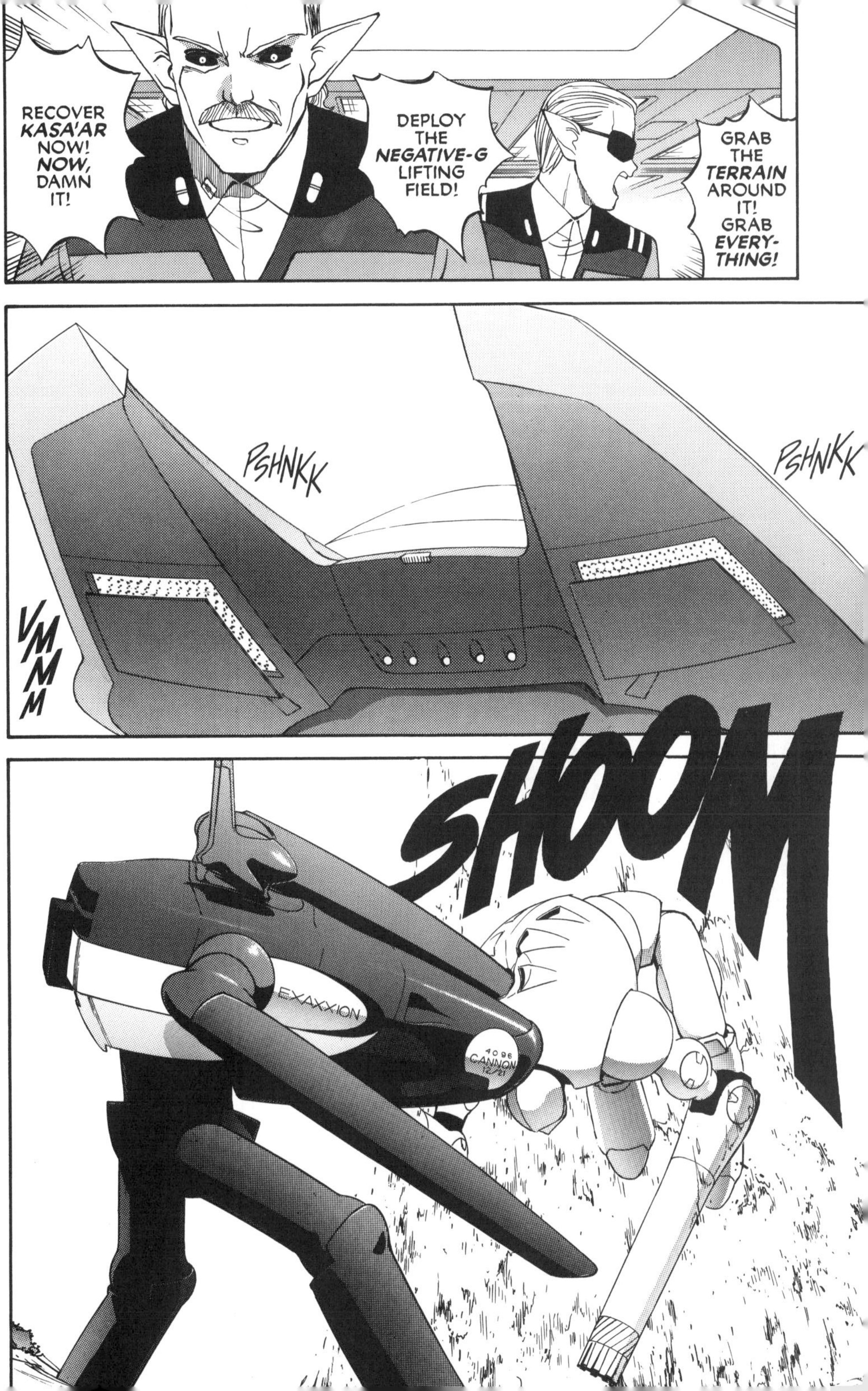
RECOVER KASA'AR NOW! NOW, DAMN IT!
DEPLOY THE NEGATIVE-G LIFTING FIELD!
GRAB THE TERRAIN AROUND IT! GRAB EVERYTHING!
PSHNKK
PSHNKK
VMMM
SHOOM
EXAXXION
4096 CANNON 12/21

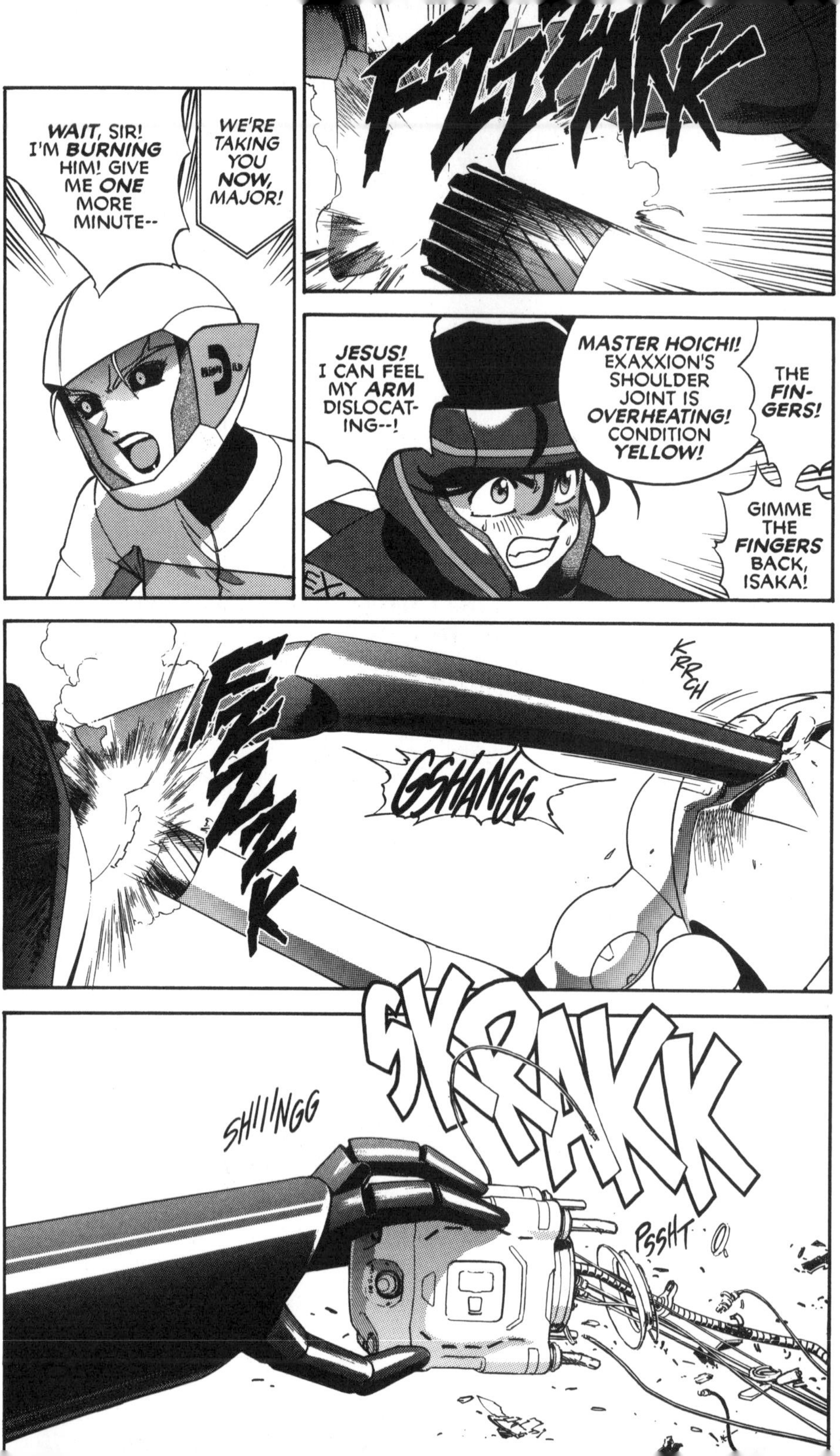
WAIT, SIR! I'M BURNING HIM! GIVE ME ONE MORE MINUTE--
WE'RE TAKING YOU NOW, MAJOR!
FZZZAKK
JESUS! I CAN FEEL MY ARM DISLOCATING--!
MASTER HOICHI! EXAXXION'S SHOULDER JOINT IS OVERHEATING! CONDITION YELLOW!
THE FINGERS!
GIMME THE FINGERS BACK, ISAKA!
KRRCH
GSHANGG
SKRAKK
SHIIINGG
PSSHT

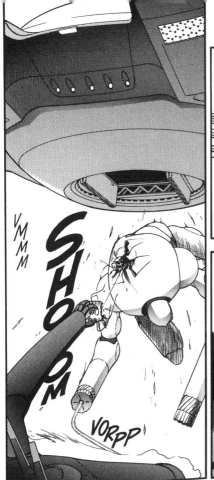

COLONEL! I CAN SEVER ITS ARM!

LET ME DOWN! *PLEASE!*

IT'S *OVER!* SHUT DOWN YOUR LASER!

OH, NO YOU *DON'T--!*

LEFT ARM TEMPERATURE IS NOW *CRITICAL...!*

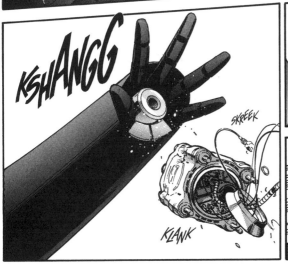

KSHANGG

SKREEK

KLANK

MASTER HOICHI IS *OPENING FIRE,* SIR!

AH! *THAT'S* THE SPIRIT, LADDIE!

KCHIK!

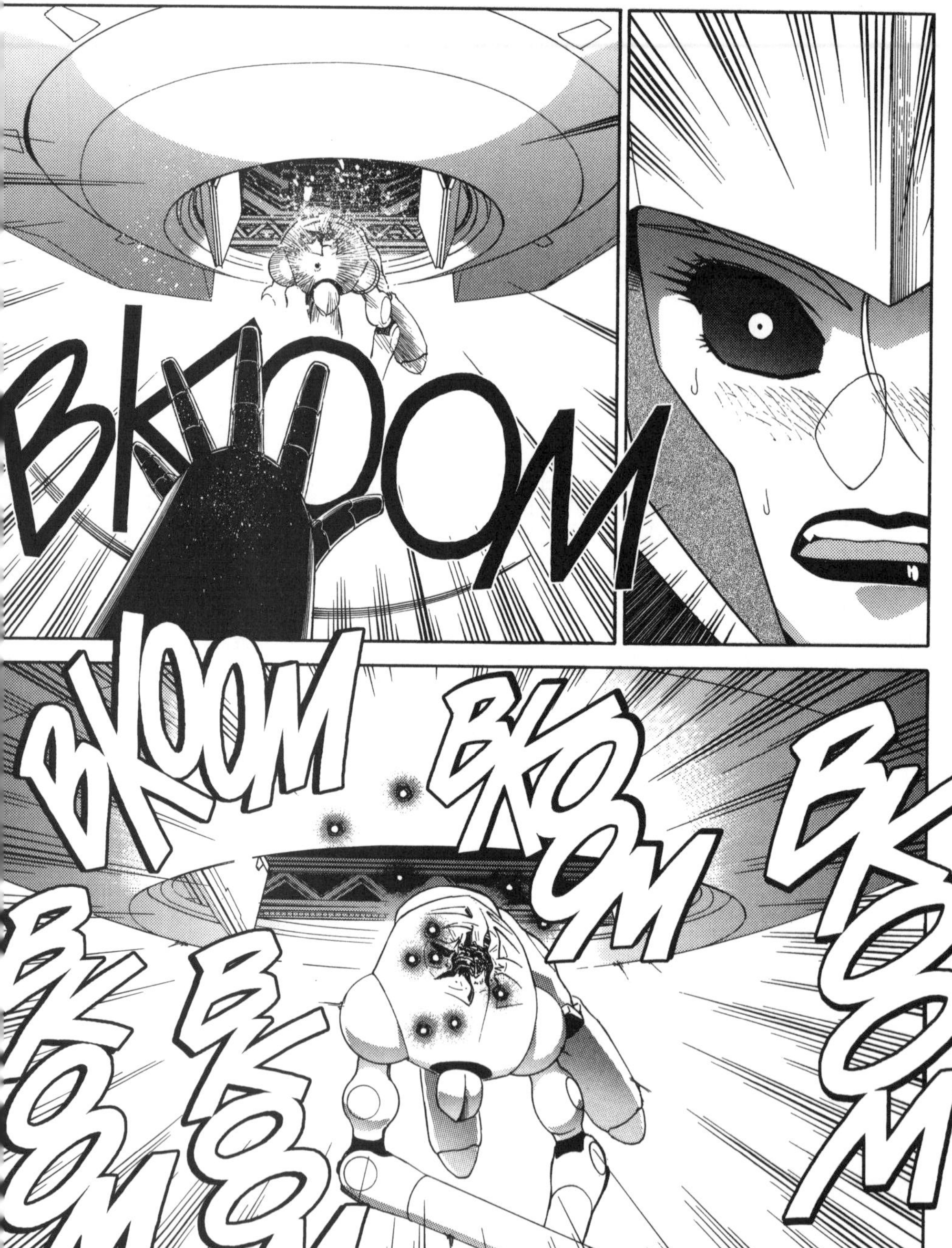
BKOOM
BKOOM
BKOOM
BKOOM
BKOOM
BKOOM
BKOOM

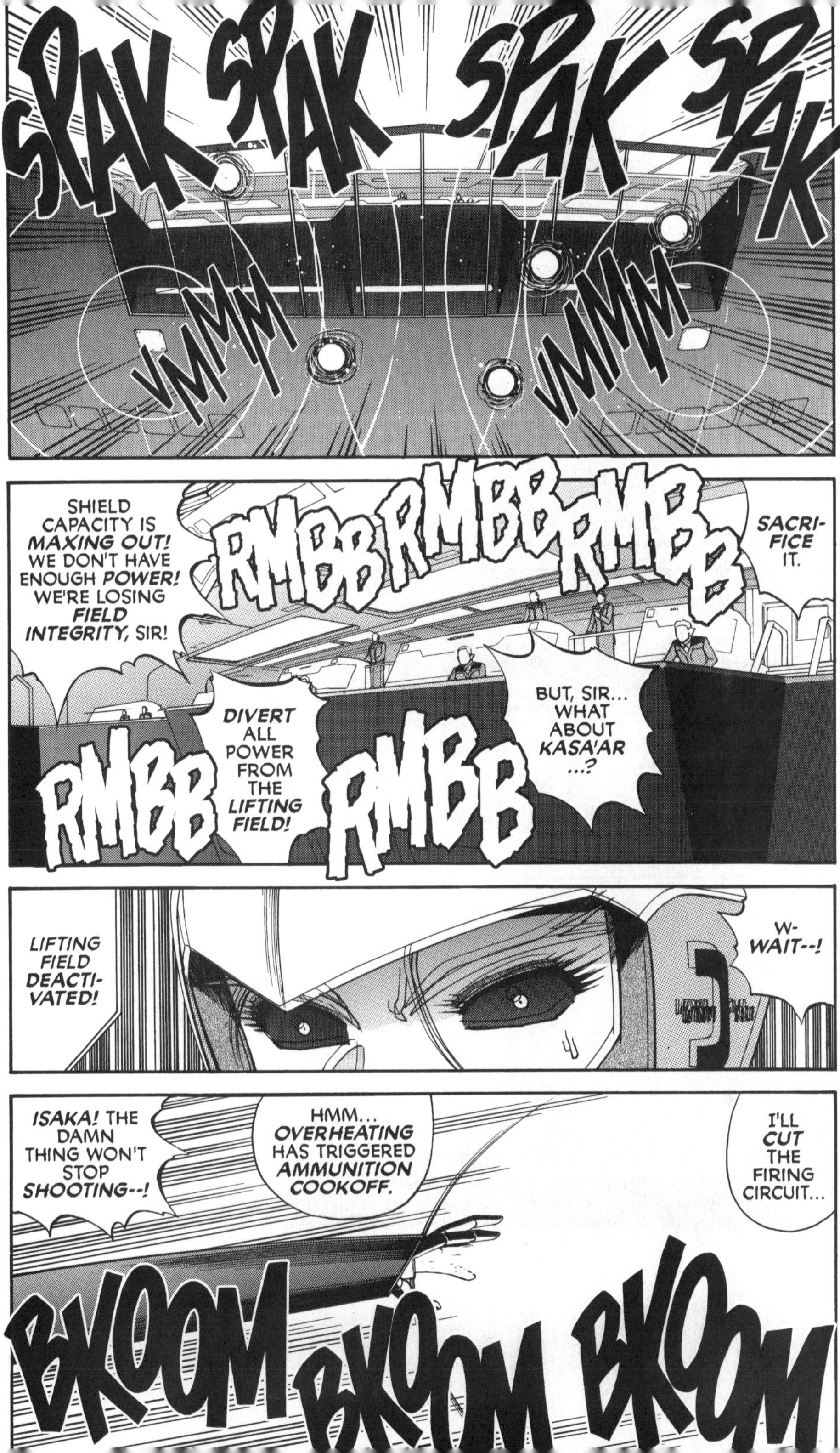
SPAK SPAK SPAK SPAK
VMMM
VMMM
SHIELD CAPACITY IS MAXING OUT! WE DON'T HAVE ENOUGH POWER! WE'RE LOSING FIELD INTEGRITY, SIR!
RMBB RMBB RMBB
SACRI-FICE IT.
RMBB
DIVERT ALL POWER FROM THE LIFTING FIELD!
RMBB
BUT, SIR... WHAT ABOUT KASA'AR ...?
LIFTING FIELD DEACTI-VATED!
W-WAIT--!
ISAKA! THE DAMN THING WON'T STOP SHOOTING--!
HMM... OVERHEATING HAS TRIGGERED AMMUNITION COOKOFF.
I'LL CUT THE FIRING CIRCUIT...
BKOOM BKOOM BKOOM

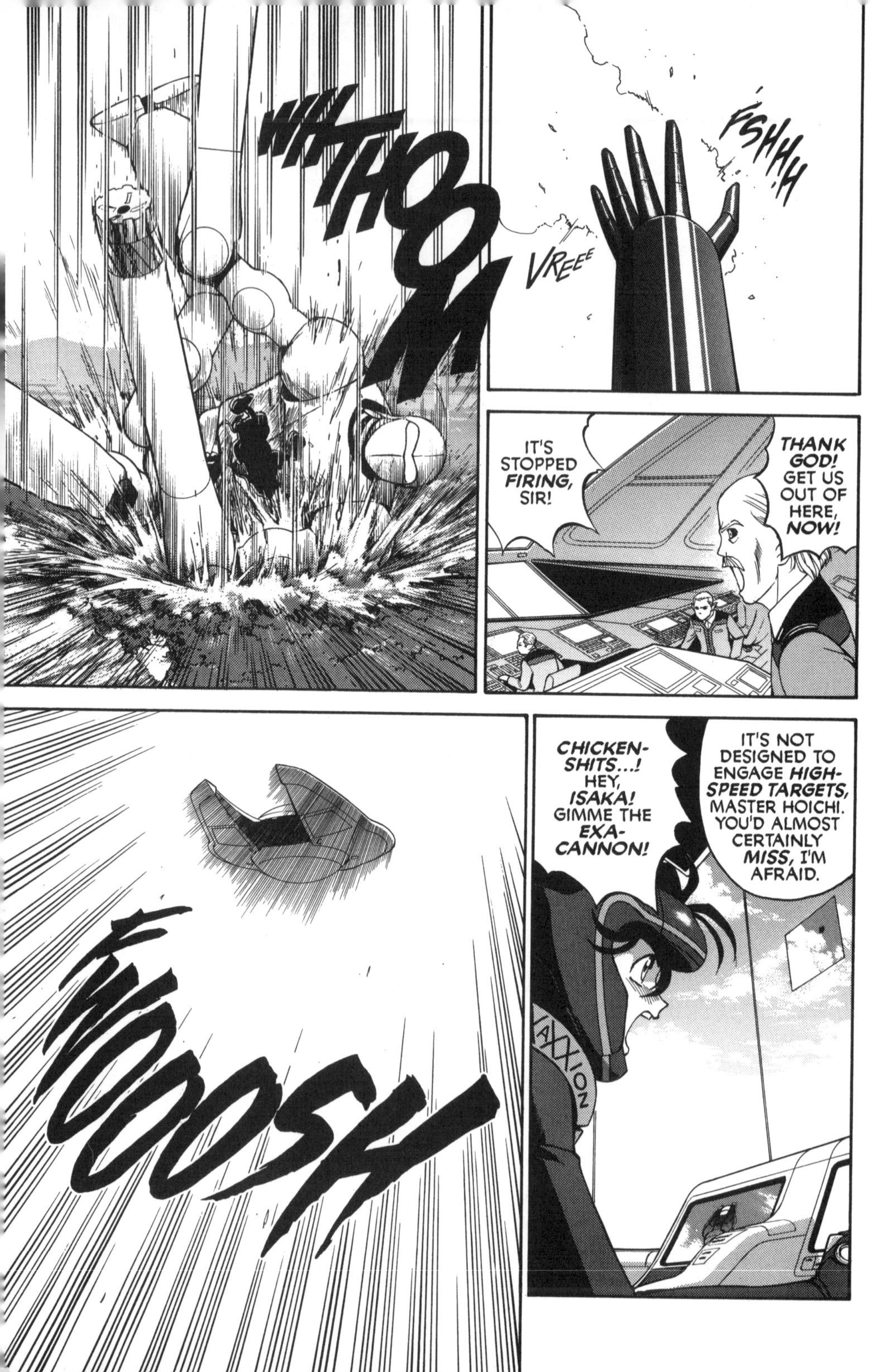
WHTHOOM
VREEE
FSHHH
IT'S STOPPED FIRING, SIR!
THANK GOD! GET US OUT OF HERE, NOW!
FWOOSH
CHICKEN-SHITS...! HEY, ISAKA! GIMME THE EXA-CANNON!
IT'S NOT DESIGNED TO ENGAGE HIGH-SPEED TARGETS, MASTER HOICHI. YOU'D ALMOST CERTAINLY MISS, I'M AFRAID.

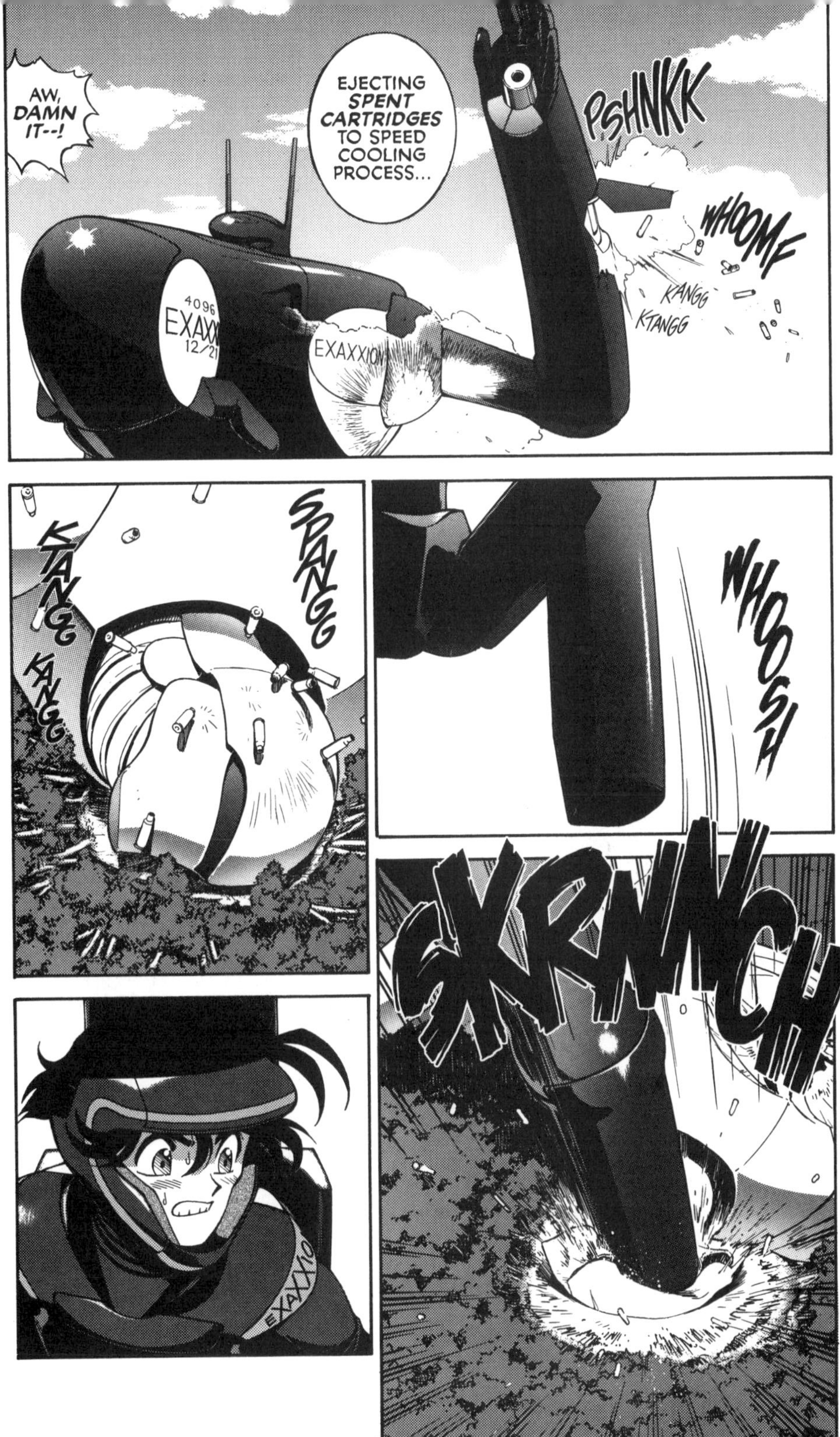
PSHNKK
EJECTING SPENT CARTRIDGES TO SPEED COOLING PROCESS...
WHOOMF
KANGG
KTANGG
AW, DAMN IT--!
4096 EXAXX 12/21
EXAXXION
WHOOOSH
SPANGG
KTANGG
KANGG
SKRWNCH
EXAXXIO

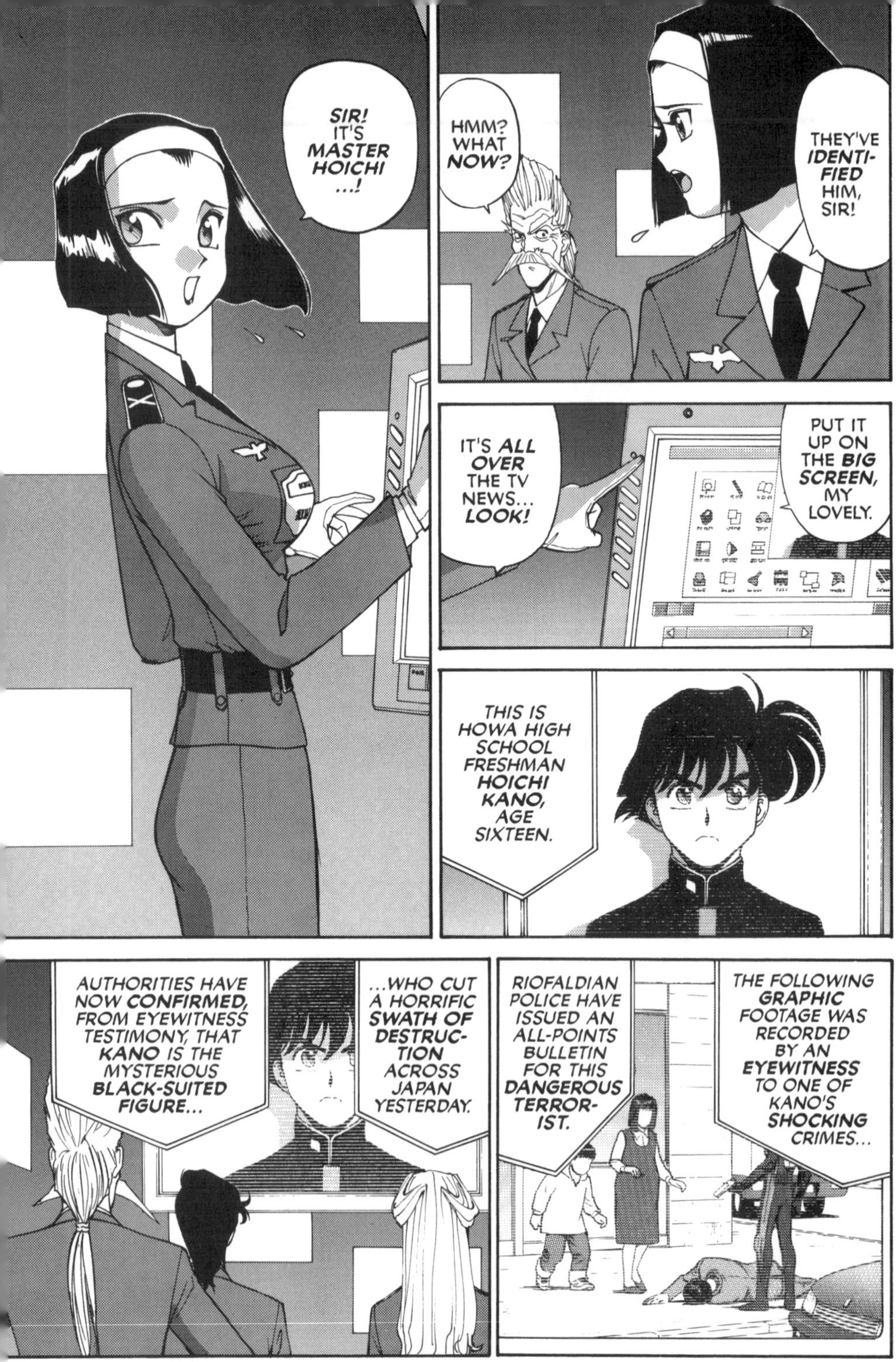
SIR! IT'S MASTER HOICHI ...!
HMM? WHAT NOW?
THEY'VE IDENTIFIED HIM, SIR!
IT'S ALL OVER THE TV NEWS... LOOK!
PUT IT UP ON THE BIG SCREEN, MY LOVELY.
THIS IS HOWA HIGH SCHOOL FRESHMAN HOICHI KANO, AGE SIXTEEN.
AUTHORITIES HAVE NOW CONFIRMED, FROM EYEWITNESS TESTIMONY, THAT KANO IS THE MYSTERIOUS BLACK-SUITED FIGURE...
...WHO CUT A HORRIFIC SWATH OF DESTRUCTION ACROSS JAPAN YESTERDAY.
RIOFALDIAN POLICE HAVE ISSUED AN ALL-POINTS BULLETIN FOR THIS DANGEROUS TERRORIST.
THE FOLLOWING GRAPHIC FOOTAGE WAS RECORDED BY AN EYEWITNESS TO ONE OF KANO'S SHOCKING CRIMES...

OH, *MY*... THAT'S *VERY* EFFECTIVE PROPAGANDA...!

THE WOMAN AND HER SON WERE RUSHED TO THE HOSPITAL, BUT THEY WERE BOTH PRONOUNCED *DEAD ON ARRIVAL*... ALONG WITH HER *UNBORN CHILD.*

HUH. THEY'RE *GOOD* ...!

CRANKING OUT THAT *HYSTERICAL SWILL* WITHIN ONLY A FEW HOURS? *BRAVO!*

AND WITH *GREAT* EMOTIONAL TOUCHES... *LOVE* THAT BIT ABOUT THE *UNBORN CHILD!*

SO... A *LIE* FOR A *LIE,* THEN, SIR ...?

YEP. YOU KNOW WHICH ONE TO USE.

FLOOD THE TV CHANNELS WITH IT.

YES, *SIR!* ♥ SHOULD I PUT IT ON THE *NET,* TOO, SIR?

YEP.

OH! YOU'RE GOING TO USE THAT *THINGY* I MADE LAST YEAR...?

THAT'S *RIGHT*... LET'S SEE...

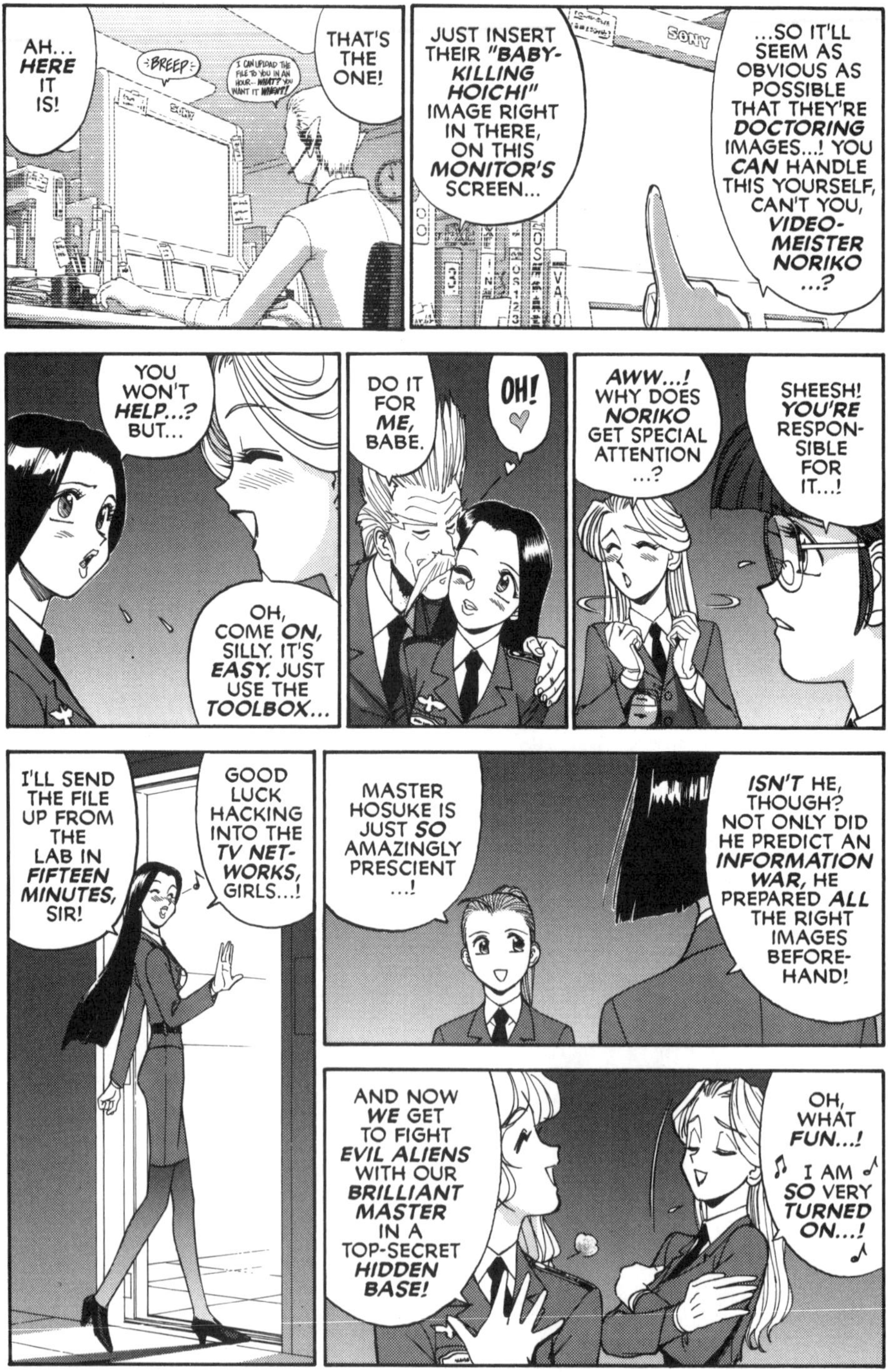
AH... HERE IT IS!
BREEP
I CAN UPLOAD THE FILE TO YOU IN AN HOUR... WHAT? YOU WANT IT WHEN?!
THAT'S THE ONE!
JUST INSERT THEIR "BABY-KILLING HOICHI" IMAGE RIGHT IN THERE, ON THIS MONITOR'S SCREEN...
...SO IT'LL SEEM AS OBVIOUS AS POSSIBLE THAT THEY'RE DOCTORING IMAGES...! YOU CAN HANDLE THIS YOURSELF, CAN'T YOU, VIDEO-MEISTER NORIKO ...?
YOU WON'T HELP...? BUT...
OH, COME ON, SILLY. IT'S EASY. JUST USE THE TOOLBOX...
DO IT FOR ME, BABE.
OH!
AWW...! WHY DOES NORIKO GET SPECIAL ATTENTION ...?
SHEESH! YOU'RE RESPONSIBLE FOR IT...!
I'LL SEND THE FILE UP FROM THE LAB IN FIFTEEN MINUTES, SIR!
GOOD LUCK HACKING INTO THE TV NETWORKS, GIRLS...!
MASTER HOSUKE IS JUST SO AMAZINGLY PRESCIENT ...!
ISN'T HE, THOUGH? NOT ONLY DID HE PREDICT AN INFORMATION WAR, HE PREPARED ALL THE RIGHT IMAGES BEFOREHAND!
AND NOW WE GET TO FIGHT EVIL ALIENS WITH OUR BRILLIANT MASTER IN A TOP-SECRET HIDDEN BASE!
OH, WHAT FUN...!
I AM SO VERY TURNED ON...!

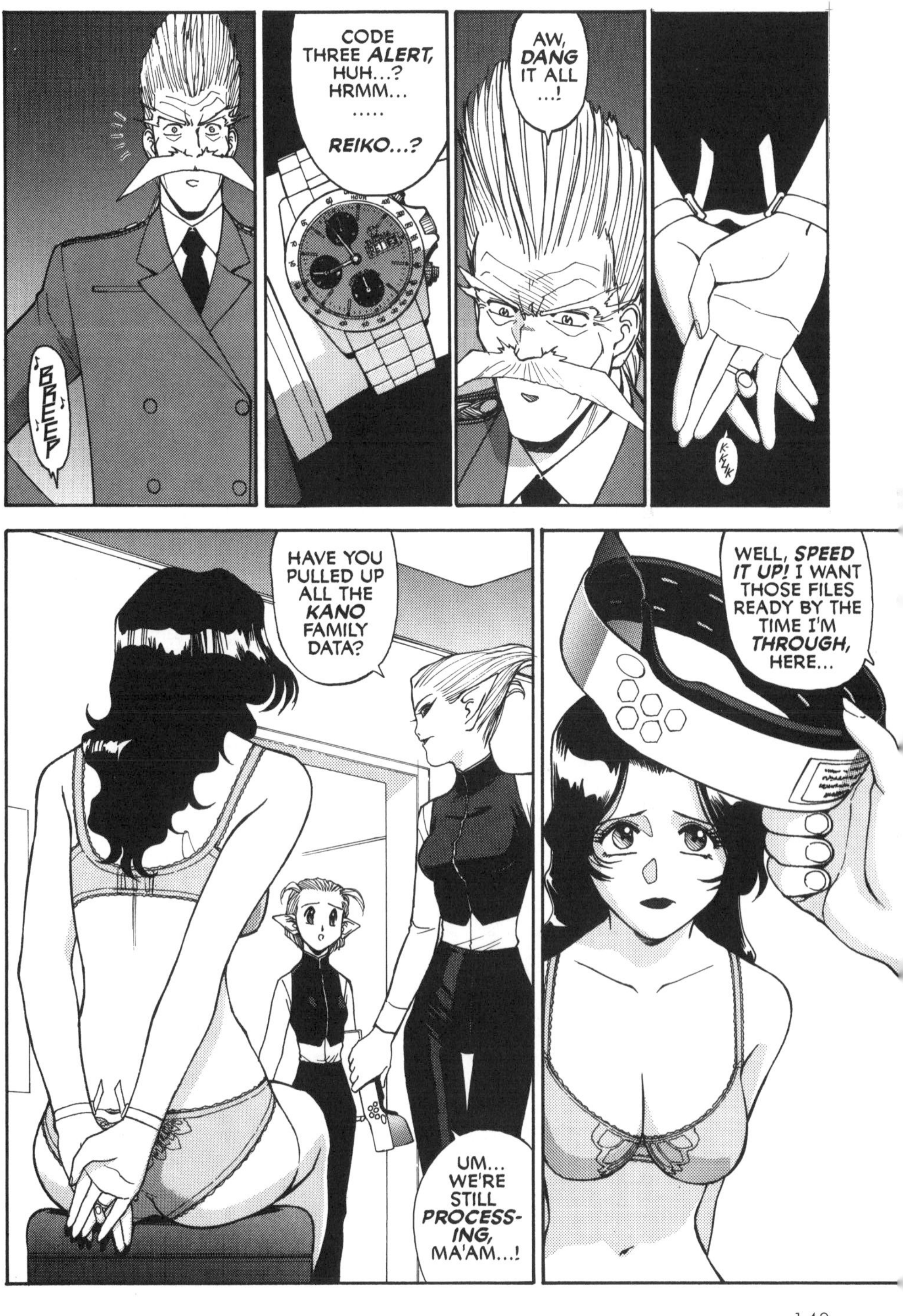
BREEP
CODE THREE ALERT, HUH...? HRMM... ..... REIKO...?
AW, DANG IT ALL ...!
K-KLIK
HAVE YOU PULLED UP ALL THE KANO FAMILY DATA?
UM... WE'RE STILL PROCESS-ING, MA'AM...!
WELL, SPEED IT UP! I WANT THOSE FILES READY BY THE TIME I'M THROUGH, HERE...

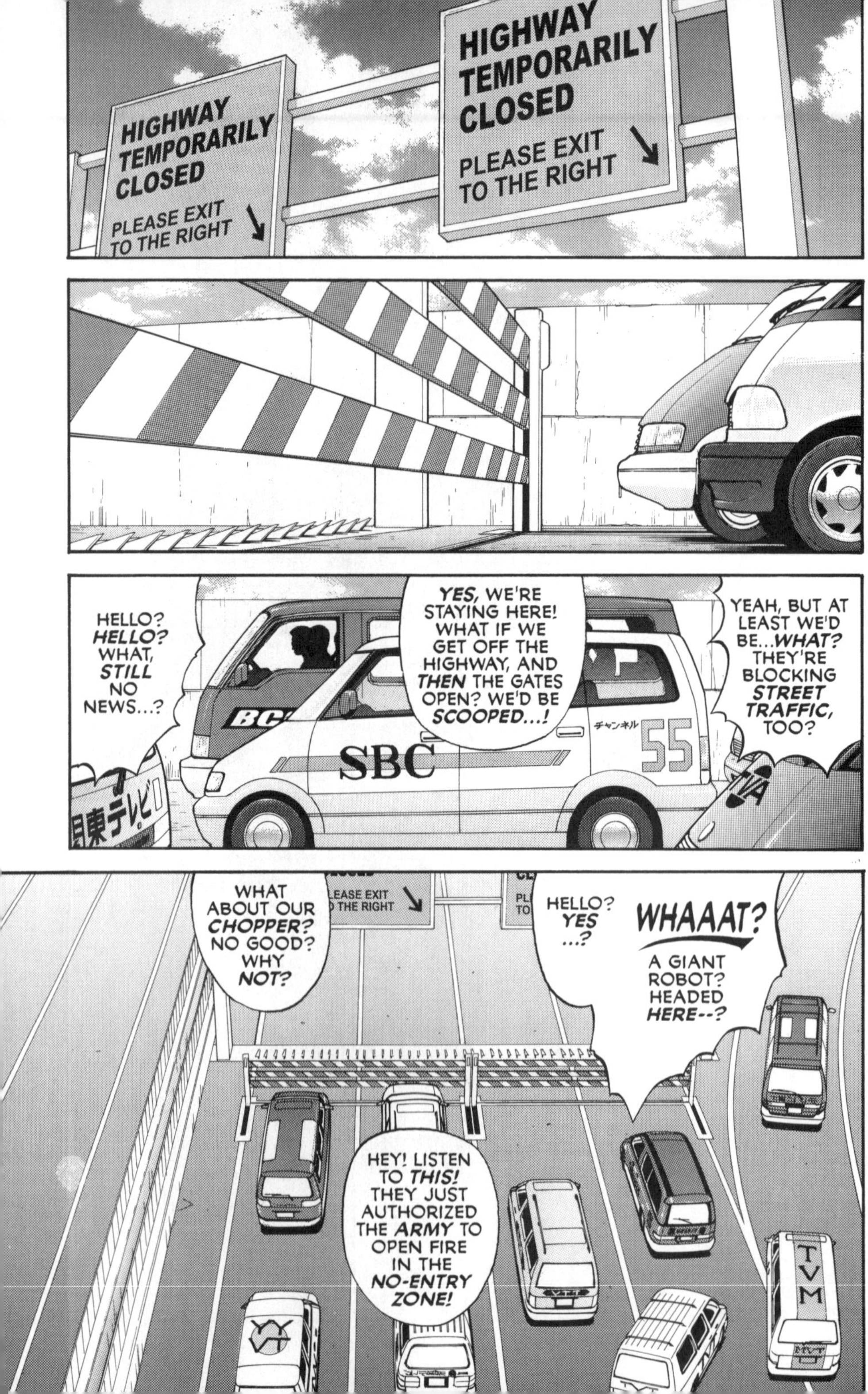
HIGHWAY TEMPORARILY CLOSED
PLEASE EXIT TO THE RIGHT
HIGHWAY TEMPORARILY CLOSED
PLEASE EXIT TO THE RIGHT
HELLO? HELLO? WHAT, STILL NO NEWS...?
SBC
チャンネル
55
YES, WE'RE STAYING HERE! WHAT IF WE GET OFF THE HIGHWAY, AND THEN THE GATES OPEN? WE'D BE SCOOPED...!
YEAH, BUT AT LEAST WE'D BE...WHAT? THEY'RE BLOCKING STREET TRAFFIC, TOO?
WHAT ABOUT OUR CHOPPER? NO GOOD? WHY NOT?
HELLO? YES ...?
WHAAAT?
A GIANT ROBOT? HEADED HERE--?
HEY! LISTEN TO THIS! THEY JUST AUTHORIZED THE ARMY TO OPEN FIRE IN THE NO-ENTRY ZONE!
TVM

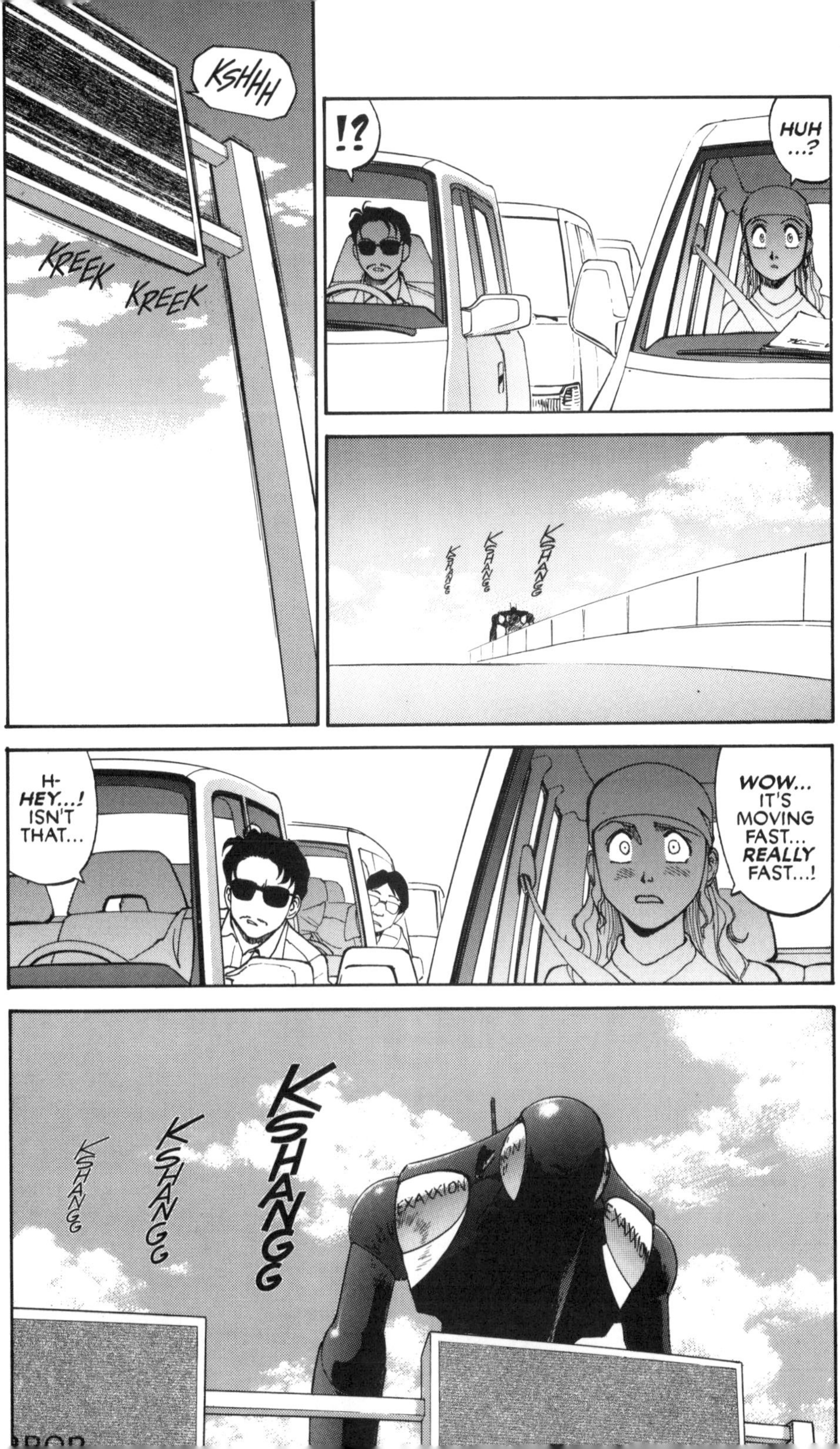
KSHHH
KREEK
KREEK
!?
HUH ...?
KSHANG
KSHANG
KSHANG
H-HEY...! ISN'T THAT...
WOW... IT'S MOVING FAST... REALLY FAST...!
KSHANGG
KSHANGG
KSHANGG
EXAXXION
EXAXXION
EXAXXION

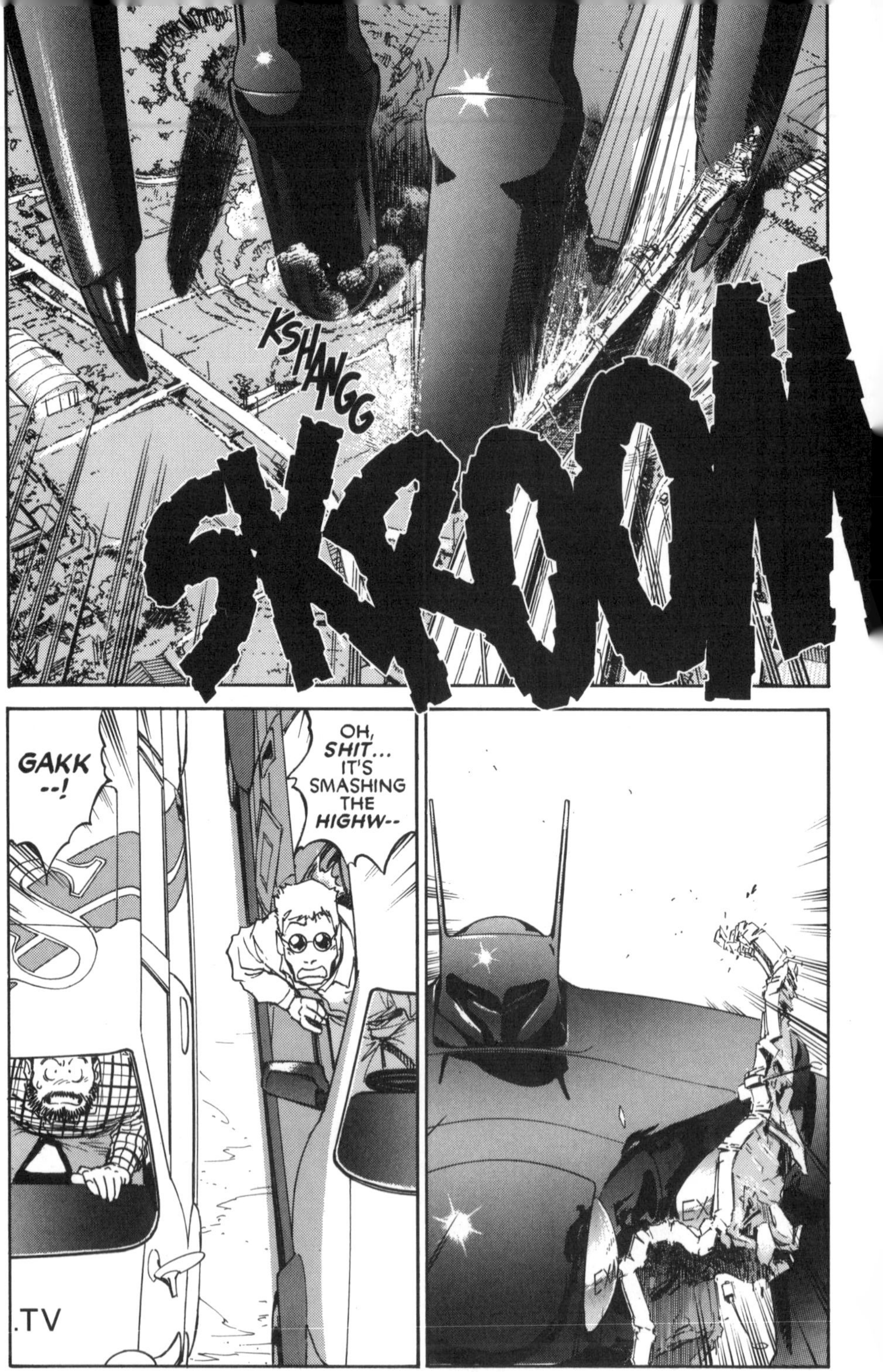
KSHANGG
SKROOM
GAKK--!
.TV
OH, SHIT... IT'S SMASHING THE HIGHW--

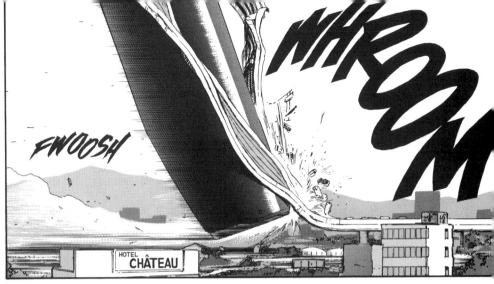

FWOOSH

WHROOM

HOTEL CHÂTEAU

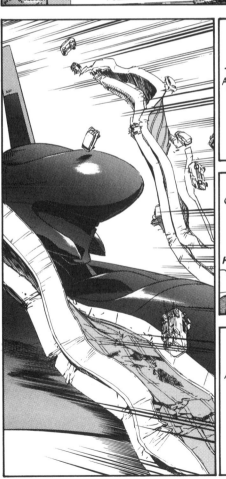

HOICHI, LADDIE! YOU'RE PEELING UP THE *HIGHWAY,* AND SMASHING THE HELL OUT OF ALL THE POOR BASTARDS IN THOSE *CARS...!*

YOU HAVE TO *TAKE MORE CARE,* MY BOY!

WHAT *IS* THIS, GRANDPA? ALL OF A SUDDEN, YOU'RE GETTING *TENDER-HEARTED?!*

WE'RE CONDUCT-ING AN *INFORMA-TION WAR* HERE, HOICHI!!

EXAXX

DON'T COMMIT ANY *ATROCITIES* THAT WE CAN'T *COVER UP,* UNDER-STAND?

ALL *RIGHT,* AL-READY! *DAMN!*

SHNKK

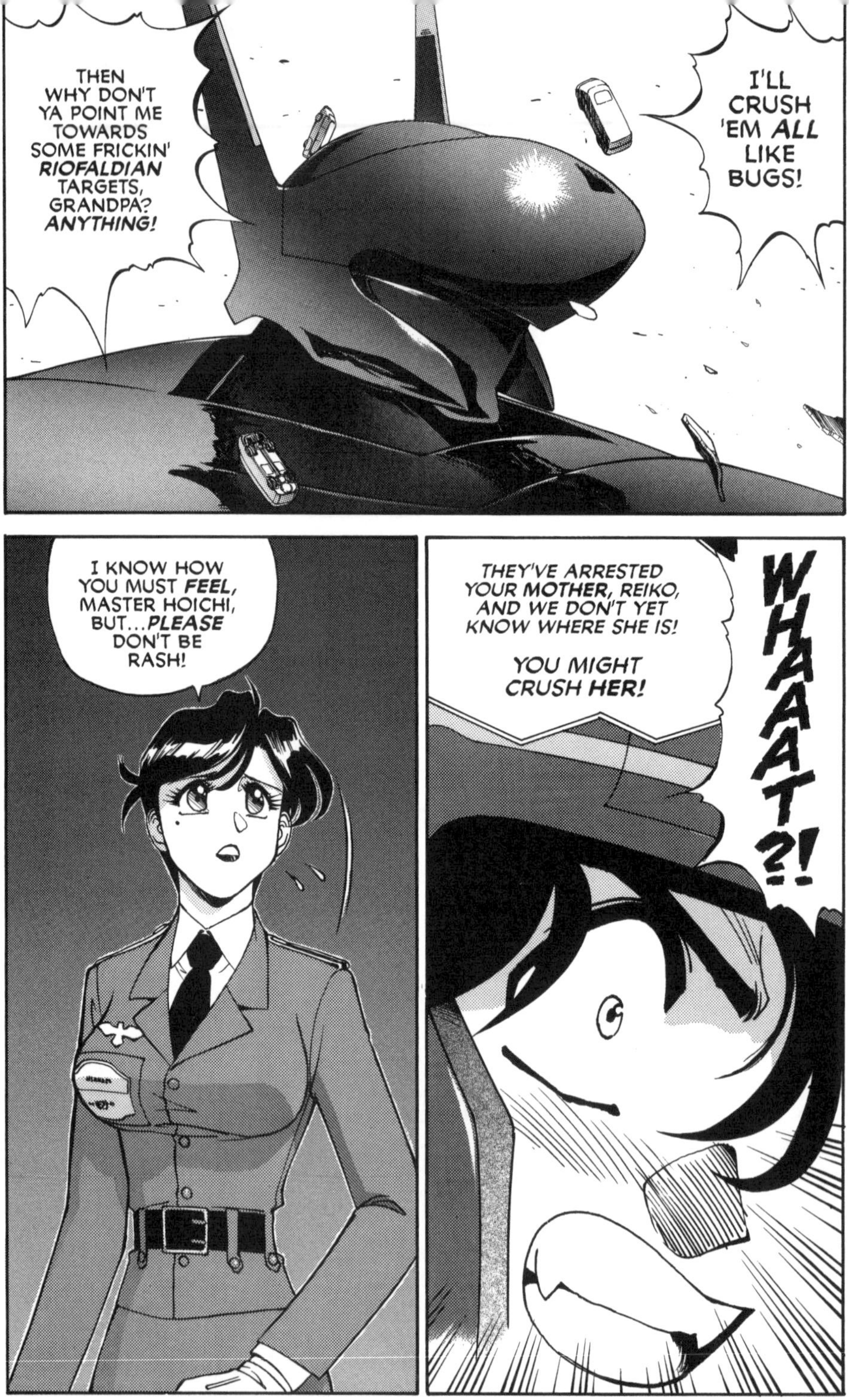

THEN WHY DON'T YA POINT ME TOWARDS SOME FRICKIN' ***RIOFALDIAN*** TARGETS, GRANDPA? ***ANYTHING!***
I'LL CRUSH 'EM ***ALL*** LIKE BUGS!
I KNOW HOW YOU MUST ***FEEL,*** MASTER HOICHI, BUT...***PLEASE*** DON'T BE RASH!
*THEY'VE ARRESTED YOUR **MOTHER,** REIKO, AND WE DON'T YET KNOW WHERE SHE IS!*
*YOU MIGHT CRUSH **HER!***
WHAAAT?!

2.8

CANNON GOD EXAXXION: STAGE 2.8

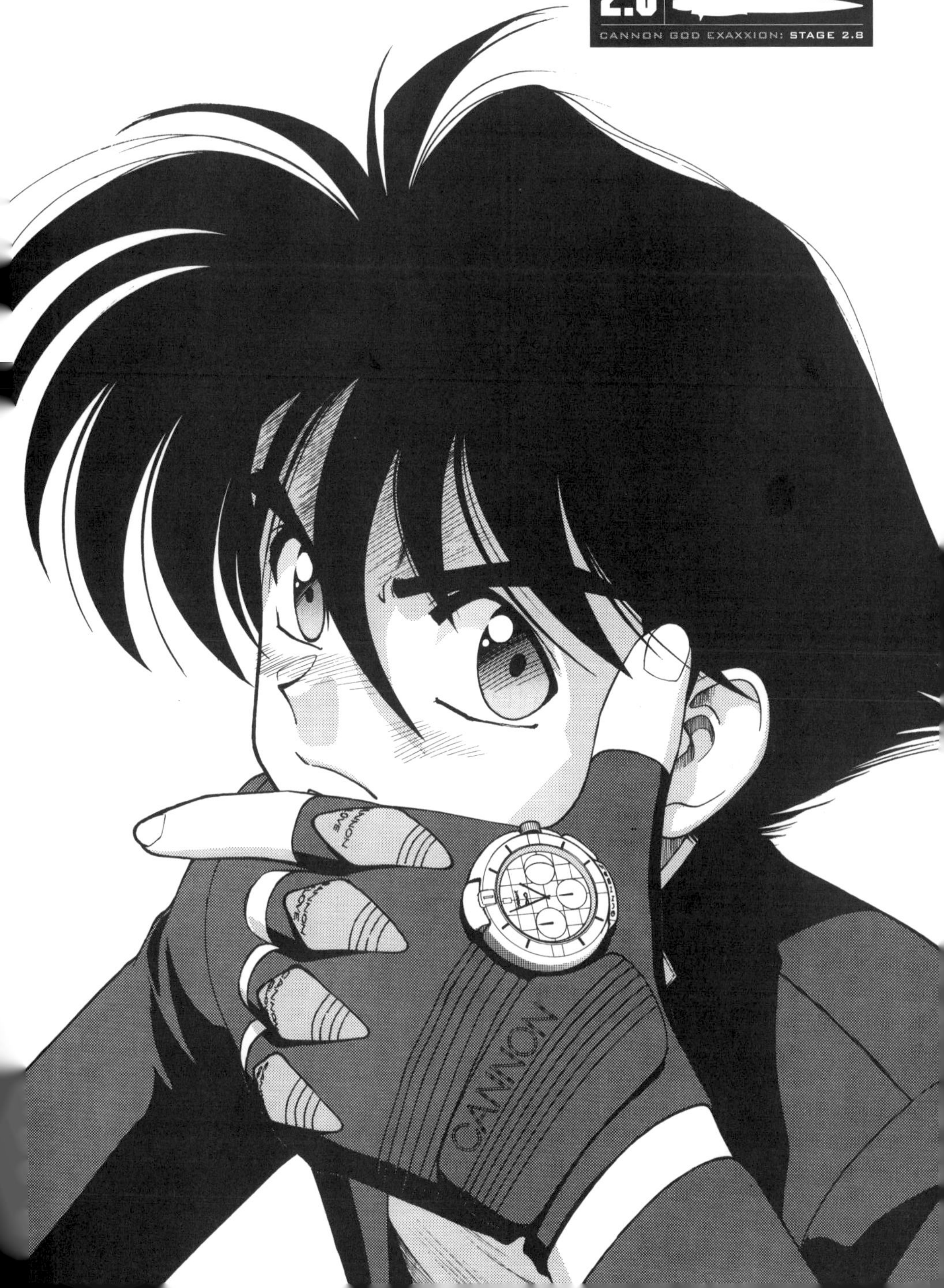
CANNON

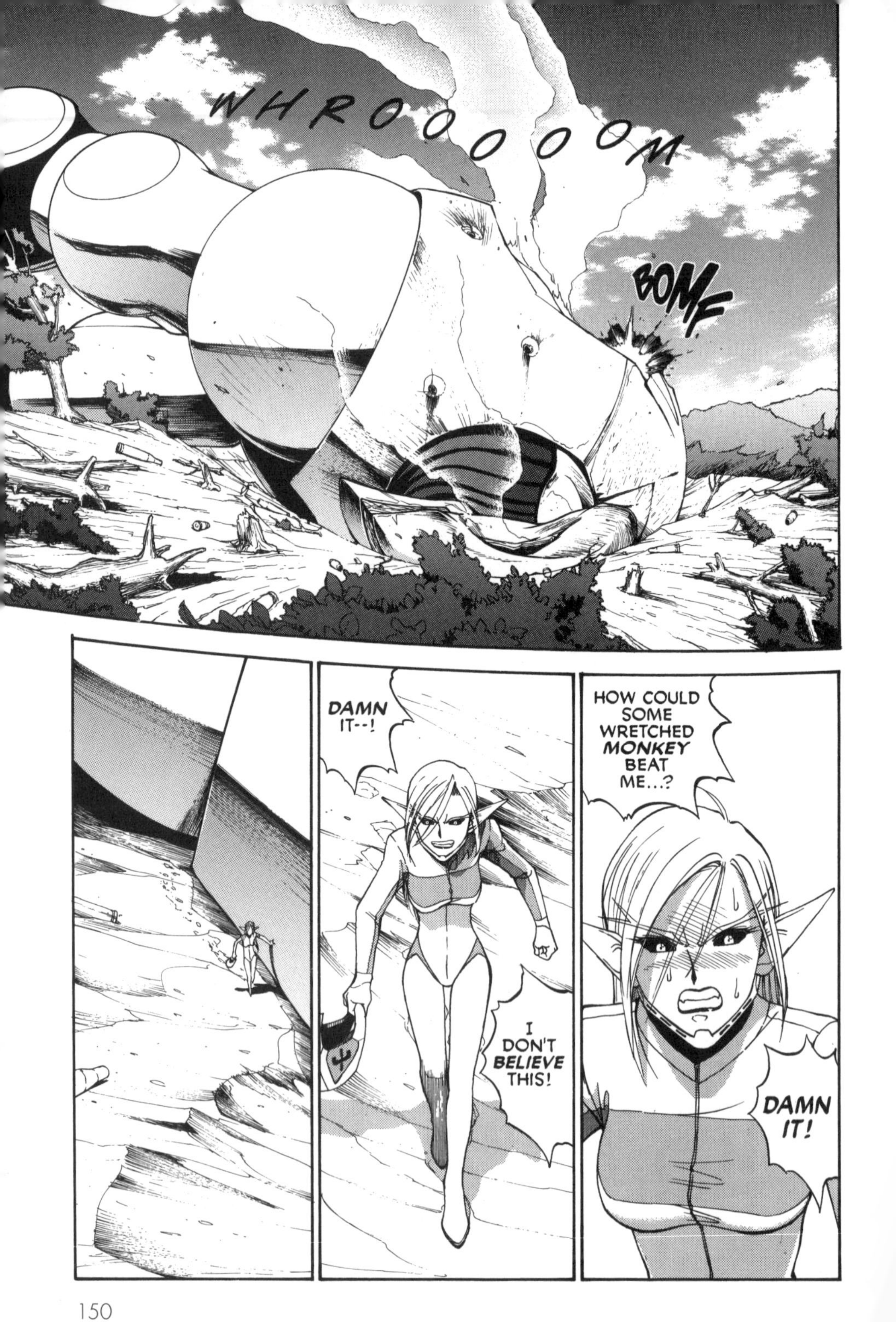
WHROOOOOM
BOMF
DAMN IT--!
I DON'T BELIEVE THIS!
HOW COULD SOME WRETCHED MONKEY BEAT ME...?
DAMN IT!

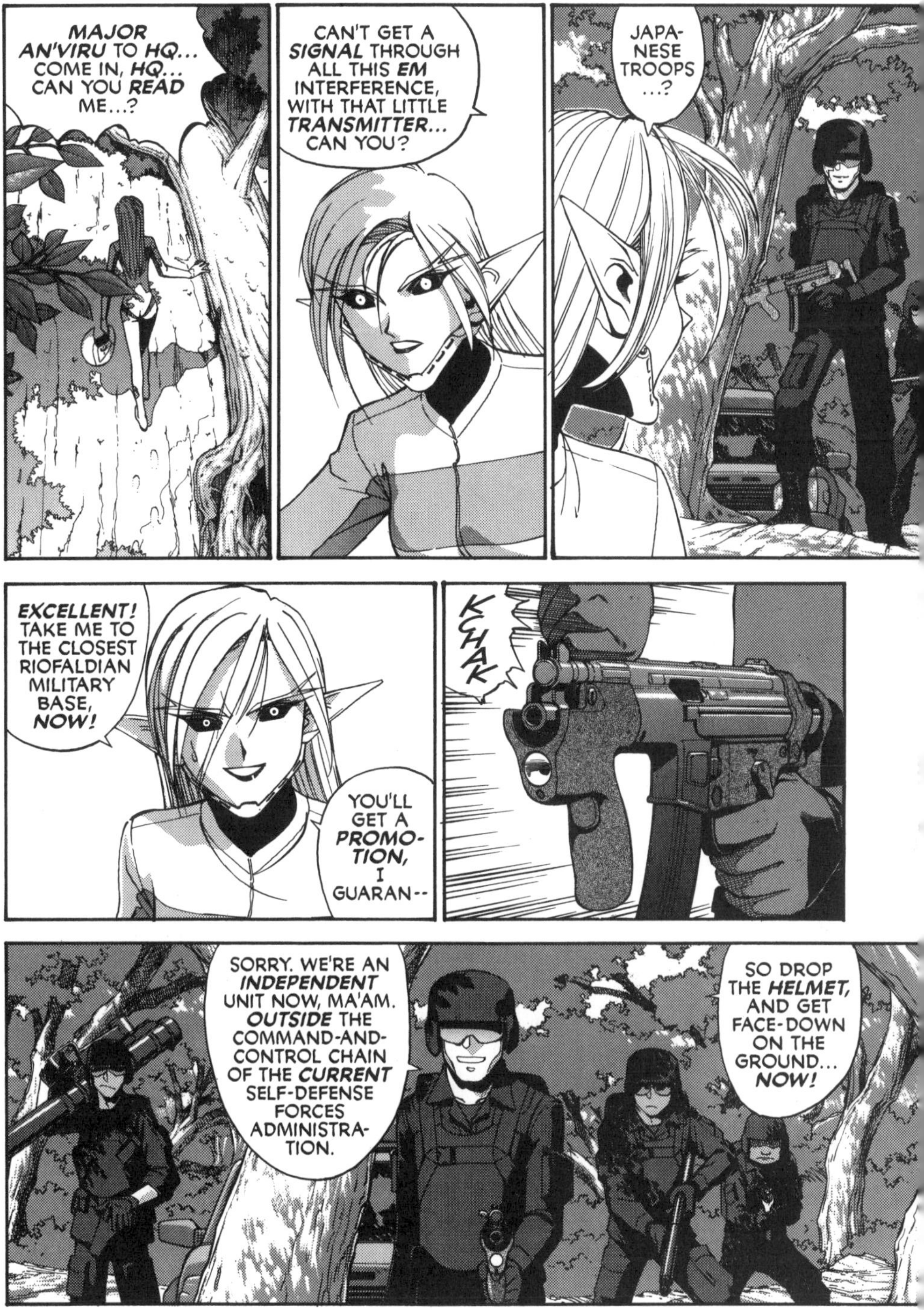
MAJOR AN'VIRU TO HQ... COME IN, HQ... CAN YOU READ ME...?
CAN'T GET A SIGNAL THROUGH ALL THIS EM INTERFERENCE, WITH THAT LITTLE TRANSMITTER... CAN YOU?
JAPA-NESE TROOPS ...?
EXCELLENT! TAKE ME TO THE CLOSEST RIOFALDIAN MILITARY BASE, NOW!
YOU'LL GET A PROMO-TION, I GUARAN--
KCHAK
SORRY. WE'RE AN INDEPENDENT UNIT NOW, MA'AM. OUTSIDE THE COMMAND-AND-CONTROL CHAIN OF THE CURRENT SELF-DEFENSE FORCES ADMINISTRA-TION.
SO DROP THE HELMET, AND GET FACE-DOWN ON THE GROUND... NOW!

WHA ...?

IDIOTS! EVEN IF YOU'RE STUPID ENOUGH TO REBEL... WHAT CAN A SINGLE UNIT POSSIBLY HOPE TO ACCOMPLISH?

WELL, YOU MIGHT JUST SAY THAT WE'RE FANS, MA'AM.

"FANS" ...?

WHDD

AAH!

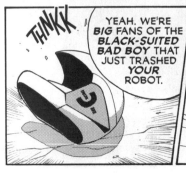

THNKK

YEAH. WE'RE BIG FANS OF THE BLACK-SUITED BAD BOY THAT JUST TRASHED YOUR ROBOT.

FDD

—HGKK S-STOP THIS, YOU... YOU BARBAR-IANS!

WE CONTROL MORE MILITARY ASSETS THAN THE COMBINED ARMED FORCES OF YOUR ENTIRE *PLANET!*

ONE ROBOT CAN'T TURN THE TIDE OF A WHOLE WAR, NO MATTER *HOW* STRONG IT IS!

WE'RE THINKIN' YOU MIGHT BE *WRONG* ABOUT THAT.

OTHERWISE, WHY ARE YOU 'FALDIES THROWING *EVERY* LAST BIT OF FIREPOWER YOU'VE *GOT* AT IT?

WE *RECORDED* YOUR LITTLE BATTLE. JUST WAIT UNTIL *THIS* FOOTAGE HITS THE NET...!

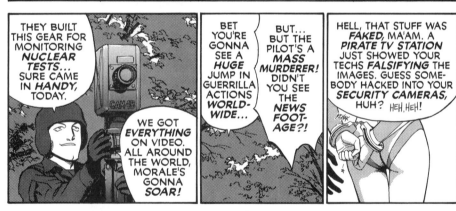

THEY BUILT THIS GEAR FOR MONITORING *NUCLEAR TESTS*... SURE CAME IN *HANDY*, TODAY.

WE GOT *EVERYTHING* ON VIDEO. ALL AROUND THE WORLD, MORALE'S GONNA *SOAR!*

BET YOU'RE GONNA SEE A *HUGE* JUMP IN GUERRILLA ACTIONS WORLD-WIDE...

BUT... BUT THE PILOT'S A *MASS MURDERER!* DIDN'T YOU SEE THE *NEWS* FOOTAGE?!

HELL, THAT STUFF WAS *FAKED*, MA'AM. A *PIRATE TV STATION* JUST SHOWED YOUR TECHS *FALSIFYING* THE IMAGES. GUESS SOMEBODY HACKED INTO YOUR *SECURITY CAMERAS*, HUH? HEH, HEH!

WHAT? THAT MUST HAVE BEEN FAKED!

WHATEVER. IF *THAT* STUFF WAS FAKED, THEN THE *ORIGINAL* MURDER VIDEO PROBABLY WAS, TOO. NOW... GET IN THE *TRUCK!*

WE'RE GONNA HAVE A NICE, LONG *CHAT*...

I'M AN *OFFICER OF RIOFALD!* DO YOU ACTUALLY THINK I'LL *TALK?*

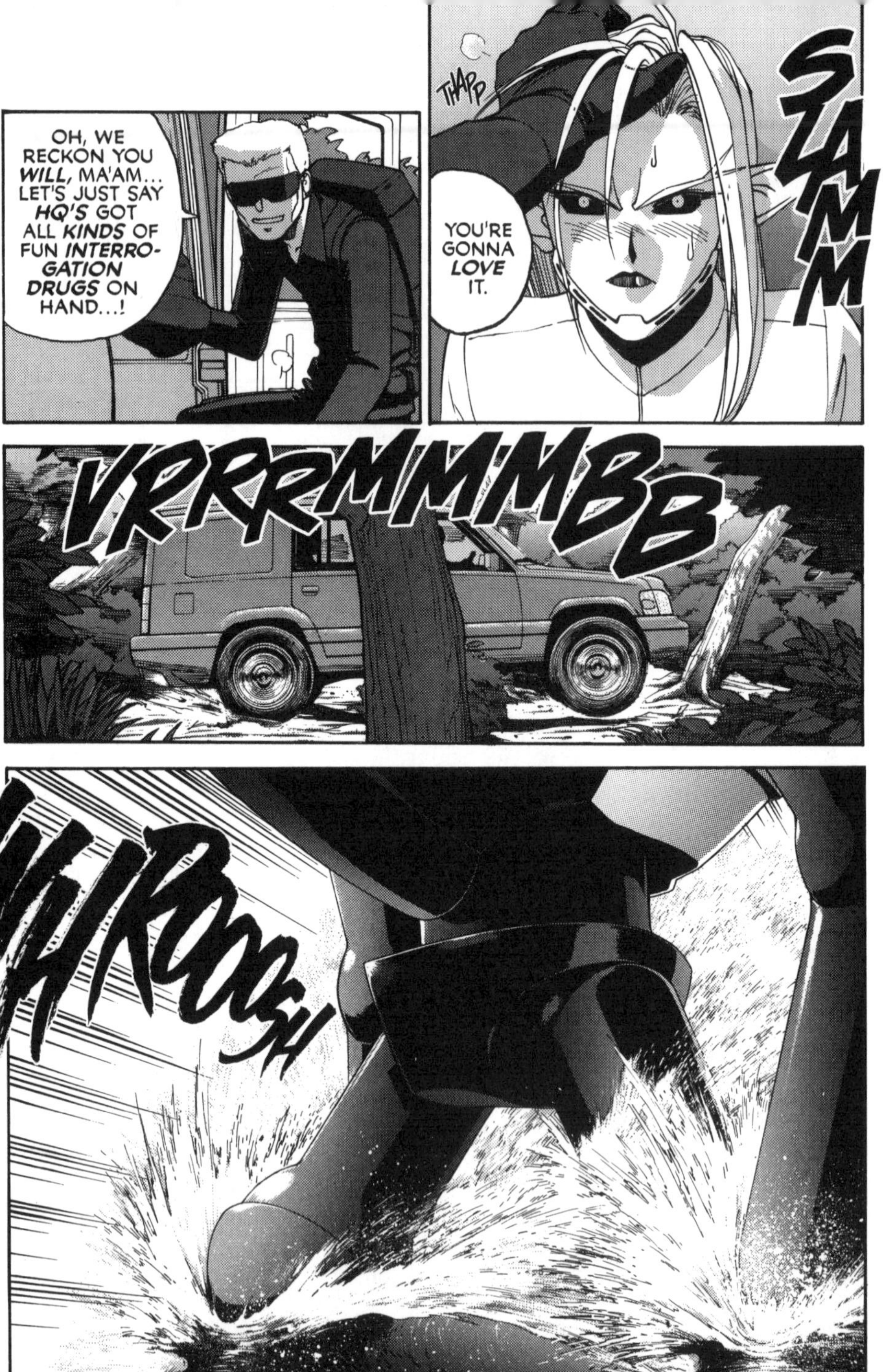
OH, WE RECKON YOU *WILL*, MA'AM... LET'S JUST SAY *HQ'S* GOT ALL *KINDS* OF FUN *INTERRO-GATION DRUGS* ON HAND...!
THAPP
YOU'RE GONNA *LOVE* IT.
SLAMM
VRRRMMMMBB
WHROOOSH

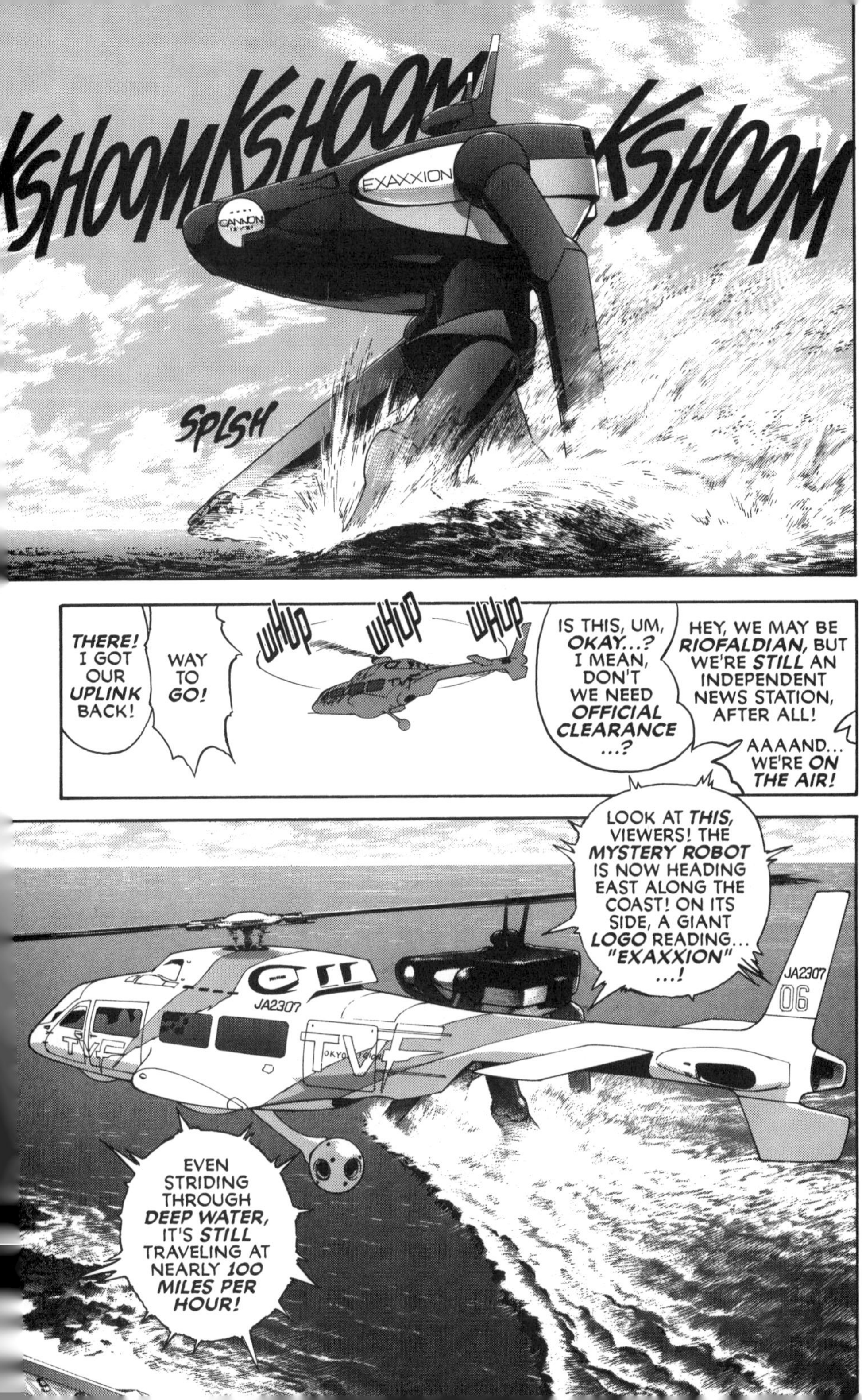
KSHOOM KSHOOM KSHOOM
EXAXXION
CANNON
SPLSH
THERE! I GOT OUR UPLINK BACK!
WAY TO GO!
WHUP WHUP WHUP
TVF
IS THIS, UM, OKAY...? I MEAN, DON'T WE NEED OFFICIAL CLEARANCE ...?
HEY, WE MAY BE RIOFALDIAN, BUT WE'RE STILL AN INDEPENDENT NEWS STATION, AFTER ALL!
AAAAND... WE'RE ON THE AIR!
LOOK AT THIS, VIEWERS! THE MYSTERY ROBOT IS NOW HEADING EAST ALONG THE COAST! ON ITS SIDE, A GIANT LOGO READING... "EXAXXION" ...!
JA2307
JA2307
06
TVF
EVEN STRIDING THROUGH DEEP WATER, IT'S STILL TRAVELING AT NEARLY 100 MILES PER HOUR!

IS A **BOY** REALLY CONTROLLING THIS ROBOT, JUST LIKE IN AN **ANIME** ...?

RUMOR HAS IT THAT ITS **PILOT** IS NONE OTHER THAN THAT NOW-INFAMOUS BLACK-SUITED TEENAGER, **HOICHI KANO!**

IN ANY EVENT, THIS **REAL-LIFE** GIANT ROBOT IS **ENORMOUS!**

IT'S KICKING UP **MASSIVE WAVES** EASILY THIRTY FEET HIGH!

NO, MAKE THAT **FIFTY FEET** HIGH!

RMBB RMBB RMBB RMBB RMBB

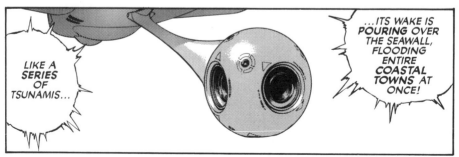

LIKE A **SERIES** OF **TSUNAMIS...**

...ITS WAKE IS **POURING OVER** THE SEAWALL, FLOODING ENTIRE **COASTAL TOWNS** AT ONCE!

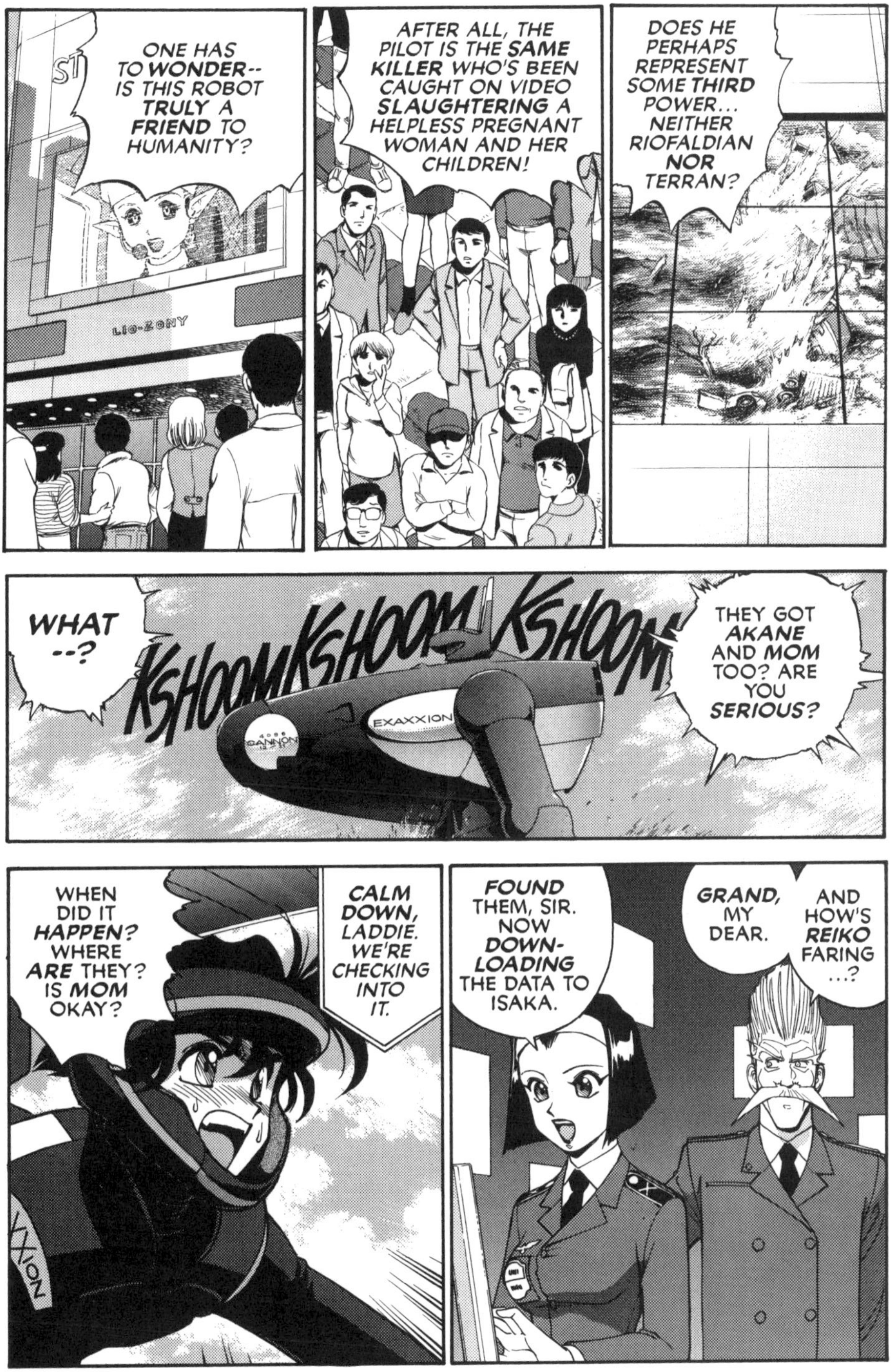
ONE HAS TO WONDER-- IS THIS ROBOT TRULY A FRIEND TO HUMANITY?
AFTER ALL, THE PILOT IS THE SAME KILLER WHO'S BEEN CAUGHT ON VIDEO SLAUGHTERING A HELPLESS PREGNANT WOMAN AND HER CHILDREN!
DOES HE PERHAPS REPRESENT SOME THIRD POWER... NEITHER RIOFALDIAN NOR TERRAN?
WHAT --?
KSHOOM KSHOOM KSHOOM
EXAXXION
THEY GOT AKANE AND MOM TOO? ARE YOU SERIOUS?
WHEN DID IT HAPPEN? WHERE ARE THEY? IS MOM OKAY?
CALM DOWN, LADDIE. WE'RE CHECKING INTO IT.
FOUND THEM, SIR. NOW DOWN-LOADING THE DATA TO ISAKA.
GRAND, MY DEAR.
AND HOW'S REIKO FARING ...?

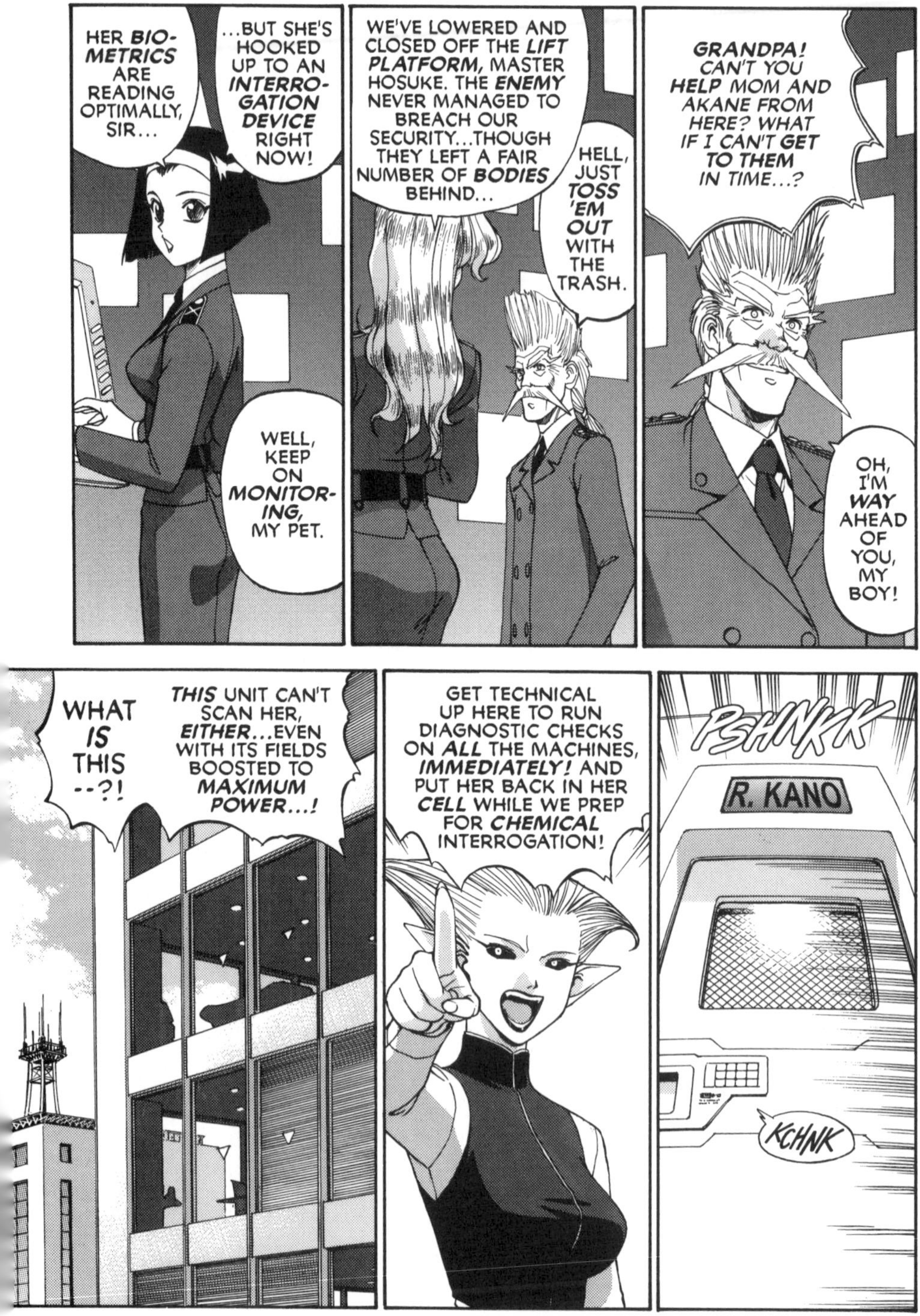
HER BIO-METRICS ARE READING OPTIMALLY, SIR...
...BUT SHE'S HOOKED UP TO AN INTERROGATION DEVICE RIGHT NOW!
WELL, KEEP ON MONITORING, MY PET.
WE'VE LOWERED AND CLOSED OFF THE LIFT PLATFORM, MASTER HOSUKE. THE ENEMY NEVER MANAGED TO BREACH OUR SECURITY...THOUGH THEY LEFT A FAIR NUMBER OF BODIES BEHIND...
HELL, JUST TOSS 'EM OUT WITH THE TRASH.
GRANDPA! CAN'T YOU HELP MOM AND AKANE FROM HERE? WHAT IF I CAN'T GET TO THEM IN TIME...?
OH, I'M WAY AHEAD OF YOU, MY BOY!
WHAT IS THIS--?!
THIS UNIT CAN'T SCAN HER, EITHER...EVEN WITH ITS FIELDS BOOSTED TO MAXIMUM POWER...!
GET TECHNICAL UP HERE TO RUN DIAGNOSTIC CHECKS ON ALL THE MACHINES, IMMEDIATELY! AND PUT HER BACK IN HER CELL WHILE WE PREP FOR CHEMICAL INTERROGATION!
PSHNKK
R. KANO
KCHNK

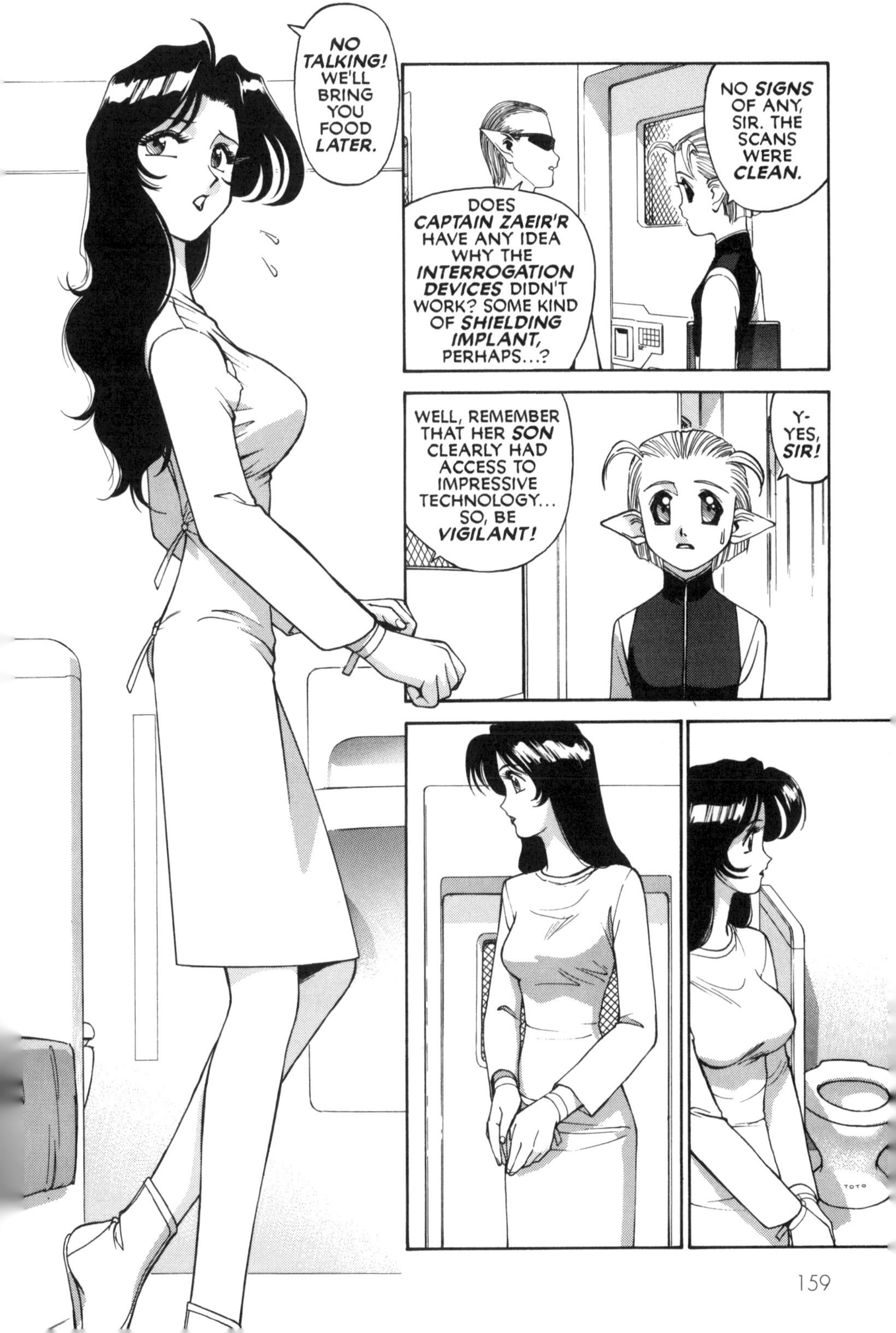
NO TALKING! WE'LL BRING YOU FOOD LATER.
DOES CAPTAIN ZAEIR'R HAVE ANY IDEA WHY THE INTERROGATION DEVICES DIDN'T WORK? SOME KIND OF SHIELDING IMPLANT, PERHAPS...?
NO SIGNS OF ANY, SIR. THE SCANS WERE CLEAN.
WELL, REMEMBER THAT HER SON CLEARLY HAD ACCESS TO IMPRESSIVE TECHNOLOGY... SO, BE VIGILANT!
Y-YES, SIR!
TOTO

THE GIANT ROBOT HAS MOVED *FARTHER OFFSHORE,* BUT IS STILL HEADING STRAIGHT FOR *TOKYO.*

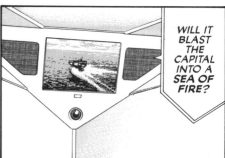

WILL IT BLAST THE CAPITAL INTO A SEA OF FIRE?

HMPH ...!

BREEP

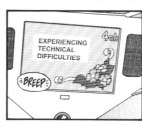

EXPERIENCING TECHNICAL DIFFICULTIES

4ch

BREEP

SIGNAL INACCESSIBLE

6ch

BREEP

DARN... I CAN ONLY GET *THEIR* MEDIA CHANNELS.

BIP OFF.

.....

.....

AND THERE'S NOT MUCH *THERE* EITHER...

FWHIP

YOUR REPORTER TONIGHT IS *AKANE HINO!*

I'M BROADCASTING FROM INSIDE A *RIOFALDIAN DETENTION CENTER.*

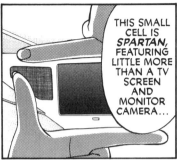

THIS SMALL CELL IS *SPARTAN,* FEATURING LITTLE MORE THAN A TV SCREEN AND MONITOR CAMERA...

...A TOILET... A SINK...

...AND A BUNK.

HERE, WE SEE A SMALL SHUTTER FOR ADMITTING *FOOD TRAYS,* SET IN THE STURDY METAL OF THE DOOR.

THIS IS MORE AKIN TO A PRISON'S *SOLITARY CONFINEMENT CELL* THAN SO-CALLED *"DETENTION QUARTERS,"* AS THE RIOFALDIANS LABEL IT.

AS WE SEE, THE RIOFALDIANS CAN SEIZE EVEN A *HARMLESS SCHOOL-GIRL* SUCH AS MYSELF...

...AND *INCARCERATE* HER WITHOUT EVER FILING CHARGES!

HOW MANY MORE *INNOCENT CITIZENS* WILL THEY IMPRISON HERE, LIKE THE *SECRET POLICE* OF OLD?

CLEARLY, RIOFALD'S MILITARY MIGHT IS *FORMIDABLE* INDEED...

...SO, SHOULD HUMANITY GIVE IN TO *DESPAIR?*

NO!

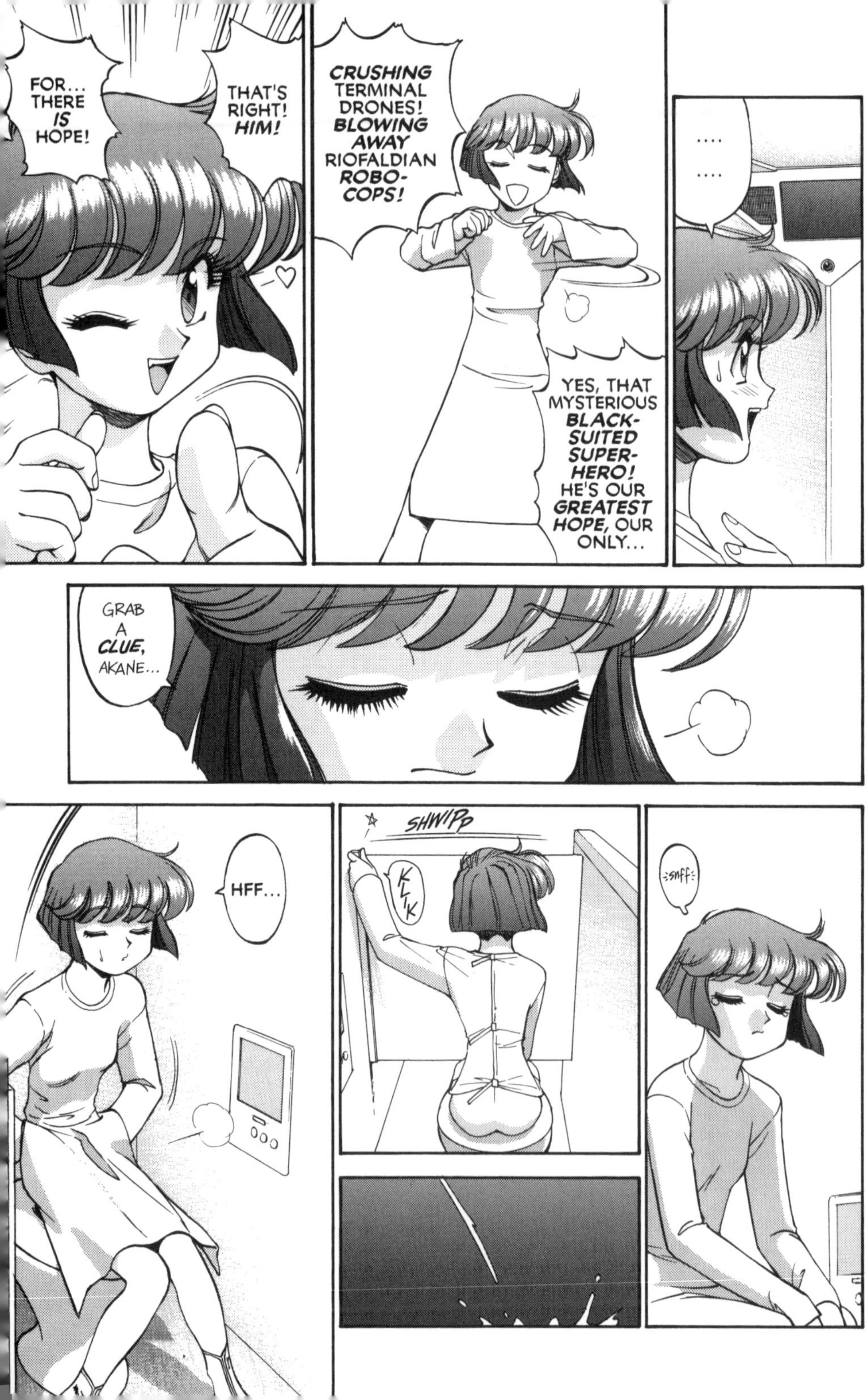
FOR... THERE IS HOPE!
THAT'S RIGHT! HIM!
CRUSHING TERMINAL DRONES! BLOWING AWAY RIOFALDIAN ROBO-COPS!
YES, THAT MYSTERIOUS BLACK-SUITED SUPER-HERO! HE'S OUR GREATEST HOPE, OUR ONLY...
....
....
GRAB A CLUE, AKANE...
HFF...
SHWIPP
KLIK
snff

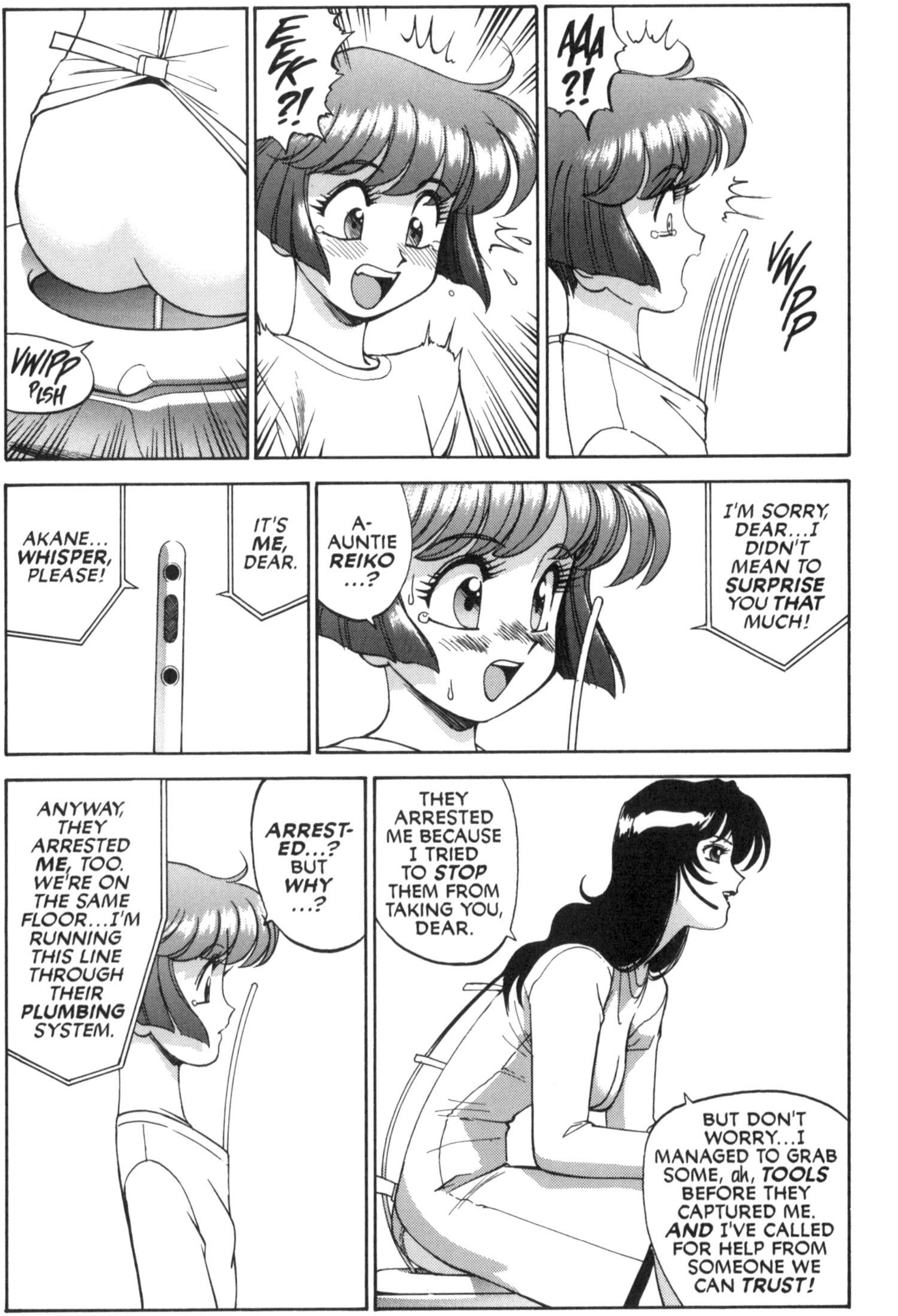
VWIPP
PLSH
EEK?!
AAA?!
VWIPP
AKANE... WHISPER, PLEASE!
IT'S ME, DEAR.
A-AUNTIE REIKO...?
I'M SORRY, DEAR...I DIDN'T MEAN TO SURPRISE YOU THAT MUCH!
ANYWAY, THEY ARRESTED ME, TOO. WE'RE ON THE SAME FLOOR...I'M RUNNING THIS LINE THROUGH THEIR PLUMBING SYSTEM.
ARREST-ED...? BUT WHY...?
THEY ARRESTED ME BECAUSE I TRIED TO STOP THEM FROM TAKING YOU, DEAR.
BUT DON'T WORRY...I MANAGED TO GRAB SOME, ah, TOOLS BEFORE THEY CAPTURED ME. AND I'VE CALLED FOR HELP FROM SOMEONE WE CAN TRUST!

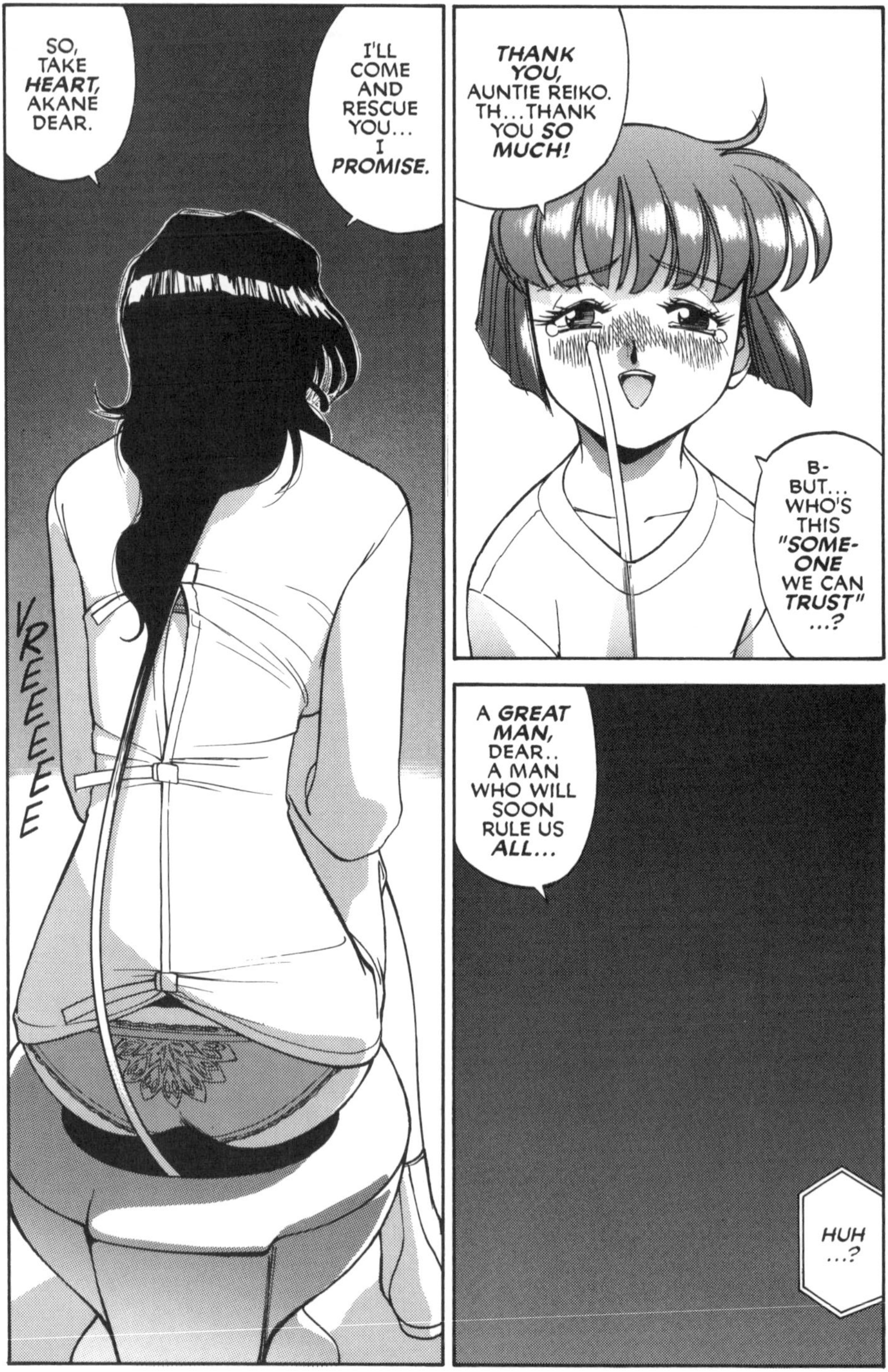
SO, TAKE HEART, AKANE DEAR.
I'LL COME AND RESCUE YOU... I PROMISE.
VREEEEEE
THANK YOU, AUNTIE REIKO. TH...THANK YOU SO MUCH!
B-BUT... WHO'S THIS "SOME-ONE WE CAN TRUST"...?
A GREAT MAN, DEAR.. A MAN WHO WILL SOON RULE US ALL...
HUH...?

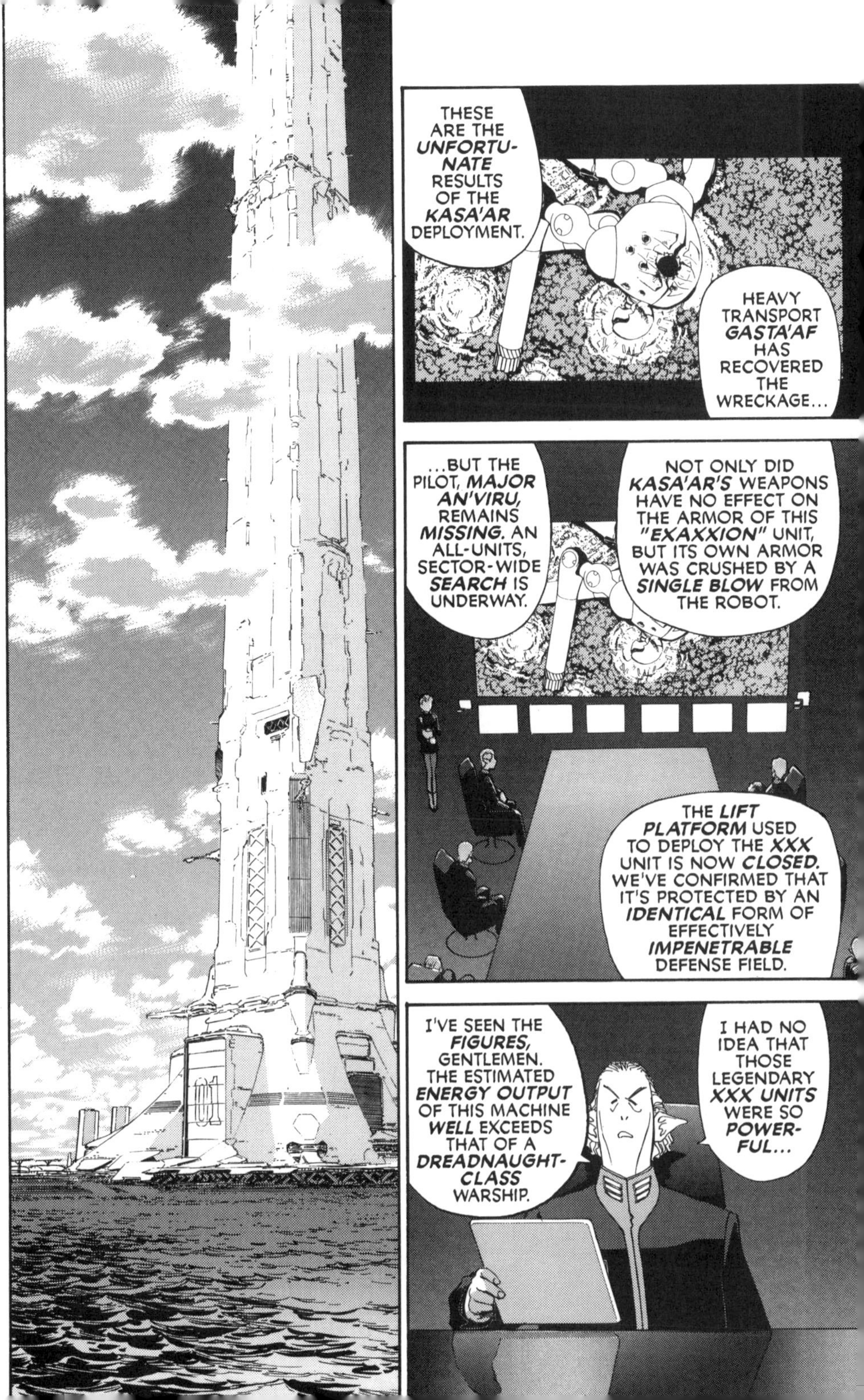
THESE ARE THE UNFORTUNATE RESULTS OF THE KASA'AR DEPLOYMENT.
HEAVY TRANSPORT GASTA'AF HAS RECOVERED THE WRECKAGE...
...BUT THE PILOT, MAJOR AN'VIRU, REMAINS MISSING. AN ALL-UNITS, SECTOR-WIDE SEARCH IS UNDERWAY.
NOT ONLY DID KASA'AR'S WEAPONS HAVE NO EFFECT ON THE ARMOR OF THIS "EXAXXION" UNIT, BUT ITS OWN ARMOR WAS CRUSHED BY A SINGLE BLOW FROM THE ROBOT.
THE LIFT PLATFORM USED TO DEPLOY THE XXX UNIT IS NOW CLOSED. WE'VE CONFIRMED THAT IT'S PROTECTED BY AN IDENTICAL FORM OF EFFECTIVELY IMPENETRABLE DEFENSE FIELD.
I'VE SEEN THE FIGURES, GENTLEMEN. THE ESTIMATED ENERGY OUTPUT OF THIS MACHINE WELL EXCEEDS THAT OF A DREADNAUGHT-CLASS WARSHIP.
I HAD NO IDEA THAT THOSE LEGENDARY XXX UNITS WERE SO POWERFUL...

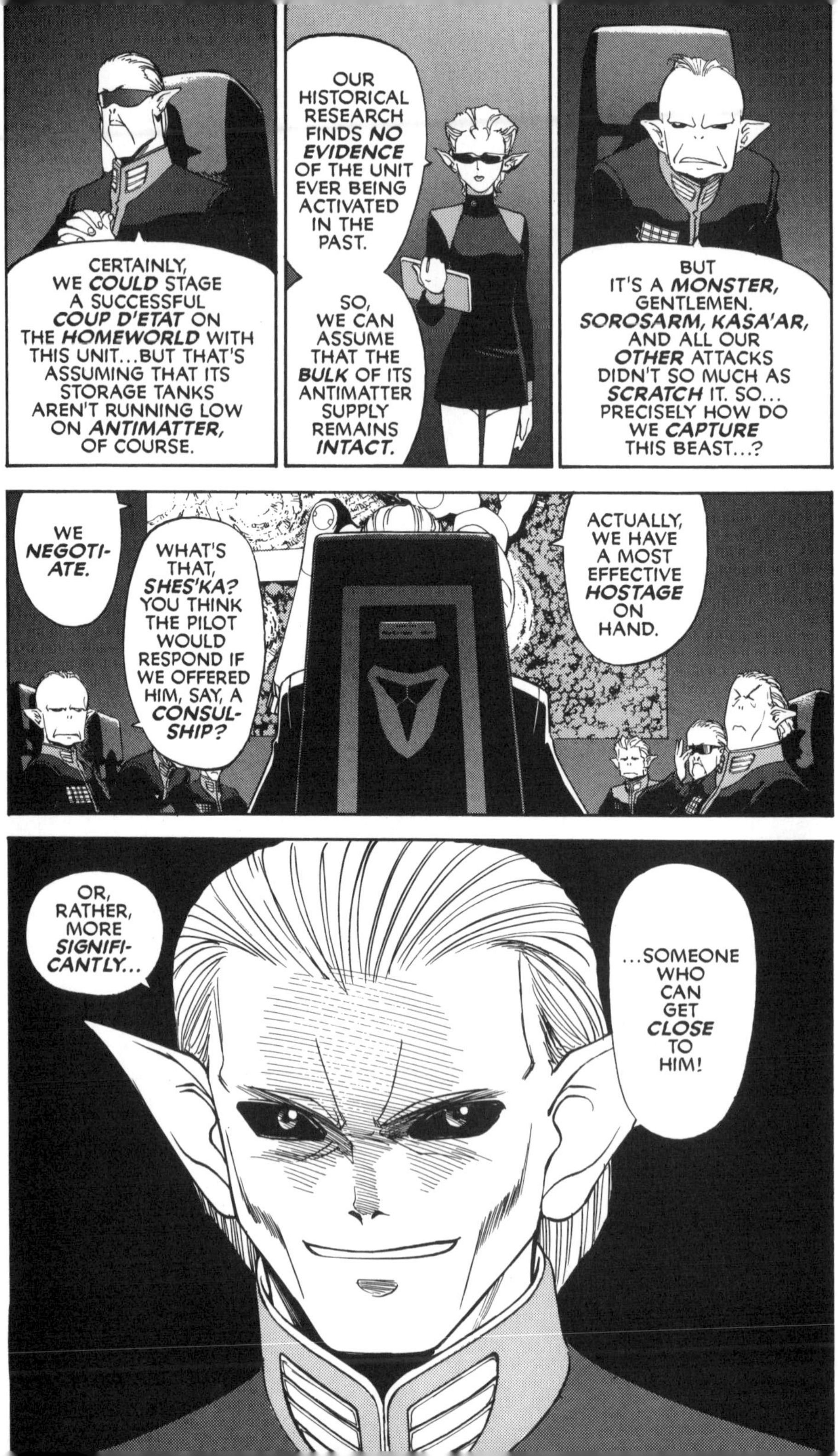
CERTAINLY, WE COULD STAGE A SUCCESSFUL COUP D'ETAT ON THE HOMEWORLD WITH THIS UNIT...BUT THAT'S ASSUMING THAT ITS STORAGE TANKS AREN'T RUNNING LOW ON ANTIMATTER, OF COURSE.
OUR HISTORICAL RESEARCH FINDS NO EVIDENCE OF THE UNIT EVER BEING ACTIVATED IN THE PAST.
SO, WE CAN ASSUME THAT THE BULK OF ITS ANTIMATTER SUPPLY REMAINS INTACT.
BUT IT'S A MONSTER, GENTLEMEN. SOROSARM, KASA'AR, AND ALL OUR OTHER ATTACKS DIDN'T SO MUCH AS SCRATCH IT. SO... PRECISELY HOW DO WE CAPTURE THIS BEAST...?
WE NEGOTI-ATE.
WHAT'S THAT, SHES'KA? YOU THINK THE PILOT WOULD RESPOND IF WE OFFERED HIM, SAY, A CONSUL-SHIP?
ACTUALLY, WE HAVE A MOST EFFECTIVE HOSTAGE ON HAND.
OR, RATHER, MORE SIGNIFI-CANTLY...
...SOMEONE WHO CAN GET CLOSE TO HIM!

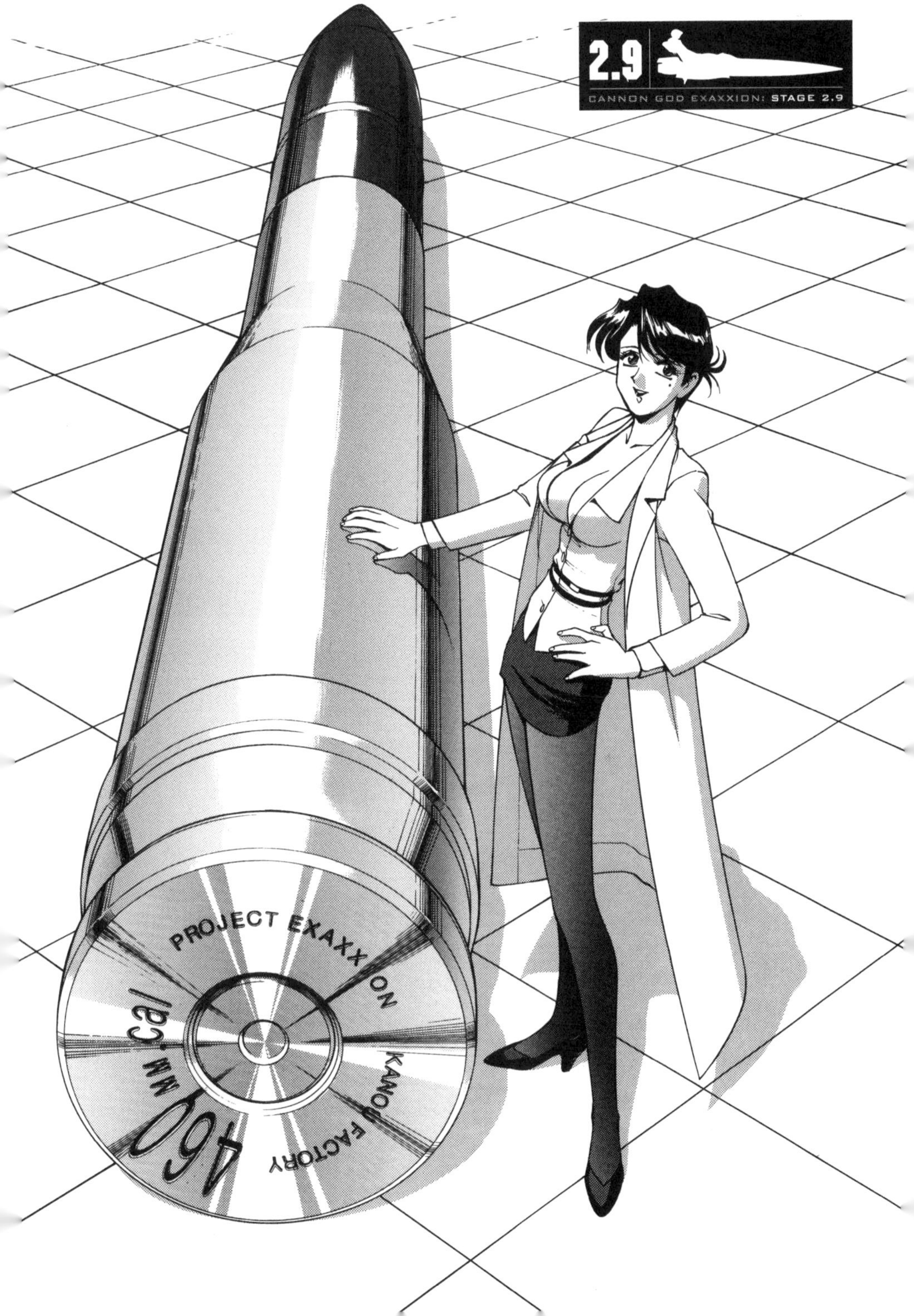
2.9
CANNON GOD EXAXXION: STAGE 2.9
PROJECT EXAXX ON
KANO FACTORY
460 mm cal

A *HOSTAGE?* WHO WOULD ABANDON SUCH AN *AMAZING* WEAPON SYSTEM FOR THE SAKE OF A MERE *HOSTAGE...?*

ALL WE NEED IS TO *BUY SOME TIME,* GENTLEMEN.

IF *ENERGY* WEAPONS WON'T WORK, THAT MEANS *INERTIAL CONTROL* WARFARE, USING *MASS*-BASED WEAPONS.

THE ISSUE AT HAND, HERE, IS THE *PEAK ENERGY OUTPUT CURVE.*

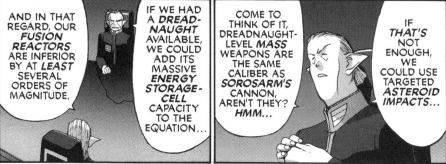

AND IN THAT REGARD, OUR *FUSION REACTORS* ARE INFERIOR BY AT *LEAST* SEVERAL ORDERS OF MAGNITUDE.

IF WE HAD A *DREAD-NAUGHT* AVAILABLE, WE COULD ADD ITS MASSIVE *ENERGY STORAGE-CELL* CAPACITY TO THE EQUATION...

COME TO THINK OF IT, DREADNAUGHT-LEVEL *MASS* WEAPONS ARE THE SAME CALIBER AS *SOROSARM'S* CANNON, AREN'T THEY? *HMM...*

IF *THAT'S* NOT ENOUGH, WE COULD USE TARGETED *ASTEROID IMPACTS...*

CONSIDERING THE SUBSTANTIAL *FUTURE INTERESTS* AT STAKE, HERE, WE SHOULDN'T EMPLOY A *SLEDGEHAMMER,* GENTLEMEN. WRECKING THIS PLANET *ISN'T* TO OUR ADVANTAGE.

I RECOMMEND THAT WE *RECON-FIGURE* A DREAD-NAUGHT'S *MAIN CANNON.*

EVEN WHILE *RETAINING* THE EXISTING CALIBER, WE CAN VASTLY INCREASE *ENERGY TRANSFER* AT IMPACT WITH A LONGER BARREL AND MORE POWERFUL ROUND.

THIS *RECON-FIGURATION* COULD BE ACCOM-PLISHED IN LESS THAN A WEEK.

SPLENDID. I'LL AUTHORIZE THAT *IMMEDI-ATELY...*

...BUT AS A *FALL-BACK* OPTION.

A *FALL-BACK* OPTION...?

WHAT, THEN, IS YOUR *PRIMARY* OPTION?

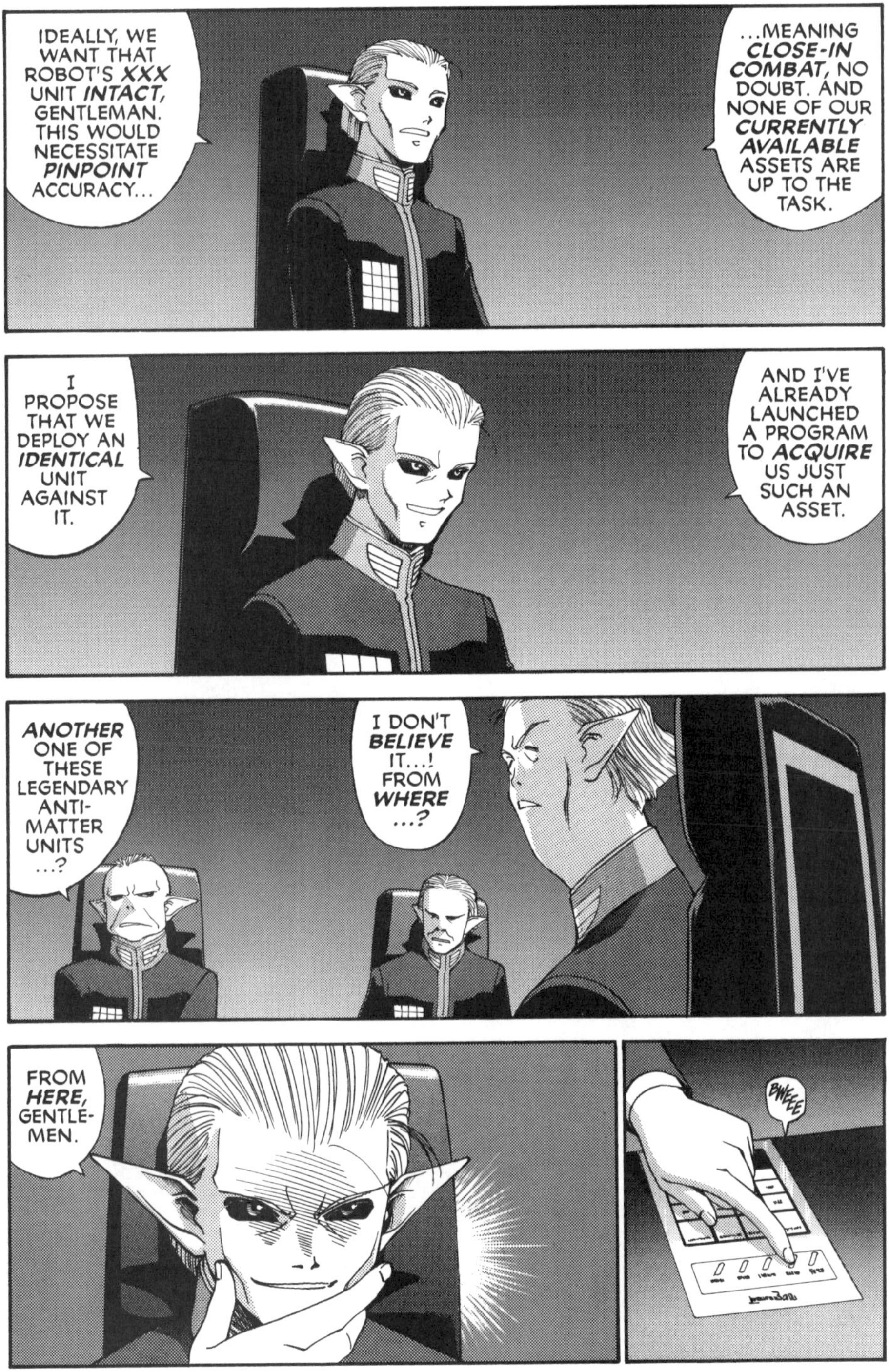
IDEALLY, WE WANT THAT ROBOT'S XXX UNIT INTACT, GENTLEMAN. THIS WOULD NECESSITATE PINPOINT ACCURACY...
...MEANING CLOSE-IN COMBAT, NO DOUBT. AND NONE OF OUR CURRENTLY AVAILABLE ASSETS ARE UP TO THE TASK.
I PROPOSE THAT WE DEPLOY AN IDENTICAL UNIT AGAINST IT.
AND I'VE ALREADY LAUNCHED A PROGRAM TO ACQUIRE US JUST SUCH AN ASSET.
ANOTHER ONE OF THESE LEGENDARY ANTI-MATTER UNITS ...?
I DON'T BELIEVE IT...! FROM WHERE ...?
FROM HERE, GENTLE-MEN.
BWEEE

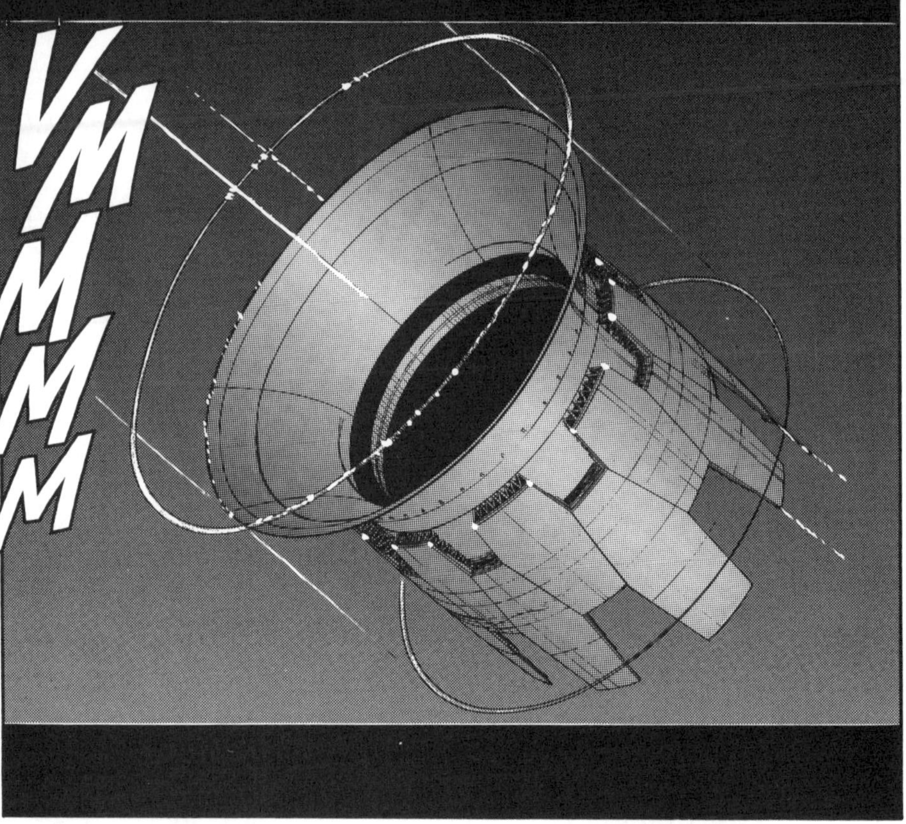
VMMMM

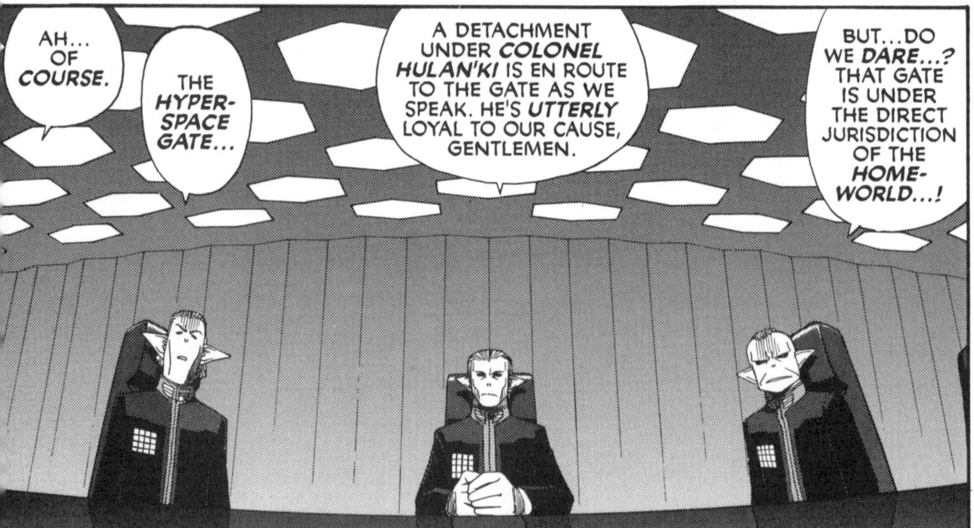
AH... OF COURSE.
THE HYPER-SPACE GATE...
A DETACHMENT UNDER COLONEL HULAN'KI IS EN ROUTE TO THE GATE AS WE SPEAK. HE'S UTTERLY LOYAL TO OUR CAUSE, GENTLEMEN.
BUT...DO WE DARE...? THAT GATE IS UNDER THE DIRECT JURISDICTION OF THE HOME-WORLD...!

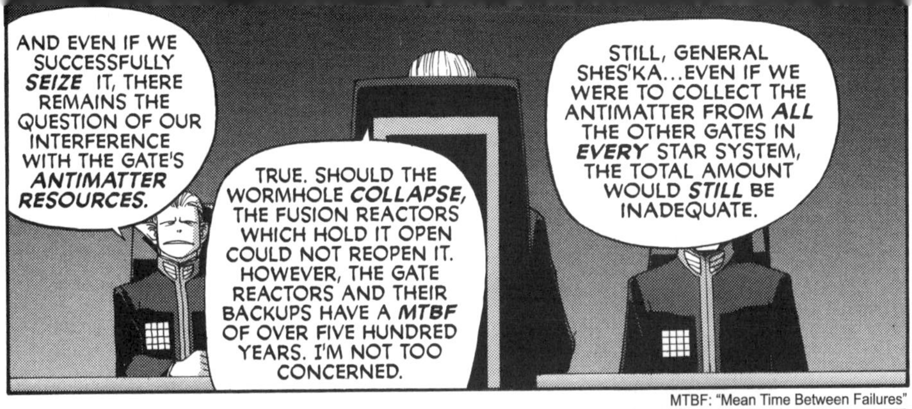
AND EVEN IF WE SUCCESSFULLY *SEIZE* IT, THERE REMAINS THE QUESTION OF OUR INTERFERENCE WITH THE GATE'S *ANTIMATTER RESOURCES.*
TRUE. SHOULD THE WORMHOLE *COLLAPSE,* THE FUSION REACTORS WHICH HOLD IT OPEN COULD NOT REOPEN IT. HOWEVER, THE GATE REACTORS AND THEIR BACKUPS HAVE A *MTBF* OF OVER FIVE HUNDRED YEARS. I'M NOT TOO CONCERNED.
STILL, GENERAL SHES'KA...EVEN IF WE WERE TO COLLECT THE ANTIMATTER FROM *ALL* THE OTHER GATES IN *EVERY* STAR SYSTEM, THE TOTAL AMOUNT WOULD *STILL* BE INADEQUATE.

MTBF: "Mean Time Between Failures"

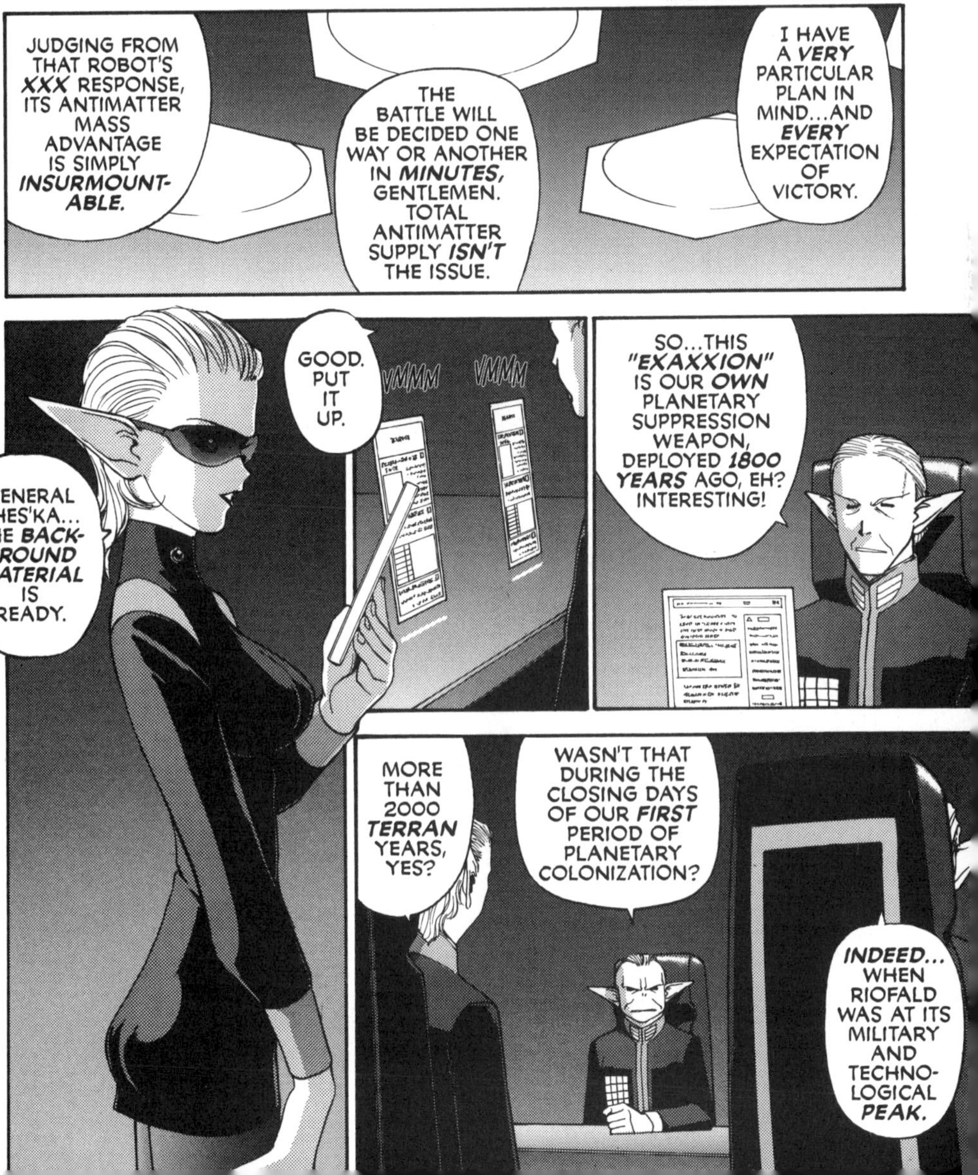
JUDGING FROM THAT ROBOT'S *XXX* RESPONSE, ITS ANTIMATTER MASS ADVANTAGE IS SIMPLY *INSURMOUNT-ABLE.*
THE BATTLE WILL BE DECIDED ONE WAY OR ANOTHER IN *MINUTES,* GENTLEMEN. TOTAL ANTIMATTER SUPPLY *ISN'T* THE ISSUE.
I HAVE A *VERY* PARTICULAR PLAN IN MIND...AND *EVERY* EXPECTATION OF VICTORY.
GENERAL SHES'KA... THE *BACK-GROUND MATERIAL* IS READY.
GOOD. PUT IT UP.
VMMM
VMMM
SO...THIS *"EXAXXION"* IS OUR *OWN* PLANETARY SUPPRESSION WEAPON, DEPLOYED *1800 YEARS* AGO, EH? INTERESTING!
MORE THAN 2000 *TERRAN* YEARS, YES?
WASN'T THAT DURING THE CLOSING DAYS OF OUR *FIRST* PERIOD OF PLANETARY COLONIZATION?
INDEED... WHEN RIOFALD WAS AT ITS MILITARY AND TECHNO-LOGICAL *PEAK.*

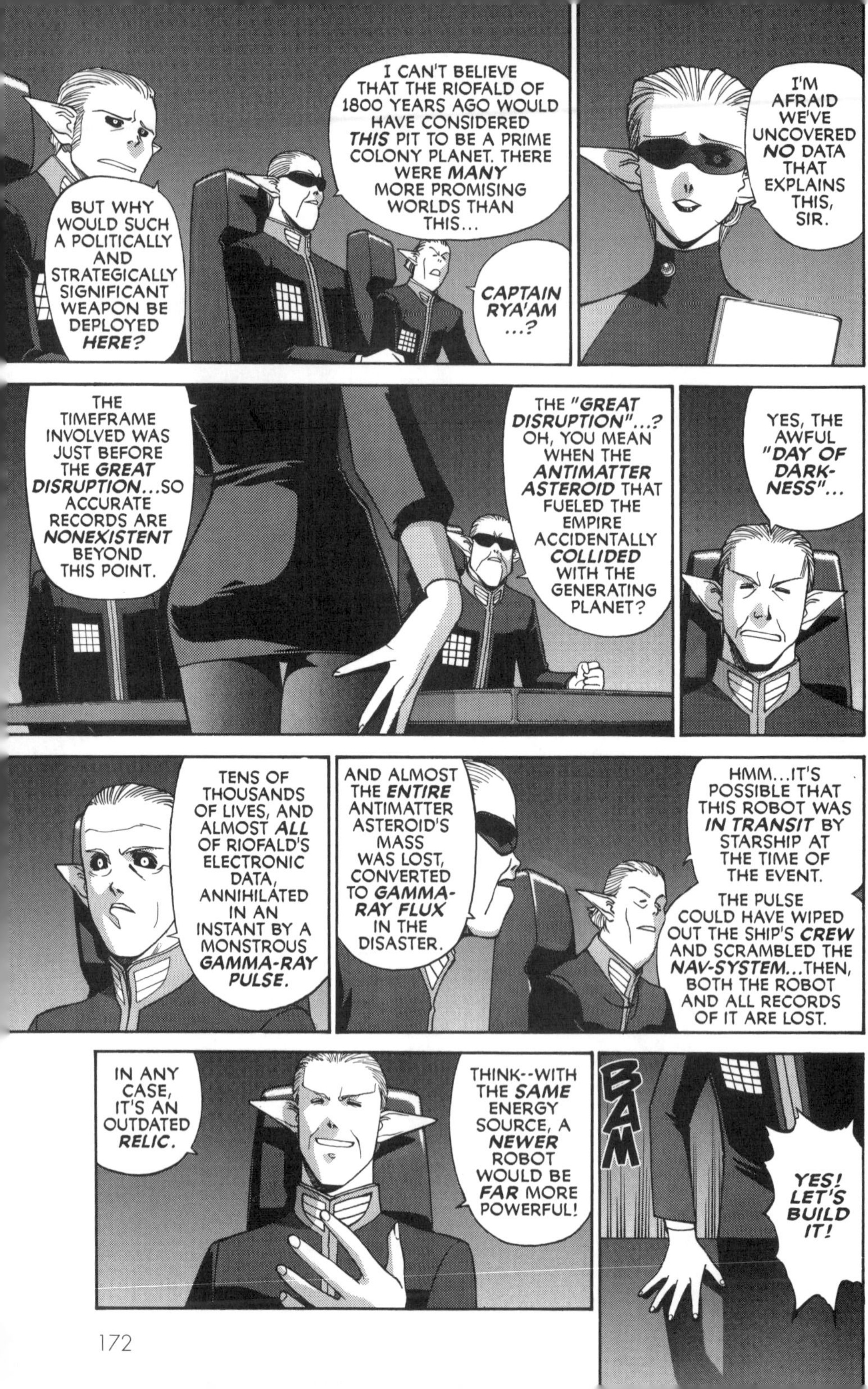
I CAN'T BELIEVE THAT THE RIOFALD OF 1800 YEARS AGO WOULD HAVE CONSIDERED THIS PIT TO BE A PRIME COLONY PLANET. THERE WERE MANY MORE PROMISING WORLDS THAN THIS...
BUT WHY WOULD SUCH A POLITICALLY AND STRATEGICALLY SIGNIFICANT WEAPON BE DEPLOYED HERE?
CAPTAIN RYA'AM ...?
I'M AFRAID WE'VE UNCOVERED NO DATA THAT EXPLAINS THIS, SIR.
THE TIMEFRAME INVOLVED WAS JUST BEFORE THE GREAT DISRUPTION...SO ACCURATE RECORDS ARE NONEXISTENT BEYOND THIS POINT.
THE "GREAT DISRUPTION"...? OH, YOU MEAN WHEN THE ANTIMATTER ASTEROID THAT FUELED THE EMPIRE ACCIDENTALLY COLLIDED WITH THE GENERATING PLANET?
YES, THE AWFUL "DAY OF DARK-NESS"...
TENS OF THOUSANDS OF LIVES, AND ALMOST ALL OF RIOFALD'S ELECTRONIC DATA, ANNIHILATED IN AN INSTANT BY A MONSTROUS GAMMA-RAY PULSE.
AND ALMOST THE ENTIRE ANTIMATTER ASTEROID'S MASS WAS LOST, CONVERTED TO GAMMA-RAY FLUX IN THE DISASTER.
HMM...IT'S POSSIBLE THAT THIS ROBOT WAS IN TRANSIT BY STARSHIP AT THE TIME OF THE EVENT.
THE PULSE COULD HAVE WIPED OUT THE SHIP'S CREW AND SCRAMBLED THE NAV-SYSTEM...THEN, BOTH THE ROBOT AND ALL RECORDS OF IT ARE LOST.
IN ANY CASE, IT'S AN OUTDATED RELIC.
THINK--WITH THE SAME ENERGY SOURCE, A NEWER ROBOT WOULD BE FAR MORE POWERFUL!
BAM
YES! LET'S BUILD IT!

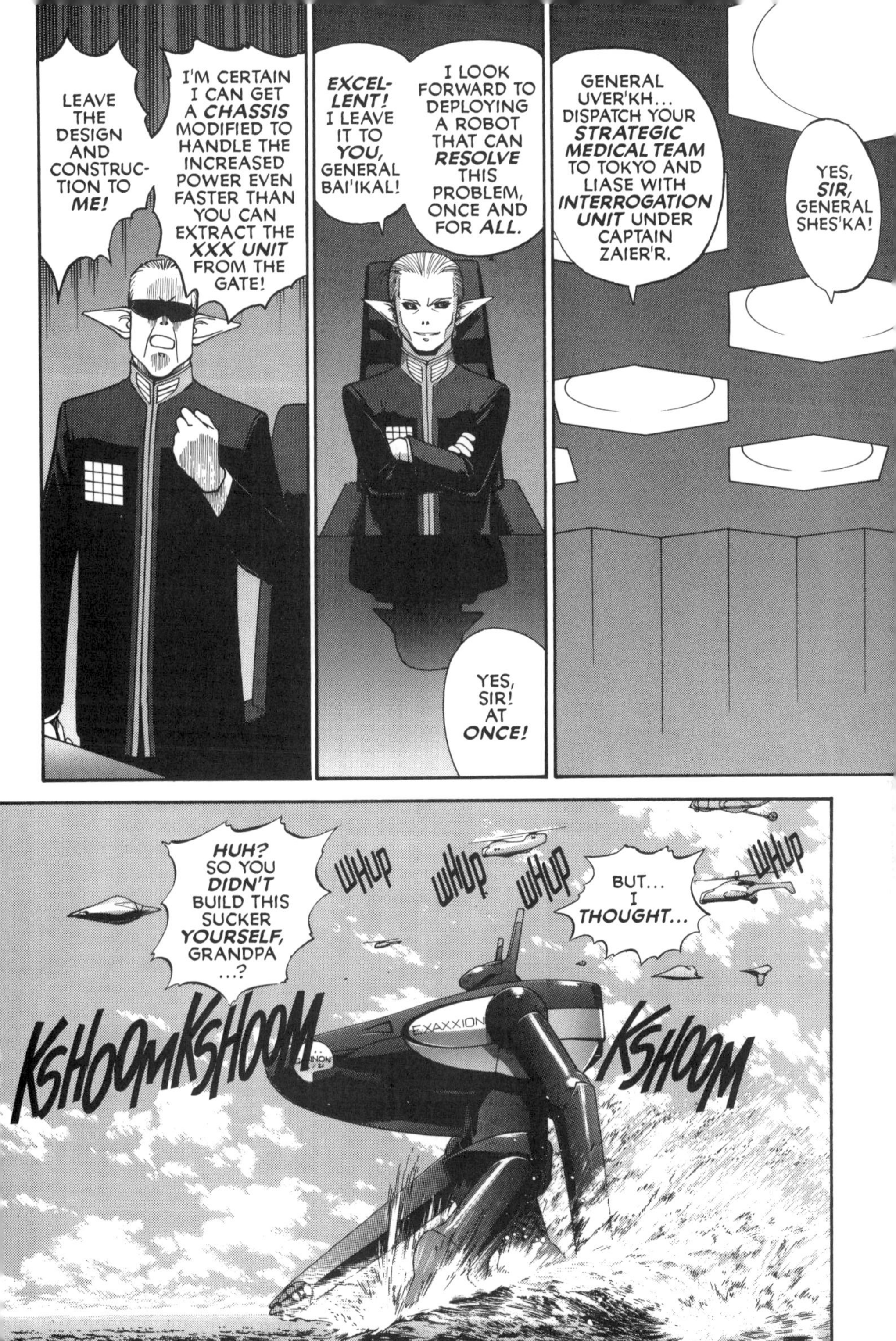

LEAVE THE DESIGN AND CONSTRUCTION TO *ME!*
I'M CERTAIN I CAN GET A *CHASSIS* MODIFIED TO HANDLE THE INCREASED POWER EVEN FASTER THAN YOU CAN EXTRACT THE *XXX UNIT* FROM THE GATE!
EXCELLENT! I LEAVE IT TO *YOU,* GENERAL BAI'IKAL!
I LOOK FORWARD TO DEPLOYING A ROBOT THAT CAN *RESOLVE* THIS PROBLEM, ONCE AND FOR *ALL.*
YES, SIR! AT *ONCE!*
GENERAL UVER'KH... DISPATCH YOUR *STRATEGIC MEDICAL TEAM* TO TOKYO AND LIASE WITH *INTERROGATION UNIT* UNDER CAPTAIN ZAIER'R.
YES, *SIR,* GENERAL SHES'KA!
HUH? SO YOU *DIDN'T* BUILD THIS SUCKER *YOURSELF,* GRANDPA ...?
WHUP
WHUP
WHUP
BUT... I *THOUGHT...*
WHUP
KSHOOMKSHOOM
EXAXXION
KSHOOM

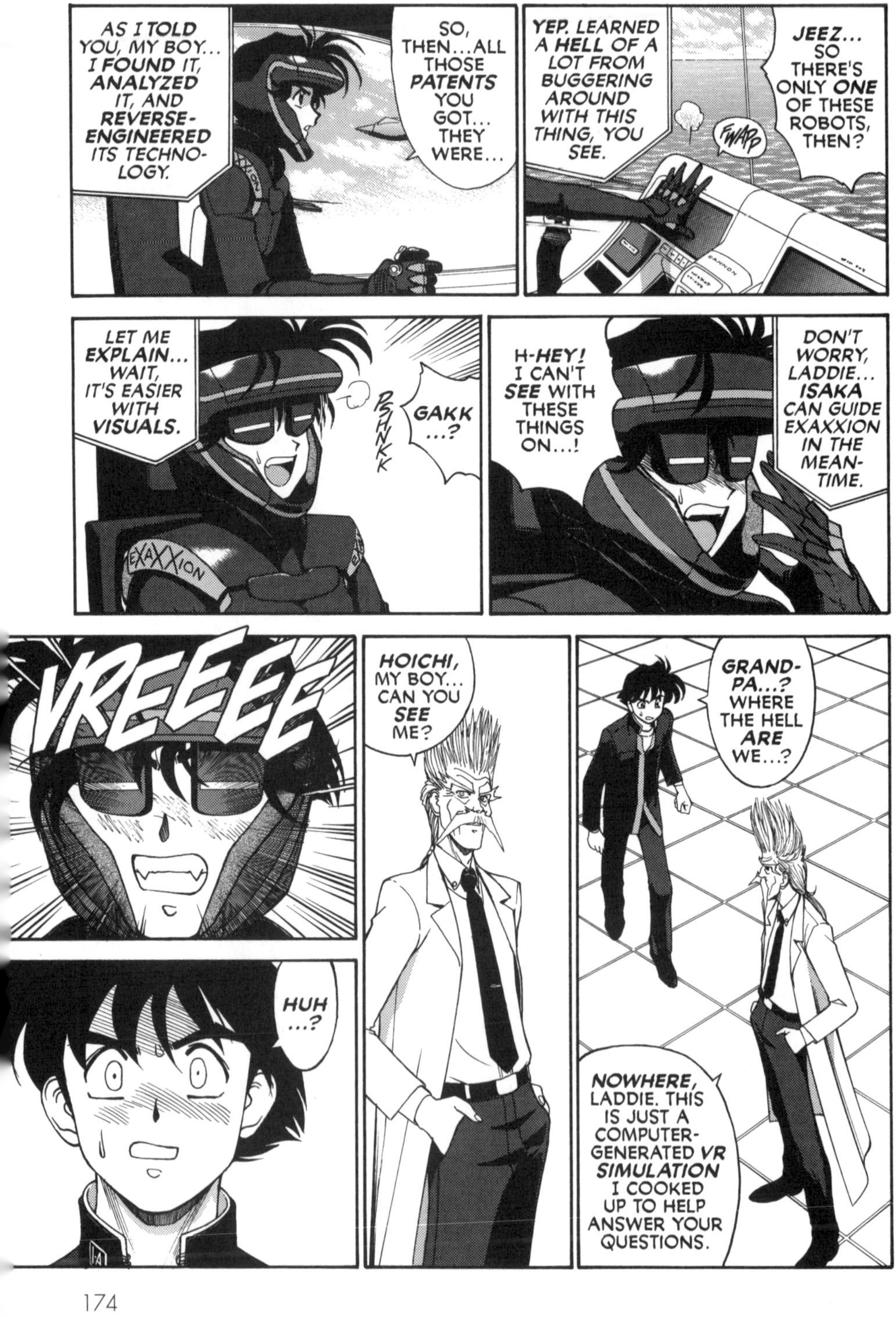
AS I TOLD YOU, MY BOY... I FOUND IT, ANALYZED IT, AND REVERSE-ENGINEERED ITS TECHNOLOGY.
SO, THEN...ALL THOSE PATENTS YOU GOT... THEY WERE...
YEP. LEARNED A HELL OF A LOT FROM BUGGERING AROUND WITH THIS THING, YOU SEE.
FWAPP
JEEZ... SO THERE'S ONLY ONE OF THESE ROBOTS, THEN?
LET ME EXPLAIN... WAIT, IT'S EASIER WITH VISUALS.
PSHNKK
GAKK...?
H-HEY! I CAN'T SEE WITH THESE THINGS ON...!
DON'T WORRY, LADDIE... ISAKA CAN GUIDE EXAXXION IN THE MEAN-TIME.
VREEEE
HUH...?
HOICHI, MY BOY... CAN YOU SEE ME?
GRAND-PA...? WHERE THE HELL ARE WE...?
NOWHERE, LADDIE. THIS IS JUST A COMPUTER-GENERATED VR SIMULATION I COOKED UP TO HELP ANSWER YOUR QUESTIONS.

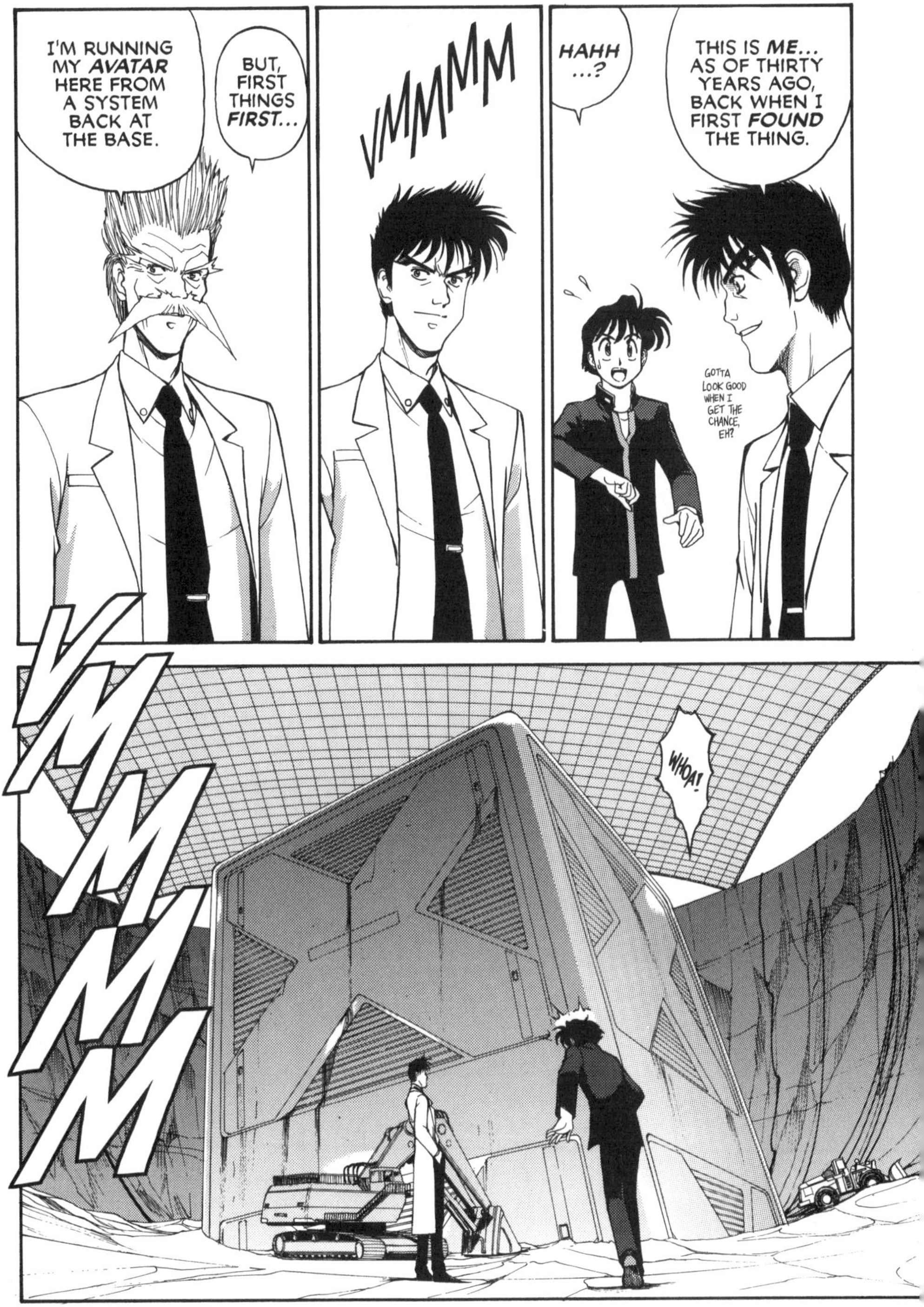
I'M RUNNING MY AVATAR HERE FROM A SYSTEM BACK AT THE BASE.
BUT, FIRST THINGS FIRST...
VMMMM
HAHH ...?
THIS IS ME... AS OF THIRTY YEARS AGO, BACK WHEN I FIRST FOUND THE THING.
GOTTA LOOK GOOD WHEN I GET THE CHANCE, EH?
VMMMMM
WHOA!

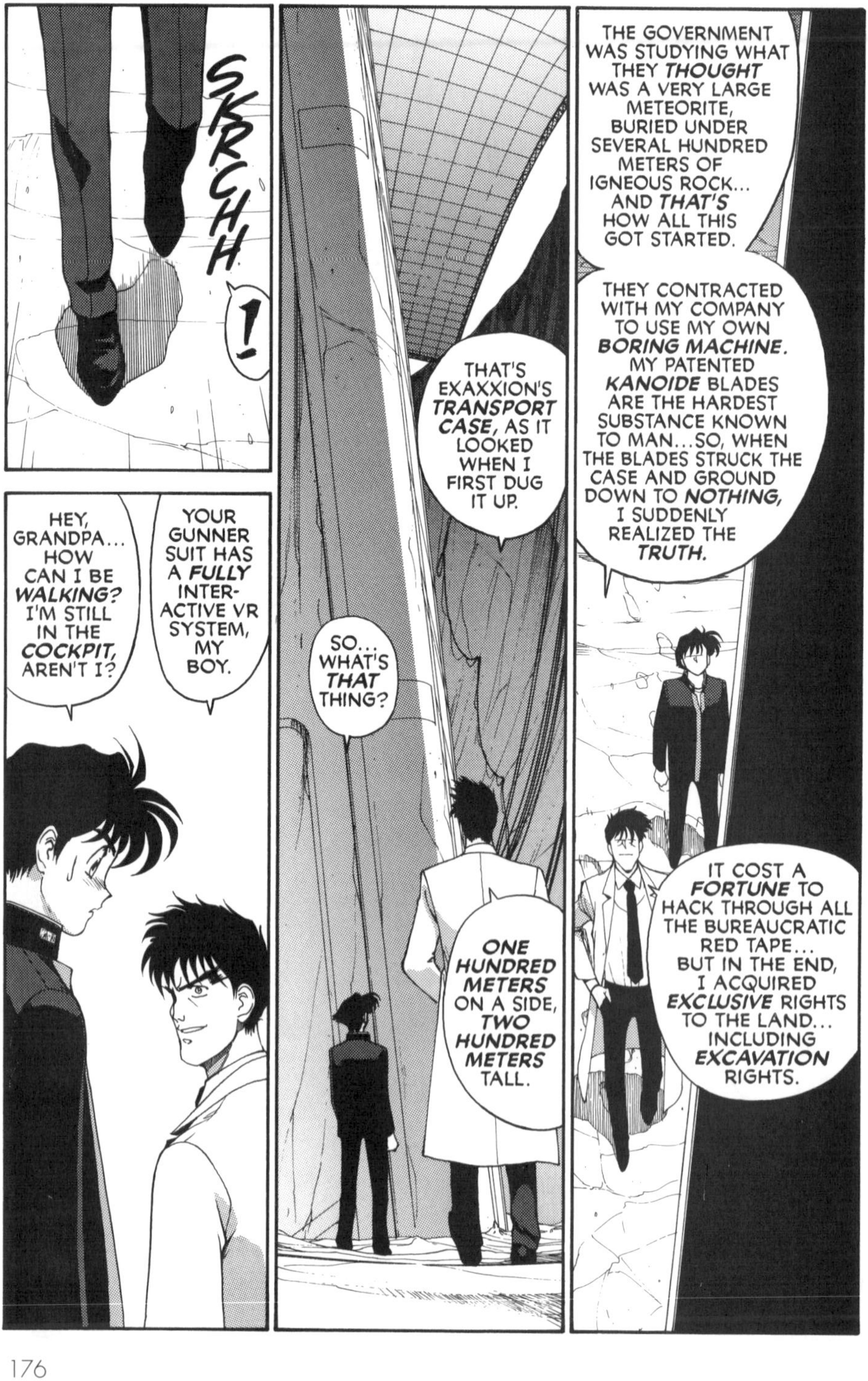
SKRCHH
!
HEY, GRANDPA... HOW CAN I BE WALKING? I'M STILL IN THE COCKPIT, AREN'T I?
YOUR GUNNER SUIT HAS A FULLY INTER-ACTIVE VR SYSTEM, MY BOY.
SO... WHAT'S THAT THING?
THAT'S EXAXXION'S TRANSPORT CASE, AS IT LOOKED WHEN I FIRST DUG IT UP.
ONE HUNDRED METERS ON A SIDE, TWO HUNDRED METERS TALL.
THE GOVERNMENT WAS STUDYING WHAT THEY THOUGHT WAS A VERY LARGE METEORITE, BURIED UNDER SEVERAL HUNDRED METERS OF IGNEOUS ROCK... AND THAT'S HOW ALL THIS GOT STARTED.
THEY CONTRACTED WITH MY COMPANY TO USE MY OWN BORING MACHINE. MY PATENTED KANOIDE BLADES ARE THE HARDEST SUBSTANCE KNOWN TO MAN...SO, WHEN THE BLADES STRUCK THE CASE AND GROUND DOWN TO NOTHING, I SUDDENLY REALIZED THE TRUTH.
IT COST A FORTUNE TO HACK THROUGH ALL THE BUREAUCRATIC RED TAPE... BUT IN THE END, I ACQUIRED EXCLUSIVE RIGHTS TO THE LAND... INCLUDING EXCAVATION RIGHTS.

OF COURSE, I HAD TO *BUY OFF* THE OLD FARTS IN THE MINISTRY WHO'D FIRST *ORDERED* THE STUDY...BUT THAT WAS A *CHEAP* INVESTMENT, IN THE LONG RUN.

I MADE THE MONEY BACK IN *NO TIME AT ALL.*

YOU KNOW, I DERIVED MORE THAN *TEN PATENTS* FROM THIS MAINTENANCE HATCH *ALONE!* WE'RE TALKING *REVOLUTION-ARY* NEW METALLURGY...

...AN ULTRA-SECURE *LOCKING SYSTEM*... AND A MAJOR ADVANCE IN *CHIP DESIGN!*

BLEW MY *MIND* WHEN THE LAB DATED THIS DAMN THING AT OVER *2000 YEARS OLD.* BUT THAT WAS *NOTHING,* COMPARED TO WHAT I LEARNED TEN YEARS AGO, WHEN THE *RIOFALDIANS* SHOWED UP--AND I REALIZED THAT THIS CRITTER WAS BUILT BY *THEM.*

WHA ....?

YOU MEAN... IT'S *THEIRS?!*

YEP! STILL DUNNO WHAT THE HELL IT WAS DOING *HERE*... BUT IT'S GOT *RIOFALDIAN SCRIPT* ALL OVER IT, DOESN'T IT?

BUT...DOESN'T THAT MEAN THAT THIS IS THEIR OWN *ANCIENT TECHNOLOGY?* 2000 YEARS OLD... H-HOLY SHIT!! THEY'LL *STOMP* US WITH THEIR *UP-TO-DATE* STUFF!!

IT'S NOT JUST A MATTER OF *TECHNO-LOGY,* HOICHI.

HEH...

I FOUND SOMETHING THAT THEY NO LONGER *POSSESS,* LADDIE.

UH... LIKE *WHAT* ...?

LIKE *THIS!*

WHDD

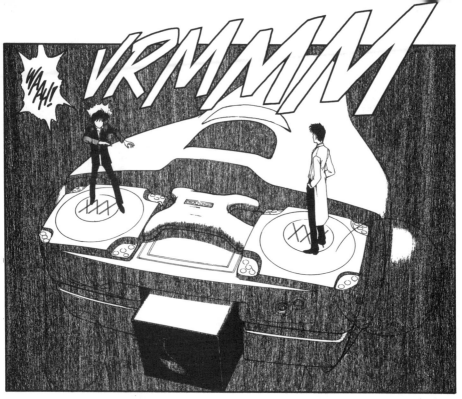

WAAH!

VRMMMM

IS THIS PART OF *EXAX-XION*...?

YEP, AS A NICE LI'L *1/8-SCALE CG* IMAGE, THE BETTER TO SHOW WHAT I'M TALKING ABOUT.

LEFT OFF ALL THE *EXTRANEOUS GADGETRY* FOR CLARITY'S SAKE...

WHAT WE'RE STANDING ON, HOICHI, IS AN *ANTIMATTER POWER PLANT.* IT CONVERTS MATTER-ANTIMATTER INTERACTIONS *DIRECTLY* INTO USEABLE ENERGY.

ANTI-MATTER...? WHAT, LIKE IN *SCIENCE FICTION*?

LIKE IN *REALITY,* LADDIE! IT'S A *DIRECT APPLICATION* OF OL' EINSTEIN'S $E=MC^2$!

AND THIS UNIT WAS STAMPED WITH A *SYSTEM NAME*...IN RIOFALDIAN, *"RA'UN META'AR,"* MEANING THREE META'AR, OR THESE *X*-LIKE SYMBOLS.

"META'AR" IS THE *FINAL LETTER* IN THEIR LANGUAGE, BY THE WAY... GIVING THIS SYMBOL SOMETHING OF THE MEANING *"ULTIMATE POWER."*

SO WHEN I HAD TO COME UP WITH A *NAME* FOR THIS PROJECT...

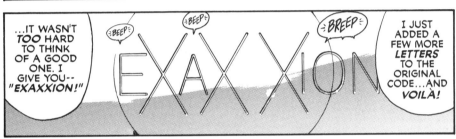

...IT WASN'T *TOO* HARD TO THINK OF A GOOD ONE. I GIVE YOU-- *"EXAXXION!"*

BEEP

BEEP

BREEP

EXAXXION

I JUST ADDED A FEW MORE *LETTERS* TO THE ORIGINAL CODE...AND *VOILÀ!*

IT'S BASED ON THE WORD *"EXACT,"* AS A VERB. AS IN, *"TO EXACT PUNISHMENT"*... *MASSIVE* PUNISHMENT! THAT'S WHAT IT'S *ALL* ABOUT, MY BOY.

AND NEEDLESS TO SAY, ALL THE BEST *GIANT ROBOTS* HAVE A NAME ENDING IN *"ON."*

IDEON, EVANGELION, GARON, VOLTRON, MEKTON, RAHXEPHON, IRON, DORAEMON, CREAM LEMON.

COOL, AIN'T IT? AND IT'S THE *ONLY ONE* OF ITS *KIND*, TOO!

HOW DO YOU *KNOW* THAT, GRANDPA? MAYBE THE 'FALDIES HAVE *TONS* OF ROBOTS LIKE THIS!

VRMMM

VRMMM

OH, BUT THEY *DON'T*, MASTER HOICHI.

!

HELLO. ♥ I'M *RYOKO TANEGASHIMA*, MASTER HOSUKE'S LEAD ASSISTANT.

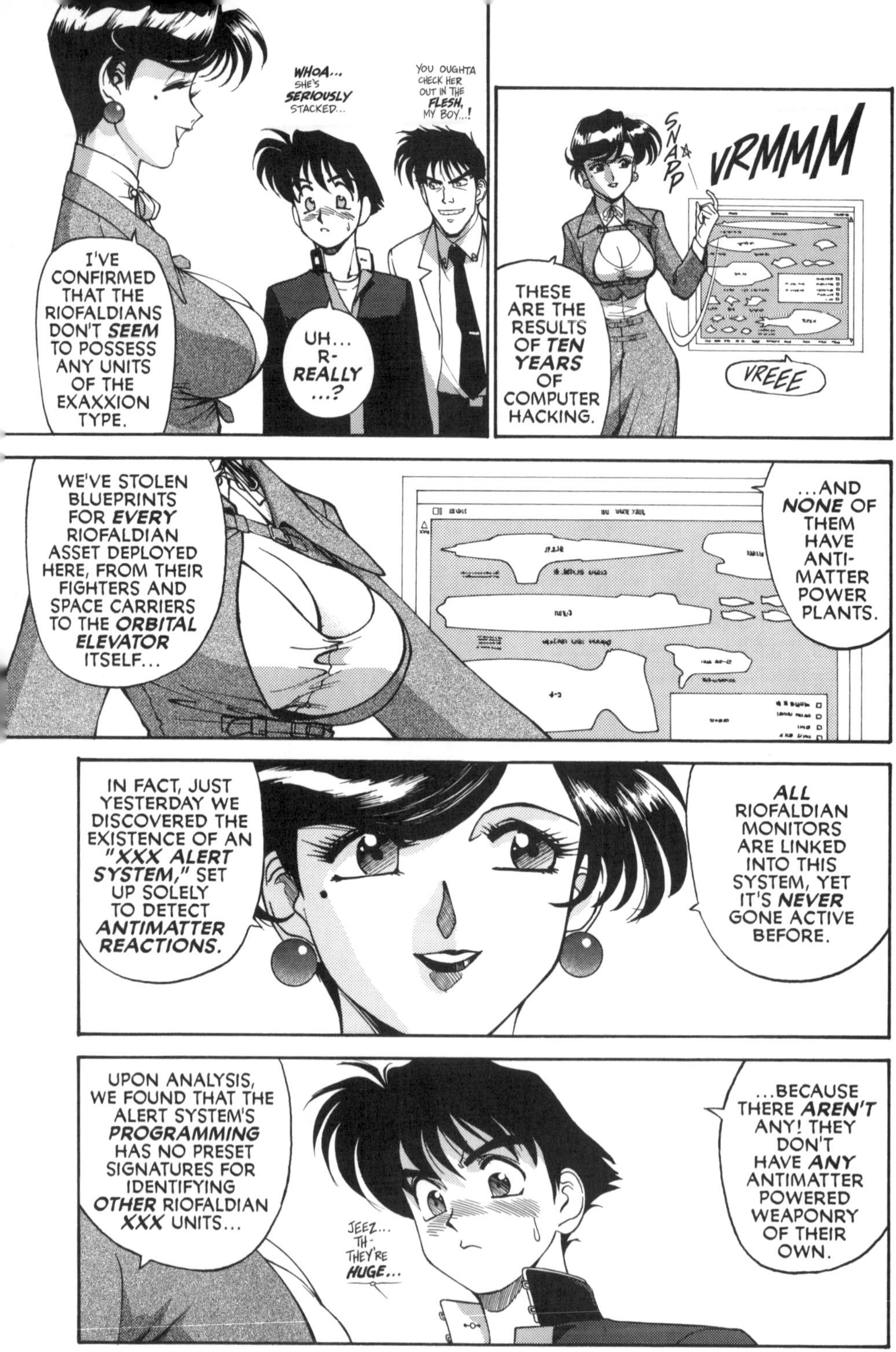
I'VE CONFIRMED THAT THE RIOFALDIANS DON'T SEEM TO POSSESS ANY UNITS OF THE EXAXXION TYPE.
WHOA... SHE'S SERIOUSLY STACKED...
YOU OUGHTA CHECK HER OUT IN THE FLESH, MY BOY...!
UH... R-REALLY...?
SNAPP
VRMMM
THESE ARE THE RESULTS OF TEN YEARS OF COMPUTER HACKING.
VREEE
WE'VE STOLEN BLUEPRINTS FOR EVERY RIOFALDIAN ASSET DEPLOYED HERE, FROM THEIR FIGHTERS AND SPACE CARRIERS TO THE ORBITAL ELEVATOR ITSELF...
...AND NONE OF THEM HAVE ANTI-MATTER POWER PLANTS.
IN FACT, JUST YESTERDAY WE DISCOVERED THE EXISTENCE OF AN "XXX ALERT SYSTEM," SET UP SOLELY TO DETECT ANTIMATTER REACTIONS.
ALL RIOFALDIAN MONITORS ARE LINKED INTO THIS SYSTEM, YET IT'S NEVER GONE ACTIVE BEFORE.
UPON ANALYSIS, WE FOUND THAT THE ALERT SYSTEM'S PROGRAMMING HAS NO PRESET SIGNATURES FOR IDENTIFYING OTHER RIOFALDIAN XXX UNITS...
JEEZ... TH-THEY'RE HUGE...
...BECAUSE THERE AREN'T ANY! THEY DON'T HAVE ANY ANTIMATTER POWERED WEAPONRY OF THEIR OWN.

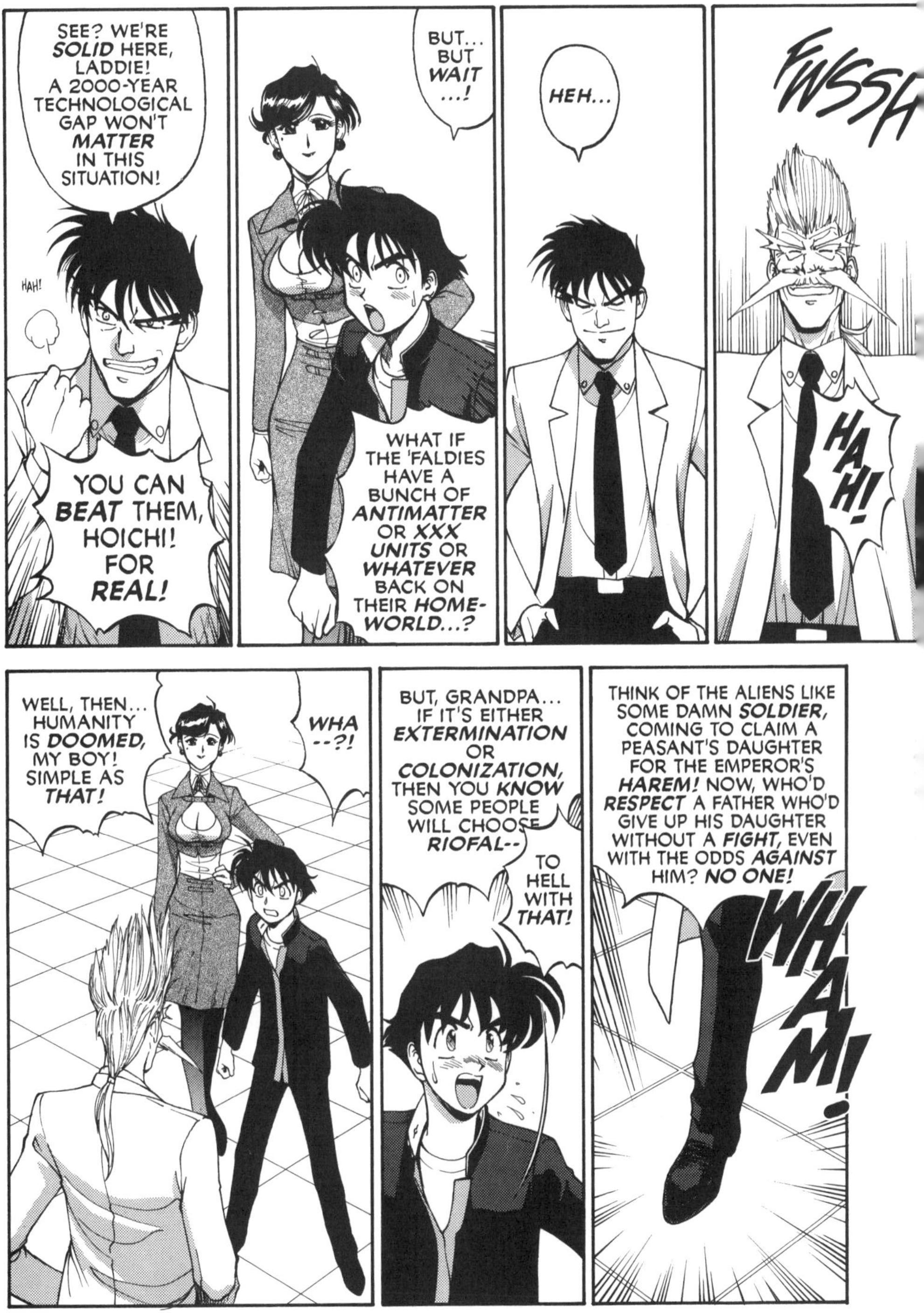
SEE? WE'RE SOLID HERE, LADDIE! A 2000-YEAR TECHNOLOGICAL GAP WON'T MATTER IN THIS SITUATION!
HAH!
YOU CAN BEAT THEM, HOICHI! FOR REAL!
BUT... BUT WAIT ...!
WHAT IF THE 'FALDIES HAVE A BUNCH OF ANTIMATTER OR XXX UNITS OR WHATEVER BACK ON THEIR HOME-WORLD...?
HEH...
FWSSH
HAH!
WELL, THEN... HUMANITY IS DOOMED, MY BOY! SIMPLE AS THAT!
WHA --?!
BUT, GRANDPA... IF IT'S EITHER EXTERMINATION OR COLONIZATION, THEN YOU KNOW SOME PEOPLE WILL CHOOSE RIOFAL--
TO HELL WITH THAT!
THINK OF THE ALIENS LIKE SOME DAMN SOLDIER, COMING TO CLAIM A PEASANT'S DAUGHTER FOR THE EMPEROR'S HAREM! NOW, WHO'D RESPECT A FATHER WHO'D GIVE UP HIS DAUGHTER WITHOUT A FIGHT, EVEN WITH THE ODDS AGAINST HIM? NO ONE!
WHAM!

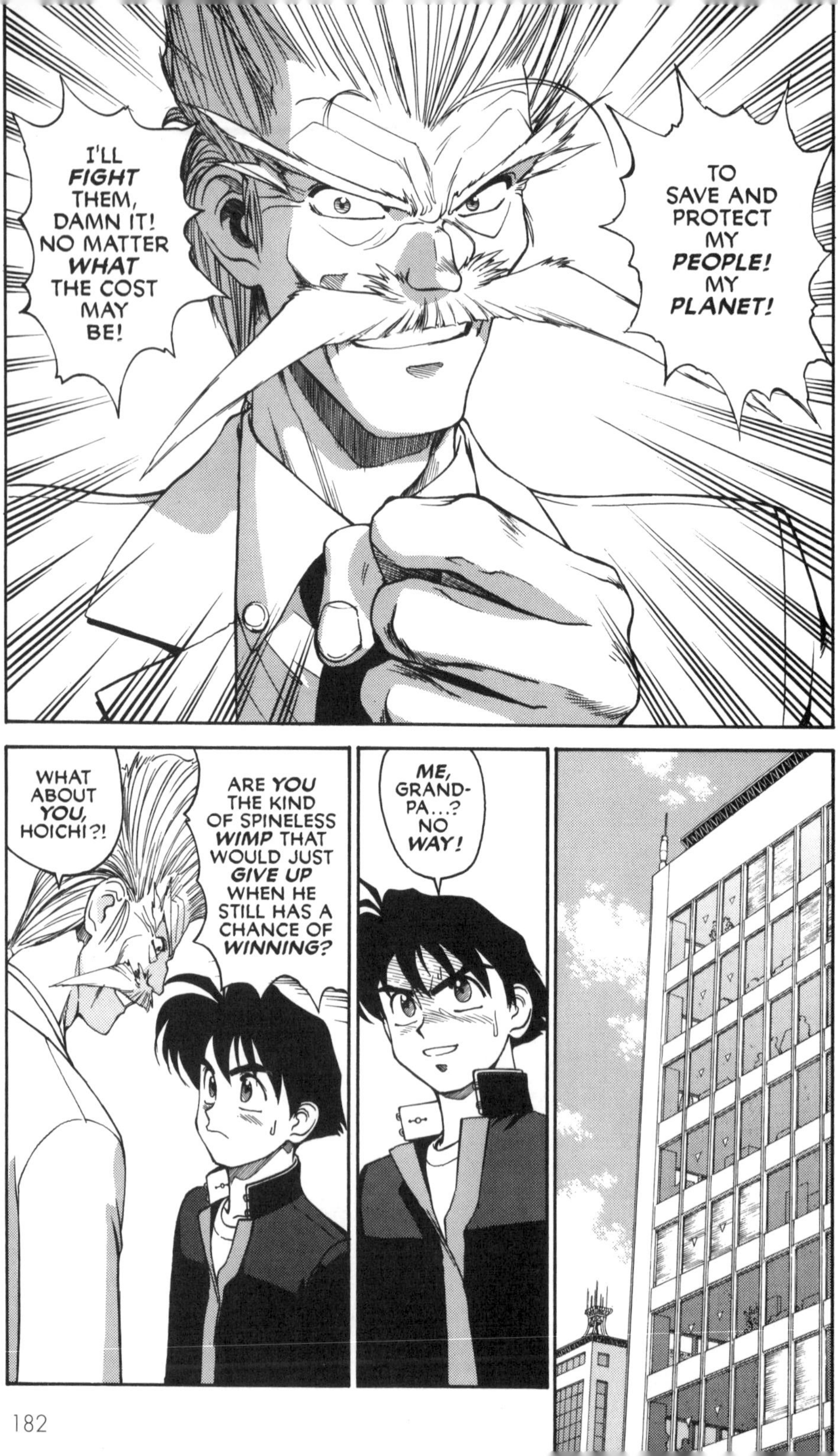
I'LL FIGHT THEM, DAMN IT! NO MATTER WHAT THE COST MAY BE!
TO SAVE AND PROTECT MY PEOPLE! MY PLANET!
WHAT ABOUT YOU, HOICHI?!
ARE YOU THE KIND OF SPINELESS WIMP THAT WOULD JUST GIVE UP WHEN HE STILL HAS A CHANCE OF WINNING?
ME, GRAND-PA...? NO WAY!

ER...IS THIS *ALL* YOUR DATA ON *REIKO KANO* AND *AKANE HINO*, CAPTAIN ZAIER'R...?

YES, SIR.

IN THAT CASE, OUR *STRATEGIC MEDICAL TEAM* WILL ASSUME CUSTODY OF THE SUBJECTS NOW, CAPTAIN. I TRUST THAT WE CAN EXPECT *FULL SUPPORT* FROM YOUR TEAM?

YES, SIR... *MAJOR RYA'AM.*

GOOD! NOW, IF YOU'D PREP AN *OPERATING ROOM* FOR US...

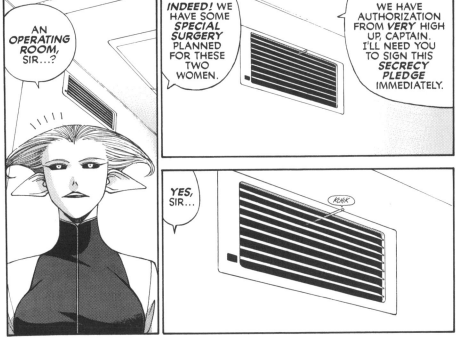

AN *OPERATING ROOM*, SIR...?

INDEED! WE HAVE SOME *SPECIAL SURGERY* PLANNED FOR THESE TWO WOMEN.

WE HAVE AUTHORIZATION FROM *VERY* HIGH UP, CAPTAIN. I'LL NEED YOU TO SIGN THIS *SECRECY PLEDGE* IMMEDIATELY.

YES, SIR...

KCHIK

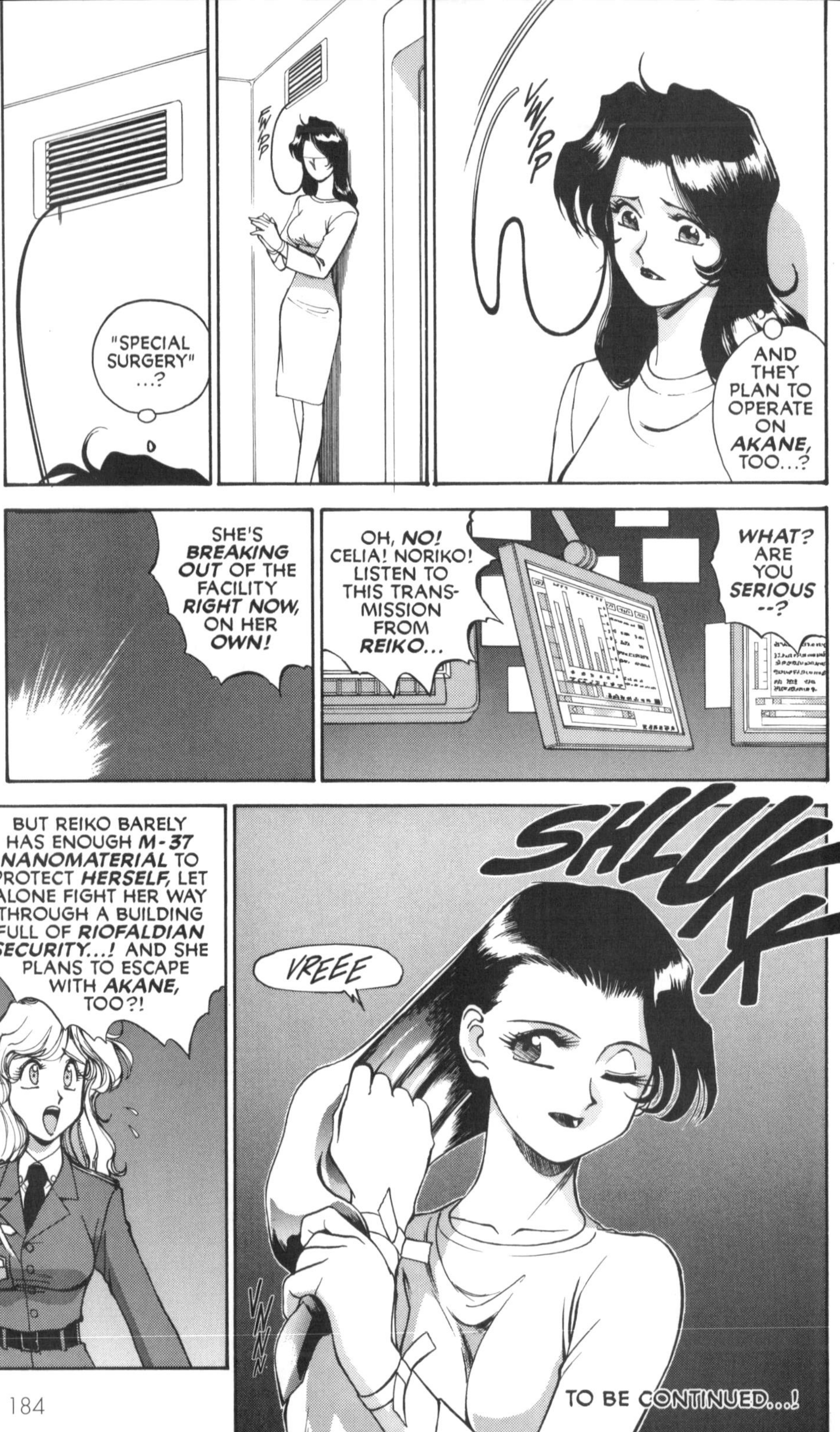
"SPECIAL SURGERY" ...?
FWIPP
VWIPP
AND THEY PLAN TO OPERATE ON AKANE, TOO...?
SHE'S BREAKING OUT OF THE FACILITY RIGHT NOW, ON HER OWN!
OH, NO! CELIA! NORIKO! LISTEN TO THIS TRANSMISSION FROM REIKO...
WHAT? ARE YOU SERIOUS --?
BUT REIKO BARELY HAS ENOUGH M-37 NANOMATERIAL TO PROTECT HERSELF, LET ALONE FIGHT HER WAY THROUGH A BUILDING FULL OF RIOFALDIAN SECURITY...! AND SHE PLANS TO ESCAPE WITH AKANE, TOO?!
SHLUKK
VREEE
VNNN
TO BE CONTINUED...!